Charisma and Community Formation in Medieval Japan

Charisma
and
Community Formation
in
Medieval Japan

The Case of the
Yugyō-ha (1300-1700)

S.A. Thornton

East Asia Program
Cornell University
Ithaca, New York 14853

The Cornell East Asia Series is published by the Cornell University East Asia Program and has no formal affiliation with Cornell University Press. We are a small, non-profit press, publishing reasonably-priced books on a wide variety of scholarly topics relating to East Asia as a service to the academic community and the general public. We accept standing orders which provide for automatic billing and shipping of each title in the series upon publication.

If after review by internal and external readers a manuscript is accepted for publication, it is published on the basis of camera-ready copy provided by the volume author. Each author is thus responsible for any necessary copy-editing and for manuscript formatting. Submission inquiries should be addressed to Editorial Board, East Asia Program, Cornell University, Ithaca, New York 14853-7601.

Part of chapter 3 originally appeared in S. A. Thornton, Review of *Alms and Vagabonds: Buddhist Temples and Popular Patronage in Medieval Japan,* Journal of Asian Studies 55 no. 3 (August 1996):729-730. Reprinted with permission of the Association for Asian Studies.

Parts of chapters 2 and 5 and Appendix originally appeared in S. A. Thornton, "Buddhist Chaplains in the Field of Battle," in *Buddhism in Practice,* ed. Donald S. Lopez, Jr., pp. 586-589. Copyright © 1995 by Princeton University Press. Reprinted by permission of Princeton University Press.

Part of chapter 4 originally appeared in S. A. Thornton, "Ippen," in *Great Thinkers of the Eastern World: The major thinkers and the philosophical and religious classics of China, India, Japan, Korea and the world of Islam,* ed. Ian P. McGreal (NY: HarperCollins Publishers, 1995), pp. 330-334 and is reprinted with permission of the publisher.

Cover design by Karen K. Smith.

Number 102 in the Cornell East Asia Series.
© 1999 S. A. Thornton. All rights reserved
ISSN 1050-2955
ISBN 1-885445-62-8 hc
ISBN 1-885445-02-4 pb
Printed in the United States of America
13 12 11 10 09 08 07 06 05 04 03 02 01   10 9 8 7 6 5 4 3 2 1

⊗The paper in this book meets the requirements for permanence of ISO 9706:1994.

To Herman Weber

Contents

Foreword

The mendicant Pure Land priest Ippen (1239-1289) is one of the most appealing figures in the medieval Japanese religious world. We are provided with brilliant glimpses of his life and teachings—wandering all over Japan with a ragged band of followers, chanting the sacred name of Amida Buddha, dancing to the chant of that name, distributing amulets guaranteeing salvation in Amida's Pure Land—in the splendid scrolls comprising the *Ippen hijiri e*. But because he did not leave the substantial written records of a Hōnen, Shinran, Dōgen, or Nichiren, Ippen's teachings and life are more fragmentary. To many he may seem to be something of a minor figure compared with other Pure Land, Nichiren, or Zen reformers of the thirteenth century. At his death there was little prospect that his teachings would survive and flourish. Some of his disciples disbanded, a few committed suicide. One disciple, Ta'amidabutsu Shinkyō, however, reorganized some of Ippen's followers into an order that would eventually emerge as the Yugyō-ha (Itinerant School), later called the Jishū (Time Sect). If Ippen's career and teachings are poorly known, the development of his teachings in what was to be one of the most vigorous branches of medieval and early modern popular Buddhism is hardly known at all.

It is here that Sybil Thornton makes major contributions. Using Weberian notions of "the routinization of charisma" and "charismatic confraternity," and Alan Bryman's analysis of charisma and leadership, she explores the development from tenuous origins of a powerful and extensive monastic community that enjoyed the patronage of Ashikaga shoguns, members of the imperial court, local warriors, and farmers. Viewing Ippen as a world-rejecting "mystic," she argues forcefully that his followers were faced, at his death, with a stark choice: to disperse entirely or to reorganize and redefine themselves as a community in closer touch with the everyday problems of local adherents eager for salvation. The study is particularly important in examining the connection between the early mendicant phase

x

focused on Ippen as *hijiri*, or itinerant holy man, and the later organization
and practices of the Yugyō-ha, which claimed to preserve the spirit of
Ippen's religious practice while institutionalizing it and in her exploration
of the interlay of legitimacy and charisma between the religious and lay
communities in the development of the Yugyō-ha/Jishū in the Muromachi
and Edo periods. Students of Japanese history, culture, and religion in the
Edo period, as well as the Muromachi and Momoyama periods, will find
much to think about in this study of community and charisma in action.
Readers who come to this work through an interest in comparative religion,
or the perspective of religion in some other place or time, will find this a
lively and stimulating introduction to the growth and transformation of
popular Pure Land Buddhism in a Japanese medieval environment. This
book considerably deepens and broadens the study of medieval and early
modern Japanese religous life by bringing the vigorous Itinerant School into
an appropriate place, at center stage.

Martin Collcutt
Princeton University
Dec. 28, 1998

Preface

Charisma and Community in Medieval Japan: The Case of the Yugyō-ha 1300-1700 examines the process by which a Buddhist confraternity was transformed into a powerful and prestigious monastic order. Because this work has application and significance beyond the sociology and history of Japanese religions and will, I hope, be read by nonspecialists, I have made every attempt to reduce the number of Japanese terms and instead to use English substitutes, capitalized in the case of important technical terms. This holds especially for the names of well-known government offices and sects.

Japanese terms are italicized except when quoted or capitalized, as in the case of titles. Important Jishū terms and texts remain in the Japanese: *nembutsu*, Yugyō Shōnin, *Jishū kakochō*, etc. Note that "Jishū" is used to refer to the name of the sect as established in the Tokugawa period, while "*jishū*" refers to the monks and nuns of the order, where it is the term used in the medieval period to indicate *nembutsu* practitioners.

The glossary covers only the most important or most-frequently used terms in Jishū texts. Nothing that might be easily found in an English-language encyclopedia has been included.

Temple names remain untranslated and often are preceded by the name of the prefecture, province, town or district in which they are located, as in "Asakusa Nichirinji," where Asakusa is a district of Tokyo. Since there are many terms for the capital of premodern Japan, the current name for the city, Kyoto, is used.

Japanese names have been written in Japanese fashion, with the family name followed by the personal name. Ages, where quoted or cited from primary sources, are also given in the Japanese fashion, where the prenatal period is also counted in the total number of years of life.

Dates given in the Japanese style are abbreviated to *nengo* (period name), year, month, day. On the whole, these are given principally in the footnotes.

It is important to keep in mind that among the documents of the Jishū or related orders, none of the narratives can be considered to provide historical evidence. The aetiologies or *engi* and biographies—no matter how old or contemporary with their subject matter—say much less about the subject of the narrative than about the people who produced them, what they wanted and how they wished to present themselves. The histories and genealogies, which date only to the Tokugawa period, present problems of their own: certainly the names, death dates, and approximate ages of the heads of the order were preserved for and through memorial ceremonies; however, war and fires destroyed records over and over again and no doubt reconstruction of them was difficult and based on memory. Some evidence is corroborated here and there in family archives. Nonetheless, reconstruction of the history of the order and sect is based on evidence that is fragmentary for some periods and rarely of the same type over a four hundred-year period. Thus, nearly all names and dates transmitted exclusively by the Jishū until the sixteenth century or even the Tokugawa period must be considered provisional.

Indeed, for the historian, the whole question of what is transmitted, how, why, and by whom is extremely problematic. Jishū studies have been dominated by apologists within the institution reinforced principally by specialists in medieval literature and in folklore. The upshot has been the credence lent by subsequently discredited theories both to the hypothesized process and to the result of transmission. My Ph.D. thesis concerned itself with the provenances of several narrative traditions of the Jishū and with the basic assumptions of the scholarship up to that time, which were demonstrated to follow no particular rule. Thus, although all scholars in the field assumed that Tokugawa period sources were suspect in terms of recreating the early history of the order, they were absolutely convinced of the credibility of medieval sources themselves. The general rule of thumb was, for example, that all literary sources (including plays, epics, and illustrated histories and biographies) preserved intact already existing and usually oral traditions. The thesis indicated otherwise and challenged the entire notion of tradition.

"Tradition" is often used in this work and it has a very specific meaning based both on Malinowski's concept of "myth as charter" and on Parry/ Lord-based theories of the transmission of narrative in predominantly nonliterate (whether preliterate or postliterate) societies. I use "tradition" to refer to any narrative or object which has been handed down, been made to be handed down, or has been presented as having been handed down; "tradition" always refers to the interests of the present rather than to the principle of pure and faithful transmission—that is, the community which both produces and receives the narrative or object as "tradition" decides its legitimacy based on its own needs and interests. In addition, I use "tradition" to refer to all factors involved in its creation and transmission: the thing or narrative which is handed down, the individual who hands down, the individuals who receive and accept as legitimate what is handed down, and the context in which the thing or object is handed down—ceremonies, rituals, or sermons, for example. Shils' discussion of tradition as a pattern of events is too limited: it does not take the realities of premodern society fully into consideration and allows for the explanation neither of changes in tradition nor of the process of legitimating those changes. Thus, when "tradition" is used in this work, it means that which is claimed to be and accepted as legitimately handed down from the past—whether it is or is not.

Acknowledgments

This book began as a Ph.D. thesis submitted in 1988 to the Faculty of Oriental Studies of the University of Cambridge. *The Propaganda Traditions of the Yugyō ha: The Campaign to Establish the Jishū as an Independent School of Japanese Buddhism (1300-1700)*, a study of the Pure Land, Ippen school order known as the Yugyō-ha (later the Jishū), traces the development of the advertising campaign of a newcomer to the salvation market of medieval Japan: this was reconstructed from the biographies, miracle stories, legends, historical documents, artifacts, and monuments which comprise the propaganda traditions of the order. I argue that the Yugyō-ha developed this body of traditions for the purpose of realizing its goals: establishing a network of temples and patrons, securing government recognition and protection, and maintaining precedence over rivals.

I wish to thank those who assisted me, from conceptualization to completion. My deepest gratitude goes to Dr. Carmen Blacker, who supervised the thesis. She never flagged in her encouragement despite the mazes, red herrings, and dead ends that seemed continuously to threaten completion. Many thanks, too, to Dr. Michael Loewe, who guided my faltering steps through classical Chinese, and to Dr. Richard Bowring, for his patience and support.

I also wish to express my deepest thanks to Dr. Kanai Kiyomitsu, who supervised my research in Tokyo, Japan. Dr. Kanai, a specialist in *nō*, was responsible for opening up the field of *jishū* studies. When I first arrived, he warned me I would be considered a fool if I took it up. Even so, it was his own intellectual rigor, a refusal to accept bad logic simply because it supported a familiar argument, that provided a compass with which to explore (for Westerners) mostly uncharted territory.

Three foundations provided me financial assistance and I am grateful for the opportunity to acknowledge their support. My work at Cambridge was partially funded by a grant from the British Schools and Universities

Foundation, Inc. (1984). A year of research in Japan (1985) was made possible by grants from the Toyota Foundation and the Asian Cultural Foundation.

I am also in debt to the priests of many temples, Jishū and others, who helped me in my research, provided materials, showed me their temple treasures, took me sight-seeing, and entertained me in their homes. Many thanks, too, go to Koyama Noboru and Michiko Matthews of the Cambridge University Library for all their help and advice, and to Andrew King, who proof-read the thesis for me. For reading and passing the thesis, I also wish to acknowledge Dr. Peter Kornicki and Dr. Martin Collcutt, who was also kind enough to write the foreword to this work.

The revision of the thesis, *Charisma and Community*, is the result of nearly eight years' work. I am indebted to Saint Lawrence University for a grant to conduct research in Cambridge in the summer of 1993. I wish to thank Katsuko Hotelling, of Hayden Library at Arizona State University, for all her help—and good cheer—in the last four years. My colleagues in the History Department, Steve McKinnon and Hoyt Tillman, were kind enough to read the draft and offered valuable advice. And, finally, I wish to thank the department's women historians' reading group for reading the first chapter in the very last week of the semester and offering helpful suggestions for making it accessible to nonspecialists: Rachel Fuchs, Susan Gray, Gayle Gullett, Tim Hodgdon, Asuncion Lavrin, and Vicky Ruiz.

1
Introduction

In 1274, Chishin Ippen (1239-1289), scion of one of the most distinguished military families of Japan, abandoned his warrior estate and took to the road to find salvation and to bring it to others. Trailed by two women and a child, he made his way to the Main Shrine of Kumano, where the god appeared to him in a vision, admonished him, and confirmed him in his religious mission to distribute to one and all a guarantee of salvation: a slip of paper on which was printed the invocation of the name of Amida Buddha. Making the final break with his family, he sent the women and child home. He spent the final fifteen years of his life tramping from one end of Japan to the other with a shabby band of men and women who braved hunger, cold, bandits, and even rape to follow him. For this small confraternity, life on the road, as hard and dangerous as it was, offered visions of Amida's Pure Land paradise in the west: itinerancy was a walking meditation whose continuous invocations of Amida's name literally fixed the practitioners' eyes on the Pure Land.

Four hundred years later, Ippen's mission was still being carried out over the length of Japan. It was, however, greatly altered. The mission was now a whole temple on the move—as many as two or three hundred religious, trainees, servants, craftsmen, and porters. Horses and palanquins were now the favored means of transport. Domainal officials and samurai escorted the train and policed the crowds. Food and lodging were provided at the domainal lord's expense. Horses and handlers were provided by the shogunate, just as they were to domainal lords in transit to and from the capital at Edo. Ippen's mission was now an ancient and venerable institution sanctioned and sponsored by the government. Only one thing did not change: the mission was still dedicated to the practice and the propagation of the chanting the name of Amida Buddha (*nembutsu*) in order to be Reborn into his Pure Land paradise in the west; Ippen's amulets were still distributed at no cost to one and all.

1

The preservation of Ippen's mission over four hundred years was accomplished by the Yugyō-ha (Itinerant School), one of several Japanese Buddhist orders tracing their origins back to the wayfaring confraternity led by Ippen. Between roughly 1325 and 1425, under the patronage principally of the warriors of eastern Japan and the shogunate (military government) led by the Ashikaga family (1336-1573), the Yugyō-ha managed to establish a position as principal representative of Ippen school Pure Land Buddhism. The shogunate recognized the order as an independent school of Buddhism and granted protection to the entourages, monks, and nuns of the head of the mission and of the head of the order. The order's position under the Ashikaga shogunate was confirmed by the Tokugawa shogunate (1603-1867), which established the Yugyō-ha as an independent sect, the Jishū (Time Sect), and gradually responded to appeals to place under its jurisdiction other temples specializing in mendicancy, itinerancy, and *nembutsu* propagation. Licensed and protected by the shogun, the head of the order's mission, the Yugyō Shōnin (Itinerant Saint), and his train travelled the length of Japan bringing a guarantee of salvation through Rebirth in paradise as well as a variety of charms against the evils and accidents one might encounter on this earth. By about 1700, with its mission subsidized by the state and its clergy received at the shogunal and imperial courts, the Jishū was one of the most prestigious Buddhist institutions in Japan.

IPPEN AND HIS SUCCESSORS: THE ROUTINIZATION OF CHARISMA

This study focuses on two processes manifested in the development of Ippen's mission from a mendicant-itinerant confraternity to a monastic institution: preservation and transformation. It is clear that Ippen's mission survived within a social organization different from that in which it had originally evolved. And, there is good reason to think, that new social organization was necessary to the mission's survival. Concomitantly, that new organization, the Yugyō-ha, could not itself have survived had it not preserved intact Ippen's mission.

The necessity for change was dictated by the very nature of Ippen's religious career and, thus, of his confraternity. Ippen was a mystic; his confraternity was based on communal meditation practices dedicated to realizing previews of and eventual entry into the Pure Land of Amida Buddha. Max Weber underscored the unlikelihood of long-term survival for such communities based on "'world-rejecting asceticism'" and an "abhor[rence of] all rational economic conduct."[1] He even attributed the disappearance in India of Buddhism to a failure to develop an organization based on more than consociation, seniority, and master-disciple relationships.[2] These were the very characteristics of Ippen's confraternity. In addition, Ippen handed out his amulets without even requiring an invocation of Amida's name: economic support of his mission would always be "voluntary, unregulated and irregular."[3] Thus, upon Ippen's death in 1289, the surviving confraternity members realized that they had two options: to disperse or to reorganize. The decision was actually made by the local feudal lord, who pursued to a remote temple those members of the confraternity who had decided to rejoin Ippen by starving themselves to death. He demanded an amulet and would not take "no" for an answer.

This story, if it is true, makes clear that the motivation was indeed to continue Ippen's mission and that it came from outside the confraternity.[4] Thus, the confraternity needed to address the problems posed by the mission itself: succession to Ippen's leadership, responsibilities to those outside the confraternity, and economic security. The very contemplation of these issues must have shaken the early leaders of the confraternity to the core, for they were being asked to reevaluate and even to redefine the basis of the religious authority to carry on the mission, to lead the confraternity, to minister to adherents and their this-worldly concerns, and even the religious authority of the mission itself. Had they realized the depth and scope of the problem confronting them, they might have decided it was really easier to starve to death.

In redefining themselves as a community, Ippen's successors were forced to question the meaning of religious authority, the very thing that had kept them together in the first place. In other words, they had to redefine "charisma." Charisma is Weber's term for the ties that bind a religious leader like Ippen and his consociates, the authority that is claimed and the authority that is acknowledged.[5] Ippen's authority was based on his ability to realize the Pure Land and on his followers' belief in it. Now, however, Ippen was gone and the real world was crushing them up against the gates to paradise. The confraternity was forced—in a way Ippen never was—to turn around and face the ordinary men and women of this world who clamored also to be guided into the Pure Land. As reluctant as Ippen's follower's originally may have been to postpone their reunion with him in the Pure Land, they committed themselves in all mercy to their mission to the laity. Moreover, the laity were not to be merely purchasers of specific religious services; through the rigorous application of the fundamental principle that bound each *nembutsu* practitioner to Amida and to each other, the laity were made part of the religious community as equal Fellow Practitioners.

This redefinition of the religious community—of its goals, its membership, and the principles of consociation in order to adapt to the demands of the real world—the need for food, clothing, lodging, and the needs of the wider community served by the religious organization—Weber termed the "routinization of charisma."[6] This study examines the efforts of Ippen's successors over four hundred years—and beyond—to meet the demands of a constantly changing world on a voluntary organization while preserving the original spirit of Ippen's revelations and mission.

These problems and the solutions to them were typical—so typical as to make the history of the Yugyō-ha a model for Weber's analysis of the transformation from "charismatic communities" to monastic institutions. The Yugyō-ha's closest comparand might be the Franciscans: they both originated in the mystic impulses of their thirteenth-century founders, evolved as confraternities of itinerant-mendicant proselytizers, and survived as endowed monastic institutions virtually indistinguishable from others. For all the similarities, however, one fact remains ineluctable: Ippen's mission and confraternity originated and developed within a religious tradition that was distinctively Japanese. Further, it was that religious tradition which made possible the transformation of the confraternity to a viable, perennial institution comprising both religious and laity that could perpetuate Ippen's mission. The strategy pursued by Ippen's successors was provided by a distinctively Japanese tradition of religious authority.

THE *HIJIRI* TRADITION: CHARISMA AND COMMUNITY FORMATION

According to Alan Bryman's analysis of charisma and leadership, the charismatic leader is one who, in fact, chooses and exemplifies a traditional religious career, who follows a "'cultural model of charismatic leadership'."[7] This is as true for Northern European saints who have followed the example of Christ and chosen suffering as it is for North African Muslim saints who have begun, like the Prophet Mohammed, by learning to read or for Theravada monks in Thailand who have followed the Shakyamuni Buddha into the forest.[8] Ippen, who founded the original confraternity, and the Yugyō-ha, which preserved and perpetuated it, followed a cultural model of response to personal and social crisis provided by the Pure Land School of Buddhism in premodern Japan: the traditional model of retreat from the world established by the Buddha Gautama Siddhartha in India and exemplified in Japan by the so-called holy men or *hijiri*, religious aspirants outside but paralleling the formal institutions of the Buddhist church.

The *hijiri*, as independent religious practitioners and temple fundraisers identified by specific religious practices, provided Ippen with the tradition on which to base his religious career. This relationship to Ippen has been long recognized, but principally in terms of providing him a package of what seemed unrelated practices: amulet distribution, enrollment in a register, and adoption of common names. However, the significance of this background and these practices to the organization and religious authority of the Yugyō-ha has until recently never been analyzed. The publication in 1994 of Janet Goodwin's *Alms and Vagabonds: Buddhist Temples and Popular Patronage in Medieval Japan* demonstrated the importance of the *hijiri* background to the organization of the order—the establishment and regularization of relationships among head of the order, religious, and lay adherents. Goodwin's summation of *hijiri* fundraising activities in terms of "a search for power," "validating new social arrangements in a changing secular world," "voluntary cooperation," "associations" or "community," and "collective" dovetails very neatly with Bryman's articulation of charisma as well as Weber's concept of the routinization of charisma, in terms of both diction and concept.[9] The *hijiri* movement, based on active involvement with and dependence on the laity, provided Ippen's successors with the model and rationale for their own mission to the laity.

Drawing on the works of Bryman and Goodwin, this study is the first to draw the connection between the *hijiri* movement and the organization and practices of the Yugyō-ha. Indeed, the Yugyō-ha/Jishū achieved its success by identifying itself thoroughly with the *hijiri* movement and skillfully adopting and adapting *hijiri* methods of fundraising and community formation. Their religious practices, such as itinerancy, distributing salvation in the form of paper slips imprinted with the *nembutsu*, granting religious names, and enrollment, formed the very core of their strategies for community formation and eventually came to be identified exclusively with the Yugyō-ha and Jishū. The rise and success of the order were connected with the way the so-called First, Second, and Fourth Patriarchs of the Yugyō-ha developed the tradition of the career of the head of the order, in whom was vested principal responsibility for perpetuating the religious practices and traditions of the *hijiri*. These three established the career of salvation that formed the basis of the religious authority of the order and at the same time developed a way to pass on the authority of the head of the order through a formal organizational structure and a procedure for deciding succession.[10]

Further, although charisma has been discussed principally in terms of a personal attribute, Weber himself tried to address the principle of reciprocity in the formation of charismatic communities by indicating the importance of acknowledging charisma as a principal function of its viability in establishing the community.[11] As articulated by Bryman, charisma is a "social relationship" of "reciprocal interdependence" based on an exchange of power.[12] It is less a product than a process. In the case of the Yugyō-ha, a religious community was formed on the basis of the exchange between the head of the order and monk or nun of a guarantee of salvation for absolute obedience: the religious (*jishū*) exchanged absolute obedience not only for salvation but also for a share of the power to guarantee salvation. Both extended this guarantee of salvation (in different forms) to the laity, who responded with economic support and political protection—and thereby became part of the religious community. The result of this exchange system was the recognition of the religious authority of and the attribution of charisma to the head of the order and to the entire order itself.

While the order saw itself as firmly within the tradition of the Pure Land School of Buddhism and the *hijiri* movement, the early Patriarchs or Founders of the order were very conscious of the special requirements for establishing and perpetuating a distinctive religious community within that tradition. The charisma of the head of the order was based on specific doctrinal principles and on the strategies for the perception, by religious and lay, of that charisma. If charisma is conceptualized as a social formation based on a system of exchange which favors the leader in terms of power, then in the Yugyō-ha the exchange was predicated on the absolute authority of the head of the order to guarantee Rebirth, which was established by identifying the head of the order as (a) Buddha.[13] The process of effecting perception of this status was carried out on two levels. On the one hand, great attention was paid to defining and refining the principle of religious life, Same Practice (*dōgyō*, also Fellow Practitioner), which would ritualize the relationship between the head of the order and the rest of the religious community. On the other hand, the order produced illustrated scrolls and other texts which not only made claims for the status of the order's head but also supported those claims with reports of miracles.[14]

As Bryman indicates, religious organizations do not survive unless the power or the charisma of the leader is shared with or somehow extended to followers.[15] The concept of delegation was essential to the organization of the order. The head of the order secured religious authority by means of itinerancy, that is, his tour of duty in leading Ippen's mission, after which he assumed the position of head of the order's main temple. By creating a religious order in which Ippen's mission of itinerant proselytizing was delegated to the chosen successor while the head of the order managed the order from a permanent residence, the Second Patriarch clearly saw a model of a religious organization in which bureaucratic functions and religious charisma were separated and, thus, he managed to institutionalize Ippen's original mission and charisma—preserve their original force—while at the same time perfecting the organization and management of the order.[16] That is, the order and Ippen's mission were not necessarily coterminous: the Second Patriarch founded an order *within which* Ippen's mission was preserved and perpetuated.

Further, in the case of the Yugyō-ha, absolute obedience or submission directed up the organizational hierarchy was translated into empowerment directed down; the order was based firmly on a precise balance of dependence and empowerment. This power, the power to save by securing Rebirth, was, however, transformed as it was passed on to the order as a whole. Indeed, one thread running through the history of the establishment and development of the order as an organization is the struggle of the head to define a source of religious authority vested solely in himself even though shared, with some limitation, and characterizing the order as a whole.[17] Thus, only the head of the mission, accompanied by his train of disciples, practiced itinerancy; however, the basis of Ippen's itinerant confraternity, Same Practice, was made the basis of chaplaincy or assignment to the person of a lay patron with the primary object of securing his Rebirth. Only the head of the order and the head of the mission practiced distribution of salvation in the form of amulets printed with the *nembutsu*; nevertheless, chaplains were entitled to participate in the extension of salvation by administering the last ten *nembutsu* at death, the *saigo no jūnen*. Only the head of the order could guarantee Rebirth in the western Pure Land, which was indicated by enrollment in the death register which he carried; even so, the custom of keeping a roll of the dead was widely adopted in Yugyō-ha and related temples. Thus, although the functions of itinerancy, amulet distribution, and guaranteeing Rebirth were vested in the heads of the order, members of the order were authorized to extend salvation in exchange for obedience to the heads of the order. Not only the heads of the order but the entire Yugyō-ha had the religious authority to guarantee salvation.

Acknowledgment of this religious authority to guarantee salvation was manifested by the widespread participation at different levels of large segments of the warrior class. Some individuals secured from the order chaplains to whom they provided their personal chapels; others called upon Yugyō-ha chaplains to provide services in the field; and still others merely had their names enrolled in the order's death register. Just as the relationship between head of the order and followers was based on a social exchange, so the relationship between the order and lay patrons was based on an exchange. In recognizing this, one must admit the implicit acknowledgment of the power and legitimating function—the charisma—of the laity in the very solicitation and acceptance of their economic support and protection.

In its relationships with traditional political power centers, the Yugyō-ha locked itself into a system of legitimation more extensive and perhaps more important than that provided by the Pure Land and *hijiri* traditions.[18] From the imperial court the order received legitimation in the forms of the inclusion of poems by their leaders in imperial poetry anthologies, the conferral of the title "Saint" or *shōnin*, and the designation of at least one temple as a temple at which prayers on behalf of the emperor were made (*gokiganjo*). Poetry as much as salvation figured in the relations with the Kamakura shogunate and its vassals. The Ashikaga shogunate extended legitimacy in the form, among other things, of protection to the trains of the current and retired Yugyō Shōnin. The order participated in the New Year ceremonies as well as the funerals and memorial services of the Ashikaga house; both the order and the Ashikaga house benefitted in terms of prestige by staging these grand occasions. The relationship between the order and the house of the Ashikaga *kubō* (governor-general) in Kamakura was especially close and religious in nature: the Kamakura *kubō* were converts; a Kamakura temple of the order was selected as a mortuary temple for the house.

By the time of the Warring States period (1492-1568), the Yugyō-ha/Jishū was so closely identified with the Ashikaga house and government that warlords enhanced and legitimated their positions by taking over the shogunate's function of protecting the trains of the current and retired Yugyō Shōnin and even by expanding patronage to include subsidies. After the joint headquarters in Fujisawa was burned down, successive heads of the order, known as Fujisawa Shōnin (Fujisawa Saints), found hospitality and new temples with various warlords. Even Oda Nobunaga (1534-1582), notorious for his suppression of Buddhist institutions that challenged his authority, patronized the Yugyō Shōnin and his temples.

The mutual exchange of legitimacy and charisma between religious community and lay community was best and most fully exemplified in the order's relationship with the Tokugawa shogunate. Not only did the order assist the founder of the dynasty, Ieyasu (1543-1616, shogun 1603-1605), in acquiring a Nitta pedigree but it also institutionalized that pedigree in its temples. In exchange, the order was recognized briefly as the sole surviving house of the Southern Court, for whom the Nitta had fought, with a title equivalent to that of "prince imperial abbot" or *monzeki*. The Tokugawa legitimated its position as shogun by continuing shogunal patronage of the Yugyō Shōnin's missionary tour. The chief priest of the order's temple in Edo, the Nichirinji, participated yearly in the shogun's New Year's poetry ceremonies. Temples of other orders specializing in itinerancy, mendicancy, and *nembutsu* propagation were placed under Yugyō-ha jurisdiction. By 1700, the Yugyō-ha, now the Jishū, was well on the way to accomplishing all its goals.

Intensive interaction with the lay community did not come without a price. Predictably, as Weber might have noted, the order found itself coopted by the ruling elite into legitimating various claims to political authority.[19] Relations with the politically-weakened imperial court were harmless enough, limited as they were to poetry and official receptions. Nevertheless, involvement with the military houses compromised the order in various ways. Accepting the shogun's and domainal lords' protection facilitated the mission's progress from province to province; however, such protection did exploit the mission to demonstrate political clout over vassals and other subordinates. The order even found that involvement with the military houses quickly resulted in interference in matters such as promotion and succession in the leadership on the one hand and, on the other, the suborning of ordinary monks and nuns for paramilitary duties in the field—among other, lesser abuses. Lay challenges to the jurisdiction of the order over its religious were met by a "radical elevation of its . . . dignity": the order made assertions of ever higher religious authority and imposed ever more specific "reglementation of all spheres of conduct."[20] Through continuous and intensified involvement with the military class, the order took on the features of military society.[21] Discipline, maintained by means of fearsome oaths and dire consequences, was equally effective in regulating relations between the head of the order and ordinary religious and in normalizing relations between the order and its patrons among the military houses.

THE JUDGMENT OF HISTORIOGRAPHY: "DECLINE"

The Yugyō-ha's rise through the good offices of the military houses has been a central concern of Japanese scholars, most notably Akamatsu Toshihide, Kanai Kiyomitsu, Ōhashi Shunnō, and Tachibana Shundō.[22] Their work has stressed that the success of this religious community in securing political recognition and power over similar communities was based on its strong ties with the warrior class, especially those warriors serving the Ashikaga shogunate in Kyoto and Kamakura during the fourteenth and fifteenth centuries and the Tokugawa house itself in the sixteenth and seventeenth centuries.[23] Their work has also discussed the reasons for this extraordinary success with the warriors of the late medieval and early modern periods: doctrine and practices guaranteeing Rebirth in paradise even to those who have killed, personal attendance on warriors in the field, reconciliation of *nembutsu* practices and the worship of native tutelary deities, publicity of signs of divine sanction of the heads of the order, the role of the temples in the religious and cultural life of the upper class, and, last but by no means least, the role of the Jishū in establishing the early history and genealogy of the Tokugawa house.[24] This emphasis on relations with warrior houses informed the first history produced by someone outside the order, Isogai Tadashi's 1937 *Jishū kyōdan no kigen oyobi hattatsu* (The origins and development of the Jishū order).[25] This work established the framework for all later research and set the goal: to retrieve the order's "lost" history, prestige, and significance in pre-modern Japanese society.

In considering the history of the Yugyō-ha over a period of some six hundred years, one can observe a pattern of rise and fall, from its origins as a rather shabby band of itinerant-mendicant *nembutsu* practitioners and proselytizers to its height as overall head of a sect composed of several temple lineages—some derived from Ippen, some not—and finally to a much diminished status as one of the smallest sects of Buddhism to survive dismantling and near obliteration under the Meiji government during the nineteenth century. Thus the story of the Jishū seems to confirm the theme of rise and fall (whether as decline, degeneration, or deterioration) in the historiography of Buddhism itself.[26]

The most famous articulation of this theme was made by Tsuji Zennosuke in his 1955 *Nihon Bukkyōshi* (*History of Japanese Buddhism*) in his pejorative characterizations of Muromachi and Tokugawa Buddhism.[27] Nevertheless, the effect on Jishū historiography had already long been felt. Isogai Tadashi, in his then definitive study of the Jishū of 1937, calls the fifth and penultimate chapter "The fifth period: the age of decline" (*Daigoki fushin jidai*). Citing an earlier incarnation of Tsuji's thesis, he characterizes the Buddhism of the Tokugawa period as one of decline, corruption, formalism, and, especially, collusion with the shogunate and domains and the various systems for organizing religion and thereby controlling the population; he accuses Buddhism of alienating itself from the people in favor of the aristocratic titles and ornate robes to be gained by a close association with shogunate and court. This tendency is supposed to go back to the Muromachi period and the concomitant estrangement ("minshin no rihan") and contempt of the people ("jimmin no keibu") and to have laid the basis for the anti-Buddhist sentiment that surfaced in the Tokugawa period, inflamed by Confucian and Shinto Revival scholarship and the bad economy of the times. The Jishū is by no means exculpated in his work.[28]

Even after the war, the theme of decline continued to inform the history of the Jishū. For example, in 1969, in an article titled "Jishū no suibiki ni oite" (On the decline of the Jishū), Nakayama Nobuyuki summarizes the research and reasons for characterizing the Tokugawa period as a time for the decline of the Jishū. First, following Tsuji, Nakayama perpetuates the characterization of the Kamakura period as the high point in Japanese Buddhism, the period of reform by new sects of Buddhism, which are credited with spreading Buddhism to the "people" with Ippen as the "anchor" of this movement. Nakayama identifies the orders claiming Ippen as founder as the principal representatives of Pure Land Buddhism, and he carries through with the main theme of the contemporary academic narrative of decline: cooption by the power centers and alienation from the common people beginning in the Muromachi period. As proof, he offers the following evidence: 1) the drop in the number of enrollees in the order's death register, the *Jishū kakochō*, after about 1500; 2) a complaint from farmers in Wakasa Province to the magistrate concerning extortion by *jishū* from the capital; and 3) Akamatsu Toshihide's emphasis on the roles of the rise of the True Pure Land sect or Ikkō-shū under Rennyo (1415-1499) and of the fall of sixteenth-century daimyo (warlords) in the decline of the order.[29]

The problem of decline, however, is attributed principally to interaction with the warrior class. Nakamura summarizes Ishida Yoshitō's thesis on the three main internal problems of the Jishū due to such interaction: formalism ("keishikishūgika"), authoritarianism ("ken'ishūgika"), and increasing emphasis on the arts.[30] Like his predecessors, Nakamura assumes that, since ordinary people had been the original objects of Ippen's mission, patronage of the upper classes led to the neglect of ordinary people. His complaints against the order are many: accusations of spying for the shogunate, using the *Jishū kakochō* for fundraising, secularization or the role of Jishū temples as imperial vow or shogunal vow temples, the turning of ritual into a sideshow, and isolated cases of immorality, embarrassing because they were reported by foreign observers in the sixteenth century.[31] He points his finger too at the incorporation of popular practices and shrine worship, Shingon, and Zen into Ippen's version of Pure Land Buddhism, which is opposed to a "pure" Pure Land doctrine of absolute dependence on Amida. Thus, problems are built into Ippen's doctrines from the very first: Nakamura places the blame on doctrine rather than on the functions of social organization in voluntary organizations. Rennyo is credited with more doctrinal appeal without any concession to the role of successful social organization at the time.[32] Nor does he make mention of the devastation of Buddhism at the hands the Meiji government.

This assumption of an irreconcilable dichotomy between the religion of the common people and that of rulers also underlies Tamamuro Fumio's approach to the Jishū in the Tokugawa period. Although he sees the sect as incorporated completely into the system by which the shogunate intended to control both religious institutions and the people, for Tamamuro the Yugyō Shōnin represents a long and deep tradition of the religion of the common people. In his discussion of this interaction between church and state, Tamamuro exposes an acute hostility to the Tokugawa regime which has informed Japanese historiography since the Meiji period. The great paradox for Tamamuro is that the Tokugawa shogunate vested in the Jishū the responsibility of acting as sole representative of popular (Buddhist) religion by subsidizing the tours of the Yugyō Shōnin with their typical forms of popular practice: *nembutsu* charms, charms against bad luck and illness, ceremonies for suppressing hungry ghosts, and class-mixing dancing *nembutsu*.[33] What Tamamuro identifies as popular religious practices—and therefore an identification with the common people—indeed exemplifies the *hijiri* tradition preserved in Ippen's mission. At the same time, however, in order to conform to the "decline" argument, Tamamuro must distinguish between the Yugyō Shōnin and the Jishū. He can point out all the ways in which the Jishū was coopted by the Tokugawa regime in its efforts to keep the people under close surveillance; however, "decline" means neglect of the common people and popular religion, and this, of course, does not apply to the Yugyō Shōnin. Tamamuro apparently does not see a problem either in the paradox represented by the Tokugawa shogunate's support of the Yugyō Shōnin or in the paradox represented by the coexistence of two institutions, the Yugyō Shōnin and the Jishū, with what he sees as such mutually exclusive interests.

Mochizuki Kazan avoids this problem by refraining from defining "decline" in terms of "feudalism" or "formalism," that is, the putative characteristics of the Tokugawa shogunate as a political institution, but by implying that the Jishū's difficulties were part and parcel of an overall decline in the economy and the overdependence on the agricultural sector as a tax base of domains and shogunate, the principal patrons of the sect and its mission.[34] The problem with this line of argument is that the "overall economic decline" of Japan—even in the north—is no longer taken for granted. For example, Diana Wright's dissertation on the relationship among the Yugyō-ha Mantokuji, the shogunal harem, and prosperous middle-class or peasant women desperate for divorces gives a rare glimpse of how one Jishū institution survived and thrived in the growing commercial economy of premodern Japan.[35] In truth, as an institution exemplifying the *hijiri* tradition of exchange, by offering goods and services—especially status-enhancing goods and services—the Jishū was better positioned to tap the relentlessly emerging commercial economy than was the "feudal" government system. It is more than probable that this was true of the Buddhist church as a whole and a fundamental reason for its suppression by the Meiji government: it was not enough to confiscate land and to secularize clergy to put them back on the tax rolls; it was also necessary to prevent the diversion to religious services and festivals of potential donations to government-inspired modernization projects.

For the most part, however, the history of the Yugyō-ha has been squeezed into a model for writing the history of Japanese Buddhism and, consequently, squeezed out of most of the histories themselves, since it is just one example among many. The acceptance of the rise-and-fall model for the history of the Yugyō-ha has even resulted in a serious neglect of the history of order during Tokugawa period by Jishū specialists themselves. Kanai, Ōhashi, and Tachibana (and many others) have researched the Yugyō-ha up to the Tokugawa period. Few, notably Tamamuro Fumio and Mochizuki Kazan, have done any in-depth study of the order during that period. Even so, there is so much Tokugawa period material available that it is surprising that not more work has been done in the area.

The neglect of the Tokugawa period in Jishū historiography seriously impinges on the ability to explain how the study of the Jishū contributes to an understanding of the history of Buddhism in Japan. Hopefully, this work on the Jishū will provoke a reexamination of the persistent themes and assumptions informing Buddhist historiography. First, it views Jishū history from a different vantage point, that is, the period of the Yugyō-ha's height under the Tokugawa (c. 1700), and asks how the Yugyō-ha got *there*. This study, then, is premised not on a pattern of decline, but rather of adaptation and survival, which is the ultimate measure of success. What then, were the strategies for survival in other schools of Buddhism? Was the Jishū unique or atypical in its success? Second, the study focuses on the Yugyō-ha's development as a social organization, on the way it formed and regularized relationships among the order's leaders, religious, and lay adherents. Since this book is limited in its scope, it can only suggest further questions: What then were the strategies of community formation in other schools of Buddhism? Was the Jishū unique or atypical in its approaches? If the *hijiri* tradition was the harbinger of voluntary community formation in late medieval Japan, and if Buddhist institutions, including the Jishū, were positioned to develop in tandem with an increasingly commercialized economy, and if this commercialism is a principal characteristic of modern society, then what was the role of Buddhism in laying the foundation for the modernization of Japan in the second half of the nineteenth century?

Certainly, the study of the Yugyō Shōnin begs a serious reconsideration of the role of Buddhism in community formation at the national level. It is already a familiar argument that Buddhism, because in "decline," was safely in the pocket of the Tokugawa shogunate. Nevertheless, there is something unnerving about a grand prelate of the Buddhist church, followed by a train numbering in the hundreds, on progress like some medieval German king throughout the whole of Japan: moving from one of his temples to the next, drawing crowds in the thousands, and distributing blessings to one and all, men and women, living, dead, and yet to be born, peasant, merchant, samurai, domainal lord, shogun, and emperor. There was, for all intents and purposes, no one in Japan who accepted his blessing who did not belong to the parish of the Yugyō Shōnin. Indeed, it could be said that through its patronage, even the state had been absorbed into the order. Thus, the Yugyō Shōnin was perhaps the only really viable national institution in a politically-fragmented society throughout the Muromachi and Tokugawa periods. Perhaps the Yugyō Shōnin, despite their commitment to salvation in the Pure Land, realized the worst fears harbored by the old sixteenth-century unifiers of Japan and the new unifiers, leaders of the Restoration Movement and early Meiji government of the nineteenth century: the Buddhist sects, singly or conjointly, as a rival center of power, political, ideological, and economic.

2
The Yugyō-ha and Jishū:
From Itinerancy to Monasticism

The history of the Pure Land Buddhist order called the Yugyō-ha (Itinerant School), later the Jishū (Time Sect), is closely tied to that of the warrior class of premodern Japan. There are several reason, of which two are especially important. Firstly, whether in illustrated scrolls or official submissions to the shogunate, the order found it expedient or simply necessary to advertise the social connections which would enhance its position. Secondly, the bulk of independent documentation of the order's early history was preserved by warrior houses or warrior governments. Thus, we are left with a story of a religious order born of the warrior class, serving the warrior class, and, ultimately, declining with the warrior class.

IPPEN: THE HOLY MAN FROM A MILITARY HOUSE
The order's connections with the warrior class begin with Chishin Ippen Shōnin (1239-1289). Ippen was the scion of a great warrior house which had contributed significantly to the establishment of the Kamakura shogunate (1185-1333): the Kōno, who held Takanawa Castle in Iyo Province on the island of Shikoku. Ippen's great-grandfather Michikiyo died in battle against the Taira. His grandfather Michinobu (1156-1223) brought his navy to assist Minamoto Yoshitsune (1159-1189) at the battle of Dannoura in 1185. As a reward for his services, the first shogun Minamoto Yoritomo (1147-1199; shogun 1192-) gave Michinobu his coat of arms, still borne by Jishū temples, confirmed him in possession of Takanawa Castle, enrolled him as a vassal (*gokenin)* of the shogunate, made him Constable (*shugo*) of seven districts, and presented him with his sister-in-law, Hōjō Masako's younger sister, in marriage. As a loyal supporter of Yoritomo, Michinobu also took part in the 1189 campaign against Fujiwara Yasuhira at Hiraizumi.[1]

Despite his connections with the shogunate, martial and marital, Michinobu was close to the Cloistered Emperor Gotoba (1180-1239; r. 1183-1198): a son and grandson were in Gotoba's palace guard; another son had received a princess in marriage and he and another of Michinobu's grandsons were received at court. As a result, Michinobu broke with the shogunate in the Shōkyū rebellion of 1221 and sided with Gotoba, for which the Kōno were harshly punished. Michinobu and a son were exiled and another son executed. All his holdings, private and government, were confiscated as were the holdings of 149 members of the family.[2]

Ippen's father Michihiro apparently did not follow his father Michinobu but was left nevertheless with very little. It is not clear just what he lived on, perhaps even his wife's property. At some point, Michihiro shaved his head, took the name Nyobutsu, and studied Pure Land Buddhism under Ketai and Shōku (1177-1247), a disciple of Hōnen and founder of the Seizan school of Pure Land Buddhism. When his wife died, he shaved the head of his ten-year-old son and sent him to Daizaifu to study with Shōku's disciple Shōdatsu, who sent him to Ketai.[3] According to Kanai, Nyobutsu's ambitions for his son in the Buddhist church rather than in the shogunate can be inferred from his decision to remain with a school of Pure Land still closely tied to the Tendai school and its emphasis on learning. One of the factors very likely influencing this choice was the fact that this was not a movement of celibates: Shōdatsu was a married man: his wife was in fact the widow of a Kōno who had brought into the marriage a son, who became the Seizan school scholar Dōkyō Ken'i.[4] Pure Land Buddhism was not just a retreat; it provided an alternate and parallel path for the ambitious, one that obviously allowed for the maintenance of family and lineage.

In 1263, Ippen's father died and he was summoned home. In 1271, however, after living the life of a layman, Ippen shaved his head. His two biographies give two different reasons, but the *Ippen Shōnin ekotoba den* points to a problem endemic among warrior families, the incessant squabbling over land.[5] One can imagine that among the Kōno, dispossessed as they were and perhaps desperate, the rows were murderous: Ippen was attacked by a relative with a sword.[6] For whatever the reason, Ippen began his life as a *hijiri*, an unordained pilgrim, ascetic, and *nembutsu* practitioner. Ippen apparently abandoned the institutions of the Buddhist church as well as warrior society. In 1274, he received an oracle at the Kumano Main Shrine: the god of Kumano, the Kumano Gongen, an incarnation of Amida Buddha, appeared to him dressed in the robes of a mountain ascetic (*yamabushi*) and instructed him to distribute his amulets (*fuda*), slips of paper printed with the invocation to the Buddha Amida, "Namuamidabutsu," without requiring faith or purity of the recipient. Reassured in his mission,

vassal and lord of Tamanawa Castle, Hōjō Tsunanari (1515-1587), swearing to return to Fujisawa to rebuild the temple when his term of office was over and requesting the site in its entirety be secured.[56] The site was, however, divided between the order and the tradesmen and craftsmen in the service of the Hōjō.[57]

Taikō assigned a supervisor for the temple, who died in 1560, shortly before Taikō himself; another died in 1593.[58] Attempts were made to build and to rebuild.[59] When Fukō (b. 1543; YS 1584-89, FS -1626) became Fujisawa Shōnin, he appointed the head of the Ichirenji in Kōfu to supervise the Shōjōkōji and left for Mito. It was this Hō'amidabutsu who rebuilt the Shōjōkōji before dying in 1604.[60]

Under the thirteenth Fujisawa Shōnin Fukō, the Yugyō-ha came under the protection of Tokugawa Ieyasu (1543-1616; shogun 1603-1605). In 1590, Toyotomi Hideyoshi (1537-1598), greatest warlord in Japan and soon master of the entire country, had defeated the Hōjō and transferred Ieyasu to the Kantō. As the new lord of the domain, Ieyasu endowed the Shōjōkōji with a yearly stipend of one hundred *koku* of rice in 1591 and in 1603 Fukō and the Yugyō Shōnin Mango (b. 1543; YS 1589-1612) paid a call on Ieyasu at Fushimi Castle.[61] In 1607, accompanied by the eighteenth head of the Ichirenji and the nineteenth head of the Kyoto Konkōji, Fukō went to Sumpu to seek Ieyasu's assistance in dealing with a recalcitrant twentieth head of the Kyoto Konkōji: on Ieyasu's order, the Kyoto Magistrate Itakura Katsushige (1545-1624) expelled the disobedient priest.[62]

In this year, Fukō took up permanent residence in the Shōjōkōji. Ieyasu had transferred Fukō's relatives and patrons, the Satake, to Akita in 1602 and reduced their income by more than half: they left vassals and temples behind.[63] Fukō looked to Ieyasu, a richer and more powerful protector. In 1613, the Yugyō Shōnin's train first came under the protection of the Tokugawa shogunate, which gave him the right to use fifty post-horses.[64]

Patronage of religious institutions in order to assert claims of political continuity and legitimacy was not the only goal of the Tokugawa: in direct continuity with the policies of warlords during the Warring States period (1492-1568), the aim was to control religious institutions by suppressing their economic power, decreasing their number and size, and defining and regulating their activities. At the same time, the Tokugawa shogunate coopted the Buddhist institutions by making them part of their strategy to control Christianity and therefore the population on the whole. All temples were to be controlled by organizing them according to the *honmatsu* (main temple-branch temple) system and having them act as surveillance over the population through the *terauke* system, by which all were required to register as parishioners of Buddhist temples. This was done over a long period of time through a series of laws and orders: first under the guidance of Buddhist priests such as Tenkai (1536-1643) and then directly under the office of the Magistrate of Temples and Shrines (*jisha bugyō*), first established in 1635. In 1665, with the publication of the *Soshūin hattō*, the unification and the standardization of regulation of all religious institutions were accomplished. In 1631 the shogunate banned the building of new temples, and in 1632 the government asked all the temples for lists of their branch temples. In 1633, Shōjōkōji submitted its own list of 274 branch temples in thirty-nine provinces, the *Jishū Fujisawa Yugyō matsuji chō*. (There is no evidence of such rolls from Taima-ha or Shijō-ha.)[65]

Recognition of the Shōjōkōji alone as the collective-main head temple (*sōhonzan*) of the Jishū reduced the political status of the Kyoto Konkōji vis-à-vis the shogunate.[66] This effectively reasserted the system established by Shinkyō whereby the head of the order was the resident head while the itinerant head functioned principally to preserve Ippen's mission. As such, the absolute authority of the Shōjōkōji was guaranteed in its right to select the head priests of the Edo Asakusa Nichirinji (temple through which the instructions of the shogunate were to be disseminated or *furegashira*), Kōfu Ichirenji (180 *koku*), Yamagata Kōmyōji (1,760 *koku*), Kyoto Hōkokuji (134 *koku* from Miidera), and Ōhama Shōmyōji (just over 32 *koku*). The abbess of the Mantokuji (100 *koku*) reserved the right to select her disciple (*deshi*).[67]

In the subsequent years, other temples and temple lines were assigned to the jurisdiction of the Shōjōkōji. The Shijō-ha, the Taima-ha, the Reisan-ha, and the Pure Land (Jōdo) school Ikkō- and Tenryū-ha were placed under Jishū jurisdiction.[68] The 1788 list of the sect's temples, *Kakuha betsu honmatsu shōjōkaku* produced by the Nichirinji, includes the following schools and the numbers of their temples:

Mieidō-ha	22
Koku'a-ha	8
Gei-ha	7
Ichiya-ha	2
Ikkō-ha/Tenryū-ha	98
Reisan-ha	55
Shijō-ha	64

This represents a total of 217 as opposed to 564 listed for the Yugyō-ha.[69] These temples are not included in the 1633 list. They are first claimed in 1697, when Donryō identified them in his *Jishū yōrakufu* as Ippen lineages.[70] It is thought that the Ikkō-ha and Tenryū-ha were added after1687 using shogunate leverage because of their similar *hijiri* activities.

Indeed, Ōhashi assumes that all were absorbed in the time around 1687, the year in which Sonnin conducted the 350th anniversary celebrations for Emperor Godaigo at Yoshino and appeared at court in crimson.[71] These temples were allowed their own succession systems and other traditions. For the Shijō-ha, this meant a tradition mixed with the Pure Land school and, for the Tenryū- and Ikkō-ha, a Pure Land doctrinal position despite its *hijiri* practices (except for amulet distribution).[72] The reason that the *jishū* communities at Mt. Kōya and Zenkōji were not transferred to the Jishū is that they were abolished by the shogunate in 1606/1615 and 1685 respectively.[73]

Where the *honmatsu* system accomplished the organization and supervision of temples, the *terauke* system extended that supervision to the population at large. The *terauke* (parish or Buddhist adherent certification) system was based on the legal requirement for the entire population to register as parishioners of temples and to have funerals and memorial services conducted by those temples and no others. This was published in 1635, around the same time the office of the Magistrate for Shrines and Temples was being planned and established. It is clear that this system was established to suppress Christianity. In that year (1635.9), the shogunate published the rewards for informing against priests ("bateren"), monks ("iruman"), and converts.[74] Temples sent certificates of temple affiliation to parishioners to sign and then submitted lists of parishioners to the domain representative (*daikan*). Jishū temples were required to do the same.[75]

However, in 1665, the functions of Christian investigation and family registration were transferred to village officials. Temples were left with no real function other than mortuary and memorial services. Financially secure, so the argument goes, there were no incentives for religious to apply themselves either to spiritual development or to the welfare of their parishioners; thus, complaints against the temples became more frequent.[76]

The economic burden of Buddhist funerals was a particular object of criticism and as a result some domainal lords, or daimyo, tried to shift their domains from Buddhism to Shinto. Temples, mostly those connected with popular religion (*kitō shinkō*), were abolished. The Mito domain destroyed 1089 (including two Jishū) out of 2,377 temples. The Okayama domain went after Tendai and Nichiren temples: 1957 religious were laicized, 1414 temples abolished, and over 377 *koku* reclaimed to the treasury. Daimyo of domains such as Aizu, Okayama, and Mito took advantage to reorganize shrines all the way down to the village level and to establish Shinto funerals.[77]

Nonetheless, the Jishū reached its height in the 1670s and 1680s. The Yugyō Shōnin even enjoyed the privileges of a *monzeki*, a rank accorded those temples usually headed by imperial princes and high-ranking aristocrats. Until the end of the Tokugawa period the Jishū, headed by the Yugyō-ha, maintained a high profile in Japanese life. Every new Yugyō Shōnin was issued the document licensing his tour and entitling him to the use of fifty post-horses. Every domainal lord through whose lands he and his train passed was required to absorb the cost of feeding and housing them, as well as the costs for rebuilding and refurbishing temple apartments.[78] The Nichirinji in Edo acquired new prestige not only as the sect's official liaison with the shogunate (*furegashira*) but through its participation with the Kanda Shrine in holding festivals and ceremonies in honor of the Tokugawa capital Edo's protective deity Taira Masakado and through its participation in the poetry calendar of the Tokugawa shogun.[79] Even the heads of branch temples were awarded the title "Shōnin" and received in audience at the shogunal court. By the Genroku period (1688-1703), the Jishū was one of the most prestigious Buddhist institutions in Japan.

ensure Rebirth were developed. Ryōnin (1073-1132), the founder of Yūzū Nembutsu, advocated the exclusive worship of Amida and working for mutual Rebirth; he enrolled those committed to Rebirth in a register. Hōnen (1133-1212), of samurai stock and son of a man killed as a result of a dispute over land, advocated the chanting of the *nembutsu* as the sole practice suited to the times and established Pure Land (Jōdo) Buddhism as an independent school.

To estimate the influence of Pure Land Buddhism at this time of trouble, one has only to read the thirteenth-century *Heike monogatari* (The tale of the Taira house) to note that in this text Pure Land Buddhism is presented as the response of choice for those about to die, whether in their beds or in battle, for those in mourning for the dead, and as a service for the dead. The *Heike monogatari*, in fact, reads very much like a "Lives of the (Contemporary Japanese) Pure Land Saints." This should be no surprise: the *Heike* was used in the early thirteenth century as a prompt book for surreptitious preaching of the Pure Land faith because it was proscribed and the proscription was enforced in the capital.[7]

ARISTOCRATIC RETREATANTS AND POPULAR HOLY MEN

By the twelfth century, a culturally-determined response to social and personal anxiety had been established under the influence of Pure Land Buddhism while it was still merely a body of practices in the Tendai school: the removal of the individual from society, secular and religious, by nominal tonsure and retirement. Among the aristocrats of the capital, this was the practice of becoming a *tonsei no mono*, taking the tonsure but not ordination, and retiring to a more-or-less permanent but secluded abode somewhere within the confines of or at least in reach of the capital. The *tonsei* movement extended from the ninth to the thirteenth century but reached its peak in the eleventh. The function of becoming *tonsei* was retreat from the world as a social order and its bonds: the court, the family, and even the cloister, any and all aspects of society defined by the Japanese system of legal codes and regulations (*ritsu-ryō*).[8] Control by the *ritsu-ryō* system of formal Buddhist institutions of retreat encouraged eremitism (not to mention a new literature of recluses).[9]

The popular comparand was the *hijiri*, the unordained street preacher and *nembutsu* practitioner who took to the road often in the service of a religious institution.[10] The most famous fundraising campaign managed by *hijiri* was on behalf of the imperial institution, the Tōdaiji in Nara, which had been burned down in 1180. The fundraising holy men or *kanjin hijiri* operated as a body of experts in management, technology, and fundraising. High-born or low, ordained monks or retreatants, hermits and householders, named or anonymous, they were usually outsiders to the monks of the temples that commissioned them and outsiders to the lay communities they solicited for funds. Nevertheless, they provided essential services to both. For example, Chōgen (1121-1206), sixty-one when commissioned to rebuild the Tōdaiji and of comparatively low status, had already established himself as an experienced fundraiser and construction supervisor. In his position he was required to be "skilled not only in *kanjin* methods, but also in shepherding artists, managing revenue, and setting the project's priorities."[11] The anonymous *hijiri* who did the legwork built bridges and irrigation dikes for the villages and communities; they dug tunnels, wells, and ponds. Some would provide entertainment by telling stories about the temple from illustrated scrolls or by singing hymns.

Some, such as fundraisers from Mt. Kōya and Zenkōji, exchanged amulets in return for donations. Upon receiving a contribution, the *hijiri* would hand out a charm or *fuda*, supposedly printed from a block carved by the founder of Mt. Kōya and the Shingon school in Japan, Kūkai (Kōbō Daishi, 774-835).[12] Similar *kanjin* was conducted by the monks of Zenkōji in Nagano Province, who established a network of about one hundred branch temples, several of which were eventually converted to Ippen school Pure Land Buddhism.[13]

The communities of lay believers formed by such exchanges were referred to as *kechienshū*, or group of people who have made a connection leading to salvation or entry into Buddhism. The group was made up of the living and the dead and performed rituals to secure the salvation of both. These groups are known by the names of donors listed in subscription rolls (*kanjinchō*) often enclosed in statues or other objects for which the funds had been collected. The meaning of enrollment in such lists was extended to mean the enrollment of the saved and eventually led to the keeping by temples of lists of the deceased whose salvation was in their care. To indicate their corporate identity as religious practitioners, the members of such communities might take a common name, such as a name including the name of Amida Buddha.

Fundraising was not just a matter of advertising campaigns and collecting donations but of trust built up by carefully negotiated exchanges of practical assistance. Therefore, fundraising practices involved more than just donations; they culminated in the creation of community, the community of the saved. Such communities, based on voluntary association rather than family, clan, or land-tenure ties, were, as the inevitable result of the breakdown of the land-tenure system centered in the capital, the harbingers of new social organizations, lay and religious, of the fourteenth through sixteenth centuries.[14]

SAIGYŌ HŌSHI AS RETREATANT AND HOLY MAN: THE LITERARY TRADITION
The tradition of the aristocratic recluse converged with that of the travelling preacher and healer in the figure of Saigyō Hōshi: Satō Norikiyo, an imperial guard in the service of the Cloistered Emperor Toba (1103-1156, r. 1108-1123), entered religious life at twenty-three. Although Saigyō Hōshi is an historical figure, the story of his life has been reconfigured in the pattern of the life of the Buddha, and therefore he has come down in history as a legend.[15] Saigyō was received originally as the first and foremost of the literary hermits. Recognition as such is seen in the imperial anthologies: *Senzai wakashū* (Collection of a thousand years, 1187/8, *Shin kokin wakashū* (New Collection from ancient and modern times, 1205/1235), and the *Shin chokusen wakashū* (New imperial collection, 1232/1234). In this context he was seen as a loner and an outsider.[16] That is, he was seen as a *tonsei no mono*. However, Saigyō was also intimately connected with centers of the *hijiri* movement: he spent thirty years on Mt. Kōya—he even participated in its fundraising activities—and visited another *hijiri* center, Ōmine in Kumano, as well.[17]

This image of Saigyō as both *tonsei no mono* and *hijiri*, preserved in a variety of texts, is seen by Keiko Hartwieg-Hiratsuka as evidence for the reception of the process of the mixing of *tonsei* and *hijiri*, specifically as a process of the cooption of Saigyō by the *hijiri* movement to represent itself.[18] A *hijiri* element has been added to a broad variety of stories and legends about Saigyō in the *Saigyō monogatari* (c. 1254).[19] There is a description of the *hijiri* center Kumano in the earliest biography, the *Saigyō monogatari emaki* (before 1219).[20] Three stories about Saigyō take place on Mt. Kōya in the *Senjūshō*, a collection of stories about hermits in the Heian and early Kamakura periods from the second half of thirteenth century.[21]

Hiratsuka-Hartwieg sees the original distinction between noble *tonsei* and popular *hijiri* beginning to be bridged in the tenth century and finished by the time of the *Saigyō monogatari* and *Senjūshō*.[22] However, we must consider that the texts might not preserve existing traditions but might indeed have initiated them and that the connection between *tonsei* and *hijiri* was accomplished by and through these texts. Nonetheless, what is critical to this study is that Saigyō had been coopted as representative of the *hijiri* movement only shortly before the time that Ippen was active.

IPPEN AS SAIGYŌ: THE LITERARY TRADITION
Ippen was a *hijiri*. Unlike Hōnen and Shinran (1173-1262), founders of the Pure Land and True Pure Land schools respectively, although trained

formally as a priest, Ippen was never ordained. A layman, he left his family to seek salvation for himself and to preach it to others. According to the *Ippen hijiri e* (Illustrated [life] of Ippen the Hijiri), also known as the *Rokujō engi* (Origins [of Ippen the Hijiri of the temple on] Sixth Avenue), after a period of austerities, contemplation, and pilgrimage begun in 1271, in the summer of 1274 he went on pilgrimage to Mt. Kōya and from there to Kumano. On the way he had been distributing amulets to those who would believe, even for a moment, and chant the *nembutsu*. A monk's refusal on the grounds he could not believe threw him into some confusion. The monk was persuaded to accept an amulet without believing. Thinking he needed divine confirmation of his amulet distribution ("kanjin no omomuki myōryo o aubeshi to omoitamaite"), he proceeded to Kumano and went to the main shrine. There he received an oracle: the god of Kumano, an incarnation of Amida, dressed in the robes of a mountain ascetic (*yamabushi*), appeared to him and admonished him saying,

> Hijiri who preaches the Yūzū Nembutsu, why do you preach the nembutsu wrongly? All Sentient Beings will not be Reborn in the Pure Land only because of your preaching, monk. The Rebirth in Pure Land of all Sentient Beings was determined with Namuamidabutsu when Amida attained enlightenment ten kalpas ago. Do not choose between believers and unbelievers, do not distinguish between the pure and impure; distribute these amulets.[23]

His mission confirmed and sanctioned by an incarnation of Amida, Ippen pursued and eventually came to represent a religious career based almost entirely on *hijiri* practices: amulet distribution, itinerancy, and community formation (taking in common Amidabutsu names, names ending in -amidabutsu, and entry in registers). One must, however, acknowledge a gap between what Ippen said and did and the way his words and deeds were transmitted by his followers. Since there is no contemporary documentation of Ippen, one must face the fact that what one knows of Ippen is a posthumous reconstruction, a reception and interpretation influenced by considerations other than pure and faithful transmission.

For example, the *Ippen hijiri e* played a critical role in influencing the reception of Ippen as a *tonsei no mono* by identifying him with Saigyō. This was taken up by Shinkyō and, at the end of the fifteenth century, the identification had been transferred to the office of Yugyō Shōnin. By the sixteenth century, Ippen's identification with Saigyō had been accepted by the lay community.

As Laura Kaufman has demonstrated, the *Ippen hijiri e* is the product of two separate impulses. On the one hand, there is the text, produced by

Shōkai and instructed him to use it to make karmic connections to salvation or *kechien* (as noted above, the word for communities created by such karmic connections with *hijiri* were called *kechienshū*).[50] Before this, he may have been writing out the Name by hand for the same text notes that, when Ippen parted with Shōkai, he "wrote the Name and granted [him] the ten *nembutsu* and so forth."[51] Apparently, Ippen made a wooden block or two in the time between beginning the pilgrimage and leaving the Kumano shrine.

The expressions for Ippen's amulet distribution in the *Ippen hijiri e* are varied but they all refer to *kanjin hijiri* practice. On just one page of one printed edition can be seen the variety of expressions used throughout the text. Some descriptions are concrete: Ippen hands out the amulet ("fuda o watashitamaikeri") or distributes the amulet ("fuda o kubarubeshi"); people receive the amulet ("fuda o uketamau-beshi") or take the amulet ("fuda o torite"). Some are a bit more general: Ippen begins to encourage the Single Nembutsu ("ippen no nembutsu o susumete" [when he leaves Tennōji]); the god of Kumano asks him why he encourages the *nembutsu* badly ("ika ni nembutsu o ba ashiku susumeraruru zo"), by which he refers to the amulet distribution; Ippen asks the attendants of the god to extend their hands and receive the *nembutsu* ("te o sasgete, sono nembutsu ukemu, to iite"). After the incident with the monk on the road, who at first refused to accept an amulet, Ippen decides he needs confirmation of his mission from a divine source; this mission he calls "kanjin" (later on in the text, as a verb ["kanjin shite"], as a verb with *nembutsu* as the object ["nembutsu o kanjin shitamaikeru"], and even as a compound ["kanjin hijiri"]). The god of Kumano, identifying Ippen's mission with Ryōnin's, calls him the holy man who encourages the Yūzū Nembutsu ("Yūzū nembutsu susumuru hijiri" [later comes the reference to "rokujūmannin yūzū nembutsu"]).[52] Thus, by means of its diction, the text places Ippen's activities in the tradition of *kanjin hijiri* practices. However, Ippen's practice of *kanjin* differed significantly from that of other *hijiri*: the amulets were given out freely; they were not exchanged for contributions. In this, Ippen was following the instructions of the god of Kumano to make no distinctions. In effect, Ippen was to act strictly as Amida's agent in offering the ultimate interpretation of *tariki* or Salvation by the other. Later followers did sell special autographs of the Name. Nevertheless, the small, printed charms have always been free.[53]

The second important *hijiri* practice was itinerancy. In order to reach as many people as possible, Ippen had to travel. The *Ippen hijiri e* and *Ippen Shōnin ekotoba den* both use the term *shugyō* (practice or austerity) for this activity. However, each uses the term *yugyō* once and once only; although this term would acquire importance later, its exceedingly rare appearance in early important texts indicates that even by 1306 the disciples of Ippen had not distinguished their activity from that of other *kanjin*-derived groups. *Yugyō* appears to be an abbreviation of the phrase *yuge gyōbō*, which T'an-luan used to refer to the fifth stage of religious development, that in which training has ended and one goes out among the people to bring them the benefits of Buddhism rather than ascend to the next stage, nirvana.[54] Itinerancy had a double function for Ippen: wayfaring was both the way for himself to make contact (*kechien*) with deities in the places in which they had manifested themselves (pilgrimage) and the way to extend that contact, to bring salvation, to other Sentient Beings. Where itinerancy was a matter of practicality for fundraising *hijiri* who looked to sources of income sometimes far from their bases, itinerancy for Ippen was a much more complicated religious practice based on meditation and mysticism. (I will discuss this further in the next chapter).

A practice initiated by Ippen and allied with itinerancy was the dancing *nembutsu*, chanting the *nembutsu* while walking in a circle, or *odori nembutsu*. With Ippen, it began as a spontaneous end to a service performed at a warrior's home in Odagiri, Shinano Province in 1279: a joint chanting of the *nembutsu* by *jishū* and laymen ended as a wild, ecstatic dance.[55] However, even during Ippen's lifetime, it was gradually transformed into a staged performance used to attract audiences to whom Ippen could distribute the amulets.[56] Dancing *nembutsu* can not as yet be proven to be a standard *hijiri* practice or going back further than Ippen's time. The *Ippen hijiri e* traces its origins to Kūya Shōnin, whom he venerated: "As for the dancing *nembutsu*, Kūya Shōnin began [the] religious practice at places like Ichiya and the crossroads at Fourth Avenue [in the capital]."[57] The ambiguous reading of this passage leads one to think that the dancing *nembutsu*'s connection with Kūya is contrived or that the real object is to place Ippen in the line of popular street preachers of the *nembutsu* exemplified by Kūya. There is no mention in relevant sources of such an activity by Kūya himself.[58]

Ippen followed *hijiri* practice of forming communities by establishing a confraternity. Before the revelation at Kumano, Ippen had been accompanied by Shōkai to Iwayaji, where he had undertaken austerities (the beginning of his life as "tonsei"), and two women and a child (Chō'ichi, Chō'ni, possibly mother and daughter, and Nembutsu-bō, perhaps a maidservant) to Kumano.[59] After breaking completely with family, he gradually formed a small group of around twenty men and women with whom he made special pacts to seek salvation together.[60] The first to follow Ippen after his revelation was Ta'amidabutsu Shinkyō, whom he met in Kyushu just after meeting and converting the warrior Ōtomo Yasuyori: "beginning with Ta'amidabutsu he made vows of Fellow Practitioners and of mutual affection."[61] Shinkyō's position in the confraternity as first disciple was indicated by his position as *chōshō*, leader of the chant.[62] Ippen did not form an order but a community of wayfarers on the same spiritual path. Taking his inspiration from a passage in Shan-tao's *Hymns on the Hanju Meditation*, he called his followers "Fellow Practitioners (*dōgyō*)."[63] Like all other groups of practitioners of the *nembutsu* at six hours of the twelve-hour day (*rokuji nembutsu shū*), they called themselves *jishū*.[64] This confraternity of both men and women (*nishū*) travelling and living together is apparently the only known example of such an arrangement in Japanese Buddhism.[65]

The community of Fellow Practitioners was reinforced through other *hijiri* practices: entry in a register and the use of Amidabutsu names. *Kanjin hijiri* kept lists of contributors, members of a community of the saved, which were placed, for example, in statues paid for with funds donated by them.[66] Ryōnin, founder of Yūzū Nembutsu, a form of mutual work toward mutual salvation, had individuals record their commitment to the movement by entry in his register, as noted above. Under Ippen, a similar register, the *Jishū kakochō*, was kept by Shinkyō of those *jishū* who had died, of those who had attained Rebirth. The first entry is dated 1279.[67] Two entries in 1319 of "kechienshū"[68] indicate the continuation of the *hijiri* tradition of community formation and the role of registers in helping to create community.

Another practice going back to Chōgen is the granting of Amidabutsu names (*amigō*) to members of the community. Ippen granted those joining the *jishū* a religious name of one syllable followed by -amidabutsu for men and women, and later, -ichibō or -butsubō for the women: the forty-eight single syllables and characters for men and forty-eight for women represented the forty-eight vows of Amida.[69] The earliest recording of the practice, a document dated 1278 in the hand of Ta'amidabutsu Shinkyō and called the *Ichigo fudan nembutsu ketsuban*, lists forty-eight *jishū* in six groups for a ceremony. These names and rankings apparently remained more or less fixed.[70] It is presumed that the Amidabutsu names were given because those who chanted the *nembutsu* became the *nembutsu* or Amidabutsu.[71] Ippen never took such a name for himself; "ippen" was very likely synonymous with the single chanting of Namuamidabutsu.

Ippen based his own propagation practices on those already in use by Kōya and Zenkōji *hijiri*. Reception of Ippen as a principal representative of the *hijiri* movement is demonstrated by the fact that so many Kōya *hijiri* were converted to Ippen school Pure Land Buddhism that ninety per cent of them were *jishū* based at chapels at Mt. Kōya (the Kayadō, Senjūin, and Rengedani), while monks serving at the front door or *tsumado* of Zenkōji were converted and known as the *tsumado jishū*.[72]

SHINKYŌ: *HIJIRI* PRACTICES AND THE CREATION OF A RELIGIOUS ORDER

When Ippen died in 1289, some of his disciples committed suicide, some returned to their homes, and a group under Ta'amidabutsu Shinkyō continued the mission. Ippen had made it clear, according to Shōkai in the *Ippen hijiri e*, that "[his] mission was to last his lifetime only." He had given some texts to a monk from Mt. Shosha, founded by Shōkū, one of his predecessors and models, and burned others; he had left to his disciples "nothing but Namuamidabutsu."[73] Thus, when Shinkyō began practicing amulet distribution and thus took over Ippen's mission, practically speaking, he formed his own, separate confraternity.[74]

Itinerancy and amulet distribution were the core functions of Ippen's confraternity, and Ta'amidabutsu Shinkyō faithfully preserved Ippen's mission. However, Shinkyō's career diverged significantly from Ippen's: he made permanent residence in temples a regular practice not only for rank-and-file monks and nuns but even for the head of the religious community. Thus, Shinkyō did not simply continue and develop Ippen's confraternity of *nembutsu* practitioners; he established his own order.[75] This was an independent order *within which* Ippen's doctrines and practices were preserved and perpetuated.

If one insists on seeing Shinkyō strictly as Ippen's disciple, then there are problems in accepting Shinkyō's continuation of Ippen's mission.[76] However, if one sees Shinkyō as a *nembutsu/kanjin hijiri*, the problems are resolved. If Ippen was only one—including Shōkai—of many practitioners of the *nembutsu*, amulet distribution, and itinerancy, then Ippen could claim no monopoly of the practices in his own lifetime except among those in his group; once he had died, the members of his confraternity were free to do as they pleased.

Shinkyō clearly saw himself as continuing the *hijiri* tradition. He also continued Ippen's concept of the leader as the sole *kanjin hijiri* in the confraternity, confirming Shōkai's reception of Ippen's role in the *Ippen hijiri e*. Throughout the *Ippen Shōnin ekotoba den* (produced c. 1305 under Shinkyō's auspices), Ippen is referred to as "hijiri" about thirty times. He is addressed as "Shōnin" usually by someone outside the confraternity.[77] For example, the report of the dream oracles received by various functionaries at the Mishima Shrine instructing Ippen to visit this his family shrine have the god refer to Ippen as "Ippen Shōnin" and "Shōnin." Very rarely, as in the same passage, does the narrator of the text refer to Ippen as "Shōnin," as in the crucial scene describing the death of Ippen which has Shinkyō and the "Shōnin" shedding tears. Again, when Shinkyō and the other *jishū* move to Mt. Tanjō to die, the text refers to their "tears of attachment to the Shōnin" (*shōnin renbo no namida*). After Ippen dies, the text refers to him twice as the "late *hijiri*" (*koshō*; the character for the second syllable is that for 'hijiri') and as the "late Shōnin" (*koshōnin*). This terminology is also followed in the 1306 *Hōnō engi ki*, written to accompany an illustrated scroll presented to the Kumano Main Shrine: *koshō*, Ippen the Hijiri, *hijiri*, not to mention the title of the *Ippen Shōnin ekotoba den*.[78] This indicates that "Shōnin" was used as a respectful form of address by those outside the confraternity and as a term of respect within the confraternity for the dead rather than as a formal title of office.

Shinkyō position as head of the newly-formed confraternity— and as Ippen's heir—is indicated by the over forty references in the text to him as "hijiri," including "*hijiri* who abandons [everything]" (*sutehijiri*), and "*hijiri* of many itinerant confraternities" (*yugyō tashū no hijiri*). The address of "Shōnin" as in "Ta'amidabutsu Shōnin, the *nembutsu* propagating saint who practices throughout the provinces" (*shōkoku shugyō no nembutsu kanjin hijiri Ta'amidabutsu Shōnin*) makes clear that the title was used as a polite form of address, exactly as it was with Ippen even though Shinkyō is occasionally referred to by the narrator as "Shōnin." For example in the scene describing the confraternity's crossing of a river, the narrator notes that "beginning with the Shōnin" (*shōnin o hajimete*), they chanted the *nembutsu*.[79] Thus, one sees a practice of addressing the head of the confraternity by his position, *hijiri*, or with particular respect by non-confraternity members while alive or by the community when dead as "Shōnin." We cannot be certain about the inconsistencies: the available text (donated to the Kōmyōji in 1594[80]) is a copy of the original and it is possible that the copyist replaced "hijiri" with "shōnin" or even added it because of contemporary use of the term.

Although Shinkyō has confirmed the status of the leader of the confraternity as sole *hijiri* and the practice of referring to the leader as such, with Shinkyō the title "Shōnin" takes on a completely different meaning. The *Ekotoba den* makes clear in the story of the miracle at Ise that Shinkyō, on account of the miracle of rays of light emanating from his person, was formally and officially vested by the court with the title "Shōnin" through recommendation by the Ise Shrine.[81] This contradicts the testimony of the *Jō'a Shōnin den*, as discussed below, that Shinkyō received his title through the good offices of a disciple who had received the title first. It should be noted, however, that, although early sources refer quite regularly to individual heads of the order as Shōnin (that is, the title follows the personal name), it is not clear when the title Yugyō Shōnin itself first became common, perhaps even as late as the early sixteenth century.

Another indication of Shinkyō's divergence from Ippen is seen in the increased emphasis on the concept of *chishiki*. *Chishiki* is a term closely associated with Pure Land Buddhism, going well back to the Heian period, when it meant guide in religious matters, guide to salvation and to paradise at death.[82] There is also indication that the term *chishiki* was used in *hijiri* communities for lay adherents or their leaders.[83] Ippen called himself the "Rokujūmannin chishiki" to indicate his status as one who causes the masses to chant the *nembutsu*.[84] In the *Ippen hijiri e* and *Ippen Shōnin ekotoba den*, Ippen is described as taking the role of *chishiki*, or religious guide, when assisting at a tonsure or at a death or when his *jishū* drown themselves to follow their religious guide.[85] In traditional Pure Land Buddhist practice, the chief function of the *chishiki* was to guide others in the chanting of the last ten *nembutsu* before death, the *saigo no jūnen*.[86] In the *Ekotoba den*, as in the *Ippen hijiri e*, there is not much emphasis on the last ten *nembutsu* in Ippen's career. One rare example is that of the story of the lay priest Ajisaka, who commits suicide by drowning: he chants the ten *nembutsu* as he enters a river ("jūnen tonaete kawa ni irikereba"). In addition, one of Ippen's hymns (*wasan*) cited in the text also refers to the "saigo no jūnen."[87] However, there seems to be somewhat more emphasis on the *jūnen* in the section on Shinkyō—and not merely in terms of numbers of references. On the one hand it is presented as something for which Shinkyō is famous. He is at one point addressed by someone outside the confraternity who says, "I have heard that [you are] the *hijiri* by whom I should be encouraged [to chant] the ten *nembutsu*."[88] More importantly, the ten *nembutsu* are carefully integrated into the story of the miracle at Ise Shrine, which, it is related, is the reason Ise Shrine recommended Shinkyō to the court for advancement to "Shōnin." When Shinkyō and his *jishū* are observed outside the shrine, they are described as "chant[ing] the ten *nembutsu*" (*jūnen o tonaetamau*). The Ise Shrine attendant, witnessing the miracle of light emanating from the hand(s) of Shinkyō ("hijiri"), "folded his hands in prayer . . . and received the ten *nembutsu*" (*te o awase . . . jūnen o uketatematsuru*). When the *jishū* are invited to enter the shrine, they are "chanting the ten *nembutsu*" (*jūnen tonaete*).[89]

We can perhaps see in the *Ekotoba den* a tentative attempt gradually to identify Shinkyō more as an orthodox Pure Land preacher than as a *kanjin hijiri*. This is certainly clear in comparing contexts established by the opening passages of the *Ekotoba den* and the *Hijiri e*. The *Hijiri e* opens with "Ippen the Hijiri" and his background. The *Ekotoba den*, however, begins with a standard analysis of Buddhism, its division into two main attributed to the fact that Donkai had been Shinkyō's disciple, had been given permission by Shinkyō to practice amulet distribution, and was founder and head of an important temple in Kyoto and its branch temples. Whether Chitoku had any authority over Donkai, de jure or de facto, is not apparent.

In 1320, having appointed Nai'a Shinkō as his successor to Muryōkōji, Chitoku died. The subsequent protest and then secession of Donkai resulted in a clarification of the *hijiri* career. The problem was not necessarily succession to Muryōkōji but the taking of the name Ta'amidabutsu. Donkai's position was that Shinkyō had established the principle that the name Ta'amidabutsu ("myōji") was to be inherited only by the Yugyō [Hijiri]; because Nai'a had not practiced *yugyō*, he was not eligible.[119] He later accused Nai'a of having repented ("eshin," by which may be inferred reconciliation and giving up the title Ta'amidabutsu) and then of apostatizing, of having made up the story that Chitoku had chosen him as his successor, of styling himself the Yugyō Chishiki, and denying Donkai's position as such. Just as there were "no two suns in the sky," there was only one Yugyō [Hijiri] and that was Donkai.[120]

The important thing is not the truth of the matter but Donkai's claim. Donkai, who established the Yugyō-ha, considered *yugyō* the main attribute of Shinkyō's heir and the main prerequisite for succession to the name Ta'amidabutsu. For him, as for Shinkyō, *yugyō* and Ta'amidabutsu were inseparable, and there was only one. *Yugyō* now definitely established the term for the touring mission: not "shokoku shugyō" but "shokoku yugyō."[121] Amulet distribution was something else entirely or he would have had to acknowledge serious problems with the former Yugyō Hijiri Chitoku and with Jō'amidabutsu Shinkan, the third of Shinkyō's disciples given the right to distribute amulets. There is no evidence of a quarrel with Shinkan: he is entered in the *Jishū kakochō*.[122]

The succession dispute forced further clarification. Donkai was the first to create a clear line of succession: Ippen the Hijiri, Shinkyō (Daishō or "Great Hijiri," the second generation), Chitoku (Chūshō or "Middle Hijiri," the third), and the fourth, himself. His own words indicate clearly that he saw a system of having the head of the order choose the Yugyō Hijiri as the basis of establishing a seamless continuity of will and intent from one leader to the next, from Ippen to Ta'amidabutsu to Ryō'amidabutsu to the fourth generation (himself). However, he would not choose from among his own, personal disciples: "Thus, because the succession of the fourth generation must [carry on] a mission [following] a single principle, [as] the Daishō [Shinkyō] said, the disciples of the *hijiri* who abandons [everything] must not have a principle of succession by inheritance," and so the mission "has maintained [the continuity of] Nonduality for more than fifty years."[123]

Donkai's contribution to the principle of succession was a concept of the career that served as a model for future generations, but one whose intent was to secure the position of Yugyō Hijiri to the Shichijō-ha (Seventh Avenue school), later called the Yugyō-ha. In 1325, Donkai left his base in Kyoto, the Shichijō Konkōji, and established the Shōjōkōin in Fujisawa, ostensibly as a challenge to the Muryōkōji and a base from which to lobby the powerful warriors of the Kamakura shogunate. As the next Yugyō Hijiri, Donkai had chosen not his own disciple but Chitoku's disciple, Ankoku (b. 1270; YS 1325-1337, FS -1337).[124] A Tokugawa period source indicates that Ankoku was the second head of the Konkōji.[125] One presumes he was made head of the Konkōji when Donkai took up *yugyō* after Shinkyō's death in 1319 and Yugyō Hijiri when Donkai took up residence at the Shōjōkōin. On Donkai's death, Ankoku took up residence at the Shōjōkōin and died there. The next Yugyō Hijiri was Shinkyō's disciple Yo'amidabutsu Itchin, head of the Ichijō (First Avenue) Kōshōji (b. 1276; YS 1327-1338, FS -1335); he is noted also by the same source as the third head or Ji'amida-butsu of the Konkōji.[126] Itchin took up residence at the Shōjōkōin on Ankoku's's death and died there. The seventh was Chitoku's disciple Shuku'amidabutsu Takuga (b. 1284; YS 1338-1354), at Konkōji, but not its head priest, since 1317-1319.[127] He died before Itchin and did not succeed to the Shōjōkōin. The eighth was Donkai's first and only disciple to take office, the fourth head of Konkōji Tei'amidabutsu Tosen (b. 1305; YS 1354-1356, FS -1381). He chose Itchin's disciple from the Jōrinji in Hakuseki, Kai'amidabutsu Hakuboku (b. 1313; YS 1356-1367).[128]

The pattern that one sees emerging is that the head of the Shōjōkōin chooses the Yugyō Hijiri, who then succeeds to Shōjōkōin. But the choice of the Yugyō Hijiri has been carefully negotiated to deal with a number of conflicting claims and interests based on office, teacher-disciple relationships, and that age-old problem in Japan, group inheritance rights and the right of the most senior to decide succession. As Kanai sees it, Donkai subordinated discipleship to office in his choice of Ankoku, a man who had served with him no more than five or six years and yet was his brother disciple's disciple. His choice may have disappointed Yo'amidabutsu Itchin, a man to whom he had turned to during in his fight with Muryōkōji, and, to compromise, Donkai must have designated Itchin as the next Yugyō Hijiri. Ankoku may have wanted to establish the career pattern of moving from the position of head of Konkōji to that of Yugyō Hijiri and thus to choose the third head of the Konkōji. Tokugawa sources list Yo'amidabutsu Itchin as the third head of Konkōji, but there is apparently no proof of his having ever been there.[129] The apparent compromise was the choice as Itchin's heir of Ankoku's long-time colleague, Takuga. The brief reference in Itchin's letter to Takuga to the "time when for some time [Takuga] had [shown] some hesitation" (*Maemae wa isasaki shinshaku no jibun*) indicates to Kanai a problem between Ankoku and Itchin concerning the succession.[130] When 1354 Takuga died, Itchin chose Tosen, Donkai's disciple and Konkōji's fourth head. Matters had come full circle, rivalry had been overcome, and the succession regularized.

Truly speaking, we really have no clear idea of what is going on—or what is supposed to go on—until Tosen appears on the scene. According to his travel diary, *Yugyō hachidai Tosen Shōnin kaikoku ki*, when Takuga died, Tosen was apparently summoned to Fujisawa.[131] On 1354.9.18, he received the announcement ("yogon") of succession and the name Ta'amidabutsu from the sixth founder ("sō") Itchin and then distributed amulets for the first time as the ceremony of succession. Between the twentieth and twenty-fifth, he sent his name ("gomyōji") Yū'amidabutsu back to Konkōji.[132] On 1355.12.22, Itchin died. On 1356.2.7, Tosen had still not returned to Fujisawa. Shortly after, a letter from the shogun arrived with instructions to proceed to the Shōjōkōin. On the thirtieth a letter from Takauji's son, the Kamakura *kubō* Motouji (1340-1367), arrived with the same instructions. On 3.21, he chose Kai'amidabutsu of the Shichijō Konkōji to style himself Yū'amidabutsu.[133] On the next day, his succession to the position of Yugyō Hijiri and to the name ("gomyōgo") Ta'amidabutsu was announced.[134]

Ideally, then, when the head of the order, the head priest of Shōjōkōin, died, his appointed successor, the Yugyō Hijiri, would make his way to Fujisawa to take up residence and leadership of the order. On the whole there seems to be no indication that the Yugyō Hijiri chose his own successor. Further, if a Yugyō Hijiri died before the head of the Shōjōkōji and before his successor could be chosen, the head chose a new Yugyō Hijiri, who performed his first amulet distribution—the ceremony of succession—at Fujisawa.[135] This is how the "unity of the mission" was preserved as was the authority of the head of the order over the head of the mission.

The custom of nominating candidates only from the Konkōji could not be continued; there would be resentment if only those from Konkōji could be eligible. Even so, the master-disciple relationship seems to have been considered very important; until the eighteenth century, the overwhelming majority of Yugyō Shōnin were disciples of previous Yugyō Shōnin. Until then, according to existing sources, the number of Yugyō Shōnin whose masters had not been Yugyō Shōnin was small—five (the twenty-second, twenty-seventh, thirty-third, thirty-sixth, and forty-fourth). Nevertheless, Konkōji would remain the joint headquarters of the Yugyō-ha and the base of the Yugyō Shōnin. The position was so important that the head of Konkōji, not the Yugyō Shōnin, represented the order at shogunal and Ashikaga house ceremonies.

While Donkai had established the career pattern of succession from Yugyō Shōnin to Fujisawa Shōnin, he also inadvertently added a new element to the career of the Yugyō Hijiri. The development of the position of Yugyō Hijiri was intimately connected with the functions of amulet distribution and itinerancy. Enrollment in a register, an old *kanjin hijiri* practice, was a function but not necessarily an important one. Certainly, as a *kanjin hijiri* function, registration, like amulet distribution, could not form a basis of authority. Although Shinkyō had begun a register of *jishū* of the confraternity who had achieved Rebirth by keeping their vows until death, there is no evidence that the *Jishū kakochō* had any special significance in the mission. Although it is the oldest surviving register, it was not necessarily the only one in use at the time.[136] Chitoku entered no names: apparently, he had never taken it on *yugyō*. Shinkyō wrote in his own name just before he died; Donkai wrote in the date and took it with him as one of several souvenirs in Shinkyō's hand. Donkai entered only thirty-seven names through 1324, the year he took up residence in Fujisawa; he apparently did not take the register with him on *yugyō* and left it at the Konkōji when he moved to Fujisawa.[137] Ankoku entered only six names, if any, in the nun's section.[138] Apparently, it was Itchin who entered Donkai's death date and was the first to make the register the register of the Yugyō Hijiri: place names indicate that he took the register with him on *yugyō*.[139] In twelve years he entered sixty-eight men and sixty-four women, including Ankoku's name and his date of death.[140] When he took up residence at the Shōjōkō-in, he handed over the *Jishū kakochō* to Takuga, the seventh. Takuga's successor Tosen, head of Konkōji, where Takuga died, wrote in Takuga's name and death date; he became the next Yugyō Hijiri.[141] The *Jishū kakochō* continued to be passed on from one Yugyō Hijiri or Yugyō Shōnin to the next.

What is clear from the entries in the *Jishū kakochō* is the concept of the community of *jishū*. At first only members of the confraternity were entered. A distinction was made between those who had kept vows and those who had not; those who had not kept their vows had not achieved Rebirth and their status was indicated by "fu" (not). "Kechienshū," or lay members, were gradually introduced, some while still alive as "gyakushū." Some *jishū* were entered while still alive as "genson." Even the long-time dead were entered, such as Taira Kiyomori and the legendary Benkei, as were members of the

Ashikaga family, *nō* and *sarugaku* actors, "bikuni," pirates and sculptors of Buddhist images.[142]

One might see the change in the sort of people entered as an indication of the change in social support of the order: warriors in the fourteenth century, shogunate and court in the fifteenth, commoners in the sixteenth. However, this does not take into account the fact that the shogunate had literally taken the Yugyō Shōnin hostage at one point and kept him in Kyoto, where, of course, the warrior officials could easily monopolize him.[143] A Yugyō Shōnin in the provinces would more likely meet with different sorts of people. At the same time, the Fujisawa Shōnin tended to take care of the Kantō and so reduced the geographical scope of the Yugyō Shōnin's duties and thus the number of entries in the *Jishū kakochō*. Again, during the latter fifteenth and sixteenth centuries, as the Ashikaga shogunate collapsed and power was localized, so the local temple became more important and its *kakochō* a better record of the order's community.

Further, the decreasing number of "fu" (none after 1388) is seen as an indication in the weakening belief in the power of the *Jishū kakochō*.[144] Other factors can be considered in the decreasing necessity to punish *jishū* posthumously: increased shogunal sponsorship and, no doubt, authority over *jishū*, tightening of regulations (i.e., under Taikū in 1412), and, of course, delegation of the authority as Chishiki to local temple heads, who, no doubt, would assume the general responsibilities of discipline. The *Jishū kakochō* can not be used to make any judgments about the order without considering other *kakochō* and documents (now existing or not) and historical circumstances in general.

Some see the community in terms of numbers: the more the entries, the more prosperous and successful the community. Thus, in Jishū scholarship, beginning with Akamatsu Toshihide, the high point of the Yugyō-ha is generally seen as reached in the thirteen years under the fifteenth Yugyō Shōnin Sonne (b. 1364; YS 1417-1429); 5,789 people are entered, men and women, living and dead, religious and lay.[145] By the time of the twenty-second Yugyō Shōnin Igyō (b. 1465; YS 1497-1512, FS -1518), the order is seen as in a serious decline because of the low number of entries: one.[146] However, considering that Shōjōkōji had burned down only three months before Igyō had become Yugyō Shōnin and that the Fujisawa Shōnin Chiren had died only five days after, it is not surprising that he had not entered very many names—he would have been expected to start using the Shōjōkōji's death register, the *Tōtakusan kakochō* (see below). Again, the delegation of authority to local temples means one has to look at their *kakochō*, too, before making any evaluation of the order as a whole.

Nor can one depend on the *Jishū kakochō* or *Tōtakusan kakochō*, lost, burnt, retrieved, and restarted, to estimate the size of the community: what is left of either is far from complete. Apparently, when Yūsan (1512-1583; FS 1573-) succeeded as thirtieth Yugyō Shōnin in 1563, he started a new roll. This he handed over to the thirty-second Yugyō Shōnin Dōnen in 1573 when he succeeded as "Fujisawa Shōnin" and sent or took the rest of the rolls to Saihōji in Kaga, Echizen Province, where he died in 1583. There, between 1588 and 1592, eleven nuns' names were entered by a single hand, perhaps that of the head priest of Saihōji.[147] Unfortunately, in 1581 pirates attacked Dōnen's train as he was sailing to the west ("Saikoku") and made off with, among other things, the part of the *Jishū kakochō* he was carrying.[148] Succeeding Yugyō Shōnin continued to use their own rolls.[149] In 1644, while in Kyoto, Nyotan (b. 1578; YS 1641-1644, FS - 1646) heard that the parts of the register started by Shinkyō and continued by generations of Yugyō Shōnin was at the Saihōji and the next year it was brought to him at Fujisawa, whereupon he immediately sent it to Edo to the thirty-seventh Yugyō Shōnin Takushi (b. 1590; YS 1645-1647, FS - 1658).[150] Some time after that, most likely after he succeeded to the Fujisawa Shōjōkōji, Takushi put the original *Jishū kakochō* in its present form of one folding volume (about nine by three inches) and added explanatory comments (these included all the "X-sō Shōnin" and "Yugyō X-dai" after the death dates of Yugyō Shōnin).[151] During an interview with the retired Emperor Gomizunoo (1596-1680; r. 1611-1629) in Kyoto in 1644 he may very well have mentioned the discovery of the *Jishū kakochō* and, upon receiving an inquiry from Gomizunoo, submitted a copy.[152] The text from Saihōji, with contemporary entries through 1592, none of which was entered by the Yugyō Shōnin after 1563, survives; the other, later rolls or volumes were apparently destroyed in a massive fire at Konkōji in 1858.[153]

It is easy to think of the *Jishū kakochō* as the main register of the order. However, as Kanai has pointed out, registers were probably quite common and it took some time for the *Jishū kakochō* to achieve a singular status as the register of the Yugyō Shōnin.[154] Moreover, the head of Shōjōkōji also maintained a death register, which more or less served the lay and religious of the eastern part of Japan, the Kantō. The original was lost when Shōjōkōji was burned in 1513 (1.29). It was begun anew by Igyō, who had taken up permanent residence at a new temple in Futaiwa in Mino Province.[155] It was lost again in 1557 in a fire at Tsuruga in Echizen Province which destroyed the Saihōji, where Butten was in permanent residence, as well as Kehi Shrine and several hundred houses and temples. Butten then started the present, existing *Tōtakusan kakochō*.[156] A folded book, 29.8 centimeters by 12.5, it was divided by Butten into two sections, one for religious (last entry 1800/Kansei 12.5.13) and one for lay ("kechien-shū," last entry 1773/An'ei 2.11.13, except for a series of mixed-date entries from one family), with mixing of sexes rather than having men's and women's sections. A few religious and lay are entered while alive as "gyakushū."[157] Its historical value, in particular, lies in the way it fills in gaps left by the *Jishū kakochō* in determining what support and sponsorship the order was receiving in the East: the Kōsaka family of Mino, the Asakura, the Nihonmatsu, and the Satake.[158]

Charisma is a career determined by social and historical circumstances and the career followed by Ippen was that of the *hijiri*. Of all eremitic institutions in the Japanese middle ages, the *hijiri* were most widely involved in the formation of voluntary religious communities by virtue of their activities as fundraisers for temples. Ippen was not a fundraiser, but he modelled his religious life on that of *hijiri* and used *hijiri* practices in his mission: itinerancy, amulet distribution, Amidabutsu names (*amigo*), and entry in registers. Much of the vocabulary describing his activities comes from *hijiri* practices and, therefore, diction: *hijiri, shugyō, kanjin, fuda, chishiki*, and *kechienshū*.

Shinkyō demonstrated a recognition that *hijiri* practices could not be the basis of his authority and ultimately he subordinated *hijiri* practices, especially itinerancy and amulet distribution, to the master-disciple relationship: he passed down his name to represent the creation of his own order, an order within which Ippen's mission was preserved and perpetuated. Most importantly, he stressed his role as Chishiki, guide to salvation, to promote himself as a more orthodox preacher of Pure Land Buddhism.

Even so, *hijiri* practices remained the core of the image of the order. Although Shinkyō shared *hijiri* practice, amulet distribution, with three disciples (but his name with only one), *hijiri* practice became the focus of the conflict between Donkai and Shinkō regarding the use of the name Ta'amidabutsu: Donkai insisted that only one (himself) who had practiced itinerancy was eligible to take the name. Thus, in the Yugyō-ha, itinerancy was the defining function of the head of the order: amulet distribution was shared among three head priests in the order. As the importance of amulet distribution by itself was diminished as the distinguishing attribute of the head of the order, the death register, as a variation of the fundraising roll or register of a particular religious community, gradually became more and more important in defining the head of the mission. Entry in the *Jishū kakochō* carried by the head of the mission became one of three defining functions of the order and demonstrated reception of the belief in the authority of the head of the order to guarantee Rebirth in the Pure Land.

A secondary issue in the definition of the *hijiri* career is the history of its development. This was preserved in the career of the Yugyō Shōnin. Ostensibly, to follow Donkai's career, based on Ippen's and Shinkyō's, one would have to go from the Konkōji to *yugyō* to the Shōjōkōji. Because 1) the Yugyō Shōnin could not manage Konkōji and manage *yugyō* at the same time and 2) because restricting access to those from Konkōji would encourage jealousy and fragmentation among all the head priests of the order, disciples and brother disciples of various Yugyō Shōnin, the role of Konkōji in the history of the order and the career of the head of the order was "sublimated" in the function of Konkōji as joint head temple of the order and base of the Yugyō Shōnin—being head priest of the temple was not required for succession to the position of Yugyō Shōnin. However, the career route from Yugyō Shōnin to head of Shōjōkōji was clearly established.

Shinkyō gave permission to three disciples to practice amulet distribution. However, with the establishment of the Yugyō-ha, the right to amulet distribution (*fusan*) was vested principally in the Yugyō Shōnin, although the Fujisawa Shōnin had the right to practice *fusan* in the six eastern provinces of Japan (Kantō) and Jō'a Shōnin of the Shijō-ha temple Konrenji had the right to practice amulet distribution within the city of Kyoto.[159] Amulet distribution was not to be the basis of authority in Shinkyō's order; it could not be monopolized and was indeed practiced by other *nembutsu hijiri* and temples, including, very likely, other disciples of Ippen. No *hijiri* practices were to be the basis of Shinkyō's religious authority. Nevertheless, the *hijiri* tradition came to define and eventually to be exemplified by the Yugyō-ha.

4

The Charisma of the Leader: Institutionalizing and Transforming Religious Authority

Ippen's authority as teacher and leader of a confraternity of religious practitioners was based on his ability to produce incontrovertible evidence of contact with the divine: letters, poems, and hymns describing his experiences of previewing the Pure Land and unification with Amida Buddha through the *nembutsu*. Ippen was a mystic.

The experience of a mystic, however, is a problematic basis for the preservation of a community beyond the first generation of followers. Only a few are capable of sharing this sort of experience; most simply live in hope of it. Thus, in the order deriving from Ippen's confraternity an immediate transition was made to other, traditional strategies of community formation to establish the authority of the leader: master-disciple relationships, oaths of obedience, and stricter regulations to define the community. All this depended on an increasing reliance on interpreting basic Seizan school concepts of the mystical unification of Amida, *nembutsu*, and practitioner to vest in the Chishiki of the order an absolute authority: that of representative of the Buddha and, finally, of Buddha on this earth.

IPPEN THE MYSTIC: THE HOLY MAN WHO ABANDONED THE WORLD

Ippen was the last of the six most famous religious figures, including Hōnen, Shinran (1173-1262), Eisai (1141-1215), Dōgen (1200-1253), and Nichiren (1222-1282), of the Kamakura period (1185-1333). Along with Hōnen and Shinran, he helped make Pure Land Buddhism an independent school in Japan. Pure Land Buddhism is generally associated with populism and simple practice.[1] However, Pure Land Buddhism both in China and in Japan functioned principally as meditation practice, the most important guide to which was The Pure Land Meditation Sutra (*Kanmuryōjukyō*).[2]

The great figures of Japanese Pure Land Buddhism were dedicated to meditation practices and the dreams and visions they produced. Genshin wrote extensively on meditation in the *Essentials for Rebirth [in the Pure Land]* and specified that the benefits of the *nembutsu* included seeing Buddhas, as well as purification of sins and Rebirth in the Pure Land at death.[3] Hōnen's own visions of Amida and the Pure Land between 1198 and 1206 were recorded in the *Sammai Hottokuki* even when he declared meditation, a "perfect vision of Amida[,] to be impractical."[4] Shinran was a devotee of Perpetual Meditation (*jōgyō zanmai*), a principal Tendai practice, all the years he was on Mt. Hiei. His decision to leave Mt. Hiei was the result of a revelation in a dream on the fifty-ninth day of a one hundred-day retreat. And even after he had accepted the Single Practice of the *nembutsu*, a major religious experience confirming the single recitation of the *nembutsu* resulted on the fifth day of fulfilling a vow to recite the three major Pure Land sutras (he stopped).[5]

Ippen is best understood as a mystic in the Pure Land tradition of walking meditation: a ceremony of circumambulating an image of Amida for ninety days while reading sutras and chanting the name of Amida meant to result in full visualization of Amida and other Buddhas.[6] It entered the practices of the Tendai school as Perpetual Meditation (*jōgyō zanmai*), Nembutsu Meditation (*nembutsu zanmai*), and Continuous Nembutsu (*fudan nembutsu*). Hōnen's disciple and founder of the Seizan school, Shōkū, promoted the Continuous Nembutsu.[7]

Ippen's life was a perpetual walking meditation culminating in occasional and varying mystical experiences—dreams, visions, and even ecstasy. For Ippen, the possibility of previewing Rebirth in the Pure Land, of seeing Amida and all other Buddhas and Bodhisattvas face to face, could be realized through pilgrimage and its extension, dancing *nembutsu* (*odori nembutsu*).[8]

Pilgrimage is walking meditation.[9] In pilgrimage, Ippen found a concrete expression of traditional Pure Land purification practices necessary to achieve or merely to preview Rebirth. Preserving the precepts and saying the *nembutsu* would negate sins and lead to purity.[10] Maintaining purity—i.e., keeping one's priestly vows—was proof of Rebirth in a Buddha's land.[11] Pilgrimage purifies the individual before the approach to the divine. The dangers of the road (and Ippen faced hunger, sleeping rough, and even attack) operate to prepare an individual for a new state in respect to a previous social life—in this case, for Rebirth in the Pure Land. Pilgrimage purifies the individual of traces of the human world: pilgrims tend to share a common way of life for the duration, one which creates a group not divided by wealth, status, or goals. The community one forms with fellow pilgrims is a result of purification. This achieved unity is a state of purity because it is not connected with the reality of social life: it is whole (holy), not divisive, not divided. Ippen did not form an order, but a community of wayfarers, of equals on the same spiritual path. Taking his inspiration from a passage in Shan-tao's *Hymns on Meditation in the Presence of All Buddhas*, he called his followers "Fellow Practitioners" (*dōgyō*).[12]

Ippen's version of the Continuous Nembutsu tradition was the dancing *nembutsu* (*odori nembutsu*): chanting the *nembutsu* while walking in a circle. It started in 1279 spontaneously at the end of a service in a layman's house: this was the first and probably the last "ecstatic" version of this meditation.[13] Although typically analyzed against the background of folk practices involving dance and funerals, driving out pestilence, and planting crops, the dancing *nembutsu* should also be understood in the context of Tendai/Pure Land walking meditation which was meant to result in a mystical experience.[14]

These experiences of mystical revelation confirmed for Ippen the traditions of meditation and mysticism in the Tendai school and in the esoteric doctrines he had formally studied as a child and youth in the Seizan school of Pure Land Buddhism. Established by Hōnen's disciple Shōkū, the Seizan school maintained very close ties with the Tendai school. Tendai Buddhism teaches the Nonduality of Buddha (or Buddhas) and all other Sentient Beings (*shujō*) based on the Buddha Nature (*busshō*) inherent in all. This Buddha Nature is what makes beings strive for enlightenment and makes enlightenment possible for all. Indeed, according to the teachings of Original Enlightenment (*hongaku*), the Nonduality of Buddha and Sentient Beings is stressed in the assertion that "all human actions . . . are . . . the actions of the Buddha."[15]

Pure Land Buddhism affirms the principle of universal salvation but through Rebirth (*ōjō*) in the western Pure Land paradise of Amida Buddha, who has vowed to save all Sentient Beings who invoke or reflect on his name (*nembutsu*). As a Pure Land school, the Seizan school identifies Amida with Buddha Nature and maintains the Nonduality of Amida's Enlightenment and the Rebirth of all Sentient Beings past and present through the invocation of Amida's name.[16] This relationship between Amida's Enlightenment and the Sentient Being's Rebirth was confirmed by one of Ippen's most important mystical experiences. His revelation came in 1271 after a pilgrimage to Zenkōji temple in Shinano Province, which enshrines an image believed to be the living body of Amida in this world. He brought back to his native province an illustration of Shan-tao's Parable of the White Path and Two Rivers: the Buddhas Shaka and Amida guide a poor soul across a slender bridge over fire and flood to the safety of Amida's Pure Land. After some eight months of contemplating this picture and invoking Amida's name, Ippen produced the "Jūichi funi ju" (In praise of the Nonduality of the ten and one), which expresses the mystical transcendence over time, space, life, and death in traditional terms of the Seizan school:

> Enlightenment [achieved] ten kalpas ago
> [Is in] the world of Sentient Beings
> Rebirth [through] the single [chanting of] the *nembutsu*
> [Is in] the land of Amida
> [Through] the unity of the [Enlightenment achieved] ten
>   [kalpas ago]
> [We] achieve [a state of Rebirth] in life [and] at death
> [Where Amida's] land and [Sentient Beings' world] are one and the
>   same
> [We] are seated in the Great Assembly [which is Amida]

> (Jikkō shōgaku shujō kai
> Ichinen [n]ōjō Mida no kuni
> Jūichi funi mushō o shōsu
> Kokkai byōdō daie ni zasu)[17]

This poem is crucial to understanding the cultural context and doctrinal basis of Ippen's mysticism: the Seizan school's concept of the Nonduality of Amida's Enlightenment and the individual Rebirths of Sentient Beings. As related in the Longer Pure Land Sutra, ten kalpas (aeons) ago, the Indian king Dharmākara (in Japanese, Hōzō), an aspirant to buddhahood or Bodhisattva, achieved full Enlightenment (*shōgaku*) and became the Buddha Amida after making and fulfilling forty-eight vows to make a buddhaland or paradise and cause to be Reborn there all who wished or invoked or meditated on his name. By the single chanting of the *nembutsu*, the practitioner or Sentient Being achieves Rebirth. Amida, in his vows, makes two conditions: one for himself, that he will fulfill his vows or not achieve full Enlightenment; and one for Sentient Beings, that they reflect on Amida or that the desire to be Reborn rise up in them. For Ippen, following Shōkū, if Amida has achieved Enlightenment, then all Sentient Beings past, present, and future (since Amida is the Buddha of infinite life) have already achieved Rebirth. Equally important is the understanding that Amida's Enlightenment and the Rebirth of Sentient Beings are mutually dependent. Without Amida's vows, each of which ends with the promise not to enter Enlightenment if the vow is not fulfilled, the Sentient Being cannot achieve Rebirth. Unless Sentient Beings think or chant Amida's name, Amida cannot achieve Enlightenment.[18]

Ippen, as mystic, transcends time. The word Ippen uses for "one chanting," *ichinen*, means a short moment, the very opposite of aeon (kalpa). Yet, Amida's Enlightenment ten aeons ago and the moment of chanting the *nembutsu* are one and the same. Ippen is speaking of an experience, a state of consciousness in which the single moment and the eternity of the kalpa are fused in a *nembutsu*.[19]

The mystic also transcends space. For Shōkū and Ippen, this world and the Pure Land into which one was Reborn is one and the same ("kokkai byōdō"). As Ippen expresses it, they are equal in terms of seeking Enlightenment or Rebirth.

The mystic also transcends life and death in his experience. For Shōkū, Rebirth in life (*sokuben ōjō*) was achieved through belief while Rebirth at death (*tōtoku ōjō*) was manifested in the appearance of Amida and his train to welcome the believer into paradise (*raigo*). For Ippen, there was no difference in the experience.[20]

The revelation expressed in this poem left Ippen secure (*anjin*) in his beliefs and doctrines handed down from Shan-tao, Hōnen, and Shōkū. This sense of security would be confirmed by further revelations. However, Ippen was more than just a mystic in the tradition of the Seizan school. His experience of divine revelation resulted in an expansion and refinement of Seizan school doctrine: while the Seizan school identified Amida's Enlightenment with Sentient Beings' Rebirth, Ippen identified Amida with Sentient Beings through the transcendent and absolute power of the Name (*myōgō*).

In 1274, trailed by two women and a child, Ippen went to Kumano. On the way, he was tested when a monk refused to accept from him a slip of paper or amulet (*fuda*) printed with the invocation to Amida. Because, the monk said, he could not believe, Ippen told him to take it without believing. At Kumano, Ippen had a vision of the main god enshrined there, a manifestation of Amida, who gave him instructions to make no conditions for accepting the amulet. Confirmed now in his mission, Ippen sent the women and child back home and formally began his career of handing out these amulets. They read: "Namuamidabutsu rokujūmannin ketsujō ōjō" or "I entrust my soul to Amida Buddha, Rebirth in paradise determined [for] six hundred thousand people." The poem he produced as a result of his revelation is the following:

> The six characters of the Name
> > are the Dharma of the single *nembutsu*
> The living beings [born into] the Ten Realms [of existence] are the
> > body of the single *nembutsu*

> The single *nembutsu* [chanted] without thought of [other] myriad
> practices is Enlightenment [itself]
> [The one who becomes] the single *nembutsu* is exalted among men,
> a lotus marvelous and excellent
>
> (Rokuji myōgō ippen bō
> Jikkai eshō ippen tai
> Mangyō rinen ippen shō
> Ninjū jōjō myōkō ge)[21]

This "Rokujūmannin ju" (In praise of the six hundred thousand people) is a statement of Ippen's mystical experience that Amida and the practitioner become one in the chanting of the *nembutsu*. Shōkū, in the Tendai tradition, maintains that Amida and Sentient Beings become one at the moment of salvation. This unity is expressed in the Six Character Name, "Namu-amidabutsu." "Namu" is the vow of ordinary Sentient Beings to achieve salvation, to be Reborn, to become a Buddha. "Amidabutsu" represents the vows made and fulfilled by Amida to save Sentient Beings; becoming Amida Buddha is the reward for the Specific Vows (*betsugan*) he made. Thus, all are Buddhas, all are the same through the mutual accomplishment of making and fulfilling vows to become Buddhas.[22]

The poem is Ippen's first statement on the absolute power of the Name to save. Traditionally, from Shan-tao to Hōnen, the Name had been "Amida" or "Amida butsu." For Shōkū, the name was the Six Character "Namuamida-butsu." The difference was based on the interpretations of the source of the Name's power to save. In the Tendai school, the Name was not seen as having power to save superior to that of other aspects or manifestations of the Buddha. Shan-tao and Hōnen saw the source of power as Amida's transcendent Enjoyment Body, the reward for merits earned as a Bodhi-sattva; therefore, the source of the power of the Name was Amida himself. Shōkū saw the source of the power of the Name in the merits Amida had earned and turned over to Sentient Beings, not in Amida himself.[23] Amida and Sentient Beings, again, were mutually dependent in seeking Enlighten-ment and Rebirth.[24]

Thus, Ippen saw that something transcending Amida himself was the source of his power, as it was the source of his Enlightenment: the Six Character Name. Ippen maintained that Dharmākara was saved and became Amida precisely when and because Sentient Beings chanted the Six Character Name. Both Amida's Enlightenment and Rebirth for Sentient Beings were made possible by the Six Character Name, Namuamidabutsu. All three, Amida, Sentient Beings, and Name, are one—when the practitioner chants the *nembutsu*. The practitioner becomes Amida; the practitioner becomes Namuamidabutsu. Ippen himself was Namuamidabutsu because he chanted "Namuamidabutsu."[25]

Ippen gave an absolute and transcendent position to the Six Character Name. As he saw it, Amida had been rewarded for the Six Character Name itself. Amida was not only within the Name (Namu*amida*butsu [my emphasis]), but he was Amida by the Name—the Name or *nembutsu* was said for Amida, too, who is Amida only as long as Sentient Beings say the Name.[26] The god of Kumano emphasized this point: "The Rebirth in paradise of mankind was determined with Namuamidabutsu when Amida attained Enlightenment ten kalpas ago."

The power of the Name was present in the slips of paper printed with the Name. Although one can read the "six hundred thousand people" as the number Ippen initially intended to save, one must also recognize that the ideographs for "six hundred thousand people" are the first ideographs of the four lines of the poem: with them, Ippen was also declaring the absolute power of the Name. Printed on the slips of paper, the Name works in and of itself. One does not need even to chant the *nembutsu*; the full benefit is obtained merely by coming in contact with it.[27] This is the ultimate expression of reliance on the power of the other (*tariki*). Distributing these paper slips, Ippen acted as, indeed, was Namuamidabutsu. He saw his mission, as mandated by the god of Kumano, to save the Sentient Beings of this world without making any conditions—whatever personal reservations he might have had about believers and unbelievers. Distribution was to be with as little consciousness (a form of self-reliance or *jiriki*) as chanting the *nembutsu* itself: the *nembutsu* could not be chanted with any conscious calculation of benefits or results, even Rebirth in the Pure Land.[28]

This poem expresses the meaning of Ippen's name. The word, like its variant "ichinen," has two meanings: the single invocation of Amida's name, the single *nembutsu*; and the single moment of a *nembutsu*. Ippen is Namuamidabutsu, which is Amida, which is Rebirth in the Pure Land; it is life, it is death, it is transcending life and death as experienced in the moment the *nembutsu* is chanted.[29] "Ippen" expresses the all-inclusive sense of unity experienced as a mystic.

Ippen's doctrines and experiences were summed up in one long hymn, which is too long to reproduce here.[30] The "Betsugan wasan" (Hymn on the Specific Vow [of Amida]) was composed in 1287 in Harima Province, when Ippen visited the shrine at Matsubara to Hachiman, also a manifestation of Amida. Simply put, the hymn describes the suffering of human life, the inability to look to the Buddha in any form for salvation because of the enormous sinfulness of Sentient Beings, and the sole opportunity for salvation in the Name.

Again, the Name is posited as the primary and most efficacious way to obliterate sins. The first *nembutsu* results from suffering, the last *nembutsu*, death, ends suffering. The end of suffering is to become a Buddha, which is Namuamidabutsu. Life is death; every minute is death; every *nembutsu* is the last *nembutsu*; every *nembutsu* is Rebirth in the Pure Land. Abandon everything, even thought of Rebirth, and say the *nembutsu* continuously.[31] For Ippen, life was a continuous *nembutsu*. The confraternity he founded was dedicated to preserving a constant state of Rebirth.

THE WEAKNESS OF THE CONFRATERNITY AS AN ORGANIZATION

Ippen's status as a mystic and thus his doctrines as expressions of his experience were used only minimally in the organization of the confraternity. It was limited to the organization of ritual of the *nembutsu*, the regulation of equipment to be carried on the road, and the vow taken to pursue the religious life.

The organization of the confraternity is indicated by a document in Shinkyō's hand from 1278, the *Ichigo fudan nembutsu ketsuban* in the Shōjōkōji collection.[32] It is the list of participants and their places for the six hours of the *nembutsu* throughout the day (*rokuji nembutsu*). First in the list comes "Ippen bō" and then come six groups of eight Amidabutsu names, making forty-eight for the forty-eight vows of Amida Buddha when still the Indian king Dharmākara. None are repeated. The first name in the first group is "Ta'amidabutsu"; Shinkyō was the first disciple, and thus one may assume that position in the groups corresponded to seniority. According to the *Ippen hijiri e*, there was a corresponding number and grouping of female religious and countless others in four groups.[33] Corroborating evidence is scanty: the earliest existing list for female religious is dated 1721.[34] Shinkyō's *Hōnō engi ki* confirms the grouping of forty-eight in six groups of eight.[35] However, another such list by Shinkyō for male religious dating from 1306, the *Betsuji banchō*, a list for the positions for the Special-hour Nembutsu ceremony on the twenty-fifth of each month, indicates changes made to accommodate increasing numbers. It begins with Ta'amidabutsu and continues with five groups of fourteen and the sixth with eighteen for a total of eighty-eight. In addition, another eighty-eight *jishū* names are recorded.[36] As the order grew and the number of participants in rituals increased, the tendency was to keep six groups and increase the numbers in each group rather than to increase the number of groups. By the Tokugawa period, however, the number of groups had been increased. The 1721 *Jimyōchō chūshaku* indicates an initial organization of forty-eight monks and forty-eight nuns and two additional groups of six with sixteen names in each of those for a total of 192.[37] The last were very likely lay.

The regulation of ritual seems to have been fairly minimal although clear enough to distinguish Ippen school *nembutsu* ritual from that of other Pure Land schools. For example, the *Heike monogatari* 3.13 (the Kaku'ichi version [1370s] as well as later ones), describes Taira Shigemori's building of a forty-eight bay temple on Higashiyama and placing in each bay a lantern. During the *nembutsu* services held there, six ladies were stationed in each bay for a total of 288. This association of lanterns with *nembutsu* practitioner was identified as Yugyō-ha in the Muromachi period: a contemporary text, the *Teikin ōrai shō* (compiled after 1444), quotes the story and then notes,

> Now [they call] Ippen the founder. The present [head of the] Fujisawa [Shōjōkōin] is the fourth [successor] to Ippen.[38]

The reference to the fourth successor, Donkai, places this between 1325 and 1327, the traditional dates of Donkai's residence in Fujisawa. Needless to say, the events described in the *Heike monogatari* took place long before Ippen was born.

Another example of Ippen's limited extension of authority over his Fellow Practitioners is the establishment of the number and type of equipment to be carried by the members of the confraternity. This list, written out by Ippen in 1287, is found in the *Ippen hijiri e*, but not in the *Ippen Shōnin ekotoba den*.[39] It is, however, in the *Ippen Shōnin goroku*, by which one may understand it as generally accepted by Shinkyō and/or his followers since it also includes excerpts from Shinkyō's *Hōnō engi ki*.[40] The twelve pieces of equipment were limited to alms bowl (*hikiire*), chopsticks and container (*hashizutsu*), hemp overrobe (*amie*), surplice (*kesa*), summer robe (*katabira*), hand cloth (*shukin*), sash (*obi*), paper robe (*kamiko*), prayer beads (*nenjū*), monk's robe (*koromo*), wooden clogs (*ashida*), and hood (*zukin*).[41] Mentioned (and shown in illustrations) in the *Hijiri e*, the *Ekotoba den*, and the *Hōnō engi ki* are the boxes in which the members of the confraternity carried their possessions on their backs.[42] According to the *Ekotoba den*, illustration and text, the boxes were painted with three stripes, white, red, and green, to symbolize Shan-tao's Parable of the White Path and Two Rivers. During sermons and at night, they were lined up to separate the nuns from the monks—indeed "to prevent attachment or abhorrence [between] men and women."[43] The symbolism of the boxes derived meaning from Ippen's first revelation, which resulted from months of practice before the illustration of the parable which he had brought from Zenkōji. Later, under Shinkyō the boxes acquired meaning more concretely applicable to the organization of the order. According to the *Ekotoba den*, in a dream of the priest of the Ono Shrine the body of the god ("goshōjin") entered one of the boxes and became the protective deity ("shugojin") of the order.[44] Again, according to the Tokugawa period *Jishū yōgi monben* (Inquiries and clarifications of the essentials of the Jishū, c. 1700), the Kumano Gongen was enshrined in the first box, called the *oichi* (honorable first), dedicated to the Budddha of Eternal Light (Muryōkōbutsu). In the Tokugawa period, succession to the position of Yugyō Shōnin was determined by lot in front of the shrine—the god decided.[45]

The boxes were called *jūnikō no hako* (box of the twelve lights) for the twelve articles they contained. Each article was given correspondence with the virtue of one of the twelve names for Amida in the Larger Pure Land Sutra (*Muryōjukyō*).[46] For example, the surplice is identified with belief in the Name and the Buddha of Incomparable Light.[47] Each article, in its identification with Amida and a way of walking with, bearing, wearing, and even calling on Amida, derives meaning from meditation practices, the basis of Ippen's practice. Even in the necessities of everyday life, the *jishū* joined Ippen as equals in the life of meditation.

The third and last example of Ippen's limited extension of authority over his Fellow Practitioners is the vow he wrote at Taimadera in 1286, the "Seimon," found both in the *Ippen hijiri e* and the *Ippen Shōnin ekotoba den*, as well as in the *Ippen Shōnin goroku* as the "Seigan gemon."[48] The first line shows Ippen's view of himself as member, rather than leader, of his community: "We disciples [of the Buddha]."[49] The rest of the text is a statement of rather general belief and practice of the *nembutsu* six hours of the day. Thus, Ippen and his Fellow Practitioners are fellows because of their common commitment to religious practice and desire for Rebirth.

Ippen's authority gave him only a tentative hold on his followers. For example, Ippen had difficulties in addressing the problem of what he called lack of faith (*fushin*) among his own followers. Surely there were those who had simply given out after years on the road. However, for Ippen, lack or loss of faith was lack of faith in the Name and lack of faith in the practice of the Name.[50] Shōkai noted in 1283, when after a disappointing period the representatives of the gods of the Ise Main Shrine and the Mountain God (San-Ō) approached Ippen at Kayazu in Owari Province "to make a karmic connection toward salvation" (*kechien no tame ni*), that lack or loss of faith was punished: a storm blew up and the next morning thirteen *jishū* were reported ill.[51]

No sexual misconduct is noted in the *Ippen hijiri e*. However, the attachment between women and men seems to have been of some concern to Ippen, according to Shōkai. Ippen's second entry into religious life (*shukke*) is described in the *Hijiri e* as triggered by the sight of a top turned by children at a time when he was beset by everyday problems and personal trouble from attachments.[52] One might even mention the legend in the *Chronicle of Nine Generations of Hōjō* (*Hōjō kudai ki*) about Ippen's leaving home because of the jealousy of his two wives from whose hair he saw snakes emerge, a standard Mt. Kōya narrative theme.[53] However, the nature of Ippen's concerns is manifested at least once in the *Hijiri e*. In a letter of 1284 responding to an inquiry, Ippen stresses that it is the attachment between men and women which leads to rebirth in the Three Worlds of pain and suffering. The only response is to destroy the forms of men and women, await Rebirth, and chant the Name of Amida.[54]

Ippen's method of dealing with lack of faith and attachment is difficult to assess. As Imai notes, it would be difficult for Ippen to deal with problems after the fact: he was a teacher; he had no absolute authority. Absolute authority was vested solely in the Name. In fact, Ippen had no answer but the Name. He could exhort, perhaps prevent. Nevertheless, he could not punish.[55]

Speaking in the language of the Pure Land tradition in which he had been educated, Ippen offered no new revelation. What Ippen did offer was a religious path in which traditional practices such as pilgrimage gave concrete expression to highly esoteric teachings on the meaning and method of achieving Rebirth in this life. Most importantly, Ippen's revelations on the nature of the role of the *nembutsu* in the relationship between Amida and Sentient Beings would form the basis of the religious authority of the heads of those orders deriving from his confraternity.

SHINKYŌ: FEARSOME OATHS, DIRE PUNISHMENTS

For every successful mystic or visionary there is an organizer who is principally credited with institutionalizing and securing the transmission of the founder. Christ had Paul, St. Francis had Elias, and Ippen had Ta'amidabutsu Shinkyō. It was only natural that, if the mission were to continue despite Ippen's statement that the mission was for his lifetime only, it would continue under the leadership of Ippen's most important disciple in the confraternity: Shinkyō was his first disciple after the sanction of the mission by the dream oracle at Kumano Main Shrine and subsequently leader of the chant (*chōshō*) in *nembutsu* rituals.[56]

Shinkyō advertised his claims to authority by means of illustrated scrolls. In 1303-04, when he took up permanent residence at the Muryōkōji in Taima, he sponsored the production of the *Ippen Shōnin ekotoba den* (The story of Ippen Shōnin in pictures and words) in ten rolls.[57] The text was a collation of sources by one Sōshun, about whom nothing is known.[58] The original is lost, but ten copies (of various dates and completeness) exist: at least one goes back to an original of 1307.[59] The *Ekotoba den* may have been written in direct response to the 1299 *Ippen hijiri e*, whose author Shōkai had achieved such success in the capital and might very well have been Shinkyō's greatest rival. The *Ekotoba den* was composed as the main scripture for *jishū* and lay persons; each temple may have had one to display, read, and explain the history and tenets of the order.[60]

In 1306, Shinkyō sponsored the production of another ten-roll biography of Ippen, illustrated by Kammonnosuke Nyūdo Shinshō and his son Fujiwara Arishige. It has since been lost. The dedication letter, the *Hōnō engi ki* (The record of the dedicated biography), on the other hand, which accompanied the scroll presented to the Kumano Main Shrine, has survived. It was specifically written to ask the god of the Main Shrine to recognize Shinkyō as Ippen's heir and to ask for the god's patronage and protection.[61]

In general, these two texts constitute the argument offered by Shinkyō in his claims, some of which have been mentioned, for the recognition of his authority by his order, the Ippen school community, and the wider Pure Land community: Shinkyō as Ippen's one, true heir; Shinkyō as incarnation of a Bodhisattva and messenger or representative of (Amida and/or Shaka) Buddha; Shinkyō as sanctioned by gods and Buddhas/Bodhisattvas; and Shinkyō as guarantor of Rebirth in the Pure Land.

However, Shinkyō faced potential problems in asserting his position as Ippen's successor—Shinkyō's leadership could be contested. Texts produced by Shinkyō make clear that he saw it necessary to assert his authority in the face of real (or anticipated) challenges from several quarters: the Pure Land community outside the Ippen school, potential rivals within the Ippen school community, and members of his own order.

Shinkyō apparently anticipated a challenge from the wider Pure Land community, a challenge that Shōkai did not address. This can be seen in a comparison of the opening sections of Shōkai's 1299 *Ippen hijiri e* and Shinkyō's 1303-1304 *Ippen Shōnin ekotoba den*. Since Shōkai's text is the earlier, Shinkyō's text can be seen as a response. The *Hijiri e* begins immediately with "Ippen the Hijiri" (*Ippen hijiri wa*), his antecedents, birth, and early education under the guidance of Seizan school clerics. On the other hand, the *Ekotoba den* begins with an analysis of Buddhism and its two paths, summarizes the orthodox interpretation of Pure Land Buddhism as the only path to take in this, the Latter Age [of the Decay] of Buddhist Doctrine (*mappō*), and only then introduces Ippen as a primary teacher of the *nembutsu*. The effect is to place Ippen firmly in the ranks of the wider Pure Land Buddhist community. Even the Seizan school is ignored: the

Ekotoba den says not a word about Ippen's years with Shōdatsu and Ketai of the Seizan school.

The second challenge to Shinkyō may have come from other disciples of Ippen, among the most important of whom was Shōkai, one of two relatives who had followed Ippen (the other was Sen'a, a brother).[62] Shōkai had accompanied Ippen on various pilgrimages and retreats early in his religious career; however, Ippen made a clean break with his family and Shōkai apparently ended up at the temple on Sixth Avenue (Rokujō Dōjō) Kankikōji in Kyoto. As a preacher of the *nembutsu*, he was famous enough to have a poem entered under his name in an imperial anthology (see chapter 6) and to obtain sponsorship for the very expensive production on silk of the famous and eponymous illustrated biography of Ippen, the *Ippen hijiri e*. Shōkai felt that Ta'amidabutsu was important enough to Ippen's story to mention him three times: once in the description of their first meeting and exchange of vows to seek salvation together and twice in the description of the events leading to Ippen's death.[63] On the other hand, the *Ekotoba den* never mentions Shōkai at all. In fact, where the *Hijiri e* describes Shōkai as taking the dictation of Ippen's last sermon, the *Ekotoba den* has Ippen write it himself.[64]

However real or imagined the challenge presented by Shōkai or others, Shinkyō was apparently conscious of one. Otherwise he would not have felt it necessary to assert his position as Ippen's appointed successor in both the *Ippen Shōnin ekotoba den* and the *Hōnō engi ki*. According to the *Ekotoba den*, on his deathbed Ippen indicated Shinkyō as his successor.[65] Among the reasons stated is that he had best heard or understood Ippen's words and was therefore able to pass his teachings on without error, a standard argument.[66] When Ippen turned to Shinkyō and asked, "As for Namuamida-butsu, are you not happy?" Shinkyō burst into tears. Then Ippen wept and said, "You are the person who must continue the ministry."[67] The reason for bursting into tears is not well understood except perhaps as a well-known motif drawn from the sutras to indicate perfect transmission of the Dharma.[68] In addition, the weeping does place the two in opposition to the others present: it identifies Shinkyō with Ippen and, in effect, makes him his equal. In addition, the *Ekotoba den* presents Shinkyō as one cut above the others, as the description of his manner and of his compassionate face in the same section indicates.[69] Shinkyō even claims to have been the only one paying sufficient attention to Ippen to notice that he had actually died.[70] Needless to say, there is nothing of the sort in Shōkai's *Ippen hijiri e*.[71]

According to Shōkai, Ippen burned or gave away all the texts he owned and stipulated that his mission was for his lifetime only ("Waga kadō wa ichigo bakari zo").[72] Ippen had no disciples in the ordinary sense but only

Fellow Practitioners of the Name. Therefore, he had no heir and no intention of founding a permanent institution. According to Shinkyō, however, as one of Ippen's followers who had decided to starve themselves to death in order to rejoin Ippen, he had been persuaded by the lord of Ōgo to give him an amulet. He had told him that the "hijiri" Ippen was dead, but Ōgo had pleaded that he was a Sentient Being who had not yet received the benefits of Ippen's mission and that he too ought to be allowed to make a connection toward salvation. That is, Shinkyō had been forced to take up the mission: he thought he had heard the call of Ippen. And that was how he came to become the Chishiki.[73]

Shinkyō's claim to be Ippen's heir is also recorded in the *Hōnō engi ki*. Whereas the *Ekotoba den* was composed as the main scripture for *jishū* and lay persons, the *Hōnō engi ki*, sent to the Kumano Main Shrine, had a much more limited audience. Here, too, Shinkyō states his special status with Ippen when, in explaining the relationship between himself as Chishiki and the *jishū*, he declares, "At that time, Ippen explained this to me, saying . . ."[74] Shinkyō's claim to be Ippen's successor is based on the assertion that Ippen had told only himself.[75]

Shinkyō claimed to be not merely Ippen's heir but co-founder of the order. Here, he depended on Pure Land teachings going back to Shan-tao of the *nembutsu* practitioner as a disciple of Shakyamuni.[76] Shan-tao's Parable of the White Path and Two Rivers is the most important model for Shinkyō: Ippen brought back an illustration from Zenkōji in 1271 and long months of meditation in front of it resulted in the "Sacred poem on the Nonduality of the ten and one." In this illustration, Amida and Shaka guide a poor soul beset by troubles across a bridge over a river of fire and flood. Thus, both Amida and Shaka are needed for salvation. If Ippen was Amida, then Shinkyō was to be Shaka.

Ippen had received divine sanction for his mission from the god of the Kumano Main Shrine, a manifestation of Amida. Shinkyō did not attempt to win recognition from the Shrine or to take his place as Ippen's successor until 1306. Rather, Shinkyō looked for an avatar of Shaka to provide the necessary sanction; his own official divine sponsor was Ono Daibosatsu (the Great Bodhisattva of Ono), tutelary deity of the ancient and still relatively powerful Wani and Ono families.[77] The *Ekotoba den* relates that while Shinkyō was in Tsuruga, Echizen Province in the spring of 1302, he received a letter from the head priest of the Ono Shrine in Ōmi Province stating that he had received an oracle in a dream from the Ono Daibosatsu. According to the god's oracular message, Shinkyō was a *gongen*, an avatar of Shaka, and he was summoned to Ono to make a karmic tie (*kechien*) with him. This Shinkyō did.[78] While Shinkyō was in Asadai in Musashi

Province, another letter from this same priest was brought to him. This priest had had another dream, in which the god had announced that he wished to become the protective deity of Shinkyō's temple; in compliance with the message, he was sending a "mirror" or physical body of the god, who was to be the protecting deity of Shinkyō's order.[79] Various explanations have been given for Shinkyō's relationship with this particular shrine.[80] However, the most important is publicly declared by Shinkyō himself in the *Hōnō engi ki*: "Kumano and Hachiman are the manifestations of Mida; Ono Daibosatsu is an incarnation of Shaka. These two objects of worship are our father and mother of mercy."[81] Shaka is certainly the equal of Amida, and therefore, Shinkyō's ministry, sanctioned by Shaka, is equal to that of Ippen: Shinkyō is to be seen as co-founder with Ippen of the order.

The protection of the gods and Buddhist deities is indicated throughout the *Ekotoba den*, both for Ippen and for Shinkyō. In a dream, the statue of Bishamon honors the fasting Ippen by descending from his pedestal. Bishamon and Fudō protect Shinkyō and his *jishū* when they cross a flooded river. The god of the Echizen Sōsha in Kokufu appears on the shoulder of the head priest to hear Shinkyō's sermon at the Saimatsu Betsuji (Year's End Special Ceremony).[82]

Sanction in terms of distinctly Pure Land Buddhism is to be found throughout the *Ekotoba den*. These include descriptions of those who attain Rebirth in paradise, such as the lay priest Ajisaka, who drowned himself in the Fujisawa River and was dragged out of the water with his hands still pressed together as if in prayer, and the priest of the Gokurakuji in Echigo Province. In 1297, while Shinkyō was staying at the Shinzenkōji at Oyama, flowers fell from and purple clouds hung in the sky; this is the sign both of the approach of Amida and of the presence of an extraordinary holy man. And finally, due to Shinkyō, Chūjō Shichirō Kurōdo of Hatakisho in Echigo Province achieved Rebirth in paradise; this was announced by purple clouds, music, and the turning of his bones to five colors.[83] The whole of Shinkyō's career is presented, like that of Ippen's but even more so, as characterized by communication with deities through dreams, wonderful signs, and even the presence of the gods. Most importantly of all, Shinkyō is presented as a successful mediator and guide to achieving Rebirth in paradise.

Shinkyō's position as Ippen's heir, his position as co-founder, and sanction and protection of the gods were not enough. In contrast to Ippen, whom Shōkai reports as having rejected attempts to identify him as the Bodhisattva Seishi, Shinkyō claimed status as incarnation of a Bodhisattva.[84] In the *Ekotoba den*, he claimed to be a manifestation of Shaka and he is described as being an avatar or *gongen* of an unspecified Buddhist deity.[85] However, the most aggressive assertion of Shinkyō's exalted status is the *Ekotoba den*'s promotion of Ippen as the incarnation of Seishi and Shinkyō as the incarnation of Kannon, nothing the like of which is to be found in the *Ippen hijiri e*. Again, it places Shinkyō on the same level as Ippen, and, like the sanction of Ono Daibosatsu, signifies that Shinkyō was a co-founder of the order. The *Ekotoba den* relates that a high-ranking cleric, Tōkyō Hōin, reported that he had had a dream in which he was told that Ippen was the incarnation of Seishi. When told, Ippen rejected this outright.[86] Indeed, this would have compromised his identification with Amida. If there was only one Amida, there were two Bodhisattvas serving him. Years later, however, in his sermon at the Year's End Special Ceremony at Taima, Shinkyō informed the surprised congregation that he was the incarnation of Kannon. Miraculously, at that very moment, a letter from a certain Onodera in Shimotsuke Province arrived:

> On the night of the twenty-seventh last, I saw Amida Nyorai in a dream. The Bodhisattva Seishi was beside the Savior, but the Bodhisattva Kannon was not. When I asked why, the Buddha answered me that he had sent Kannon to the human world to extend his salvation. There he is known as Ta'amidabutsu [Shinkyō]. He further told me that he had already sent the Bodhisattva Seishi, who was called Ippen there, but that Seishi had returned already.

If Ippen was Seishi and Shinkyō Kannon, then the status of one was equal to that of the other. Oblivious to the political implications, the congregation, religious and lay, could only weep tears of happiness.[87]

For all the claims concocted for public consumption, when it came to authorizing the principles which now informed the organization of the order, Shinkyō's last resort of appeal was to Ippen as founder. Shinkyō claimed that the institution entrusted to him by Ippen had been designed by Ippen.

First, Shinkyō had to establish a hierarchy of authority to facilitate regularization along institutional lines of the relationship among the members of Ippen's confraternity. Position based on seniority had been well established in Ippen's time, but this applied to rituals and not necessarily to a hierarchy of authority. This was accomplished by reinterpreting the nature of the "vow" (*chigiri*) first made between Shinkyō and Ippen. In the *Ippen hijiri e*, Shōkai describes their meeting in Kyushu: "Shinkyō was the first to bind himself in a vow of Fellowship in Practice and mutual affection."[88] Shinkyō's later *Ekotoba den*, however, says nothing about the vow.[89] However, his *Hōnō engi ki* describes the vow as that between "master and disciple" (*shitei o keiyaku o nashi*).[90] Thus, in characterizing the oath taken with Ippen as a master-disciple relationship, Shinkyō created a precedent for a hierarchy, the pattern for an order rather than that, equality, for a confraternity. In particular, it reenforced his status as Chishiki, guide in religious matters, by defining his relationship in terms of a social relationship already obtaining in existing Buddhist organizations.[91]

The authority that Shinkyō as Chishiki had was based on the vow that every novice made upon entering the order and which proceeded from the novice's needs, not the Chishiki's. Shinkyō explains, whether the attribution to Ippen is true or not, that although it is easy enough to enter a temple, sit before a statue or painting of the Buddha, and commit oneself to becoming a Bodhisattva, it is not so easy once one has left the temple to maintain one's resolve, which, "like drawing in water, leaves no trace." Further, a "Buddha of wood" does not speak, cannot be asked questions, and cannot guide the aspirant. Thus, the truly committed seek out a teacher, specifically the Chishiki of Ippen's line (Shinkyō, of course), and "making (treating) him as a messenger of the Buddha, accept from him the words of the vow and precepts and thus strike the gong of the [order's] rules."[92] Thus, one takes a Chishiki as a "living rule" and heeds his admonishments because

> "as for the Chishiki his precepts are in his very body . . . as for instruction for Rebirth and the path of instruction for Release . . . there is nothing that surpasses a single phrase of the Chishiki . . .," said [Ippen].[93]

Shinkyō claims that Ippen had determined the words of the vow taken upon entering the order. The applicant would in the presence of the Chishiki make an oath now and forever to surrender one's life to the Chishiki, to obey his orders, never to leave the order or to break the rules on pain of white leprosy and black leprosy in this life and, in the next, eternal rebirth in the realms of the hell-bound, hungry ghosts, and animals. Then the applicant struck a gong.[94] This ritual is described fully in the *Ekotoba den* beginning with "from now until the end of [your] life surrender your life to the Chishiki" and ending with "being dead while alive, surrender your life to the Chishiki."[95] In the *Hōnō engi ki*, however, the entire ritual is invoked solely by means of the formula "surrender your life to the Chishiki" (*shimmei o chishiki ni yuzuru*).[96] This oath in the ritual of ordination created by Shinkyō was the principal form of acknowledging the religious authority of the Chishiki. Shinkyō stressed it over and over again as the very basis of achieving Rebirth:

> . . . nuns and monks, who make a vow to surrender their lives to the Chishiki, who strike the gong, who do not entrust [matters] to their own will . . . who follow the orders of the Chishiki, who do not break the

gong of the principles [of the order] will achieve the Rebirth Determined [for them]).[97]

The importance of this oath of obedience to Shinkyō is demonstrated by the
fact he attributes it to Ippen in the section where Shinkyō has Ippen explain
the meaning of the oath as *kimyō*: "[one] surrenders one's life to the
Chishiki. The words [for doing this] are the two ideographs of *kimyō*."[98]
"Kimyō" is an alternative reading of "namu."[99] "Namuamidabutsu" has a
formulaic substitute, "Kimyō Muryōju kaku," which has exactly the same
meaning. "Kimyō" is translated variously, but is best understood as "dedicate
body and soul to [the Buddha]."[100] As such, "kimyō" had a literal and
concrete application for Shinkyō in defining his relationship with *jishū*. It
is clear from Shinkyō's *Hōno engi ki* that "kimyō" means "surrender one's
life" (*shimmei o yuzuru*) in the sense of entrusting oneself totally and
completely to the guardianship of another. "Kimyō" means "namu"; even if
Shinkyō uses "kimyō" alone, since it is understood in the Pure Land schools
as "Kimyō Muryōju kaku," then by analogy one entrusts one's Rebirth to the
Chishiki as if to the Buddha himself. Thus, since Shinkyō already identifies
Chishiki with Buddha for anyone who enters his order, if "Namuamidabutsu" means "I rely on Amida Buddha for my Rebirth" then what will later
be called "Chishiki kimyō" means "I rely on the head of the order for my
Rebirth."[101]

In choosing this term, both as a contracted formula and as its literal
translation into Japanese, for the initial oath of obedience upon entering the
order, Shinkyō very carefully set up a functional identification of Chishiki
with Buddha. The one is freely substituted for the other in the important and
often-used formula, "Chishiki/hotoke ni shimmei o yuzuru" and its variants.
If, as Shinkyō states, one gives up one's life to the Chishiki ("shimmei o
Chishiki ni yuzuru") and gives up one's life to the Buddha ("inochi o Butsu
ni tatematsuru"), then the Chishiki functionally is or represents the
Buddha.[102] "[If one] worships Amida Buddha with one's very life, even
though the body is for a time in this polluted world, the heart will become
a Bodhisattva of the Pure Land."[103] Since Chishiki and Buddha are
interchangeable, one is given to understand that by giving up one's life to
the Chishiki, one will achieve Rebirth in the Pure Land. However, this
applies only to those who join the order; a contract is made to treat them the
same. One does not enter Shinkyō's order because he "is" the Buddha but
because he will function for the aspirant as a Buddha. Even so, since
Shinkyō does tend to use "Chishiki" and "Hotoke/Buddha" interchangeably
in formulae, as in "leaving everything to the Buddha" (*manji o hotoke ni nin*

se) and "leaves everything to the Chishiki" (*manji o chishiki ni nin suru nari*), the identification of one with the other is very strong.[104]

Shinkyō also claims that Ippen established the precepts of the order ("seikai no kotoba"), established severe prohibitions ("sono kinkai kengo nari"), and demanded that his disciples "preserve the rules [he] bequeathed them until the end of time."[105] These vows or precepts, said to have been written at Tennōji in 1286 and called the *Jishū seikai* in the *Ippen Shōnin goroku*, are found neither in the *Ippen hijiri e* nor in the *Ekotoba den*. Compared with Ippen's "Seimon" (Verse of Aspiration), these eighteen precepts are much more concrete in terms of defining not only practice but self-reflection: "Perform the office of chanting the Name, do not perform various austerities. . . . Raise up the heart of equality, do not raise up thoughts of discrimination. . . . Demonstrate a heart of compassion. . . . Wholeheartedly abide by the rules of the Chishiki" (*Moppara chishiki no okite o mamorite*).[106]

Indeed, it is very possible that the core of these eighteen precepts were the precepts that Shinkyō wrote in 1298 while ill in Muraoka in Musashi Province, now called *Ta'amidabutsu dōgyō yōjin taikō* (Ta'amidabutsu's great outline of admonitions on Same Practice).[107] It is made up of nine couplets of eight characters each and one line of ten. Some themes sound very familiar: "Preserve the heart of entry into religious life, do not return to lay status . . . forever do not break [your] vows." It must be noted that these precepts do more to describe the life of Fellow Practice than to structure the order as a functioning social organization:[108]

> Abandon [even] a hut, do not begrudge life [as fleeting] as dew
> Preserve the heart of entry into religious life (*shukke*), do not return
>   to lay status
> Do not neglect the gods, revere the Three Treasures [of Buddhism]
> Lest you fall into hell forever, forever do not break [your] vows
> Associate with believers, do not turn your back on disparagers
> [For the] teachings depend on Ta [amidabutsu], sin is the sensation
>   of comfort or discomfort
> Despise life as you would rubbish, do not [seek to] postpone death
> Chanting the Name depends upon birth, [in] the heart is deep faith
> The body worships the Buddha, the mouth always [chants] the
>   *nembutsu*
>
> Addition: the entry into religious life which catalyzes the *nembutsu*
> practitioner is the Specific Vow [of Amida] alone

Shinkyō, in order to strengthen his authority to establish these precepts, claims in the *Hōnō engi ki* that Ippen established certain forms for the organization of the order.[109] The making of the twelve light boxes (discussed above) is confirmed by the *Hijiri e* and *Ekotoba den* (without the list).[110] Shinkyō attributes to Ippen the organization of men and women religious in groups of six and the names of the forty-eight in each group, all to represent the forty-eight vows of Amida. He claims, indeed, that this was done to accommodate the increasing number of monks and nuns.[111] The *Hijiri e* confirms that "according to the roster, [in rituals] the [total assembly of] *jishū* was organized into groups of forty-eight monks and forty-eight nuns, with numberless others in four more groups."[112] This might well be said to confirm at least the assertion of increasing numbers of members.[113]

Indeed, one can ascribe Shinkyō's attempts to enhance his authority as Chishiki to the need to get a tighter grip on the order whose very nature was changing due to expansion. Obviously Shinkyō felt that he was facing some sort of challenge to his authority: either it was not strong enough to deal with specific issues or else he was contemplating developments for which he needed to prepare. An appeal to the god of the Kumano Main Shrine indicates a problem concerning the entire Ippen school community, not all of which was under his jurisdiction or under his immediate supervision: the communities at Mt. Kōya and Zenkōji were independent, as were many smaller communities. He may even have been considering the possibility eventually of consolidating the entire Ippen school community. The god of the Kumano Main Shrine represented the highest authority he could appeal to for sanction; the compromise was that, even if only in the *Hōnō engi ki*, he had to ask for recognition of his authority in Ippen's order rather than in his own.

It is more likely, however, that he was faced with problems concrete and at hand. His *jishū* were settled in about one hundred temples, but he had established permanent residence at Taima and was conducting his administration of them from there. He had disciples he could trust to act for him: Chitoku was now the "Yugyō Hijiri," Donkai had been sent to Kyoto to found a temple, and others had been despatched as private chaplains. In short, Shinkyō may have feared that his personal authority was declining in direct proportion to the rate of growth and, of course, delegation of authority. Thus, he was a point in his career, and in the development of his order, when he recognized that a hierarchy of authority had to be established and that the position of the head of the order had to be secured. This was done by asserting his ultimate authority to define the standards of religious life in the order.

Shinkyō complained about the drop since Ippen's time of the quality of *jishū* in provincial temples.[114] As demonstrated by the number of letters concerning the problem, there was more than potential mischief brewing between monks and nuns.[115] Kanai attributes the escalation of problems among monks and nuns to the ease of living off the donations and sponsorship of usually powerful patrons and parishioners. Thus, concomitant with the success of the order in the wider world was a tendency to corruption within the order. And, for this, Kanai asserts, Shinkyō must bear the responsibility.[116] More importantly, Shinkyō took responsibility. He encouraged the expulsion of miscreant *jishū*.[117] He advised men and women to keep away from each other and to "leave everything [that concerns salvation] to the Chishiki" (*manji o chishiki ni nin su nari*).[118] He admonished them, "Priest Shan-tao never raised his eyes to look at women."[119] He even tried praising examples of repentance. Shinkyō describes the experience of a nun who had been batting her eyes (or worse) at monks and laymen. Falling severely ill and thinking better of it, she repented to her head priest ("chōrō"), performed water purification, and died in peace.[120] Nevertheless, the situation deteriorated so badly that he had to forbid monks and nuns to live in the same establishment or to mix at all.[121]

The problem was so great, apparently, that in 1306 Shinkyō wrote a memorandum, the *Dōjō seimon* (Temple regulations) which he distributed to the temples.[122] Here, in his introduction, Shinkyō reviews the problem of love and attachment between men and women as the principal reason for rebirth in the realms of suffering and delusion. He states what will be reiterated in the *Hōnō engi ki*, that "Namu" is the vow of the gong to surrender one's life to the Chishiki, that "Amidabutsu" is the Buddha who made the vow to save those who say the *nembutsu*, and that those who keep their vows to say the *nembutsu* will achieve Rebirth, and that those who do not will be expelled.

If Rebirth depended upon obedience to the Chishiki and his definition of Rebirth, that is, keeping the precepts, then the Chishiki had the right to define the status of the *jishū* as Rebirth or not. The repentant *jishū*, monk or nun, could be forgiven and returned to the state of Rebirth.[123] The recalcitrant *jishū* could be punished by expulsion and the state of Rebirth rescinded. Reevaluation of status was extended even to those *jishū* whose Rebirth had been recognized at death and registered in the *Jishū kakochō*. Shinkyō, following *kanjin hijiri* practice, had while Ippen was still alive begun keeping a list of those in the confraternity who had died and achieved Rebirth, represented by enrollment of the Amidabutsu name. Shinkyō entered the names of *jishū* in his order who had died having kept the vows.

Now, if it was found out after death and registration that the vows had been broken, the Chishiki would cancel the Rebirth in paradise by writing "not" (*fu*) above the *jishū*'s name. If a mistake had been made, the cancellation itself would be cancelled. There were, it seems, cases of jealousy and posthumous backbiting. Between 1281 and 1398, eight men and sixteen women had their status of Rebirth rescinded or cancelled with a "not" (*fu*) written over their Amidabutsu names (in all but one case with the Chinese character).[124] This was a concrete demonstration of the absolute power of the head of the order to guarantee or to cancel Rebirth.

Nonetheless, Shinkyō recognized that his own status as Chishiki depended on guaranteeing Rebirth to his followers and Rebirth meant living according to the precepts; especially for an order of both men and women, this meant celibacy. Shinkyō claimed, as Chishiki, the last word in all things pertaining to salvation and as such the authority to establish the rules and regulations of life in the order. Not only could he teach but also punish. The basis of his authority was not, however, Ippen's: it was not the result of a divinely-inspired revelation; it was not personal. Shinkyō developed a social organization with an emerging hierarchy of functions and at the same time claimed authority by virtue of his position in that hierarchy, his "office" as Chishiki. The organization and the authority both, he claimed, had been bequeathed to him by Ippen. Once his claims had been sanctioned by the god of Kumano Main Shrine, his authority was absolute. Or so, one imagines, he hoped.

TAKUGA: THE CHISHIKI AS BUDDHA ON THIS EARTH

The consolidation of the religious authority of the Yugyō Shōnin was accomplished by the seventh, Takuga, in office 1338-1354.[125] Perhaps the finest scholar produced by (or attracted to) the Yugyō-ha, Takuga wrote many theoretical works that became standard sources of reference for the order. For example, Takuga's writings are cited extensively in Chiren's *Shinshū yōhō ki* (c. 1500).[126] A significant indicator of his importance to the order is the tradition that he, a member of the Yano family of Kazusa Province, was a cousin of the famous Zen priest Musō Soseki (1275-1351).[127]

Takuga was Yugyō Shōnin during what was perhaps the most turbulent period in Japanese history. By the end of 1338, the year he took office, Emperor Godaigo had destroyed the Kamakura shogunate, failed in his attempted restoration of imperial rule, and been deposed by Ashikaga Takauji, who assumed the office of shogun. Fighting would continue until 1392 with the unification of the Northern and Southern Courts. During this period, the order expanded dramatically and its numbers were swelled by defeated warriors and, no doubt, by the widows of others.[128]

By the time Takuga became Yugyō Shōnin, Shinkyō's eighteen admonitions no longer sufficed: discipline was terrible. One has only to look at Takuga's attempt to regulate clerical mores and manners, the 1342 *Tōzai sayō shō* (Summary of conduct at all times and places), to see what he was up against as a result of a rapid expansion, very likely exacerbated by the civil war conditions of the times: wearing outdoor clogs in the corridors, entering the temple by banging the shoulder against the sliding doors, going to the bathroom with the door open; during services chanting too loudly, leaning against the pillars and walls and gossiping, pushing and shoving to get in the first rows and looking every which way but front; rumpled clothing, fancy clothing, fancy fans, sloppy posture; ogling the nuns and other women, visiting the nuns alone; running around with parishioners, favoring the talented and high-born among them, getting involved in their fights; talking about the time before becoming a *jishū*; rudeness to the elderly; telling naughty stories about monks and nuns in front of the Chishiki, improper posture before the Chishiki, insufficient attendance on the Chishiki, insufficient gratitude to the Chishiki, and insufficient zeal and alacrity in obeying the orders of the Chishiki.[129]

In this text, through the enumeration of 254 items of proper and improper (mostly improper) conduct, Takuga sought to coerce a demonstration of respect for himself as Chishiki, for the *jishū* as a religious community of Fellow Practitioners, for the laity as spiritual responsibilities.[130] In regulating the smallest details of *jishū* life, Takuga attempted to make sure that the *jishū* acted out before themselves and others the deference to the religious authority of the Chishiki and veneration of entire order itself. Takuga wrote extensively on the *jishū* way of life: among others, a commentary on Shinkyō's first eighteen admonitions of 1286, the *Ta'amidabutsu dōgyō yōshin taikō chū* (Commentary on Ta'amidabutsu's great outline of admonitions on Same Practice, and the 1342 *Jōjō gyōgi hōsoku* (Articles of the rule of deportment).[131] The battle, however, was never ending.

Takuga's concerns were much the same as Shinkyō's and therefore so was his response: to create a hierarchy within the order based on a hierarchy of religious attainment at the peak of which was the Chishiki. Takuga reemphasized Shinkyō's point in the *Hōnō engi ki* that the critical issue was the identification of the Chishiki with the Buddha as a contract undertaken by the *jishū* in the vow taken at ordination:

> Although you make the oath [to entrust your salvation] to the Chishiki, the one relied upon is the Buddha in human form. Thus, you must know

that the gong [you strike] to make your vows [is] the forty-eight vows [by which] the Buddha and the Chishiki become a single body.[132]

Ippen's doctrine of the Nonduality of Amida and *nembutsu* practitioner notwithstanding, in the Yugyō-ha only the Chishiki has the function corresponding to that of the Buddha Amida. The Nonduality or unity of practitioner and Amida Buddha through the Name was used to buttress the authority of the Chishiki when Takuga equated the name Ta'amidabutsu with the Name itself: Ta as Sentient Being, Amida as the Name, Butsu as the realization of the vow.[133]

Takuga carries the application of the principle of Nonduality to the extreme in defining the authority of the Chishiki. The Nonduality of Sentient Being and Amida in the chanting of the Name underlies a term first introduced into Ippen school texts by Takuga: "shōbutsu ittai." This too refers to the Nonduality of Sentient Beings (*shūjō*) and Amida**butsu** [my emphasis]. It is apparently a formula based on the models of *shōbutsu ichinyo* and *shōbutsu funi*, where *ittai* means a single thing or entity.[134] However, since *shōbutsu* is commonly read as *iki butsu*, living buddha or buddha in human form, the idea of the Chishiki functionally as a Buddha on this earth is reenforced.

This identification of the Chishiki with the Buddha is further reenforced by Takuga's use of other terms. Again, for Shōkū, Namuamidabutsu was the concrete expression of the Nonduality of Sentient Beings (*shūjō*) and Amida.[135] In the Seizan school, this is coded in the formula *kihō ittai* and in its variant *nōki shoki ittai*, both of which terms are found in the *Ippen Shōnin goroku*.[136] *Ki* represents Sentient Beings and *hō* Amidabutsu. *Nōki* is the one who relies on, calls on, disciple, or Namu, while *shoki* is one relied upon, called upon, master, or Amidabutsu.[137] Thus when Takuga, as above, asserted that the Chishiki was the "shoki," the master one turned to for salvation, he was reenforcing the identification of the Chishiki with Amida. Takuga notes that this is indeed an interpretation different from that of other schools. He iterates often enough that this is a feature of the Yugyō-ha: "In other schools, they do not set up Buddha on this earth" (*nikujin no butsu*).[138]

If the Chishiki is the body of the living Buddha/Buddha in human form, the *jishū* is a Bodhisattva.[139] The oath and keeping the oath are critical: "the *jishū* of our order [who] practice the virtue of *kimyō* . . . are Bodhisattva."[140] Again, the monks and nuns in the Chishiki's train are nonretrograding Bodhisattvas.[141] The Bodhisattva is indeed the one who has made the vow and is faithful (*dōshin*) as defined above by Ippen, one who believes in the Name and practices the Name or, as defined by Shinkyō, one keeping his precepts.[142]

As with Shinkyō, for Takuga the contract undertaken by the Chishiki and the order's *jishū* made Chishiki and *jishū* mutually dependent for their status as Buddha and Bodhisattva. Just as Amida could not become Amida unless all Sentient Beings were born into his Pure Land paradise, so the Chishiki could not be the head of a religious order composed of monks and nuns who could not keep their vows, especially that of celibacy, the true sign for Ippen and Shinkyō that one existed in a state of Rebirth. Thus, it was not merely the responsibility of the *jishū* to keep the vows; it was the responsibility of the Chishiki to provide those instructions and conditions conducive to Rebirth.

Moreover, increased reglementation was made necessary in order to protect the order. It is important to note that claims of ever higher authority on the one hand and ever tighter regulation of *jishū* life on the other came at the same time as *jishū* were subjected to abuses at the hands of their patrons. Takuga asserted his religious authority with lay adherents as well as with monks and nuns in order to secure conditions for the Rebirth of his *jishū*. This demonstrated most concretely in his intervention to deal with the abuse of *jishū* serving as chaplains in the field. There is no evidence that priests accompanied armies as chaplains, that is, those whose main function was to attend the warrior at his death, until the outbreak of civil war in 1331. The earliest references for *jishū* in the field are for 1333, when two hundred "*dōdō no jishū*" (same road *jishū*) and other religious were reported as being with the Hōjō army besieging Akasaka and Chihaya Castles.[143] The last reference to *jishū* activity in the field is in the *Ihon Odawara ki* (Variant chronicle of [the Hōjō of] Odawara), a late sixteenth-century work on the Ise Hōjō:

> In general, *jishū* monks have from times of old been experts in *waka* and have made their business the treating of weapon wounds. Therefore, they have gone to the front lines, have treated battle wounds; they have disposed of the corpses and have accepted the last ten *nembutsu*. That is why, they say, every general has them accompany him and greatly appreciates them.[144]

This entry refers to Yugyō-ha *jishū*, for it describes the poetry relations between a domainal lord, Hōjō Ujitsuna (1487-1541), and the head priest of the local Yugyō-ha temple.[145] Evidently, Yugyō-ha *jishū* provided entertainment and medical, religious, and mortuary services to the warrior in the field.

Yugyō-ha *jishū* in the field were referred to either as "dōdō no jishū" (same road *jishū*) or as "shōban no jishū" (accompanying *jishū*)"[146] They were either the warrior's own chaplain, assigned by the Yugyō Shōnin, or a monk or nun summoned from a Yugyō-ha temple. Yugyō-ha *jishū* were expected to perform religious ceremonies and to seek their own and the warrior patrons' Rebirth in paradise. They were permitted to wear armor to protect themselves, to protect the defeated and the noncombatants, and to perform a variety of related duties: informing and comforting family survivors, amusing patrons with poetry, and practicing medicine.

However a *jishū* was secured and whatever the duties to the warrior patron, the Chishiki made no objection as long as the principal religious objective was being met: the Rebirth of warrior and *jishū*. However, by the 1350s, Yugyō-ha *jishū* in the field were subject to so many abuses that in 1350-1351 Takuga was forced to circulate a directive to *jishū* in the field. This has not survived; however, in 1399 it was reissued by the eleventh Yugyō Shōnin and current Fujisawa Shōnin Jikū (b. 1304; YS 1381-1387, FS -1412) and is therefore known as the "Jikū shōjō."[147]

Jikū reasserted that the "purpose of *jishū* going on the same road (*dōdō*) is to administer the ten *nembutsu* at the time of death." *Jishū* were to secure the Rebirth in paradise of their patrons and of themselves. They were to perform religious ceremonies. They were permitted to do what was necessary to protect themselves in battle and to protect noncombatants. They might not touch weapons, they might not act as couriers, they might not act as their patrons' servants. Any infringement of the rules would result in the loss of Rebirth in paradise both for the *jishū* and for his patron.

The suborning of the *jishū* for paramilitary services, as a breach of discipline, was seen primarily as a problem for internal regulation, where the main point of contention was the transfer of commitment from the Chishiki to the patron (*danna*) at the risk of both their souls. But the problem of a conflict in jurisdiction over *jishū* activities had been present from the very beginning, when Shinkyō first began to assign *jishū* to adherents as chaplains. Not only was it difficult to refuse a powerful patron, especially if the *jishū* was entirely dependent on him, it was difficult for a *jishū* to define the line between commitment to Chishiki and that to patron, if both were dictated by the Chishiki. Takuga and Jikū determined to resolve the conflict by insisting that the *jishū* recognize their principal commitment as that to Chishiki and by giving them a standard set of regulations.

Internal regulation alone would not solve the problem. This became all too clear in 1353, when the problem became an issue in the relations between a shogunate warrior and the order. Nikki Yoshinaga (d. 1376), Military Governor (*shugo*) of Ise Province and relative of the shogun

Ashikaga Takauji, tried to have the *jishū* of the Nagano temple Senjuji expelled and replaced because they had protected some of the defeated in the aftermath of the siege of Nagano Castle. Takuga immediately despatched a letter, the "Nagano gosho."[148]

In this letter, Takuga stressed that it was a common assumption of both warrior and *jishū* that the *jishū* would, if necessary, aid and protect the warrior patron. If *jishū* refused to aid the defeated warrior in his time of most desperate need, warriors would not be requesting him, Takuga, for *shōban no jishū* at the rate they were. *Jishū* were the enemies of no one, the allies of no one. They belonged to the Chishiki. Each *jishū* had a mission to his warrior patron, given by the Chishiki and quite independent of the military situation, and would be aided by *jishū* nuns. This was recognized by everyone. The Nagano *jishū* had acted in a capacity recognized and accepted by all warriors. Nikki was interfering with their religious functions. Takuga asked Nikki to consult his relative, the shogun Ashikaga Takauji. Takuga was confident that Takauji would support him lest he risk his own Rebirth in paradise; he made sure to let Nikki know that he had met Takauji at Kayazu that year.

Apparently, Takuga won that bout. Takuga and Jikū were concerned that the *jishū* act in a strictly religious capacity. Failure to restrict the *jishū*'s activities would result in a threat to the order, its discipline, and its activities. The prohibition of paramilitary functions was meant to prevent the *jishū* from following, however inadvertently, the patron instead of the Chishiki and thereby losing Rebirth in paradise.[149] At the same time, it was difficult even for Takuga to draw the line between religious duties and paramilitary functions: commitment to save the life of a warrior might be seen as aid to the enemy. Therefore, it was absolutely crucial that the warrior recognize the neutrality of the Yugyo-ha and its right to offer asylum as part of its religious duties. The conflict was apparently resolved in favor of the Yugyō-ha: Jikū's 1399 directive is the last reference to *jishū* activity in the field until the entry praising *jishū* in the late sixteenth-century *Ihon Odawara ki*. Either the activity was strictly curtailed or else it was so prevalent that it hardly merited mentioning. Although most scholars would tend to agree with the second proposition, I propose the first as more valid. If the warrior could not command the services of his *jishū*—if he could not force him to engage in paramilitary activities or prevent him from aiding the defeated enemy—the warrior would cease to employ the Yugyō-ha *jishū* and turn to the *jishū* and monks of other schools. This, I propose, is exactly what happened.

One of the principal reasons that the Yugyō-ha was able to protect the activities of its *jishū* was that the Yugyō Shōnin Jikū, Taikū (b. 1374; YS

1412-1429, FS -1439), Sonmyō (b. 1349; YS 1401-1412, FS -1439), Sonne (b. 1364; YS 1417-1429), and Kiyū (b. 1398; YS 1440-1466) had particularly strong influence over the Ashikaga shogun Yoshimochi, Yoshikazu, and Yoshinori. These are also the leaders of the Ashikaga shogunate at the height of its power. As long as the Yugyō-ha had enough influence over the Ashikaga shogun and the shogun were strong enough to support the Yugyō-ha in its conflict with shogunate warriors over the abuse of *jishū* services, then it seems only reasonable to assume that warriors ceased to look to the Yugyō-ha for their "shōban no jishū."

An indication of lay adherence and therefore belief in the Yugyō Shōnin's religious authority is given in the order's death register, the *Jishū kakochō*, which was the physical expression of the Chishiki's authority to confirm or rescind Rebirth status for the living and the dead. Although warrior names are not unknown in the sections entered by previous Chishiki, beginning with Takuga, Yugyō Shōnin entered warriors more and more regularly. Takuga himself entered on 1351.2.26, for example, members of the important Kō family, who served Takauji: Moronao (killed on the run) together with his adopted son Morofuyu (killed the year before) and Moronao's brother and adopted son Moroyasu and his son Moroyo (both assassinated).[150] By the 1390s, warriors were quite regularly entered, including long-deceased members of the Ashikaga house: the first shogun Takauji's brother Tadayoshi (1306-1352); Takauji's son Motoujii (1340-13-67), first Kamakura *kubō*; and Takauji himself.[151] Up through the mid-fifteenth century, there were very few important warrior houses serving the Ashikaga who were not represented in the death register. Thus, the more the warrior class believed in the religious authority of the Yugyō Shōnin, the more secure from service in the field were the *jishū* of the order. What they believed was that the *jishū* was a single body with the Chishiki and the Chishiki was Buddha and the Buddha was Amida.[152]

5
The Charisma of the Religious Community

Throughout its history, as an order made up of both men and women and as an order distinguished by its mission to and therefore involvement with lay adherents, the Yugyō-ha struggled to maintain its integrity as a religious community. This integrity was defined in terms of a religious discipline known in Ippen school orders as Same Practice (*dōgyō*), the object of Fellow Practitioners (also *dōgyō*). As with the leaders of all religious orders, the head of the Yugyō-ha had a particular responsibility to subordinates to assist them in realizing specific spiritual goals. The last chapter surveyed the authority of the head of the order to define these spiritual goals and to establish the regulations of the order that would lead to them. Thus, the integrity of Same Practice depended on the ability to render absolute the religious authority of the head of the order, the Chishiki.

As indicated in the first chapter, religious authority, or charisma, is not a hypostatic property. It is rather a "social relationship" of "reciprocal interdependence" based on an exchange of power.[1] In the Yugyō-ha, this reciprocal interdependence between Chishiki and *jishū* was based on the bald fact that the integrity of the order, its religious discipline, was just as important to the head of the order in perpetuating the mission and the perception of charisma of the rest of the community, lay and religious, as it was to the subordinate in the pursuit of the religious career. Thus, in order to maintain discipline, a principal strategy of sharing religious authority was employed on the assumption that the individual religious would commit to the mission of the order and all formal institutions which maintained it if offered a role in the mission to the wider community; absolute obedience was exchanged for a share of religious authority.

In the Yugyō-ha, religious authority was derived from Ippen's mission, which was preserved and perpetuated by the order. Specific expressions of religious authority were reserved to the Chishiki, especially those characterizing the career of the *hijiri*. In the Yugyō-ha, only the Yugyō Shōnin, the

Fujisawa Shōnin, and the Shijō Shōnin of the Kyoto Konrenji were recognized as having the authority to distribute *nembutsu* amulets. In addition, only the Yugyō Shōnin (supported by his train) practiced itinerancy and only the Yugyō Shōnin had the right to guarantee Rebirth (and to rescind it) through enrollment in the order's death register, the *Jishū kakochō*.

However, a certain measure of religious authority was extended to the wider religious community. Firstly, temple heads were given the status of Chishiki. Secondly, all *jishū* had the right to extend the possibility of Rebirth in the form of the last ten *nembutsu* (*saigo no jūnen*). And, finally, based on the status of their heads as Chishiki, individual temples imitated the practice of enrolling believers—more specifically, parishioners—living and dead, in a register.

REDEFINING SAME PRACTICE AND FELLOW PRACTITIONER

As seen in the last chapter, one of the most serious threats to the integrity of religious life was the lack of direct supervision by the Chishiki, and the main contributors to that problem were the expansion of the order and its settling in temples. That there were during Ippen's lifetime communities of adherents served by some sort of religious guide is made clear by Shōkai's report that some of these leaders, called *chōrō* ("Reverend Elder," commonly used to refer to temple heads), made their way to Ippen's side as he lay dying.[2] As much as Ippen recognized the importance of serving the laity (*zaike*), it is not clear how he intended to do so.[3] The relationship of religious in the lay communities or of *chōrō* to Ippen is not clear. Not even Shōkai's relationship to Ippen, for that matter, is clear. Moreover, the doctrinal justifications for providing chaplains to lay adherents are not clear. After all, as Takuga noted, "the laity . . . have nothing to rely upon but the chanting of the Name as taught by this school." That is, they could not look to reliance on the order's vow (*kimyō*), the keeping of which made *jishū* Bodhisattva.[4]

As seen in the second chapter, Shinkyō made the decision to settle the confraternity. There were apparently several practical reasons for doing so. The first was the problem of the number who wished to follow in Shinkyō's train. Illustrations in the *Ippen hijiri e* indicate as many as about twenty in Ippen's train. This may have been the maximum number that a small village or hamlet could possibly afford to take in at any one time.[5] Thus, settling *jishū* made possible the absorption of a larger number of full-time religious.

The second reason was the number of *jishū* too old or just too tired to continue *yugyō*. Settling down without permission remained a problem encountered sporadically throughout the entire history of the order. For example, in the sixteenth century the Fujisawa Shōnin enlisted the assistance of Hōjō domainal vassals to expel monks and nuns who had settled without permission on Shōjōkōji property. (See chapter 6.)

A third reason was the Kamakura shogunate's harassment of itinerant bands of *nembutsu* practitioners and other religious, who were considered beggars and undesirables.[6] Even Ippen in 1282, as seen in the *Ippen hijiri e*, was forbidden entry into Kamakura by an official clearing the streets in advance of a shogunal procession.[7]

No doubt these reasons made the requests for resident chaplains very attractive. One must not forget the number of temples and their religious who were converted and no doubt stayed to provide services to the local community, but there were indeed requests. As Shinkyō noted in a letter to such a chaplain, he had sent him because the patron "Kurogoma-dono had made a request to send one to [him] because of the depth of his faith."[8] Shinkyō stated three reasons for sending chaplains. The first was to prosper the faith of the patron like Kurogoma-dono who had requested the *jishū* as chaplain:

As for the reasons for sending monks to those who have requested *jishū*, one is to assist the faith (*shinjin*) of the patron (*ganshū*) and to cause him to achieve Rebirth.[9]

The second reason for sending *jishū* to patrons had as much to do with the spiritual development of the *jishū* as with that of the patron, as Shinkyō explained to one such chaplain:

When you were here [with me] with the object of relying on the Chishiki, you may not even have known the extent of the karmic effect of your actions; you did not even [truly] revere the blessings of the mercy of the Buddha. You did not [really] even appreciate the blessings of [practice with] the Chishiki. Therefore, in the time you are separated from [me], if you apply [yourself] body and soul, you will also [come to] have an understanding of the [true] state of your condition and the belief in the Specific Vow [will] become even [more] precious; you [will] appreciate even more the blessings of [the supervision] the Chishiki, even more than when you were here. Because I have sent you to a person of faith, the fate of your condition [will be] happy in this life and the next."[10]

Chaplaincy, as an assignment from the Chishiki, had the same purpose, training, that *yugyō* was supposed to provide, even though it was a training in independence in order to learn the value of reliance on the Chishiki. This might be seen as a paradox, but it would hardly be sensible to entrust the order to men and women who were not trained to think or to make decisions which were in perfect accordance with the spirit of the order. Nor was it paradoxical to have others rely on them since their function was that of Chishiki.

In a sense, too, chaplaincy or temple residence offered trials as severe as any offered by the rigors of *yugyō*. Sometimes the assignment entailed a considerable sacrifice on the part of the *jishū* because of the desire to stay with Shinkyō.[11] Sometimes, no doubt, practicing obedience in just staying put was the hardest lesson. One Jū'amidabutsu, forced to "rest" in the country for two or three years, was told he might have to wait until he died and went to the Pure Land to see Shinkyō again, despite an apparent promise of an opportunity to return to Taima.[12] Some were in considerable distress, as Sai'amidabutsu of Takanomiya saw, while famine raged in Musashi and Sagami Provinces.[13] Some were simply dying of boredom.[14]

The third reason for sending *jishū* to temples was to preach the *nembutsu* to the local inhabitants, to

solicit people in the area with a connection [that they might] hear [about] our doctrines and practices and experience religious awakening; since an aspiration for Rebirth will also arise, we should also take special care for the benefits for Sentient Beings. Therefore, considering carefully this very principle, when the number of people here increases too exceedingly, according to the situation I shall just send them to other places.[15]

Thus, chaplaincy served the interests of the order as well as those of the order's mission. However, Shinkyō and his successors would have to contend with the consequences.

Despite the advantages of dispatching *jishū* as chaplains, an important problem was posed by permanent residence in temples, known as solitary residence (*dokujū*). Ippen's religious career had been based on communal itinerancy or *yugyō*. Thus, there was a possibility that a qualitative difference of religious life might develop for those Ippen had accepted to make a vow of Same Practice and to follow him on *yugyō* and those remaining in their communities. Alert to the problem, Shinkyō made a concerted effort to see to it that such a qualitative difference did not obtain in his order. This he achieved, to some extent, by shifting the focus of religious practice from walking practice or itinerancy to *nembutsu* practice and to include laity in the category of Fellow Practitioner. Through this shift he tried to ensure that *dōgyō*, Fellow Practitioner or Same Practice, was available in solitary residence (*dokujū*) in the temple as well as in itinerancy.

The main question, of course, was whether Same Practice could be achieved by *jishū* in temples away from the Chishiki as well as by those in the presence of the Chishiki or on *yugyō*, with laymen as well as with fellow religious. Shinkyō affirmed that this is indeed the case:

When one entrusts one's life to Amida there is no other thing of use than the most important thing [in life and death], Rebirth. Therefore, I have given up the arts, I have given up knowledge, and I have given up [even] virtue; thus, there is nothing I can teach another. Consequently, I have not a single disciple. If each and everyone has faith and chants the *nembutsu*, [I my]self and others will achieve Rebirth together; therefore, we are all Fellow Practitioners. That is why [this] Ta'amida-butsu has written [about] this in the *Dōgyō yōjin taikō* (Great outline of admonitions on Same Practice) in eighteen verses. Sentient Beings call a *zenchishiki* one who understands this and has thereby come to the Realization (*satori*) of Non-self (*muga*). Thus, if one says, "That is Same Practice," at that very time, one has understood the words of the Chishiki in one [hearing], [that] the Chishiki and I too indeed are Fellow Practitioners. If one thinks that this is not necessarily a teaching which ought to be venerated, that person has not achieved faith. Similarly, exchanging the heart of the learner for the heart of the Chishiki, in this way they must become one. As for the *zenchishiki*, [they] also call him the Great Cause (Daiinnen).[16] What is called "in" is Sentient Beings, what is called "en" is the Chishiki; although two, because they gain the path of Nonduality, [they become] the Great Cause—so they explain it. Usually, what [people] understand as a person's *dōgyō-zenchishiki* is that together they encourage the *nembutsu* [and] that in times of pain and trouble doing such things as nursing [the sick] is called *dōgyō-zenchishiki*; [but these] are temporary forms [taken] for a time. Truly at times [that one] knows one's mental state, when one understands as noted above, one calls too *dōgyō-zenchishiki* the Fellow Practitioners and companions with whom one becomes familiar [who are] none other than egos [trying] exceedingly to leave suffering and cause [even others] to achieve the same Realization (*satori*) as their own.[17]

All those who work together to promote the *nembutsu*, to perform acts of charity, and bring themselves and others to Realization are Fellow Practitioners, religious and lay. For, "destroying one's egoism and abandoning one's pride, priest and patron together will become *dōgyō-zenchishiki* and achieve Rebirth itself."[18] It was important for the *jishū* to understand that anyone to whom or with whom assigned by the Chishiki became a Fellow Practitioner:

> Together with the Fellow Practitioner (*dōgyō*) or religious companions (*dōryo*) I have attached to you, [you] are [all] creatures at the discretion of the Chishiki; together, without division, without neglecting practice, encourage [the *nembutsu*].[19]

Any and all the Chishiki threw the *jishū* in with, other *jishū* or laity, became *dōgyō*, Fellow Practitioners.

Involvement with laity posed problems to the religious. Although *jishū* were forced to be in the world they were forbidden to be of it. Temple administration and patrons had their needs, but *jishū* had to remember to remain *jishū*. The problems encountered by *jishū* settled in temples gave Shinkyō the opportunity to refine the idea of Same Practice which he had formulated in the *Dōgyō yōjin taikō* (Great outline of admonitions on Same Practice). For example, the economics of a temple sometimes posed considerable problems of a spiritual nature. Farming, for example, killed insects and that was a dreadful sin. Shinkyō made clear that if one farmed in order to kill insects, then one sinned. The sin was in the heart:

> Understanding this, if one farms to support the temple while cherishing the heart of the Buddha, one achieves Rebirth. If one manages [the temple] in order to live in comfort, indeed the karmic effects of the heart [are such that] even if [living solely from the income obtained from] receiving alms, one falls into hell.[20]

In the case of temples or chaplains with patrons, one could expect the patron to provide "clothes and food" for the sake of assistance in his own salvation. The question then became, considering the dependence on the patron, to what extent the involvement in the patron's affairs was permitted. Shinkyō wrote,

> Further, pay attention to the management of the daily affairs of the patron which are appropriate; since they are your provisions for the road to Rebirth you should not distance yourself from the ingredients.[21]

Again,

> . . . since it is the custom of the countryside, if it [is done out of] mercy to help in this life and the next, it is entirely appropriate to assist the patron since supporting *jishū* caused [the patron to have] to develop rice fields and to cultivate dry fields and the like. . . . Since a *jishū*, for whom the most important thing in life is Rebirth, does not know [the

difference between] morning and evening, there is nothing besides chanting the *nembutsu* even when sleeping and when awake, [and] it is reasonable that even in the single [chanting of the] nembutsu at death, after all, there must be no other words than these. Usually, when one's faith is true, Same Practice is also possible by oneself. There is no need to worry.[22]

It was the intent and not particularly the action that counted, as long as *jishū* maintained their religious obligations. Same Practice was the same for a *jishū* no matter what the circumstance: it was the *nembutsu*. Even so, the problem of interaction between lay as *dōgyō* and *jishū* would remain a standing problem in the order.

EXTENSION OF RELIGIOUS AUTHORITY TO TEMPLE HEADS

Despite the need to find places for the expanding number of *jishū*, Shinkyō could not despatch any but the most qualified: the *jishū* delegated as chaplain had to be trusted by Shinkyō to take charge of the spiritual life of the patron, someone with whom Shinkyō may already have had a close relationship. Moreover, *jishū* reflected himself: the Chishiki could not be the Chishiki of an order whose members were not living according to the precepts. If, in the Seizan and Ippen schools, "Namuamidabutsu" meant "Amida depends on my *nembutsu* to achieve Buddhahood," so Shinkyō recognized that his own status as Chishiki depended on guaranteeing Rebirth to his followers. Rebirth meant living according to the precepts and Shinkyō and his successors took personal responsibility for seeing to it that their followers did so. But *jishū* in permanent residence in temples were not under their personal supervision and there was always potential for trouble, as seen in the previous chapter.

Shinkyō was very clear in his own mind as to the *jishū* he considered qualified, those living according to the precepts and obedient to him:

. . . since nuns and monks give up their lives to the Chishiki and make the vow, [since] by striking the gong and not depending on their own wills they destroy the karmic effects of their actions, since they entrust themselves to [the divine forces] which are concerned about them and protect them that they may achieve Rebirth, [and] because they will achieve determined Rebirth (ketsujō ōjō), they cause [their spiritual charges] to go ahead [of themselves to Rebirth]."[23]

He was equally conscious that the very nature of chaplaincy demanded that he confer his own status as Chishiki on the chaplain:

Indeed, since I have sent you to Kurogoma-dono because in the deepness of his faith he had asked me to send him one, let him revere you and treat you as Chishiki and *chōrō*. . . . Even though while you were here [with me] you were [only] a *jishū*, Kurogoma, in the faith born in him, [should] revere you as the Chishiki."[24]

Thus, Shinkyō extended the status of and delegated the function of Chishiki to *jishū* he assigned as chaplains. This is borne out by external evidence in the *Taiheiki*, which describes an incident in which a lady's chaplain, referred to as a "*hijiri* who had long served as her as Chishiki," prevented her from committing suicide and took her to a well-known Yugyō-ha temple to become a nun.[25] By 1500, texts indicate that the heads of Yugyō-ha branch temples were known as Chishiki.

The ability and willingness to delegate had a firm foundation in religious doctrine. The sharing of religious authority lies at the very heart of Seizan school doctrine, followed by Ippen, in the concept of the Nonduality (*funi*) of the moment Amida achieved buddhahood ten kalpas ago and the moment the practitioner utters the *nembutsu*.[26] The determinant of this Nonduality, "Namuamidabutsu," means not only "I rely on Amida for my Rebirth" but "Amida relies on my nembutsu for his Buddhahood." This reciprocity, the interdependency of the Buddhahood of Amida and the Rebirth of Sentient Beings, is implicit in the requirements both for Amida and for Sentient Beings to meet the conditions set out in Amida's forty-eight vows. Indeed, the principle of interdependency and Nonduality embodied for Ippen in the Name ("Namuamidabutsu"), as seen in the last chapter, was used to establish the absolute authority of the Chishiki by identifying him with the Buddha.

This same Nonduality represented by the Name also became the paradigm for the relationship of interdependency and Nonduality between Chishiki (friend, teacher and guide to salvation) and *jishū* (members of the order, *nembutsu* practitioner). As noted in the previous chapter, Shinkyō identified himself as the representative of and then as the Buddha himself; indeed, he claimed to be an incarnation of Kannon.[27] In addition, he demanded from those he accepted as disciples that they accept him as *their* Buddha and, in his letters, freely substituted Chishiki for Hotoke or Amida in specific formulaic expressions meaning reliance on another for salvation. This has a long history in Pure Land thought in which the *dharmā-kāya* (Jp. *hosshin*) or Dharma Body or Principle of Becoming a Buddha is realized by *sambhoga-kāya* (Jp. *hōjin*), the manifested state of realizing Buddhahood or Enjoyment Body, which itself is manifested in this world as an Historical Body, or *nirmāna-kāya* (Jp. *keshin*). For Ippen, following the Seizan school, the Name "Namuamidabutsu" was the Dharma Body which secured both Amida's Buddhahood and the Sentient Being's Rebirth.

However, for Shinkyō as head of his order, not the Name but he himself as Buddha by consent secured the Rebirth of his *jishū* by regulating their lives in accordance with specific precepts and causing them to chant the Name. The agreement to treat the Chishiki as a Buddha shifted to acknowledgment of the Chishiki as the Historical Body of the Buddha, the form manifested in this world. The twenty-first Yugyō Shōnin Chiren explained it, stating, "Our school establishes a body of the Buddha in the flesh and makes the Chishiki [the object] of highest reverence."[28] If according to Takuga, "the Chishiki is the Buddha in human form, the *jishū* is a Bodhisattva living in ease having achieved Realization (*satori*)" or "because [the Chishiki] causes [the *jishū*] to convert and [to achieve] Rebirth, he makes *jishū* monks and nuns nonretrograding Bodhisattvas."[29]

The concept of Chishiki as Buddha and *jishū* as Bodhisattva was one expression of the hierarchical relationship between the head of the order and the other religious of the order which was meant specifically to secure discipline. However, between about 1350 and 1500, the theory of the Three Bodies of the Buddha (Skt. *trikāya*, Jp. *sanshin*) became a bit more pronounced in explanations of the doctrinal basis of discipline, that is, the relationship between Chishiki and *jishū*, and, as a result, in explaining the corporate identity of the order. As Takuga asserted in the *Jōjō gyōgi hōsoku*, "Mida is the Three Bodies of Enlightenment in the eternal past" (*Mida kuon shōgaku no sanshin nari*). The Dharma Body, the principle or essence of buddhahood (*dharmā-kāya*), is the Name ("Myōgo kore wa hosshin"). "All previous heads of the order are manifestations of Amida" (*Sōsō sude ni Mida no funjin nari*).[30] This manifestation, *funjin*, is equivalent to *keshin*, which is a kind of Historical Body (*nirmāna-kāya*) or incarnation of the principle of buddhahood.[31] The head *jishū* in temples are also Historical Bodies of the Buddha ("Dokujū mata keshin nar[i]").[32] Chiren consolidates the theme by specifically identifying Amida as the Enjoyment Body and at the same time uses it to buttress the hierarchy: "[the position of the Chishiki] is the same as that of the Enjoyment Body (*hōjin*) of Amida" and "temple heads . . . are all manifestations (*funjin*) . . . of the Chishiki."[33] That is, the Chishiki is a manifestation of Amida and temple heads are manifestations of the Chishiki. Ordinary *jishū* are not distinguished by the term *funjin*, which indicates an hierarchical but not necessarily a qualitative difference. Thus, the order of *jishū*, including the living and the dead, the Chishiki and all *jishū*, was conceived of as a unified whole—a corporate entity—identical with Amida Buddha. Since Amida Buddha and the Chishiki are one and *jishū* and Amida are one, the entire religious order represents the corporate body of Amida, made possible by the Name.[34]

Thus, Nonduality, as the doctrinal basis for the relationship between Buddha and Chishiki, together with the absolute vow of obedience to the Chishiki, rendered absolute authority to the Chishiki on the one hand and, on the other, served to bind the *jishū* to Chishiki as to form a single entity. If the Buddha and the Chishiki were a single body ("Chishiki to butsu to ittai naru koto"), then the Chishiki and the *jishū*, too, became a single body (*isshin*) with the taking of the vows at ordination.[35] On the basis of this, Yugyō Shōnin extended to the *jishū* assigned as chaplain the authority to function as Chishiki to his spiritual charges. According to Chiren's *Shinshū yōhō ki* (Record of important teachings of the Pure Land school, c. 1500), "[a]s for temple heads, because of the principle by which all separate parts (*funjin*) of the Buddha are of one body, they receive the title of Chishiki."[36] It is, however, important to remember that the linchpin of this identification between Chishiki and *jishū* was the vow of absolute obedience.

Shinkyō identified himself with the Buddha principally by virtue of his function. In the letter cited above, he stated that *jishū* delegated by him to act as chaplains would "cause [their spiritual charges] to go ahead [of themselves to Rebirth]."[37] This theme was taken up by Chiren when he asserted, "As the single body of the Chishiki, receiving the virtues of Amida, one causes Sentient Beings well to cross over."[38] The phrase "cause to go ahead" is a substitute for the formula "cause to cross over," which is the function of the Chishiki. This is a reference to an important tenet for Shantao and revealed in the Parable of the Two Rivers and White Path, to which reference is constantly made. Shakyamuni Buddha is the one who stands on *this* side of the river urging the traveller on to the other side where Amida calls. In the *Shinshū yōhō ki*, Shakyamuni is referred to as "Shaka hokken" (Shaka who urges) and "hokken Shaka" (Shaka the urger). The first appears under the section on the last ten *nembutsu*:

> Again, the teaching of Shaka who urges comes to a conclusion in the two characters of "Namu."[39]

The second comes in a discussion of the Chishiki:

> However, the Chishiki of this school [Yugyō-ha] becomes the master (*aruji*) of the chanted *nembutsu* (*shōmyō nembutsu*). . . . even though his position is the same as that of the Enjoyment Body of Amida, first of all appearing in this polluted world (*shaba*), attaching himself to all Sentient Beings, he causes them to chant Amida's Name and encourages [them to strive for] Rebirth in the Pure Land. This is why [his position]

is the same as the position of Shaka the urger (*hokken* Shaka). As for temple heads, scattered in the eight directions [the Chishiki] has sent them, they are all separate parts (*funjin*) of the single body (*ittai*) of the Chishiki."[40]

Since the temple head or chaplain as Chishiki is identified with the Chishiki of the order and the Chishiki is identified by his function of encouraging the *nembutsu* as the Hokken Shaka, because they share the same identity and function of the Chishiki, the *jishū* serving as chaplains function and are identified as manifestations of Shaka. Thus, Shinkyō's identification with Shaka was preserved in a corporate entity identified principally with Amida.

On the basis of the concept of Nonduality, the *jishū* was considered a substitute for the Chishiki and was considered a Chishiki. Nonduality remained a fundamental principle in the order. This is indicated by the *Shinshū yōhō ki*, in which Chiren stated the following:

> Considering deeply taking the measure of the words of the vow one gives up one's life to the Chishiki. Therefore a *jishū*, anywhere one might be, is solely [part of] the Single Body of the Chishiki. . . . As the Single Body of the Chishiki that receives the virtue of Amida one causes Sentient Beings to cross over [to the Pure Land].[41]

Through this identification, the *jishū* was made absolutely subordinate to and dependent upon the Chishiki—even a mere extension of the Chishiki. However, this identification also laid the basis for extending religious authority to—for sharing religious authority with—the *jishū* assigned as a private chaplain or as head of a temple. This authority shared with and by the Chishiki could never be asserted except over spiritual charges, lay and religious, assigned by the Chishiki. As Chishiki, the temple head gave permission to enter the order, took the oath of initiation, and reserved the right to affirm or to deny the state of Rebirth, and, subject to appeal to the Chishiki, to expel a *jishū*.[42] Temple *jishū* were required to treat the temple Chishiki as Chishiki of the order: to eat what the Chishiki left, to turn over alms and donations to the Chishiki, and to receive robes directly from the Chishiki.[43]

Receiving food and clothing from the Chishiki was extremely important in that it so clearly ritualized the relationship of dependence as a form of spiritual training, doctrine routinized into a rule of the order. As Shinkyō wrote,

> I provide the two things food and clothing as well as the articles of daily life etc. in order to stop other desires. [I provide clothing, etc.] so that there are no other needs and therefore there are no desires of the

heart. . . . if you receive offerings from other people, [your heart] will become separate from the Chishiki's heart.[44]

The relationship of absolute dependency in *dōgyō* demanded by Shinkyō of his *jishū*, spiritual and material, was replicated in the relationship between temple Chishiki and temple *jishū*.[45] However, this same dependency, based on the vow taken upon entering the order, did not model the relationship between *jishū* and the lay patron: although the *jishū* was to sometimes a great extent dependent on the lay patron, the laity took no vows of obedience. While one's dependence on the Chishiki was rewarded with Rebirth, the relationship with one's patron was fraught with risks to the *jishū*'s Rebirth. The religious authority extended to the individual *jishū*, which allowed one to participate in the mission of extending salvation, threatened in very real terms one's relationship with the Chishiki. As demonstrated in the last chapter, chaplains who allowed themselves to serve their patrons too well found that they had imperiled not only their own Rebirths but those of their patrons. And yet *jishū* could not refuse to serve as chaplains: they could neither refuse to obey the Chishiki nor turn their backs on the *hijiri* tradition of rendering assistance to *kechienshū*.

EXTENDING RELIGIOUS AUTHORITY TO ORDINARY *JISHŪ*

In delegating authority to temple heads and to chaplains, along with sharing the title and responsibilities of Chishiki and the status of *dōgyō*, Shinkyō shared one function: the granting of the ten *nembutsu* at death, the *saigo no jūnen*. Again, this was the custom of calling out the *nembutsu* and causing the one about to die to repeat the *nembutsu* a total of ten times, or perhaps until death. This was, indeed, a function Shinkyō could not monopolize. Even in the *Ippen hijiri e*, it is clear that when it came to assisting the dying in chanting the ten *nembutsu*, Ippen was not the only *chishiki*. When the lay priest Ninomiya died, the attending "monk acting as *chishiki*" (*chishiki no sō*) was not Ippen.[46] Thus, granting the last ten *nembutsu* was not among the functions characterizing the *hijiri* career upon which the religious authority of the Chishiki was based.

Even so, as we have seen in chapter 4, granting the ten *nembutsu* features prominently in the *Yugyō Shōnin ekotoba den* in establishing Shinkyō's religious authority. Indeed, granting the ten *nembutsu* seems to have become a feature of the order. The ten *nembutsu* administered by the head of the order had special efficacy. Shinkyō wrote that if one heard the *nembutsu* of the Chishiki and immediately died, even if the sound of the *nembutsu* did not pass one's own lips, one would achieve Rebirth.[47] The principal function of the Yugyō Shōnin, as Chishiki of the order, was to propagate the *nembutsu* and to cause people to chant the last ten *nembutsu* before death and thus to avoid rebirth in the three evil worlds:

> Shan-tao was the only master to explain that, because the sinner with the pain of death closing in on him is not able to meditate on the name of the Buddha, the good friend (*zen'u*), knowing how to forget suffering, instructs him and causes him to chant the Name of Amida. . . . The good friend (*zen'u*) . . . is the Chishiki of our order. What is called the *zenchishiki* is only the preparation for death. . . . Therefore, Shan-tao says, to be able to escape the three [evil] worlds after death is due to the kindness of the Chishiki/*chishiki*.[48]

According to the *Shinshū yōhō ki*, the ten *nembutsu* administered by the Chishiki had particular significance when administered to *jishū* departing on a journey or to *jishū* fallen dangerously ill:

> When a *jishū* departs on a journey, he receives the ten *nembutsu*; should he on his journey die in a distant place, the ten *nembutsu* which he received from the Chishiki creates the condition of death [and Rebirth]. Therefore, after [once] receiving the ten *nembutsu*, one dies without [further] word of judgment. . . . Or, after one returns from another place or recovers from illness, as for receiving the ten *nembutsu*, worship is rejoicing that one has not died this time, even more, is accumulat[ing] merits [on] returning to where the Chishiki is, [who] causes [one] to bow down [and worship gratefully the fact that] one will surely achieve Rebirth. In this school, everything in daily monastic conduct and in worship uses the ten *nembutsu*. This expresses the extreme [application] of the principle of Single-minded Exclusive Practice [of the *nembutsu*] (*ikkō senju*).[49]

Accepting the ten *nembutsu* functioned also as a form of acknowledging the authority of the Yugyō-ha, as when in 1424 the Konrenji was forced to accept the status of branch temple of the Konkōji, the Yugyō-ha headquarters in Kyoto. According to a contemporary diary entry, Jō'a, the seventh head of that temple and seventh of that name, was instructed either by the shogun himself or by one or more influential men in the warrior government to go to the temple on Seventh Avenue, the Shichijō Konkōji, to receive the ten *nembutsu* from the fifteenth Yugyō Shōnin Sonne. This is reported as having taken place in the seventh month of 1424.[50]

Most importantly, however, the granting of the last ten *nembutsu* was the single most important duty of the local *jishū* to parishioners and seems to have been identified almost exclusively with Ippen school orders. While the *jishū* secured his own Rebirth through the vow to the Chishiki, "the laity

. . . [had] nothing to rely upon but the chanting of the *nembutsu* (*shōmyō*) as taught by this school."[51] This is attested to in the propaganda narratives surviving in epics which describe the granting of the ten *nembutsu* at death on the battlefield: either the warrior's connection with Ippen school orders can be proven or the religious is identified in the text as Ippen school.

Chapter 4 has already discussed the background of service of Yugyō-ha and other Ippen-school *jishū* in the field between 1331 and about 1400. What is critical about the function of such *jishū* is that, as chaplains sent by the Chishiki to secure the Rebirth of their warrior patron-parishioners, they functioned in the capacity of Chishiki with the limited and transformed power of the Chishiki. The evidence for *jishū* activities in the field preserved in two Yugyō-ha documents and a bare handful of propaganda traditions in two or three epics indicates that this power was expressed principally as extending the possibility of Rebirth by granting the last ten *nembutsu*, the *saigo no jūnen*.

To warriors afraid of a sentence to hell as a result of death on the battlefield, Shinkyō offered only the *nembutsu*. He assured them with this consolation:

> However, if the believing practitioner of the *nembutsu* dies chanting the *nembutsu*, by the very sound of the chant he will wipe out his sins and achieve Rebirth in paradise. Because he is a practitioner without compare who tries to chant the *nembutsu* in the midst of battle in which he might lose his life, surely he will be welcomed into paradise.[52]

To another query he replied,

> Heading for the battlefield of warriors and the like where you might be killed, although you hold a weapon in your hand, should you die with the *nembutsu* on your lips, you will be Reborn in paradise. And if so, it is because only the chanting of the *nembutsu* is necessary.[53]

In line with Shinkyō's concept of the need of a chaplain to prosper the patron's faith, the chaplain became necessary to make certain that the patron actually chanted the *nembutsu* at the appropriate time: more emphasis was placed on the last ten *nembutsu* at death.

Warrior belief in the need of the Chishiki's administration of the ten *nembutsu* was clearly demonstrated in 1333. Just before the fall of Kamakura to Nitta Yoshisada's forces, the Shōjōkōin was swarming with men coming to accept the last ten *nembutsu* before death; *jishū* apparently witnessed the battle and administered the last ten *nembutsu* to those who were executed. The Fujisawa Shōnin Ankoku (b. 1279; YS 1325-1327, FS -1337) described the scene:

Although Kamakura was in a great uproar, it was particularly quiet at the temple, because all the men who had come in swarms had departed for the battlefield; the place having been deserted except for the monks, nothing untoward happened. Even in the thick of the fighting, they were all chanting the *nembutsu*, the attacking force and the defenders. In the aftermath, men were executed for fighting against their own side; our priests went to the beach, all led *nembutsu* believers in the chanting of the *nembutsu* and caused them to achieve Rebirth in paradise. Since the battle, having witnessed what we did, people have been increasing their faith in the *nembutsu*. I hope to live [long enough] to write you again.

Respectfully
Namuamidabutsu
Fifth month, twenty-eighth day
Ta'amidabutsu[54]

Some simply took their chaplains with them on campaign. In time, *jishū* were assigned directly to warriors in the field. Takuga and Jikū asserted that the "purpose of *jishū* going on the same road (*dōdō*) [was] to administer the ten *nembutsu* at the time of death."[55] And, as a previously cited quotation from the *Ihon Odawara ki* indicates, Yugyō-ha *jishū* were remembered for their service in the field administering the ten *nembutsu* long after such service had been terminated.

Evidence in epics indicates how chaplains operated. *Jishū* chaplains administered the last ten *nembutsu* just before their charges went into battle. Usually, the incident is described as already having taken place. For example, the sixth chapter of the c. 1370 *Taiheiki*, in describing the deaths of two warriors in 1333, reports that "the *hijiri* who had followed them until the end and had led [them in] the ten *nembutsu* at death" (*Kore made tsukishitagaite saigo no jūnen susumetsuru hijiri*[56]) begged the heads of Hōjō vassals Hitomi On'a and Homma Kurō Suketada from Akasaka Castle, carried them back to the camp at Tennōji, informed Homma's son, wrapped the heads in sleeves, and buried them.[57] It is very likely that this *jishū* was a chaplain assigned by Shinkyō himself. There exist two letters from Shinkyō to Hitomi On'amidabutsu, founder of the Ichijōji, in what is now Fukadani City, Saitama Prefecture, one of the great Yugyō-ha temples of the fourteenth and fifteenth centuries, and one to a Homma Gen'amidabutsu, a member perhaps of the same family or Homma himself.[58]

However, Chapter Thirty-nine actually describes the granting of the ten *nembutsu* as it happens: Okamoto Shinano no kami Tomotaka, "receiving the ten *nembutsu* at death from a *jishū*" (*saigo no jūnen jishū ni ukete*), rode to his death in battle at Itahana in Kōzuke Province in 1363. The *jishū* is presumed to have come from the Yugyō-ha Mummyōji nearby (Annaka City, Gumma Prefecture).[59]

Later references are found (so far) only in the c. 1392-1393 *Meitokuki*, which treats of the revolt of Yamana Ujikiyo against the shogun Yoshimitsu on the last day of 1391 (Meitoku 2). Both describe the granting of the last ten *nembutsu* as having taken place in the past, as an attribute of the *jishū*. It was "the *jishū* who had followed him till the end" (*Saigo made tsuketari-keru jishū no mōshikeru wa*) who explained to those who had taken Yaki Kurō's head why there was a bare patch on the side. This *jishū* is thought to have been a *jishū* from the Konrenji (if not merely modelled on one): Yaki Kurō's wife and mother are reported as hiding in the neighborhood of the Konrenji ("Shijō no dōjō"). The *jishū* brings her a letter and a lock of hair from Yaki and returns to him with a lock of her own (the word used, *mirufusa*, is found often in *jishū* texts) and assures him that he can go to his death with his heart at ease because she has become a nun.[60] And, finally, "a jishū who had been summoned from the temple in Sakai to follow Yamana Ujikiyo, the lord of Ōshū, and a messenger from [his son] Miyata the vice-commander of the horse of the left came running in together, one after the other" (*Sakai no dōjō yori Ōshū ni tsukemōsaretarikeru jishū to Miyata no Sama no suke no tsukai to futari hashirikasanete kitari*) to announce to Yamana Ujikiyo's lady her husband's terrible defeat and death at the hands of the shogunate.[61] The Yamana were Yugyō-ha adherents: the family memorial temple, the Sanmyōji (Yamanadera) in Hōki Province (now Shimane Prefecture) was Yugyō-ha and the Yamana killed in the revolt are entered in the *Jishū kakochō*.[62] The Sakai Dōjō was the Injōji, a large and famous branch temple of the Konrenji with its support in the local merchant community.[63]

These four examples are the only direct references to Yugyō-ha and Shijō-ha *jishū* in the field. They describe the last ten *nembutsu* being administered just before a battle. One more describes the administering of the ten *nembutsu* before an execution. The *Taiheiki*, the eleventh chapter, relates that a member of the Hōjō family, Sasuke Sadatoshi, called here Sakai Sadatoshi and Sakyō no suke, was recaptured after the fall of Kamakura (1333); before he was executed, he asked the "holy man who had led him in the chanting of the ten *nembutsu* at death" (*saigo no jūnen susumekeru hijiri*) to take his short sword to his wife and child; he then chanted the ten *nembutsu* again and held out his neck for the sword.[64] Sasuke Aki no kami Sadatoshi was connected with Shinkyō through poetry: a letter to Sadatoshi and a poem exchanged with Shinkyō are preserved in the *Ta'a Shōnin hōgo*.[65]

These examples are distinguished not only by the documented connections of the warriors concerned to Shinkyō and his successors but also by their diction. They use the variations of two formulae (formulaic systems), but no two use exactly the same variation:

saigo no jūnen jishū ni ukete
(receiving the last ten *nembutsu* from a *jishū*)
kore made tsukishitagaite saigo no jūnen susumetsuru hijiri
(the *jishū* who followed [him] to the end and encouraged the last ten *nembutsu*)
saigo made tsuketarikeru jishū
(the *jishū* who had followed him to the end)
Sakai no dōjō yori Ōshū ni tsukemosaretarikeru jishū
(the *jishū* summoned from the temple in Sakai to follow the lord of Ōshū)
saigo no jūnen susumekeru hijiri
(the *hijiri* who encouraged the last ten *nembutsu*)

"Jishū" and "hijiri" are interchangeable, "kore made tsuk[u]" and "saigo made tsuk[u]" ("follow till death," with some sort of resonance with "saigo no jūnen"), as are "ukeru" (receive) and "susumeru" (encourage). These are the only examples of the use of these particular formulae in epic. Formulaic diction is probably the easiest element of composition to imitate. And yet, these formulaic variations are restricted to composition in the fourteenth century and refer obviously to Yugyō-ha and Shijō-ha (and very possibly to Taima-ha) *jishū* serving as chaplains in the field. This restriction supports my contention that Yugyō-ha activity in providing chaplains in the field ended by or shortly after 1400, and, therefore, so did the production of propaganda narratives based on the activity.

However, other examples illustrate the continuing second theme of Yugyō-ha propaganda, service of a religious nature to those coming to or brought to a Yugyō-ha or Shijō-ha temple to shave their heads, to die, or to be buried. In Chapter Twenty of the *Taiheiki*, eight *jishū* accompany Nitta Yoshisada's body to the Yugyō-ha temple in Nagasaki, the Ōjōin Shōnenji, for burial. Many of his men enter the same temple.[66] The temple would later become an official temple for prayers of the shogunal house in part because the temple cared for the soul of a major enemy of the Ashikaga. (See chapter 6.) The *Meitokuki* reports that when Yamana Mitsuyuki was betrayed, captured, and executed in Kyoto in 1395, his head was sent to the shogun Yoshimitsu for inspection and Yoshimitsu gave the order for the head to be sent to the Konrenji for burial. From there, it was sent to the branch temple at the graveyard of Toribeno, identified as the Hōfukuji.[67]

Yugyō-ha chaplains tended to the survivors of warriors killed in the field. Yugyō-ha temples also became the refuges of the widows of warriors. Chapter Twenty-seven of the *Taiheiki* preserves a tradition that the wife of Uesugi Shigeyoshi, who had been exiled and assassinated in 1349 at the instigation of Ashikaga Takauji's general Kō no Moronao, was rescued from a suicide attempt and brought by her long-time chaplain ("*chishiki . . . hijiri*") to the same Ōjōin Shōnenji to become a nun.[68] Chapter Twenty-nine reports that in early 1351, a "*jishū* from Kai" brought word to Moronao that his brother and adopted son Morofuyu had committed suicide.[69] The Kō connection with the Yugyō-ha has already been discussed: it is likely that the *jishū* was Yugyō-ha from any one of the many Yugyō-ha temples in Kai Province. Along with the example in Chapter Eleven cited above, describing the activities of the holy man who had led [Sasuke] Sadatoshi in his last ten *nembutsu* and brought his short-sword to his wife only to see her kill herself with it, these represent the examples in the *Taiheiki* which illustrate services to family survivors.

The Yugyō-ha also maintained a tradition of offering refuge to warriors. According to Chapter Thirty-eight of the *Taiheiki*, in 1362, the Fujisawa Shōnin (the fourth, Tosen) gave refuge to Hatakeyama Kunikiyo (d. 1362) and his brother Yoshihiro, who had fled from the siege of Shuzenji Castle, and, giving them two horses and two *jishū* to guide them, sent them to the Konkōji in the capital. Later, their brother Yoshitō (1331-1379) was informed by a *jishū* that they had escaped to Fujisawa, was smuggled out of the enemy camp where he was a hostage, and took refuge at the Shōjō-kōji.[70]

What such narratives do not tell is the fate of some of these chaplains. Killed along with the brothers Kō Musashi no kami Moronao and Kō Echigo no kami Moroyasu were Bun'amidabutsu and Shō'amidabutsu.[71] Because of the relationship of the order with the Yugyō-ha, it is reasonable to conclude that they were Yugyō-ha *jishū*.

As discussed in the last chapter, Takuga and, later, Jikū found themselves in the awkward position of having to protect Same Practice in temples and the relationship of Fellow Practitioners obtaining between *jishū* and patron. Having given permission to save lives, especially those of non-combatants, Takuga had to defend the *jishū* of a branch temple against an Ashikaga general who wanted to expel them for protecting defeated warriors. Not only did he have to defend Same Practice from warriors, but he and Jikū had to defend it against *jishū* who had become so involved in the affairs of their patrons that they faced losing the way of the *jishū*. (See chapter 4.)

Nothing so demonstrates the problems of extending religious authority to serve laity and the ramifications as does the story of Yugyō-ha service in the field. Lay interference with the relationship between Chishiki and *jishū* remained a constant problem. A *jishū* who was committed to a patron, of course, found it difficult to disobey or to refuse a request. For example, once assigned to a temple, a *jishū* was not supposed to act as guide for parishioners going on pilgrimage. And yet, although such pilgrimages were forbidden, it was acknowledged that a *jishū* so requested by a powerful patron could not very well refuse.[72]

Although it is easy to assume that the head of the Yugyō-ha had absolute authority over *jishū* and their appointments, considerable compromise was necessary in order to maintain relations with powerful patrons. This is seen especially in the case of the Ichirenji of Kōfu, family memorial temple (*bodaiji*) of the Takeda of Kai. The Takeda, and their cadet branches including the Hemi (founders of Chōsenji), Kurogoma (Shōganji), and Nambu (Jikōji), had been converted by Shinkyō.[73] Shinkyō converted the head of the house, Ichijō Gempachi Tokinobu Butsu'amidabutsu, whose brother Shōrokurō Munenobu joined the *jishū* and followed Shinkyō for fourteen years before returning to the Ichirenji to become its first *jishū* priest. The second, third, and fourth head priests of the temple were also from the family.[74] At Ichirenji, the tutelary deity (*ujigami*) of the Takeda, the god of the Sumiyoshi Shrine (*honji* Tenjin, an incarnation of Kannon or Seishi), was worshipped in a special ceremony by the new head priest until the end of the Tokugawa period.[75] Initially the Ichirenji functioned principally as a family temple headed by a member of the family who had already married and had children before joining the order. The Yugyō-ha gained the temple permanently in 1400 when the government forbade the transfer of temples to or from the order or even within lineages. Ultimately, however, the choice of temple head depended on the Takeda, who required of head priests who were not Takeda to make a ceremonial vow when they took office that they were indeed Takeda descendants.[76] Thus, the absolute authority of the Chishiki over the temple head was compromised. Similarly, in the sixteenth century, the Mōri, as domainal lords ("ryōke"), were involved in the choice and appointment of the head priest of the Zenfuku-ji.[77] Again, the head priest was technically compromised in his absolute commitment to the Chishiki of the order.

The power of such local temples was such that considerable privileges were extended: the acceptance of such privileges was in itself acknowledgment of the right of the head of the order to confer them. For example, the thirteenth Fujisawa Shōnin Fukō extended privileges enjoyed by the head of the order to other temples: to the head priest Kaku'a of the Jōnenji in what is now Aizu-Wakamatsu City, Fukushima Prefecture the right to wear a *chakugo* surplice and to sit on a half mat and to Sō'a of the Ryūzenji in what is now Akita City, Akita Prefecture the right to use a half mat and an umbrella.[78] The goal may have been to raise the status of some temples in order to reduce that of others by expanding the total number of important temples or to strengthen the order's power in the far north by creating a base identified by its privileges with the head of the order. Fukō came from the Satake family; the Ryūzenji had been a Satake domain temple since 1591. The Satake were transferred to Akita in 1603 and the temple moved with them.[79] Thus, the elevation of Ryūzenji's status is at least logical. The particular reason for extending privileges to Jōnenji is as yet unknown.

Ranks and titles also functioned in the creation of a network of loyalties concentrated on the head of the order. In the Muromachi period, the title "Shōnin" was granted by the emperor and thus shared by several lineages founded by Shinkyō and his followers: the head of the Taima Muryōkōji, the Yugyō Shōnin, the Fujisawa Shōnin, the head of the Konrenji, and the head of the Nagasaki Shōnenji in Echizen Province. In the Tokugawa period, with the changes introduced by the government, a whole new series of ranks and titles became available to the order. In the *Tōtakusan kakochō*, the title "Oshō" appears for the first time and frequently—as does the title "Shōnin," listed for temples for which there is no evidence of imperial designation. Thus, this title was extended to—shared by—the head of the order in order to bind other religious of the order more tightly to himself. (See chapter 6.)

THE EXTENDED AUTHORITY TO GUARANTEE REBIRTH

As demonstrated in chapter 3, the *Jishū kakochō*, a register of those who had achieved Rebirth, originated in the *hijiri* practice of entering the names of donors which thereby created a community of the saved. As noted, *kakochō* were probably quite common and it took some time for the *Jishū kakochō* to achieve a singular status as the death register of the Yugyō Shōnin. Further, the head of Shōjōkōji also maintained a death register which more or less served the lay and religious of the eastern part of Japan, the Kantō. So did the major temples like the Konkōji and the Konrenji in Kyoto.

Among the registers of local temples, the most famous is the *Ichirenji kakochō*.[80] As mentioned above, the Kai [Province] Ichirenji, in Kōfu, was the family temple of the Takeda. The register is made up of three parts: one for monks (1419 to 1634) and one for nuns (1396 to 1663) started by the seventh head (Hō'a) and a third (1632 to 1702) begun for men and women, religious and lay.[81] Over 6700 names are entered. In the sixteenth century, Ichirenji was given the supervision of the reconstruction of the Shōjōkōji: the register lists names of craftsmen and members of the Horiuchi family, one of the most important supervising families of the town that formed around the temple and were involved in its rebuilding.[82] The entries and other notes of the sixteenth and seventeenth centuries indicate the geographic range of adherents, the temple's connections and branch temples, and the careers of its heads by recording master-disciple relationships and the temples to which and from which the heads had been transferred.[83] Great figures such as Ashikaga Mochiuji and Tokugawa Iemitsu are also entered.[84] Indeed, one of the studies yet to be done is an analysis of the *Ichirenji kakochō* in order to determine the nature and development of the extended Kai Ichirenji *jishū* community. According to Ishida, in the monks' section alone, most names entered, 194, are from the Nagasaki Shōnenji in Echizen, an imperial and shogunal (Ashikaga) temple for offering prayers. Names are also entered from such prominent temples as the Hitomi Ichijōji in Musashi Province (68), the Utsunomiya Ōganji in Shimotsuke Province (56), and the Kayazu Kōmyōji in Owari Province (41).[85]

But more importantly, the entries indicate the extent to which the temple functioned as the Takeda family memorial temple until the destruction of the Takeda in the late sixteenth century. In the monks' section, the list of sixteen temple heads is followed by the list of Takeda patrons through Nobuharu (Shingen, 1521-1573) and only then are ordinary *jishū* listed. The register shows the temple's initial function as family temple of the Takeda: the lists of souls of ancestors, the entry of those who had died for the Takeda in war, those whose deaths (such as that of Suwa Yorishige in 1542) the Takeda had caused. However, there are not many entries of cadet families such as Kurogoma or the Hemi with *jishū* temples of their own, of adherents or *jishū* in their villages, or head priests of the family temples (such as Kurogoma Mi'amidabutsu).[86]

The religious power of the *kakochō* is indicated by the frequency of entries of "gyakushū," entry before death to guarantee Rebirth. In the Bummei era (1469-1487), there is an exceptionally high rate with nineteen entries in the nuns' section and, in the monks' section for the same period, about twenty-five.[87] One use of entry as *gyakushū* might have been the same as the ten *nembutsu* before death: there is at least one example of entering as *gyakushū* in 1480 a man who died in battle in 1493.[88] There are no cancellations of Rebirth noted, however.

The Ichirenji represents the extremes of religious authority and political power that could accrue to a branch temple under the right circumstances. In the sixteenth century, as the Takeda rose to prominence in Kai, so did their mortuary temple. As will be discussed in detail in the next chapters, the Ichirenji acquired special prominence after the burning of Shōjōkōji: not only were the temples main images of the Amida triad installed at Ichirenji, but the Ichirenji was entrusted with the responsibility of rebuilding

Shōjōkōji. By about 1700, the head of the Ichirenji had acquired the right to succeed to the office of Fujisawa Shōnin in the case of the deaths of both Fujisawa and Yugyō Shōnin. After World War II, the Ichirenji was strong enough to secede from the Jishū as a result of a succession dispute.

Shinkyō and his successors were faced with the problem of maintaining the integrity of the religious life of followers not under their direct supervision. They met the situation by posting *jishū* whom they trusted as chaplains and temple heads. The doctrinal basis both for securing the absolute obedience of *jishū* and for extending religious authority to them was the traditional concept of Nonduality which was used to create a single corporate body: the Dharma Body as the Name, the Enjoyment Body as Amida, the Historical Body as the Chishiki, and his many parts or manifestations as the *jishū*. This was buttressed by Donkai's concept of the rule of succession as the key to creating a corporate body with a single will and intent that included the dead and therefore transcended the limits of time (chapter 3). Extremely disturbing is the extent to which the integrity of the corporate body of the order was threatened by interaction with the laity. If the order accepted warrior patronage, their temples and their relatives, the order found itself compromised and its *jishū* abused. Shogunal recognition of the order in 1400 and the prohibition of temple conversions seem to have had a temporary and limited effect. While the order was more or less successful in protecting the integrity of the religious life of obedience and practice of those *jishū* under the immediate supervision of those with the highest religious authority, the Fujisawa Shōnin and the Yugyō Shōnin, individual temples or chaplains were much more vulnerable: the very religious authority which had been delegated to them directed them to the laity and even bound them to their spiritual charges. The struggle of the Yugyō-ha to reconcile these divided loyalties was played out against the simple fact that the delegation of religious authority brought with it the threat of fragmentation.

6
The Charisma of the Lay Community

The relations of the Yugyō-ha with laity were extremely complex. The order was not a cloistered monastic community but an evangelizing community and its raison d'être was indeed its mission to the lay community. The order sponsored a mission to distribute salvation to one and all. The order despatched chaplains to patrons on request. The order offered protection and semi-religious status to a variety of social refugees and outcasts: beggars, pariahs, and retreatants followed the trains of the order or clustered around temples and obtained some sort of support as charity. Thus, practically speaking, except for the vow taken by novices at ordination, there was no real, clear-cut distinction between religious and lay in the Yugyō-ha community: all were members of the community seeking salvation.

As far as the order was concerned, its relationship with the lay community was based principally on what it offered the lay community as Fellow Practitioner: salvation. Salvation, however, was not the only advantage recognized by the laity. Thus, as we have seen, the order found itself in the truly unexpected situation of having to defend its *jishū* against a range of abuses at the hands of its patrons. Resolution was achieved by appeal only to the highest authority in the land, the shogun. Indeed, the order was particularly dependent upon external sources of authority to regularize a range of relationships: that between head of the order and *jishū* as well as that between the order and lay patrons. Conversely, those external sources of authority, emperor, shogun, or warlord, were in a sense dependent on their patronage of the Yugyō-ha and Jishū, which effectively functioned to assert claims to authority; acceptance of such patronage, as protection or even regulation, legitimated those claims to authority. Therefore, a close look at the relationship established between the order and the highest levels of authority in medieval Japan is necessary in order to understand the nature of the exchange on which that relationship was based.

109

IMPERIAL TITLES: SHŌNIN

In Japan, highest authority, if not greatest power, was accorded the imperial family: emperor, retired emperor, senior retired emperor, crown prince and their empresses, consorts, concubines, children and all descendants to the fifth generation. As high priest (or even chief object of worship) of the combined family cult and agricultural cult constituting state Shinto and as sovereign presiding over a Chinese-style government and its bureaucracy, the emperor functioned principally as a source of authority for a series of "in-law" families and warlord regimes which wielded actual power. The emperor—or more commonly whoever controlled the emperor—controlled the clerical appointments and promotions in the Buddhist institutions under the jurisdiction of the imperial government system, whose titles were known as the *sōkan* or "dignities of the Buddhist hierarchies." The titles, corresponding with positions in the official bureaucracy and first conferred in the seventh and eighth centuries, included Daisōjō (rank of Dainagon in the imperial bureaucracy), Sōjō (rank of Chūnagon), Gonsōjō (Sangi), Daisōzu, Gondaisōzu, Shōsōzu, Gonshōsōzu, Dairisshi, Chūrisshi, and Gonrisshi.[1]

Buddhism was extremely important to the imperial family in establishing bases of power outside the official bureaucracy and its institutions. During the Heian period, upon retirement an emperor took nominal orders and his residence was known as a temple (*in*). The offices of the senior retired emperor or Cloistered Emperor (*in no chō*) functioned to challenge the power of the Fujiwara in-law family by building up a private land base for the imperial family and by attracting nobles and the military to alliances with the prospect of positions in the *in no chō* and management positions on land held by the imperial family. Concomitant with this development was the gradual appropriation of a range of informal titles to confer upon clergy and thereby the assertion of the authority to do so. These titles, which, again, had no connection with the imperial bureaucracy, included the posthumous titles Daishi, Kokushi, and Hōshi, as well as Zenji and Shōnin (superior/holy person).[2] As Donryō noted in the c. 1700 *Shibazaki bunko* (Shibazaki [Nichirinji] collection), such titles were conferred by the imperial house in reverence for the virtues of the "family" of Shaka Buddha.[3] Of all these titles, the title Shōnin was of special importance to the Yugyō-ha and Jishū.[4]

The title Shōnin (superior/holy person) is found in sutras such as the Wisdom Sutra to refer to a monk excelling in scholarship or practice. The title seems first to have been used in reference to popular street evangelists such as Kūya/Kōya and then as a form of address for formally ordained monks. Gradually it was used as a term of respect for heads of temples and other high-ranking monks. At some point, apparently in the Heian period, emperors and retired emperors began to confer it as they did the titles Kokushi, Zenji, and Oshō. By the fifteenth century, interest was demonstrated by the imperial court in regularizing, indeed of monopolizing, the title Shōnin in the face of perhaps rampant arrogation of the title by clergy of various ranks, including "birdcatchers": the occasional document indicates a question on the part of an emperor leading to a request for an official inquiry. In the late sixteenth century, Tokugawa Ieyasu was one warlord at least who supported the court's assertion of the right to limit the title to those holding official grants (except those who had used the title twenty years) and even to punish with exile those a little too aggressive in pursuit of the title. As late as 1627 even the right of Chion'in, founded in 1211 by the Pure Land school founder Hōnen, to the title Shōnin was being investigated by the Tokugawa shogunate.[5]

Jishū documents indicate five Shōnin recognized in the sect; however, not one of them derived his title from Ippen. The first, it is claimed, to receive the title was Jō'amidabutsu Shinkan (1268-1341): sent to Kyoto in 1309, he is credited with the safe delivery of the future Emperor Kōgon after his mother had consumed three of his own *nembutsu* charms—delivered personally—and rewarded six months later with the title Shōnin. The tradition of the conferral of the title has been preserved by the Konrenji, founded by Jō'a Shinkan, in two sources: the documents collection and the *Jō'a Shōnin den* (Story of Jō'a Shōnin, 1463):

> The words of the order of the retired emperor say: "As for prayers for the tranquility of the world, they should be prayed with especial sincerity; keep in mind the safety of the whole country." [I] convey the orders of the retired emperor; therefore, as above. Ōchō 1 [1311] 8.27 [from Takashina] Masanaka [to] the honorable monk Jō'a Shōnin[6]

Nothing in the text of the document itself says anything about granting a title, although it does address Jō'a as Shōnin, which can be seen as substantiating the claim. The only document extant in the Konrenji collection which comes close to serving as substantiation of this claim is "The imperial order of Gokōgon" for ceremonies appealing for aid and assistance (*kitō*), addressed to "the honorable monk Jō'a" from [Yanagiwara] Sachūben Tadamitsu and dated [Embun 3 (1358)] 3.26.[7] There are problems with this tradition. First, the year of Kōgon's birth is given as 1311; most sources agree that the year was 1313. Second, the account of the conferral of the title on Shinkyō through the good offices of his disciple differs radically from that given in the *Ekotoba den*, as seen below. The biography of Jō'a was written after the temple was forced to acknowledge the authority of the

Yugyō-ha; its function is, no doubt, to assert the prerogatives of the Fourth Avenue school. In any case, this title of Shōnin would come to the Jishū when Konrenji was made a branch of the Konkōji.

The second to receive the title was Shinkyō. On the basis, it is claimed, of the miracle at Ise Shrine discussed in the last chapter, Shinkyō was recommended to the imperial court for a religious title. However, according to the *Jō'a Shōnin den*, his title was conferred through the good offices of his disciple, Jō'a: in 1312, through Jō'a's intercession Shinkyō, too, was granted the title Shōnin. The lay priest Tōnin Hatano Izumo had been sent as a messenger to Shinkyō to ask for the printing block for the *nembutsu* charms so that his ministry could be carried out in Kyoto and Shinkyō had consented:

> In addition, because Ta'amidabutsu lived in the country, he had not yet received the title Shōnin. The intention was forwarded to Jō'a Shōnin. The imperial order bestowed on this temple still exists. Its words say, "The founder [of the order] Ta'a must style [himself] Shōnin. The intention to bestow the order [on] the followers [of Ta'a] is the imperial will." Thus, [I] convey these orders as above. 3.26 [from] Sachūben Tadamitsu to the honorable monk Jō'a"[8]

There are no extant documents to corroborate this claim. Strictly speaking, the Taima-ha alone should have retained the title Shōnin when Donkai seceded. However, this title too was assumed by the Yugyō-ha and never, apparently, contested. Since there was a current Yugyō Shōnin based at the Kyoto Konkōji and a retired Yugyō Shōnin or Fujisawa Shōnin at Fujisawa, the title was shared between them even throughout the Tokugawa period.

The Shōnin titles granted to both Shinkyō and Shinkan are documented only in the tradition carried by the *Jō'a Shōnin den* and related illustrated scrolls. The claim to the third title, however, is substantiated by an official document granting it to a branch temple of the Yugyō-ha. The Chōrinsan Ōjōin Shōnenji, in what is now Maruoka City, Fukui Prefecture, was one of the most important of the Yugyō-ha temples during the middle ages but declined during the sixteenth century due, it is asserted, to competition from Shinran's school of Pure Land Buddhism.[9] In 1536, Emperor Gonara conferred the title "Shōnin" on the head of the temple.[10]

The temple enjoyed an extraordinary success in the middle ages partly due to the fact that Nitta Yoshisada, the great hero of the restoration movements of the fourteenth and nineteenth centuries, was buried there. According to the *Taiheiki*, his headless body, accompanied by eight *jishū*, had been sent there immediately after his death in battle in 1338.[11] In 1458, the temple was designated a *kiganjo*, an official temple for prayers for peace and prosperity for the Ashikaga shogunal house and then for the imperial house in 1465 (see below).[12] The shogun Ashikaga Yoshimasa endowed the temple to provide incense for Yoshisada.[13] This was one form of placating his angry spirit; honoring the temple in which he was buried can be seen as another form. While it is true that it was never emphasized in documents, no doubt the unarticulated consciousness of the order's traditional role in suppressing angry spirits of the war dead played a part in securing wealth and honors for the temple, which was charged with the keeping of the spirit of the Ashikaga's greatest enemy. In the Tokugawa period, as far as the order was concerned, Nitta Yoshisada was of little consequence; there is rarely mention of him in the texts under study. What mattered to the order was that the head of one of its branch temples bore the title Shōnin and was received at court.[14]

The title Shōnin was granted to the head of yet another temple, the Kyoto Konkōji, established by Donkai and joint headquarters of the Yugyō-ha. The *Jishū kekkishū* reports that, on the basis of the precedent established with Shōnenji, the title was granted during the Kan'ei period (1624-1643) by Gomizunoo (1596-1680, r. 1611-1629; son-in-law of the shogun Hidetada). The emperor conferred the title on the twenty-first head of the Shichijō Konkōji, Ji'a, and received him in audience. It is not clear whether this took place before or after 1629, the year of Gomizunoo's retirement.[15]

In 1657, Kaku'a, the head of the Kyōkōji in Hamamatsu, Tōtōmi Province, also received the title of Shōnin by imperial command.[16] The reigning emperor was Gosai (1637-1685; r. 1655-1663). Even so, the command very likely originated with the shogun Ietsuna (1640-1680; shogun 1651-). Originally a Tendai temple established in the early tenth century and known as the Kanma Dōjo (Kanma temple), it was converted in 1283 by Ippen while under Chitoku Hōin Kyōkō Ajari (d. 1307), from whom it derives its name. Several Yugyō Shōnin served as head priests of this temple: the fourteenth, the twenty-first, the thirty-fourth, the fiftieth, and the fifty-eighth. While Tokugawa Ieyasu was in residence in Hamamatsu, a lady in service to him had a dream and as a result, a poetry group was started, which eventually was convened regularly at the Nichirinji in Edo. The temple was important enough to receive a yearly stipend of sixty-five *koku* under the shogunate's vermilion seal.[17]

The title of Shōnin conferred by the imperial house was of importance to the order in two ways. First, it bestowed recognition and status on the order. Second, it did not involve the order in the imperial bureaucracy, thus preserving the status of *shukke/tonsei* that distinguished this order: for, as Chiren asserted around 1500, the "order [was] an order of *tonsei*."[18] The maintenance of *hijiri* status was of utmost importance in the medieval period: certainly, signs of office such as colored or silken robes were forbidden in the order up to the early seventeenth century.[19] During the Tokugawa period, however, things changed, including the attitude to silk and color. Therefore, at the end of the seventeenth century Donryō (head of the Edo Nichirinji and future Yugyō Shōnin) found it necessary to address the problem of rank and office in an order of *tonsei*. He noted that "the Yugyō [Shōnin] [was] recorded as being without rank (*mui*) and without office (*mukan*)" but that since the status of the Yugyō Shōnin was that of *monzeki* he was of the rank Provisional Assistant High Priest or Daisōzu [*sic*]. However, since all religious (*shukke*) were without rank and without office, he found it necessary to explain the history of how and why religious were part of the imperial bureaucracy. In the end, however, the fact that "Shōnin" was a suitable title for the imperial court to present the house of the Buddha Shaka without awarding an equivalent position in the imperial bureaucracy probably explained why the Yugyō Shōnin was the only one recorded as without rank and without office even though all other Buddhist schools, as *shukke*, were technically without rank and without office.[20]

During the Tokugawa period, the use of the title began to change, as can be seen in the Shōjōkōji's death register, the *Tōtakusan kakochō*. Of seventy names alone (not including Yugyō Shōnin or Fujisawa Shōnin) entered during the Genroku period (1688-1703) in the "Monmatsu sōrō" (Monks of the order) section, thirteen are listed as Shōnin.[21] Of these Shōnin, not one is from those temples noted as receiving the right to the title, Shōnenji, Konkōji, or Kyōkōji.[22] That is not to say that head priests of these temples are not listed: the twenty-third head of Kyōkōji is listed as an Oshō (preceptor, a title conferred on suitable clergy after at least ten years in orders, as in Zen schools).[23] This in itself is typical: one head of a temple might be listed as Shōnin but not another. For example, the twenty-third head of the Konkōji (d. 1706) is listed as a Shōnin and so is the head (technically a supervisor called Indai, since this is actually the Yugyō Shōnin's temple, but definitely the head because the office Amida name "Ji'a" is given) who died in 1714, but the Indai who died in 1779 (Go'a) is listed only as "Oshō." Again, the twenty-first head of the Kai Kurogoma Shōganji (d. 1689) is listed as an "Oshō," as is the twenty-second who died in 1704; however, the twenty-seventh (d. 1762) is listed both as "Oshō" and "Shōnin" as is the twenty-eighth (d. 1782).[24] Finally, the twenty-third head of Shōnenji (official name, On'a), who died in 1709, is listed as "Shōnin" and "Oshō"; his successor, the twenty-fourth, who died in 1710, is listed only as "Oshō."[25] However, the (unnumbered) head who died in 1779 is listed as "Shōnin" and "Oshō."[26] While not all problems indicated by the apparent inconsistencies can be addressed, the proliferation of this title can be interpreted in two ways. First, since Yugyō-ha/Jishū temple heads were transferred from temple to temple, once a priest had headed a temple with the title he kept it even when transferred. Or second, somehow the Tokugawa system of a confederacy of nearly autonomous domains had resulted in the sharing of a charismatic title with more and more heads of branch and other temples; that is, the title of Shōnin had been shared with more temple heads in order to raise their dignity vis-à-vis the local domainal lord. The question remains whether this means a concomitant loss of religious authority to the title or to the head of the order. The abbesses of the Mantokuji, for example, appropriated the title in their own documents but are not listed as "Shōnin" in the *Tōtakusan kakochō*, clearly a demonstration of their independence.

IMPERIAL TITLES: *MONZEKI*

Another title claimed by the order, but apparently only briefly, was that of *monzeki*. Meaning "traces of a lineage," the title referred initially to the sons of the imperial house and very high nobility who had taken orders and the temples in which they resided. The most famous of these temples, which may have numbered as many as twenty-nine, included the Ninnaji, Daikakuji, and Shōren'in, all in the capital Kyoto.[27] By the Tokugawa period, several types of *monzeki* had been acknowledged: *miya monzeki* for imperial princes, *shinnō monzeki* for the sons of the Fushimi, Arisugawa, and Katsura princely houses, *sekke monzeki* for the sons of the five houses (Konoe, Kujō, Nijō, Ichijō, and Takatsukasa) from which the Regents (for a minor or for an adult) and empresses were selected, and *seika monzeki* for the seven and later nine noble families eligible for the offices of Minister of the Right (Udaijin), Minister of the Left (Sadaijin), and Prime Minister (Dajō-daijin).[28] The last two were also referred to as *junmonzeki* (semi-*monzeki*).[29]

At some point in the seventeenth century, the Jishū began campaigning to acquire the title *monzeki*. This was accomplished under the forty-second, Sonnin, who became Yugyō Shōnin in 1668, nineteenth Fujisawa Shōnin in 1683, and died in 1691 at sixty-seven.[30] Sonnin apparently acquired the highest rank in the official Buddhist hierarchy, Daisōjō ("Senior High Priest"), and, it is claimed, was recognized as Abbot of the Southern Court, with rank equal to that of *monzeki*. (To be discussed further in chapter 7.) However, no other Yugyō Shōnin is recorded as bearing the rank of "Daisōjō" or of using the title "Abbot of the Southern Court," although the privileges gained were maintained.

Imperial Titles: *Gokiganjo*

The third title conferred by the imperial house was that of *kiganjo/gokiganjo* (prayer place) or *chokuganjo* (imperial prayer place). This referred to temples built by members of the imperial house with the public function of protecting the emperor and pacifying the state.[31] Sometimes the term *goganji* is used, as for Tōdaiji, but the tendency is for this term to be used more normally for temples built for private reasons.[32] For example, those temples built or recruited by the Office of the Cloistered Emperor in order to secure an economic base for the imperial family were called *goganji*.[33] However, "kiganjo" or "chokuganjo" refers to a variety of temples including those known as *monzeki* (Ninnaji, Daigoji), private temples such as Hōjōji (built by Fujiwara Michinaga [966-1028]), or the Engakuji (built 1282 in Kamakura by Hōjō Tokimune [1251-1284]) and Onjōji (Miidera, head of the Jimon Tendai school).[34] The *chokuganjo* has even been defined as a temple where the mortuary tablet of an emperor was kept. The first such temples were the Shitennōji (built in 593 by Prince Shōtoku) and the Yakushiji in Nara. There are documents attesting to the naming of existing temples as *chokuganjo* throughout the premodern period.[35]

What is not stated in documents but can be assumed is the role of such temples in suppressing powerful, angry spirits of the dead, that indeed such temples were commissioned to pray for the pacification of the realm in times of major unrest. For example, in 1458, the Shōnenji, mentioned above as the resting place of Nitta Yoshisada, an enemy of the Ashikaga, was created a *kiganjo* by order of the shogun Ashikaga Yoshimasa. The charter can be seen as an attempt by the shogunate to extend its authority in Echizen at a time when the province was being torn apart by the succession dispute in the Shiba house, one of the three families sharing the position of Shogunal Deputy (*kanrei*). However, in 1465, shortly before the outbreak of a civil war that would tear apart the country for ten years, an order from the Emperor Gotsuchimikado (1442-1500; r. 1464-) instructed the Shōnenji to offer prayers. Again, in 1536, the year of his official ascension, the Emperor Gonara (1497-1557; r. 1526-) issued an order to pray for the peace of the country and the eternity of the imperial throne.[36] Thus, the temple can be said to have acquired status as an imperial *kiganjo* or *chokuganjo* because it was used as one.[37]

Because the function of a *gokiganjo* is to pray for the peace of the country, such instructions may be seen as indicating *gokiganjo* status of a Yugyō-ha temple even when no document granting such status is extant. In the fifteenth century, the Shōjōkōji also received letters conveying instructions from the emperor to offer prayers. The first, from 1417, was issued by Emperor Shōkō (1401-1428; r. 1414-):

Suitable prayers for the peace of the country and the perpetuation of the emperor's reign are to be offered. [The above is] according to the will of the emperor. Therefore, [instructions are to be carried out] according to orders here conveyed. Ōei 24.7.17 [from] Ushōben Tsuneoki [to] the honorable priest Ta'a Shōnin[38]

This followed six months after the period of unrest in the Kantō from 1416.10.2 to 1417.1.5-9, the dates of the failed revolt of Uesugi Ujinori Zenshū against the Kamakura *kubō* Ashikaga Mochiuji. Dismissed from his position as Mochiuji's First Minister (*shitsuji*), Ujinori shaved his head and then revolted in league with Ashikaga Yoshitsugu (1394-1418; brother of the shogun Yoshimochi) and Ashikaga Mitsutaka (uncle of Mochiuji) with the intent of replacing Mochiuji with his brother Mochinaka. Defeated and all but deserted, they committed suicide; Yoshitsugu was killed by his brother in Kyoto.[39] The acknowledgment by the emperor of the role of the Shōjōkōji as a recognized pacifier of the land of the souls of the unhappy dead is substantiated by other contemporary evidence.

Shōjōkōji was involved in the campaign described above when Uesugi Ujisada, fighting on the Kamakura *kubō* Mochiuji's side, was routed and fled to the Shōjōkōji where he committed suicide (10.6). In addition, the body of Iwamatsu (Nitta) Mitsuzumi, one of Zenshū's generals, was brought to the temple for burial.[40] In 1418, the Shōjōkōji erected a monument dedicated to the pacification of all the dead, friend and foe, fallen in this same revolt. The original text of this "Fujisawa teki mikata kuyō no tō" reads as follows:

[Names of the dead:] Mitsutaka-kō, Mochinaka-kō, Uesugi Uemon no suke Ujinori nyūdō Zenshū, Uesugi Gorō Noriharu, Uesugi Hyōgo no suke Ujiharu, Iwamatsu Jibu taifu Mitsuuji, Uesugi Izu no kami Norikata, Takeda Aki no kami Nobumitsu, Ueda Kōzuke no suke, Imagawa Mikawa no kami, Hikita Ukyō no suke, Shiitsu Dewa no kami, Imagawa Shuri no suke, Uesugi Zenshō Shōhitsu Ujisada, Kido Shōgen Mitsuaki, Isshiki Hyōbu taifu Norimoto, Isshiki Sama no suke."[41]

Namuamidabutsu: in the revolt which lasted from the twenty-third year of Ōei [1416], sixth month, sixth day, until the twenty-fourth year of the same [1417], in various places friend and foe lost their lives by arrow and sword and by water and fire. For the departed souls of those who lost their lives, men and beasts, that they might be Reborn in paradise [we] erected this monument. Let monks and lay persons who pass it chant ten *nembutsu*. Twenty-fifth year of Ōei [1418], tenth month, sixth day.[42]

The function of the order as a whole in pacifying the angry spirits of the war dead is clear from a variety of sources. On the day in 1333 (Shōkei 2.5.22) that Kamakura fell and the last shogunal regent Hōjō Takatoki (1303-1333) committed suicide, the vassals of Nambu Uma no kami Shigetoki brought his body to the Fujisawa temple, where the Fujisawa Shōnin Ankoku performed the funeral service and gave him the posthumous name Kyōjōjiden Shō'amidabutsu. The six vassals then committed suicide and were buried alongside.[43] In addition, the fifteenth-century illustrated scroll *Yugyō engi* (Origins of the Yugyō [Shōnin]) and nō play *Sanemori* describe the pacification of the ghost of the aged warrior Saitō no bettō Sanemori, whose death in battle in 1183 is celebrated in the *Heike monogatari*.[44] References to Yugyō Shōnin pacifying the war dead (and others) are scattered throughout Jishū sources. For example, in 1520, the twenty-fourth Yugyō Shōnin Fugai (b. 1460; YS 1518-1520, FS-1526) held a service and erected a "stupa" (probably the typical wooden plaque inscribed with the *nembutsu*) at a place called Nagami in Etchū Province for the several hundred who had died there in a battle the year before.[45] He also conducted services for all killed in the siege of Kōfu in the next year (see below).

Another letter to the Shōjōkōji indicating *gokiganjo* status because of instructions from the emperor, this time the retired Emperor Gokomatsu (1377-1433; r. 1382/92-1412), also required prayers for the pacification of the country in 1430:

> Suitable prayers for the peace of the country and the perpetuation of the emperor's reign are to be offered. [The above is] according to the instructions of the emperor. Therefore, [instructions are to be carried out] according to orders as above conveyed [herewith]. Eikyō 2.11.2 from [seal of Gon'ushōben] [to] the honorable priest Ta'a Shōnin[46]

This followed upon a period of unrest due to the succession of Ashikaga Yoshinori. The fourth Kamakura *kubō* Ashikaga Mochiuji, like his father, had hoped to assume the position of shogun. When Yoshinori was appointed, Mochiuji turned on his First Minister Uesugi Norizane (1411-1466), who was supported by the shogun; the result was a humiliation for Mochiuji, who eventually raised the revolt which led to his own death in 1439.

The question remains whether these two letters in the Shōjōkōji make Shōjōkōji a *gokiganjo*. Compared with Shōnenji, it has nothing (that has survived) like an official letter conferring official status (even shogunal rather than imperial). And yet, the tradition that Gokōgon (1338-1374; r.1351-1371) had conferred an imperial autograph on the Shōjōkōji, that is, provided the calligraphy for the temple plaque, is taken as a sign of conferring "kiganji" (prayer temple) status on the temple.[47] However, both temples had the responsibility of pacifying the spirits of the dead killed in battle. That is perhaps the real reason for receiving imperial instructions to pray for the protection of throne and country.

There is however one further interpretation of the letters to Shōjōkōji: they may be covert instructions to restrain Mochiuji. Considering the close relations between the order and the shogunate, it would not be surprising for the shogun to make a very circumlocutory appeal for the Fujisawa Shōnin to do his best in his role as spiritual adviser to Mochiuji to keep him out of trouble. Even if not, then an imperial order for the main temple of an order in the East (of which there were indeed not many) to conduct prayers for the peace and pacification of the land and the carrying out of that order could not but be seen as a not-too-thinly-disguised order to Mochiuji to curb himself. Add to this the fact that in 1439 Uesugi Norizane fled Mochiuji to the Shōjōkōji and had his head shaved there in what can only be called protest and it becomes increasingly probable that the temple's role was as political as it was religious.[48]

In this context, we must also look again at the Shijō-ha Konrenji in Kyoto and indications of status as *gokiganjo*. In its collection of documents are imperial orders (up to the Tokugawa period) for prayers and ceremonies mostly for the peace of the country. This would indicate that, even though the Konrenji had not officially received designation as *gokiganjo*, it was in fact, like Shōjōkōji, used as one.[49]

IMPERIAL POETRY ANTHOLOGIES

One of the most important ways for the imperial court to assert (or arrogate) authority was by conferring status—without any concomitant depredation on the treasury—by selecting an individual's poem for inclusion in an imperial anthology (*chokusenkashū*). The first, the *Kokin wakashū* (Collection from ancient and modern times), was commissioned by Emperor Daigo (885-930; r. 897-) in 905 and was completed in 922 by an editorial board consisting of Ki no Tsurayuki (872?-945) and others.[50] Twenty more anthologies were edited through the reign of Gohanazono (1419-1471; r. 1428-1464). The inclusion or exclusion of a poem was an indication of one's position at court.[51] Sometimes the poem is included, but without naming the author, because the author was of rank too low to merit acknowledgment of his identity.

Poems of chief figures in the orders of the Ippen school were included in imperial anthologies. Indeed, the Ippen school was famous for its poets. A poem by Ippen was collected in the fourteenth imperial anthology, the *Gyokuyō wakashū* (Collection of jeweled leaves, 1312-1349).[52] It does not appear in any basic Ippen texts, such as the *Ippen hijiri e*, but it is identified as his in the private anthology of Katsumata Nagakiyo Shō'amidabutsu, the *Fuboku wakashū* (c. 1310). Ippen's name is not given. He is, according to the poem's preface "a certain person at the same [Ishikiyomizu] shrine."[53]

A poem by Shōkai was also collected in the *Gyokuyō wakashū*. He is actually identified by name as "Shōkai Hōshi."[54]

Ta'amidabutsu Shinkyō, too, was celebrated as a poet.[55] His poem, "Sadly though you leave the world, it goes merrily on; better abandon it [for the Buddhist path] while still alive" (*Awarege ni nogarete mo yo wa ukarikeri, inochi nagara zo sutsubekarikeru*), was also included in the *Gyokuyō wakashū*. Shinkyō is not named: "Poet unknown."[56] This poem, too, is identified as his in the *Fuboku wakashū*.[57]

Shinkyō had connections with the poetry world. He apparently had a good relationship with the compiler of the *Gyokuyō wakashū*, Kyōgoku Tamekane (1254-1332), who visited him in 1310.[58] His relationship with [Fujiwara] Katsumata Nagakiyo, the compiler of the *Fuboku wakashū*, resulted in thirty-one entries among the over seventeen thousand poems collected. Nagakiyo, a convert with the religious name Shō'amidabutsu Renshō, was a disciple of Reizei Tamesuke (1260-1328); he too composed poetry with Shinkyō in the years between 1308 and 1310.[59] Poetry brought Shinkyō into contact with Reizei Tamesuke, who visited him in 1316 and his brother Tamemori (d. 1328), who visited him in 1313, as well as with their nephew Tamekane.[60] It has been suggested that because Shinkyō was so intimately connected with the Reizei, the anti-Nijō school of poetry, the Nijō school treatise *Nomori kagami* (1295), which criticizes Tamekane, also makes fun of the Ippen school dancing *nembutsu*.[61] Shinkyō's reputation as a poet continued long after his death. Certainly, Kanze Nobumitsu (1435-1516), the author of the *nō* play *Yugyō yanagi* (Yugyō [Shōnin] and the willow; first presented 1514), must have been acquainted with Shinkyō's work: in the play he uses a formula created in Shinkyō's poem, "Mata haru to tanomenu rō no wakare ka na *kotoshi bakari no* [my emphasis] hana no nagori ni," which appears in the play as "*kotoshi bakari no* [my emphasis], kaze ya itowan to, tadayō ashi motomo, yoroyoro yowayowa to."[62]

Despite Shinkyō's strong connections with the poetry world, neither he nor Ippen is identified as the author of his poem; however, Shōkai is. Obviously, Shōkai was a person of consequence in the capital around 1312 and was definitely given precedence over both Ippen and Shinkyō.

Imperial recognition was extended also to the Shijō-ha. Shinkyō's disciple Shinkan Jō'amidabutsu (d. 1341), founder of the Shijō-ha Konrenji, is identified as the "Jō'a hōshi" who wrote the poem included in the *Shinsenzai wakashū* (New collection of a thousand years), the eighteenth imperial anthology, commissioned in 1356 by Emperor Gokōgon and finished by Nijō Tamesada (1293-1360) in 1359.[63] The second Jō'a, who died in 1360, was also a noted poet.[64] A poem in the same anthology also attributed to "Jō'a Hōshi" is thought to have been composed by him.[65] A poem of the third Jō'a of Konrenji is included in the *Shingoshūi wakashū* (New later collection of gleanings, 1383-1384).[66] According to temple tradition, he was originally a member of the Ashikaga family and a Tendai monk; he was converted by Shinkyō and built the Enfukuji near the Atsuta Shrine in what is now Nagoya.[67] After about thirty years as its head priest—and after establishing a reputation as a poet in the Nijō school—he became the head priest of the Kyoto Konrenji and died after ten years in 1370.[68] A poetry group under Nijō Tameshige was based at the Konrenji. Other poems by "Jō'a Shōnin" are also included in the *Shingoshūi wakashū*: number 600 and number 692 in volume seven and number 1299 in volume sixteen.[69]

The world of poetry was small and very tight and the Konrenji was part of it. For example, the celebrated Ton'a (1301-1384) was as involved both in the religious world of the Konrenji and in the world of poetry. Ton'a was one of the four main disciples (*shitennō*) of Nijō Tameyo (1250-1338). At least nine of his poems are included in the 1364 imperial anthology *Shinshūi wakashū* (New collection of gleanings), completed by Ton'a himself.[70] Born Nikaidō Sadamune, he was a member of a family high in the Kamakura shogunate and converted to Shinkyō and to the Yugyō-ha: the first set of ten *nembutsu* chanted at the Shōjōkōji were dedicated to one Nikaidō Shikibu nyūdō Shu'amidabutsu.[71] A letter to Ton'a from Shinkyō in response to a question on religion indicates that Ton'a was a disciple of the first head of Konrenji, Shinkan.[72] Ton'a, a *jishū*, lived at the Konrenji and participated in the many poetry meetings there. After Shinkan's death in 1341, the second Jō'a and Ton'a exchanged in his memory poems which were collected in Ton'a's collection *Zokusōanshū*.[73]

OFFICIAL VISITS AND RECEPTIONS

One of the most important ways that the imperial court conferred favor was through presentation at court. Jishū tradition asserts that the first Yugyō Shōnin invited to an imperial interview was the twelfth, Sonkan (b. 1349; YS 1387-1400), who was received by Gokomatsu.[74] However, an earlier tradition of the Konrenji asserts that the first of Ippen's disciples favored with an interview was Shinkan Jō'amidabutsu. As noted above, in 1311 he was summoned to present to the consort of the retired Emperor Gofushimi three of his *nembutsu* amulets in order to assist in her difficult childbirth. A text slightly later than the *Jō'a Shōnin den*, the *Jō'a Shōnin ekotoba den* (Story of Jō'a Shōnin in pictures and words; 1469-1487), reports that the retired empress became a disciple and visited the Konrenji to "make a karmic connection with the Shōnin." It is claimed that she made a robe of ramie or hemp and presented it to him; once she borrowed his robe and put it on for a *nembutsu* ceremony to pray for buddhahood (*bodai*). The text is a literary compilation of the *Jō'a Shōnin den* and various other narratives, including the *Ippen hijiri e*. So, one should not be surprised to see a standard theme also used in the *nō*: enlightenment even through the wearing of a priest's robe. Further, even the retired emperor too is reported as visiting Jō'a for a discussion on doctrine. It is also claimed that on his death (1336), he willed to the Konrenji a portrait and robe as a sign of karmic connection toward his buddhahood.[75]

Shinkyō, too, was received in audience. As noted in chapter 2, a report in the *Jō'a Shōnin den* accepted as credible is that in the ninth month of 1314 (Shōwa 3), while Shinkyō was stopping at the Konrenji on his way to Kumano, Gofushimi's consort attended a service at the Konrenji and asked Shinkyō to allow Shinkan to distribute Shinkyō's *nembutsu* amulets since the printing block had been sent to the Konrenji. Summoning three *jishū* as witnesses, Shinkyō had Jō'a distribute his amulets for the first time.

With just what frequency the Yugyō Shōnin or the Fujisawa Shōnin were summoned to an audience at the court of the reigning or retired emperor is not known. It is more likely that the relations with the heads of the Konkōji or Konrenji were more intimate because their residence in the capital permitted the development of such connections through poetry. As yet, nothing much is known. There was, however, a tradition that no Yugyō Shōnin (current or retired) since the nineteenth (d. 1496) had received an invitation to court when in 1557 the twenty-fifth Yugyō Shōnin Butten, living in residence as "Fujisawa Shōnin" in the castle town of Tsuruga in Echizen Province, received a letter of invitation to court: he was summoned to the capital to "make a karmic connection" with the Emperor Gonara, who had been unwell.[76] Despite the enticements of "the restoration of [the] order and perpetuation of [his] reputation unto eternity," Butten did not go because he "was bent with age."[77] Butten is reported as dying at eighty-five in 1571; therefore, he would have been about seventy when he received the letter.[78] His age notwithstanding, Butten, if anything, was bent with care for, as Tachibana suggests, in 1557, less than half a year before the summons, his official residence had been burned down in a great fire which took a good part of the town of Tsuruga.[79] Gonara died about a month after the letter of invitation was written. Butten missed his chance for an imperial interview. However, his disciple and thirty-first Yugyō Shōnin Dōnen (b. 1518; YS 1573-1584, FS -1587) received invitations to attend court twice, in 1579 and 1580. Dōnen, while in Mino Province, first received word brought by the head priest of the Kyoto Sanjō (Third Avenue) Sōgonji from the Kyoto Magistrate (*shoshidai*) Murai Nagato no kami Sadakatsu (d. 1582), Mokujiki Sosen, head priest of the Seiganji, and the sculptor of Buddhist images Shijō Daibutsushi Hōgan. A year later, Dōnen approached Kyoto—his entrance was quite an affair. The arrangements had been made by the Kyoto Magistrate. Some three hundred men with horses were sent to escort him. The Fujisawa Shōnin Yūsan (b. 1512; YS 1563-1573, FS -1583) sent a delegation from Tsuruga of eleven and even the head priest of the Shōnenji in Nagasaki in Echizen Province came personally. Several hundred *jishū* came from neighboring provinces to accompany him. As he approached Kyoto, *jishū* from the main temples came to escort him into the city. While staying at the Kyoto headquarters Konkōji and other temples, he was visited by throngs of people including high-ranking aristocrats.[80]

On the eleventh day of the ninth month of the seventh year of Tenshō, word came from Kajūji Dainagon Harutoyo (1544-1602), whose sister Haruko was the consort of the crown prince, that Dōnen would be presented at court on the thirteenth. He was received at the imperial residence and that of the crown prince and taken on a tour of "the throne room and office of the sacred mirror." He also "distributed more [*nembutsu*] amulets than had ever been heard of in previous generations."[81] A court lady left her own record of the interview:

> The Yugyō Shōnin came [to the palace] to pay his respects. Kajūji Chūnagon acted as escort. He presented ten quires of *hikiawase* paper, fan, and scroll. Similarly he paid his respects to the crown prince.[82]

Dōnen was again invited to court on the fifth day of the second month of the next year. Emperor Ōgimachi (1517-1593; r. 1560-1586) himself received the ten *nembutsu* and an amulet and "personally inspected the precious treasures of generations of Yugyō [Shōnin], including the ten volume illustrated life [*Ippen Shōnin engi e*], the gong of Ippen . . . and the star inkstone." Dōnen was also received at the new palace of the crown prince (built for him by Oda Nobunaga), where he was presented to the crown prince, who "[made] a karmic connection [by receiving] a [*nembutsu*] amulet and the ten *nembutsu*," and his consort. Gifts were exchanged, tea and cakes were offered, and a tour of the throne room and the imperial compound was offered on Dōnen's request to the *jishū* accompanying him. "It was the utmost experience of their lives."[83]

While the monks' notice was caught by the royal treatment and the fine appointments of the palace, the interest of the court lay in the sacred treasures which Dōnen had brought with him:

> The Yugyō Shōnin came to the palace bringing several holy objects. The interview with the emperor took place in the reception rooms reserved for the shogun; [there] he conferred the ten *nembutsu*. The nobles all personally accepted them; the imperial princess [daughter of Gonara and sister of Ōgimachi] also received the ten nembutsu. The sacred objects were all very fine. He presented ten quires of Sugiwara paper and a court fan. Afterwards he proceeded to the palace of the crown prince.[84]

As powerless as the imperial house was in the sixteenth century, the occasion of receiving a prominent Buddhist cleric offered the opportunity not only to take advantage of religious benefits but to assert authority: the power to summon, to employ some to act as messengers, to recruit others to participate—all this represented the authority of the emperor, limited as it was to the area of ceremonial. The emperor as host offered recognition and prestige; the guest offered religious benefits and legitimation. Audiences at the court of the emperor or retired emperor would continue off and on in the Tokugawa period, especially in the seventeenth century. The thirty-sixth Yugyō Shōnin Nyotan (b. 1578; YS 1641-1644, FS -1646) was received in audience by the retired Emperor Gomizunoo in 1644 and the forty-second Sonnin (b. 1625; YS 1668-1683, FS -1691) was received in crimson silk in 1672.[85]

RELATIONS WITH THE KYOTO AND KAMAKURA ASHIKAGA HOUSES

As significant as imperial patronage of the order was, shogunal patronage may well have been more important for practical reasons: the authority of the shogun reached further and wider than did that of the emperor. In addition, the order was absorbed into the official ceremonial calendar of the shogunate, which was even more important than the faith or devotion of individual shogun. Patronage was mutually beneficial: in all cases, the interests of the order coincided with the those of the shogunate. When in 1339 Ashikaga Takauji confirmed in its possessions the Seventh Avenue temple Konkōji, the joint headquarters of the order, he was demonstrating his newly-asserted authority as shogun, the first of the Ashikaga line.[86] When, it is claimed, at some time during Itchin's tenure as Fujisawa Shōnin—probably 1353—Takauji subsidized the repair of the main hall of Shōjōkōin and changed its name to Shōjōkōji (and, it is also claimed, the Northern Court Emperor Gokōgon conferred his autograph for the temple plaque, a sign of official recognition), he was appealing to the Buddhas and Bodhisattvas for protection during a particularly difficult time in his campaign.[87] Takauji's first official contact with the order was perhaps his meeting in 1353 with the seventh Yugyō Shōnin in Kayazu, Mino Province.[88] The official nature of the relationship between the order and the shogunate can be said more or less confirmed in 1356, when letters from both the shogun and from the Kamakura *kubō*, Ashikaga Motouji, summoned the eighth Yugyō Shōnin Tosen from his *yugyō* to make his way to Fujisawa to take up the position of head of "Shōjōkōin."[89]

Both the Kyoto and Kamakura Ashikaga were devoted to the Yugyō-ha. There was a very close relationship between the Yugyō-ha and the Kamakura *kubō*, the cadet house of the Ashikaga installed in Kamakura to maintain control of the eastern and northern part of the country. The fourth Kamakura *kubō* Mochiuji is especially remembered for his relationship with the order: he is mentioned in the *Yugyō engi* as having been converted by thirteenth Yugyō Shōnin Sonmyō.[90] He was remembered in the Tokugawa period as having made a significant donation to the Shōjōkōji towards construction: the second set of the ten *nembutsu* chanted at the Shōjōkōji in the evening was dedicated to Mochiuji and he was entered twice in the *Jishū kakochō*.[91] He is advertised in the order's illustrated scroll *Yugyō engi* (Origins of the Yugyō [Shōnin]) as a convert of Yugyō Shōnin Sonmyō. Finally, the *Yūki senjō monogatari* (Tale of the battlefield of Yūki, after 1451) highlights the relationship of the order to Mochiuji and his sons Haruō and Yasuō, who were executed by shogunal order after his death and a major revolt in their defense in 1441.[92]

Of the Ashikaga shogun, the sixth shogun Yoshinori seems to have been most closely connected with the order. Yoshinori visited the Konrenji in 1430 for poetry and in 1431 went there again as well as to the Konkōji where he burned incense.[93] In 1432, Yoshinori issued to Konkōji, the chief temple of the Yugyō-ha in Kyoto, a document granting land and privileges (exemptions from duties and prohibition of the entrance of Military Governors or *shugo*).[94] In 1440, he exchanged gifts with "Ta'amidabutsu," very likely Kiyū, who became the seventeenth Yugyō Shōnin that year.[95] A Tokugawa period Yugyō-ha source claims that Yoshinori was so devoted to Kiyū that he had a portrait of him in the palace.[96] According to an entry in the *Tōtakusan kakochō*, some of Yoshinori's ashes were sent by his son Yoshikatsu (1434-1443; shogun 1442-) to the head temple of the order Shōjōkōji for burial.[97]

These very friendly relations resulted in the establishment of the Yugyō-ha as an officially-recognized order. In 1400, Yoshimochi issued documents to the Yugyō-ha Konkōji and Shōjōkōji (both in the Konkōji collection) by which the branch temples of these two were forbidden to convert to other sects or other orders of Buddhism, and the temples and branch temples of other Buddhist sects and orders were forbidden to convert to Yugyō-ha; these documents effectively recognized the order as an independent school of Buddhism:

> As for the various branch temples of the Konkōji [and the Shōjōkōji] in the provinces: whether concerning the order's temples and sub-temples or whether the temples of other lines and all schools, it is said that it is quite usual to submit applications [expressing] intentions to [become] a disciple of [another] temple. This is absolutely not to be, in short every case now and hereafter is banned most stringently. Immediately preserving recent precedent, this letter [requires that you] make [your] priority Buddhist services and the like as above. Seal. Ōei 7.4.7.[98]

Here, the Yugyō-ha is defined as an independent line and order of Buddhism and its authority over its temples recognized; at the same time, its popularity as an order is indicated in the prohibition against accepting the conversion of other temples. Here, too, the Ashikaga government demonstrates its official capacity in regularizing the organization of Buddhist institutions as part of its administrative duties and, in doing so, officially recognizing the Yugyō-ha.

In 1416, the fourth shogun Yoshimochi extended official protection to Shōjōkōji and Konkōji by ordering the shogunal Deputy Hosokawa Mitsumoto to order the Military Governors of the provinces to see to it that the *jishū*, porters, horses, and palanquins of the two temples passed without trouble through their barriers:

> The passage to and from the capital [through the] various provinces of the porters, palanquins, horses, etc. of the *jishū* of the Shōjōkōji (Fujisawa Dōjō) and Yugyō Konkōji (Shichijō Dōjō): by reason of [the documents bearing official] seals and stamps, you are to pass them without [let or] hindrance and without charging a toll at the barriers. This order is to be passed on to the Military Governors of the provinces. If the law is broken, at that place, in connection with the report [to the authorities], you must punish the crime as a warning. This must be ordered. Therefore, the instructions as above. Ōei 23.4.3. Shami (Hosokawa Mitsumoto) seal. To the temple concerned.[99]

This document also herewith recognized the joint leadership of the order. From the point of view of the shogunate, the Fujisawa Shōnin and the Yugyō Shōnin were equals. Despite this official protection, there appears to have been trouble the next year, 1417, with the Enryakuji (Mt. Hiei, Ōtsu, Ōmi Province), which apparently tried to charge the entourage of the Yugyō Shōnin Sonne at its barrier. Yoshimochi shot off an order to the temple:

As for passing the Yugyō Shōnin [let or] hindrance: you have not respected the intent of the order I have given. You are to follow the order strictly that the *jishū* of the Shichijō and Fujisawa [temples] of this order be [passed through barriers] without [let or] hindrance and without paying toll [on their way] to and from the capital. Ōei 24.2.13. Ken[] seal Kan[] seal Benchō seal. [From] Togashi Hyōbu taifu-dono.[100]

The Miidera caused trouble in 1419. Again, an order was issued:

The passage to and from the capital of the porters, palanquins, horses, and various bearers, etc. [commissioned for the] round trip of the *jishū* of the Shōjōkōji (Fujisawa Dōjō), Yugyō Konkōji (Shichijō Dōjō) and their various branch temples: by reason of [the documents bearing official] seals and stamps, they are to pass without [let or] hindrance [through] the barriers of the various provinces. However, at the barrier at Miidera, it is likely that they will go as far as to protest. Shall they not invite a severe reprimand? All the more, if they break the law, they must be punished. This must again be ordered. Therefore, the order as above. [1419] Ōei 26.10.20. Shami (seal of Hosokawa Mitsumoto) [To] the temple concerned [Miidera].[101]

These orders, of course, established an official precedent for issuing documents to each Yugyō Shōnin. However, the sixteenth Yugyō Shōnin Nanyō did not receive his letter of passage until 1436, about six years after attaining the office and six years after Yoshinori had become the sixth shogun. The text is virtually identical, except for the substitution of "in" for "hangyō" for "seal":

The passage to and from the capital of the porters, palanquins, horses, etc. of the *jishū* of the Shōjōkōji (Fujisawa Dōjō) and Yugyō Konkōji (Shichijō Dōjō): by reason of [the documents bearing official] seals and stamps, you are to pass them without [let or] hindrance through the barriers. This order is to be passed on to the Military Governors of the provinces. If the law is broken, at that place, in connection with the report [to the authorities], you must punish the crime. This must be ordered. Therefore, the instructions as mentioned above. [1436] Eikyō 8.12.5. Ukyō daibu (seal of Hosokawa Mochiyuki). To the temple concerned.[102]

The last extant document issued by the shogunate was issued by the tenth, Yoshitane (1466-1523; shogun 1490-1493 and 1508-1521) through his Shogunal Deputy Ōuchi Yoshioki (1477-1528), who had reinstated him after fifteen years of exile:

> Because the Yugyō Shōnin will be on circuit throughout the provinces, the Military Governor of each province is to provide board and fifty pack horses with handlers for transport in accordance with previous duties. These orders issued according to instructions mentioned above. [Ōuchi] Ukyō daibu Yoshioki. [1513] Eishō 10.1.15.[103]

It is difficult to know how to evaluate this document, whose wording differs so much from previous ones: it sets a precedent for the Tokugawa regime rather than following the precedent of the Ashikaga. The documents issued by the Ashikaga shogunate ordered the Military Governors to see to it that the *jishū*, porters, horses, and palanquins of the Shōjōkōji and the Konkōji passed without trouble through the official barriers. In 1513, it was claimed, the Yugyō Shōnin had been given the right to meals and fifty horses with their handlers.

On the surface, the balance of power seems very one sided: the shogunate gives and thus has all the power. However, the order, as recipient, offers the shogunate the opportunity to assert—and to test—its authority over all the Military Governors and temples of the land. It offers even the representative of the shogun to arrogate authority.

One of the most significant steps taken by the Ashikaga shogunate to demonstrate its support for the Yugyō-ha was to force, in 1424, the Shijō-ha Konrenji to become a branch temple of the Yugyō-ha Konkōji.[104] According to a contemporary diary entry, Jō'a, the seventh head of that temple and seventh of that name, was instructed either by the shogun himself or by one or more influential men in the warrior government to go to the temple on Seventh Avenue, the Shichijō Konkōji, to receive the ten *nembutsu* (either from the fifteenth Yugyō Shōnin Sonne, whose base it was, or the acting head priest), a ritual form of acknowledging the authority of the Yugyō-ha. This is reported as having taken place in the seventh month of 1424 (Ōei 31). On the night of the tenth of the eighth month, the monks and nuns of the Konrenji burned down the temple in protest. The temple was rebuilt and Jō'a reinstated, for in 1430 the shogun went to Konrenji for *renga* poetry with Jō'a.[105]

The official relationship between the order and the shogunate took several forms. One form of official status was participation in the ceremonial calendars of the shogunate and the Kamakura *kubō*. In Kyoto, the heads of the Kyoto headquarters Konkōji and the Fourth Avenue (Shijō-ha) Konrenji took their places with other representatives of great Buddhist institutions in the shogun's New Year receptions: at the end of the year (*shimotsuki*) and at New Year's, first the head of Konrenji was received and then the head of Konkōji, one or more days later.[106] In Kamakura, while Kamakura *kubō*, Mochiuji's son Ashikaga Shigeuji (1438-1497), received the Fujisawa Shōnin on the eighteenth day of the New Year and on the first day of the twelfth month received the ten *nembutsu* from him. The Kamakura Ashikaga maintained a close relationship with the Fujisawa Shōnin, who was ranked the equal of the chief priest of the Rinzai Zen Kenchōji in Kamakura: on leaving the palace of the prince, he was escorted by him as far as Hakushū, and letters addressed to him were written in terms of the highest respect.[107] Shigeuji's son Masauji, the second prince of Koga (Koga *kubō*; 1466-1531), accorded to the Fujisawa Shōnin, Konrenji in Mino (the site of the graves of Mochiuji's sons), and the Yugyō Shōnin the same ranking as the head of Kenchōji and the address of highest respect in his correspondence.[108]

Similarly, the relationship between shogunate and order was maintained through ceremonial correspondence. For example, in 1411 the shogun Yoshimochi sent a letter to the Fujisawa Shōnin Jikū acknowledging receipt of gifts and sending gifts in return. In 1423, he replied to a letter from the fifteenth Yugyō Shōnin Sonne congratulating him on taking the tonsure. In 1424, he again exchanged letters and gifts with "Ta'amidabutsu" (Taikū or Sonne).[109]

In addition, representatives of the order took part in the funerals of the Ashikaga family. However, these funerals became the stage for squabbles between the Konrenji and the Konkōji. The dispute over precedence between Konkōji and Konrenji was aired at funeral ceremonies in 1463 at Tojūin for Shōchiin, wife of the sixth shogun Yoshinori and mother of the eighth shogun Yoshimasa (1436-1490; shogun 1449-1474).[110] Because of the dispute, Konkōji refused to send a representative to the funeral in 1489 of the ninth shogun Yoshihisa (1465-1489; shogun 1474-).[111] In 1490, the shogunal court attended services for Yoshimasa at both Konrenji and Konkōji and Konkōji did take its place behind the Konrenji.[112]

If one assumes that everything the shogunate did was public, then every gesture of the shogun toward the order must be seen as official sanction, even pilgrimage. When in 1431 Yoshinori went on pilgrimage to the

Hachiman Shrine and entered the purification rooms, six "jishū" in two-hour shifts offered prayers and incense on his behalf. In 1478, the retired shogun Yoshimasa and his son the shogun Yoshihisa went to the Konkōji to receive the ten *nembutsu* during the week of the equinoctial Buddhist services.[113]

Another expression of the official relationship between the order and shogunate was expressed in relationships directly with individual temples. One of the most important functions of the shogunate was to confirm a temple in its possessions. As noted above, Takauji confirmed the Kyoto Konkōji in its possessions in 1339. This confirmation was apparently renewed with the accession of each new shogun, for in 1395, a year after Yoshimitsu retired and had his son Yoshimochi assume the office of shogun, he donated ("kifu") or confirmed the Konkōji in its possessions occupying the land from Seventh Avenue to Shiokōji and from Higashitōin to Takakura Avenue, an area of about 2.45 acres just north of the present Kyoto train station. In 1409, Yoshimochi himself confirmed the Konkōji and its branch temples in their possessions.[114] Since the Konkōji was the base of the Yugyō Shōnin and joint headquarters of the Yugyō-ha, this process of confirming and reconfirming the order in its possessions constituted a civil ritual demonstrating and acknowledging the authority of the shogunate to treat the order very much as it did its vassals.

Another function was the designation of temples of the order as shogunal *kiganjo*. In 1458, at the request of the seventeenth Yugyō Shōnin Kiyū, the above-mentioned Shōnenji of Nagasaki in Echizen, as well as its branch temple the Kōmyōin, the Kamakura Kōsokuji (which does not seem to carry the tradition) and the Kōshōji of Hyōgo Province (more likely Hyūga Province) were designated *gokiganjo*.[115] According to the order under the seal of Ashikaga Yoshimasa,

Seal of Yoshimasa

In respect of the Shōnenji of Nagasaki in Echizen Province along with the Kōmyōin : they are immediately to become *kiganjo*; the temple holdings (catalog [attached] separately) are not to be disturbed; the statement of all commands which [you] ought to know are as above.

(1458) Chōroku 2.11.26[116]

The principal argument for designation was offered in the *Shōnenji engi utsushi* (Manuscript copy of the origins of Shōnenji): the founding in 721 of Shōnenji by order of the female Emperor Genshō (680-748; r. 715-724) and a subsequent failure, due to the decadence of the world, to designate the temple a *gokiganjo*. By chance, the very day that the necessary documents received the shogun's seal, the current head of the temple "On'a saw in a dream Ippen and the second founder [Ta'a], who said that this temple must be [designated] a *gokiganjo* and they recommended sending *jishū* called Na'a [and] Shun'a as messengers to the shogun [Yoshimasa]."[117] However, the advantage to the shogunate was the opportunity to express its authority at a time when Echizen was being torn apart by the succession dispute in the Shiba family, one of the three shogunal Deputy families.[118] Shiba Yoshitake (b. 1435) died in 1452 and the succession was fought over by two relatives, Yoshikado and Yoshitoshi (1435?-1508). In 1459, Yoshimasa recognized Yoshikado and then Yoshitoshi in 1466. Yoshitoshi was by that time married to the sister of the wife of Ise Sadachika (1417-1473), who was very close to the shogun.[119] Perhaps that is why Ise Sadachika was so heavily involved in the formalities of designating Shōnenji a *gokiganjo*: Sadachika is one of the chief liaison officers (including his brother and members of the Iio family) as well as a chief beneficiary of the temple's yearly tribute.[120]

Clearly acceptance of such a designation did not come without strings attached. A tray and an incense container worth 4,000 *hiki* were presented to the shogun by the Yugyō Shōnin. Every year, the temple was obliged to send "as tribute" to the shogun two hundred wax candles, one hundred to Ise Sadachika, and thirty candles and one *kan* silver to the shogun's secretary, Ise Sadamune (1444-1509). The shogun sent to the temple a portrait of the late shogun Yoshinori and several mortuary tablets.[121]

Thus, it was quite an expensive enterprise to become a shogunal *gokiganjo*, which entailed an exchange of ceremonial gifts and paying no doubt the expenses for the envoys back and forth from the capital, not to mention the apparent presentation at court.[122] It is possible, as has been suggested, that Kiyū, as a member of the Hatakeyama family, one of the three Shogunal Deputy or *kanrei* families, was in a position to secure the good offices of the Ise.[123]

The presentation of Yoshinori's portrait and mortuary tablet to the Shōnenji and Kōmyōin begs the question whether this made them official mortuary temples (*bodaiji*) for Yoshinori. The designation as mortuary temple is much clearer in the case of the Kamakura Ashikaga family. For example, one of the temples for which *gokiganji* status was claimed, the Kōsokuji, maintains the mortuary tablets of shogun Ashikaga Takauji and Kamakura *kubō* Ujimitsu, Mitsukane, and Mochiuji.[124] As the Chōshun'in, one of its titles, the Kōsokuji has the function of a mortuary temple especially for Mochiuji, whose posthumous religious name is Chōshun'in-den.[125] Indeed, a letter from Mochiuji to the Fujisawa Shōnin (identified by Tachibana as Taikū) thanks him for giving permission to take into his employ the head of the Kōsokuji.[126] The fact that it was included in the list of temples claimed to have been designated "gokiganji" makes clear the status of the temple at least in the eyes of the order itself.

The designation of a temple as a mortuary temple (*bodaiji*) was a more private form of favor and one indicating personal faith. The Kamakura Ashikaga designated as one of their mortuary temples the Yugyō-ha Betsuganji of Kamakura, one of the thirty-three stops on the Kannon pilgrimage route. This temple had a long-standing relationship through several generations of Kamakura *kubō*. In 1382, Ujimitsu endowed the Betsuganji with land "for the buddhahood (*gobodai*) of Zuisenji-dono [his father Motouji]." Although the Zen temple Zuisenji is where Motouji was buried, the Betsuganji was also dedicated to his buddhahood. In 1400, Ujimitsu's son Mitsukane endowed the Betsuganji "for the buddhahood (*gobodai*) of Eianji-dono [his father]." Here is the same situation as above: Eianji was the Zen temple where Ujimitsu was buried and yet Betsuganji was also dedicated to his buddhahood. And, finally, in 1420 Mitsukane's son Mochiuji endowed the Betsuganji "for the buddhahood (*gobodai*) of Shōkōin [his father]."[127] The Betsuganji also possesses a mortuary monument about three meters high said to be dedicated to Mochiuji.[128] Mochiuji committed suicide in the Eianji, which was burned down and later abandoned. The Zuisenji now has the wooden statues of Motouji and Ujimitsu and the grave monuments (*haka*) of Motouji, Ujimitsu, Mochiuji and their wives.[129]

Relations with the order and its temples were as much personal as official. In 1355, Motouji sent a letter to the eighth Yugyō Shōnin instructing him to proceed to Fujisawa to take up the position of Fujisawa Shōnin.[130] When Ujimitsu died, the twelfth Yugyō Shōnin sent his son a letter of condolence, to which Mitsukane sent a reply.[131]

As personal as the relationships may have been, the principal function of the shogunate was protection of the order. Indeed, because protection of the Yugyō-ha's mission was a function of the Ashikaga shogunate, protection of the Yugyō-ha—even ceremonial correspondence and exchange of gifts—became an extremely important assertion of legitimacy for dispossessed Ashikaga and powerful warlords alike throughout the sixteenth century. Correspondence with the order was part of the ceremonial of the shogunal court. The tenth shogun Ashikaga Yoshitane spent ten years in exile in Suwō Province under the protection of Ōuchi Yoshioki, under whose name the document above requiring subsidies of the mission was issued, and, after being expelled from Kyoto for a second time, died in Awa. In 1517, while still in office, Yoshitane sent a letter to the Fujisawa Shōnin Igyō congratulating him on building a temple at Futaiwa in Mino Province.[132]

Such ceremonial correspondence was also important to the eleventh shogun Ashikaga Yoshizumi (1480-1511; shogun 1495-1508), who spent several years in exile, especially the last three years of his life. At some point, he sent a public letter under his personal signature ("gonaisho" as opposed to "migyōsho," which usually go through a deputy or other official under a seal) to "Ta'a Shōnin" to thank him for a gift of candles. He also sent another letter accompanying a gift of gold brocade and a tray to one of the Shōnin to reciprocate a gift of "twenty lengths of silk and five hundred candles."[133]

Yoshitane and Yoshizumi had some pretensions to authority even in the early sixteenth century. Nevertheless, this was all but ignored in the time of the fifteenth and last Ashikaga shogun Yoshiaki (1537-1597, shogun 1568-1573). Having fled Kyoto and under the protection of Asakura Yoshikage (1533-1573), he had the opportunity to meet the Fujisawa Shōnin Butten, who in the first month of 1567/Eiroku 10 performed the funeral service for Yoshiaki's maternal uncle Daikakuji Gishun, another refugee in Tsuruga.[134] Yoshiaki performed his coming of age ceremony (*gempuku*) at Yoshikage's castle at Ichijōgatani and finally entered Kyoto under the escort of Oda Nobunaga in 1568. By 1573, Nobunaga had imprisoned Yoshiaki. From 1575 to 1587, Yoshiaki, having shaven his head, was in Tomonotsu, Bingo Province under the protection of Kikkawa Motoharu (1530-1586) as well as his father Mōri Motonari (1497-1571) and brother Kobayakawa Takakage (1533-1597). In 1588 he received a pension of ten thousand *koku* from Hideyoshi and died in 1597.[135]

It was while Yoshiaki was in Bingo Province, an exile still asserting the prerogatives of the position he hoped yet to reclaim, that the thirty-first Yugyō Shōnin Dōnen may have visited him in 1580 while on *yugyō*, for Yoshiaki wrote,

I was so happy when last you came here from so far away. Therefore, you must tell Terumitsu further about the necessity of rebuilding at last branch temples [of your order which have been destroyed]. Sincerely yours. 7.19. Signature. Ashikaga Yoshiaki. [To] Ta'a Shōnin.[136]

This letter is interesting because it demonstrates the lingering vestiges of the ceremonial relationship between the lost shogunate and the order, for this was the year Dōnen was received by Yoshiaki's enemy Oda Nobunaga. Such courtesies continued to be extended by Dōnen, as when he wrote Yoshiaki to inform him of the rebuilding of the order's headquarters in the capital and received his reply.[137] Moreover, the exchange of gifts continued: on receipt of two hundred candles, Yoshiaki sent a red lacquer incense container and a tray.[138]

The sort of relations, exchange of gifts and correspondence, established in the fifteenth century continued in the hard times for the Ashikaga shogunate during the sixteenth. Whether one is speaking of a shogun with no power or of a shogun with no office, the conclusion is the same: the exchange of correspondence and gifts between the two parties remained a system of mutually sustaining assertions through ceremonial of legitimacy at a time when the shogun had no effective power and the order had lost its Kantō headquarters. The order was now much more important to the relationship and the relationship on a much more equal footing.

While ceremonial relations were maintained with the Ashikaga, the real protection of *yugyō*, of the order, and of its temples was transferred to the warlords actually in control of the provinces. The local daimyo had absolute power in his own domain. For example, in 1582 Dōnen entered Kagoshima, capital of Satsuma Province, domain of Shimazu Yoshihisa (1533-1611). Dōnen immediately sent a formal application to Yoshihisa asking permission, because of the disturbances in the capital, to take up official residence for two or three years at two temples, the Kōdaiji and Kōshōji, in Hyūga Province (Miyazaki Prefecture, Nishitō City). The domainal lord had to approve travel and to subsidize the journey. Thus, in 1583 various vassals along the route through Hyūga were ordered to receive Dōnen. "Reception" meant transport: from Oi to Tonogōri, Dōnen was provided with eighty mounts and three hundred pack horses—and that meant anywhere from 320 to 460 men to lead the horses. "Reception" meant provisions: from one vassal, forty sacks of rice to the Yugyō Shōnin and one barrel of Kyoto saké to the head priest of the Jōkōmyōji in Kagoshima. Vegetables and firewood were also donated, all at the expense of the local vassal.[139]

The domainal lord was apprized of important events in order to secure his recognition. In 1584, Dōnen, having secured the approval ("gyoi") to conduct the ceremony advancing Fukō to the position of thirty-second Yugyō Shōnin, asked Yoshihisa to subsidize horses and porters for Fukō's *yugyō* from Tonogōri to Mimitsu. Kōdaiji and Kōshōji were recognized as "Fujisawa," the official residence of the Fujisawa Shōnin.[140]

One might ask what could possibly be gained by the patronage of a religious order which imposed on one's subordinates the enormous inconvenience and cost of protecting and maintaining several hundred people and horses at a time. There is one principal advantage: assertion—if not outright arrogation—of the right to rule. The warlord assumes the function of the shogun and asserts absolute authority within his realm. The warlord brings religious benefits to his people and earns thereby, if nothing else, a good reputation. The warlord has the opportunity to issue orders to his vassals and see them carried out; that is, he can test the effectiveness of his authority (only one vassal declined to receive Dōnen, and that was because of illness).[141] In return, the vassal has the opportunity to prove his loyalty and worth to his lord by effectively carrying out his will.

Thus, patronage of the Yugyō Shōnin and his train presented the opportunity to act out in a ritual context the contract of service between warlord and vassal and the assertion of the right to rule that it represented. In Hyūga Province, this was more important than otherwise might be considered, since this was still contested territory. One of the new "Fujisawa," the Kōshōji in Tonogōri, had originally been established by Itō Sukekuni in 1202.[142] This Itō family, the Itō related to the famous twelfth-century Soga brothers, had been connected with the order at least since the fifteenth century, when Kudō (an alternative name for the Itō) were enrolled in the *Jishū kakochō*.[143] Itō Yoshisuke (1513-1585) had been at war with the Shimazu for years. He defeated the Shimazu in 1541, moved into Ōsumi Province in 1551 and into Satsuma in 1557. However, he was finally defeated and forced out of Hyūga altogether by Shimazu Yoshihisa in 1577. The contest with the Shimazu was taken over by Ōtomo Yoshishige (Sōrin, 1530-1587) of Bungo Province, who carried on the fight with the Shimazu until Hideyoshi's campaign into Kyushu put an end to all fighting in 1586.[144] Shimazu protection of the Yugyō Shōnin and Fujisawa Shōnin functioned as an extension of political authority into Hyūga, just as raising the Shōnenji to *gokiganjo* status was supposed to extend shogunal authority into Echizen more than a century before.

Such protection of the Yugyō Shōnin or Fujisawa Shōnin could be used to assert political authority in all parts of the country. One could postulate that the very survival of the order was due to the opportunity to demonstrate the exercise of political authority that sponsorship offered. Thus, when Ōuchi Yoshitaka (1507-1551) was requested by the Yugyō Shōnin permission to pass through his territory, he made the following reply:

I received the information in your letter that [you] will be coming to my domain. [Please call on me for any assistance in making your journey as comfortable as possible for] there should be no discomfort in any part of [the journey]. In addition, I have received the folding fan, ten quires of smooth paper, and ten lengths of silk. I must express well my feeling of pleasure. Your humble servant; sincerely yours. Ninth month, twenty-eighth day. [From] Sakyō daibu Yoshitaka. Signature. Presented to [the Yugyō Shōnin's] personal retainers.[145]

This letter is not dated; however, it is likely that it was written in 1548: both the Fujisawa Shōnin and future Yugyō Shōnin passed the New Year at the Shōmyōji in Fuchū (now Chōfu) in Nagato Province (Chōshū), then under the Ōuchi, and there in the third month of the next year 1549 Hen'in (b. 1509; YS 1549-1551) assumed the position of twenty-eighth Yugyō Shōnin.[146] Yoshitaka's father Yoshioki had been Deputy under the shogun Yoshitane and thus had had the right to issue documents concerning the Yugyō Shōnin in the shogun's name. Yoshitaka's protection of the Yugyō Shōnin can be seen as an assertion of the perquisites of his father. However, in real terms, since permission was been requested to enter his domains (*bunkoku*), he was being treated as having absolute authority in his own right.

Not all cases of protection of the order were based on political considerations. In 1520, the new Fujisawa Shōnin Fugai moved the main image of Shōjōkōji from the Chōzenji in Sumpu, Suruga Province to the Ichirenji in Kōfu, Kai Province, the capital of the domain of Takeda Nobutora (1494-1574).[147] The Ichirenji, as noted above, had been the mortuary temple of the Takeda for generations. The next year, 1521, Nobutora was attacked by a vassal of the Imagawa, Fukushima Masanari, lord of Hijikata Castle (also known as Takatenjin Castle) in Tōtōmi Province.[148] Sorely pressed and fearing the worst, Nobutora summoned Fugai to return to the Ichirenji to minister to him at the end. The hard-fought campaign lasted two months and ended disastrously for Masanari. Fugai conducted memorial services for the dead, friend and foe, and persuaded Nobutora to send home the three thousand prisoners of war. Then he resumed his journey.[149] Nobutora prepared to go to Sumpu for negotiations after the war and received a letter from Fugai, to whom he sent this reply:

I had heard that you were going to the North from Shinano Province and was privately [thinking of how] I wanted to see you [again] when your messenger monk and honorable letter [arrived]—how gratifying. It was [kind of you] to send the various [gifts] especially. These too were [a cause] for celebration. No matter what, send a messenger in the spring and tell me everything. On the coming seventh, I go to visit [Imagawa Ujichika in] Sumpu. [If you suffer any] distress, inform me quickly. Do not fail to write. As for the circumstances, it will be truly as you will, [according to] the message which you gave this messenger. Your humble servant; sincerely. Twelfth month, fifth day. [From] Mutsu no kami Nobutora. Addressed to Rokunoryō.[150]

This is not a letter from a lord to a religious leader with political cachet but a letter from a grateful spiritual charge to his priest, who had stayed by his side at the worst time of his life and for whom he would continue to feel gratitude.

However, nothing reveals more the absolute authority of the domainal lord and the vulnerability of the Yugyō-ha than the series of negotiations undertaken with the Hōjō of Sagami Province to keep the land of the devastated Shōjōkōji while the Fujisawa Shōnin took up residence elsewhere and tried to gather support for the reconstruction of the temple. For forty-five years, nothing could be done. By 1577, the temple site was so overrun by renegade monks ("akusō") that the Yugyō Shōnin Dōnen sent letters to the lord of Tamanawa Castle, Hōjō Ujikatsu (1559-1611, Tsunanari's grandson), and the family vassal Horiuchi Tango no kami Shigechika, asking help in clearing them out while the chosen successor Yū'amidabutsu Fukō wrote the branch temples of Sagami and Musashi Provinces. Their efforts were met with success: Ujikatsu's father Ujishige (1536-1578), in Hitachi campaigning against the Satake, Fukō's family, sent a letter to the leaders of the community in Fujisawa to refuse permission to renegade monks and nuns or any without proper documentation to reside on temple grounds or in the town itself.[151]

However, in 1558, information reached the ears of Taikō, twenty-ninth Yugyō Shōnin, that the Hōjō apparently had it in mind, considering the failure of the Fujisawa Shōnin to relocate there after so long, to exercise their right of eminent domain over the property and to turn it into fiefs for retainers in exchange for 1000 *kanmon*. Taikō, responding immediately, sent a letter to the lord of the fief, Hōjō Tsunanari, and swore by the "the Great God of Suwa, and the other greater and lesser deities of heaven and earth in the various provinces" to return and rebuild the temple.[152]

Taikō must have felt that he had some leverage with this member of the Hōjō family, on whom he had depended for years to intercede with the main Hōjō family. Hōjō Tsunanari, lord of Tamanawa Castle and of the area in which the Shōjōkōji ruins lay, was the son of that Fukushima Masanari who had attacked Takeda Nobutora thirty-seven years before. At seven he had been entrusted to Hōjō Ujitsuna (1486-1541), who later married his daughter to him and adopted him. From this can be inferred that the Hōjō had been pulling the strings when Tsunanari's father betrayed the Imagawa and attacked the Takeda.[153] In truth, he was indebted to the order because Fugai had performed the memorial service for friend and foe, including his father, killed in the campaign against Takeda Nobutora.[154]

Tsunanari's influence must have prevailed: reconstruction was permitted. In 1587, Hōjō Ujinao (1562-1591) allowed the order to use timber from any fief in the domain to rebuild the temple.[155] However, the order could not secure the entire "fief" to the Fujisawa Shōnin. The Hōjō confiscated or bought out much land from the Shōjōkōji estate, as they did from about thirty temples. By the next year, 1559, temple land ("Fujisawa dōjō jinai") yielding 13 *kan* 726 *mon* in tax to the domain for military purposes had been donated to the "Yugyō Shōnin" while temple land ("Fujisawa jibun") yielding eleven times as much, 147 *kan* 700 *mon*, had been conferred on the sawyers of Fujisawa ("Fujisawa daigiri-biki"), comprising twenty-five houses (out of 280-290).[156] They were descended from *kakuryō* (Guest Companions), defeated warriors, traitors, disowned children, and criminals protected by and in the service of the Yugyō Shōnin, Fujisawa Shōnin, or other temples of the order.[157] After the destruction of Shōjōkōji, its *kakuryō* had shifted to business and the crafts; those twenty-five houses, perhaps because of their experience in temple construction, had been recruited to the service of the Hōjō for whom they specialized in large-scale construction necessary for castles and other fortifications.[158] They were more necessary to the Hōjō than was the Yugyō-ha and they came to be supported by the domain with income from formerly Shōjōkōji land.

Whereas patronage of the Yugyō-ha could be used to legitimize the fragmentation and decentralization of shogunal authority, it could also be used to legitimize the arrogation of shogunal power and centralization under a new authority. Between 1568 and about 1590, Japan was gradually reunified under a central administration by Oda Nobunaga (1534-1582) and Toyotomi Hideyoshi (1536-1598). Both considered the great Buddhist institutions as major political rivals and with great effort managed to bring them under control: Mt. Hiei in 1571, the Ikkō-shū in 1576, Negoro in 1585.

During this time, temples of the Yugyō-ha came under the protection and control of these two. Protection of temples asserted authority formerly accruing to the shogun and meant a transfer of authority. For example, Nobunaga issued a vermilion seal document forbidding using the temple as a camp or fortification to the Shinzenkōji in Igawa in Echizen Province, the official residence of Fujisawa Shōnin Butten from 1557 until his death in 1571. In 1581, his representative Nomura Jinjūrō endowed the temple to pay for incense to burn before Butten's mortuary tablet.[159] Protection and patronage were offered by individuals in official capacities: the right to official capacity was thus asserted and confirmed.

Even the order's mission came under new official protection. Nobunaga gave permission to the thirty-first Yugyō Shōnin Dōnen to carry the mission into his domains and even received Dōnen in Kyoto. In 1578, as soon as he arrived in Ise Province, Dōnen sent messengers (loaded down with "friendship gifts" [*immotsu*]—court dress, gold brocade, red lacquer tray, incense container—so many the same customarily exchanged with the shogun) to Oda Nobunaga (then Minister of the Left with upper-second court rank) informing him of the emperor's wishes for an escort ("goannai arubeki jōi"). The messengers were received at Azuchi Castle in Ōmi

Province. Nobunaga was delighted, it is reported—so much so that he sent back a message giving permission freely to practice within his domain ("Bunkoku goshugyō gojiyū tarubeshi omomuki [no] gohenji ari").[160] This meant that all officers in the domain were required to receive Dōnen and to assist him in securing "room and board"—no mean feat for an entourage which might well have numbered several hundred people.[161] Nobunaga's second son Nobuo (1558-1630) received Dōnen in Ise at Matsugashima Castle, and Nobunaga's brother Nagano Kōzuke no suke Nobukane (1543-1614) at Anotsu Castle. Nobunaga's eldest son Nobutada (1557-1582), then lord of Mino and Owari and Konoe chūshō, lower-third court rank) came from Gifu Castle to the Kōmyōji in Kayazu, Owari Province to watch dancing *nembutsu*, meet the head priest and the Yugyō Shōnin, and receive an amulet. After he returned to the castle, he sent back gifts and a promise to await Dōnen's arrival at Gifu. Dōnen received help from and had connections of various sorts with Oda vassals—the Kyoto Magistrate (*shoshidai*) Murai Nagato no kami Sadakatsu, Hosokawa Fujitaka's wife, Akechi Mitsuhide (1526-1582), Nara Magistrate Tsutsui Junkei (1549-1584) and his wife, and Uji Magistrate Yamaguchi Shigemasa, for whose son, killed the year before at Osaka, he performed a memorial service. Nobunaga himself invited Dōnen to Azuchi but was forced to cancel (because of the revolt of Araki Murashige); he received him later in Kyoto. It was noted by Dōnen's chronicler, no doubt with some satisfaction, that Nobunaga's control of Kyoto and suppression of Nichirenites had made it easier to preach the *nembutsu*.[162]

The order's relationship with Hideyoshi was not particularly close. There is a legend that Hideyoshi had served as a boy at a temple near his native village of Nakamura, the oft-mentioned Yugyō-ha Kōmyōji in Kayazu.[163] As overlord of many domains and national hegemon as of 1590 with the defeat of the latter Hōjō at Odawara, Hideyoshi was ultimately credited with the protection of the order's mission in any domain. For example, the lord of Echigo, Uesugi Kagekatsu (1555-1623), submitted to Hideyoshi, who made him one of the five guardians of his son Hideyori. In 1589, Kagekatsu's representative Naoe Kanetsugu (1560-1619) authorized the sponsorship of the train of the new Fujisawa Shōnin Fukō through the Uesugi domain:

> Hospitality in the form of horses and handlers, lodging, and escort is to be extended without hesitation to the Fujisawa Shōnin on his return to [his] province as prescribed. Therefore, as above. Tenshō 17.9.7. [Under the] seal of Naoe Kanetsugu. [To the] lords within [the domain].[164]

Hideyoshi's ultimate authority as hegemon and therefore credit for the document that establishes a link in the chain of precedents of patronage by military rulers is indicated by a Jishū text, the *Yugyō Fujisawa ryōshōnin gorekidai keifu* (The lineage of successive generations of both the Yugyō and the Fujisawa Shōnin), which asserts that the order came from Hideyoshi himself.[165] It is important to remember, again, that the train either of the Yugyō Shōnin or Fujisawa Shōnin was extremely large—a whole temple complex on the move—and presented a considerable policing problem. Furthermore, the order depended entirely on charity. For all the precious objects necessary for ceremonial exchange with hosts and all the contributions made by believers carried, the order did not use these to pay for food and lodging for its monks and nuns on *yugyō*. Permission to take on the responsibility for providing these had to come from the top. All the same, such duties had been those of the shogunate; appropriating such duties functioned as the assertion of authority: legitimacy is maintained by observing precedent.

However, Hideyoshi's most important actions taken concerning the order were the issuing in 1591 of a vermilion seal document endowing the Kyoto headquarters Konkōji with 197 *koku* and the donation in 1598 of land in Kyoto to Yugyō Shōnin Mango, with which he built the Hōkokuji.[166] The Hōkokuji (Temple of the country of the dharma) was founded sometime in the 1570s or 1580s as the Hōkokuji (Temple of the wealthy country) by Fujiwara Haruko Shinjōtōmon'in, the wife of Crown Prince Masahito and mother of Emperor Goyōzei, who had received Dōnen in 1580, as a mortuary temple for her father Kajūji Haruhide. The ideograph for "hō" in the name of the temple, unfortunately, was the same as that for "toyo" and could have been interpreted as an allusion to "Toyotomi" and, after the fall of the Toyotomi, it was changed to that for "dharma."[167] The Yugyō-ha's positioning in Hideyoshi's system of legitimating authority through ceremony was established in 1593 by complying with Hideyoshi's order to the Buddhist schools (including Shingon, Tendai, Ritsu, Zen, Nichiren, Jōdo and Ikkō) to provide one hundred *jishū* for memorial services for Hideyoshi's parents to be held regularly at the sutra library of the Great Buddha Hall of Hōkōji, a temple established by Hideyoshi by commandeering materials from various warlords. Only one school, the Nichiren "No give, no take" school, refused and was suppressed.[168]

Especially in its relations with the highest-ranking and most powerful members of society, the Yugyō-ha found itself in what could be an unexpectedly compromising position. Patronage involved an exchange that the order perhaps did not anticipate: sponsorship in exchange for legitimation of the sponsor—sponsorship functioned indeed to legitimate the sponsor.

Thus, what the order might assume to be the basis of its relationship with a lay patron, salvation, was not even necessary to the relationship at all. The failure to recognize this suggests a naif; but the heads of the order were hardly naive. If the order was being used, then the order would take advantage of whatever patronage was offered to further its mission. Nothing so represents the order's sense of the reality of the situation as its relationship with the Tokugawa, a minor vassal family that came to rule Japan for over two hundred and fifty years.

7
The Yugyō-ha and the Foundation Legends of the Tokugawa

In 1590, after the defeat of the Hōjō at Odawara, the last major struggle in his campaign to reunify Japan, national hegemon Toyotomi Hideyoshi transferred Tokugawa Ieyasu from Mikawa Province to the Kantō. Ieyasu established his new base at Edo. Fujisawa and the Yugyō-ha headquarters Shōjōkōji were located in his new domain, and it was then that the order as a whole began its long and close association with the Tokugawa house. Several significant events helped to shape the relationship. First, as new domainal lord, in 1591 Ieyasu demonstrated his authority by endowing the Fujisawa Shōjōkōji with a yearly rice stipend of one hundred *koku* (about five hundred bushels).[1] This grant is stipulated as an "endowment" (*kifu*) even though reference is made to "precedent" (*senki*) established by the Hōjō's grant. It is a mistake to read this as meaning that the Tokugawa endowment is in addition to or more or less equal to that of the Hōjō, even though the Tokugawa calculation is in *koku* (about five bushels) of rice and the Hōjō in currency. Rather, it is important to remember that in the land tenure system being developed, land could revert to the domainal lord with each death or transfer and it could be confiscated and reallocated at any time as fiefs or temple/shrine endowments. Thus, Tokugawa Ieyasu did not confirm the temple in its possessions but donated them anew as a demonstration of his authority as lord of the domain. All together, "rice fields, dry fields, mountain forest, houses, and temple precincts" amounted to approximately 71.38 acres.[2]

As Ieyasu completed the transition from major warlord to national hegemon and shogun, the Yugyō-ha proceeded to establish ceremonial relations. In the second month of 1603, Ieyasu received the appointment as *seiitaishōgun*. On the twenty-eighth day of the fourth month, the Fujisawa Shōnin Fukō and the Yugyō Shōnin Mango were received in audience at

Fushimi Castle in Kyoto.[3] Thus, one observes the resumption of relations between the order and the shogunate whose precedent had been established by the Ashikaga and whose purpose was the mutual acknowledgment of authority acted out in the ritual of the audience.

The order also followed precedent established in the Muromachi period of appealing to the shogunate for help in dealing with the order's internal problems. Ieyasu retired in 1605 and passed the position of shogun on to his son Hidetada (1579-1632; shogun 1605-1623); even so, it was understood that Ieyasu was still running things. Thus, when in 1607 trouble broke out between the Yugyō Shōnin Mango and his disciple the current head of the Kyoto headquarters Konkōji, the Fujisawa Shōnin Fukō, accompanied by the eighteenth head of the Ichirenji and the previous head of the Konkōji, went for help to Ieyasu at Sumpu rather than to the shogun at Edo.[4]

In addition, the order decided that Ieyasu was a reliable protector for the long term: that year Fukō transferred from Mito to take up permanent residence at the Fujisawa Shōjōkōji, the first time for the Fujisawa Shōnin since 1513.[5] And Ieyasu reciprocated: Fujisawa was designated a post station on the principal highway to Kyoto, the Tōkaidō, and thus the prosperity of the town was guaranteed.[6]

The Jishū, as the Yugyō-ha was generally known by this time, was most grateful for the shogunate's decision to follow precedent established by the Muromachi government in protecting *yugyō*. In 1613 the shogunate issued to Chōgai (b. 1561; YS 1613-1627, FS -1644) the first of the vermilion seal documents giving each new Yugyō Shōnin the right to use fifty post horses and their handlers:

Vermilion Seal

Fifty horses [and their handlers] are to be provided at the point of departure at all points from Edo to the various provinces. This is bestowed upon the Yugyō Shōnin. Keichō 18 Year of Junior Brother of the Wood-Ox 3.11[7]

This *tenma goshuin* (in one form or another, but more or less regularized) would be issued to each Yugyō Shōnin upon appointment with a regularity not evidenced by the existing documents of the Ashikaga period. The *tenma goshuin*, the document granting the right to the use daily of fifty horses and handlers, conferred privileges equivalent to those of daimyo travelling on the Tōkaidō, the highway between Kyoto and Edo. It was issued twenty-three times in the Tokugawa period.[8] This reflects the shogunate's practice of confirming feudal holdings every generation: it could be rescinded at any time; it was not a permanent grant.

Therefore, the Jishū needed continuously to reassert its rights according to precedent; this can be seen in the way that it presented its documents— over and over again if need be. The *Shibazaki bunko* (c. 1700) asserts that ever since the first imperial order to travel around the country had been issued, later emperors had followed precedent ("imitated this") and continued to issue such orders. These orders had been carried out by the shogunate: "The devotion of the shogunal house continues undiminished to this day."[9] The implication of the statement is clear: if the Tokugawa family wanted to establish legitimacy as the new shogunal house, it had to follow precedent and support the Yugyō Shōnin. A very tactful allusion to this is made in an account of the Jishū submitted in 1697 to Yanagizawa Dewa no kami Yoshiyasu (1658-1714), the favorite of the shogun Tsunayoshi: in his *Jishū yōryakufu* (Abbreviated account of the Jishū), the author Donryō refers briefly to the patronage of Ieyasu, the issue of the document granting the right to the use of fifty post horses and their handlers, and the documents issued to generations of Yugyō Shōnin by the Kamakura and Kyoto Ashikaga military governments.[10]

The appeal to precedent is sometimes implied simply by listing documents. The *Jishū kekkishū* (c. 1700), in a section entitled "Documents issued by the house of [Ashikaga] Takauji to the Yugyō [Shōnin]," lists three and labels them carefully. The first complains about the trouble caused the Yugyō Shōnin's train at Miidera, the 1419 "Document from the Shogun Shōteiin Yoshimochi, fourth generation from Takauji in the time of the fifteenth Yugyō [Shōnin] Sonne Shōnin." This is not the earliest in the possession of the Shōjōkōji, the earliest being that from 1416. It does, however, include mention of branch temples, which the 1416 document does not, and gives evidence of the degree to which the shogun was willing to back the Yugyō-ha.[11] The underlying message is, of course, that the Ashikaga gave the Yugyō-ha unconditional protection and that the Tokugawa must do the same.

Even evidence of the acknowledgment of precedent during the Ashikaga period is given. The *Jishū kekkishū* offers the "Document from Shogun Erin'in Yoshitane to the Constables of the Provinces in the time of the twenty-second Yugyō Shōnin," issued by Ōuchi Yoshioki. It ends saying, "Thus, on account of there being a precedent, in the time of the thirty-sixth Yugyō Shōnin Nyotan, in the time of the regime of the Prime Minister Lord Taiyūin Iemitsu, a vermilion seal [document] was issued [granting the use of] fifty post horses. The last time the vermilion seal, issued to each of the generations of Yugyō [Shōnin] who have succeeded since then, was issued was Kanei 18 (1641)."[12] Thus, Tokugawa patronage is attributed to the force of precedent established by previous regimes; the legitimacy of the Tokugawa regime is based on the principle of following precedent.

In gratitude for all Ieyasu's favors to the Jishū, the Jishū entered Ieyasu's name and that of his concubine Cha'a in the *Jishū kakochō*. The second shogun Hidetada (Taitokuin) and his wife (Sūgen'in) were also entered.[13]

THE ADVANTAGE TO THE SHOGUNATE: THE MINAMOTO PEDIGREE

A factor not generally recognized in the relationship between the Jishū and the Tokugawa was the degree to which the Tokugawa actually depended on the Jishū. The Jishū functioned to legitimate Tokugawa claims to the Minamoto lineage which was required to assume the office of shogun (*seiitaishōgun*).

The order's connection with the Tokugawa (formerly Matsudaira) family, who headed the shogunate from 1603 to 1867, can be traced back to the early sixteenth century. In 1503, Matsudaira Nobutada (1489-1531) protected and recognized the rights to income from possessions of the Yugyō-ha Shōmyōji in Ōhama, Mikawa Province and in 1509 further endowed it. The Shōmyōji was originally founded as the mortuary temple of the Wada, a cadet house of the Hatakeyama (one of the three Ashikaga Shogunal Deputy families) which served in the shogunal bodyguard (*hōkōshū*). The Matsudaira supplanted them at the end of the fifteenth century and, in the time-honored process of asserting authority, took over the protection of the Wada temple. The temple was used, very much as the order itself was, to pray for the souls of dead killed in battle: in 1512, following a period of three hard years fending off attacks by Imagawa Ujichika between 1506 and 1509, Nobutada endowed the temple to perform dancing *nembutsu* services every month on the eighteenth for the souls of those killed, friend and foe. Nobutada's own daughter Tōichibō is said to have been a *jishū* there until her death in 1570—this made the temple a family temple of the Matsudaira much as the Ichirenji functioned as such for the Takeda family.[14]

The temple was apparently a center of poetry at one time: the *renga* master Sōboku (d. 1545) stopped there in 1544. The head priest at the time, Go'a, had important aristocratic and therefore poetry connections: a scion of the Kazan'in family, he had been adopted by the tenth shogun Ashikaga Yoshitane; however, because of the troubles of the time, he had become a *jishū*. He had been transferred to the Shōmyōji from the Shōgonji in Ōtsu the year before. Indeed, Go'a's own poetry talents are surmised from the report that in 1543 he was invited by Matsudaira Hirotada (1526-1549), lord of Okazaki Castle, to a poetry party. That same year, Hirotada went to the

Shōmyōji for poetry: there, the name Takechiyō was chosen for his son, the future Tokugawa Ieyasu; the temple still has the writing table and writing equipment used at that party.[15] In 1559, with his father dead ten years and himself a vassal of the Imagawa, Ieyasu, while still called Motoyasu, confirmed the Shōmyōji and six other temples in possession of their lands.[16]

The Shōmyōji and the Yugyō-ha as a whole were critical to Ieyasu's pursuit of the position of shogun because they were pivotal to his claim to a Minamoto pedigree, essential to the office. Together, the order and the Tokugawa created a grand legend concerning the origins of the Tokugawa in representatives of the Nitta family who had fought for the Southern Court against the Ashikaga, survived the annihilation of their clan, and suffered exile and obscurity for several generations before settling down in Mikawa Province and founding the family which would provide one of the three great unifiers of Japan.

The initial step taken by the Yugyō-ha in creating the foundation legend of the Tokugawa family was to assist in the establishment of the Tokugawa genealogy. Tokugawa Ieyasu was born a Matsudaira. The Matsudaira family were descended from, it has been suggested, lower-ranking religious specialists connected with a shrine; they needed to establish a Nitta-Serata-Tokugawa lineage for political reasons and for prestige. Ieyasu's claim to a Tokugawa pedigree, a claim which probably went back as far as his grandfather, was shaky and not successfully pursued without a little bribery, a little forgery, and a little help from the Yugyō-ha.[17]

In 1566, Ieyasu petitioned the imperial court and received permission to change his name from "Matsudaira" to "Tokugawa," the name of a cadet house of the Nitta.[18] He was given the title "Mikawa no kami" and that of "Ukyō daibu" and Lower-Fifth Rank. However, at this time, Ieyasu actually claimed Fujiwara ancestry (although the document was later emended to read "Minamoto") and continued to use the name Fujiwara until 1586.[19]

Ieyasu was greatly assisted in this enterprise by a priest of a Jishū temple in his native province, the Seiganji (Okazaki City, Aichi Prefecture), whose connection at court was the former Prime Minister (*kampaku*) Konoe Sakihisa (1536-1612; *kampaku* 1554).[20] When Ieyasu's initial request to the court was denied by Emperor Ōgimachi, Sakihisa obtained from the head of the Shinto bureau, Yoshida Kanesuke (1516-1573), a copy of a genealogy of the Tokugawa house supposedly found among the papers of the Madenokōji family. Sakihisa submitted it to the emperor, and only then did Ieyasu receive his new name. For their services, Ieyasu promised both Sakihisa and Kanesuke money and horses every year.[21] He also, subsequently, reneged on the deal.

Between 1590 and 1595, Ieyasu was showing extraordinary interest in genealogies and having his own drawn up.[22] In 1609, six years after being appointed shogun, Ieyasu ordered emendation of the standard genealogy, the *Sompi bummyaku*. He proclaimed his Nitta ancestry by securing in 1611 a posthumous court appointment for his putative ancestor Nitta Yoshishige (1135-1202) and, in 1613, by establishing a temple in his honor.[23]

The problem of the genealogy was to connect the verifiable ancestor of the Matsudaira, one Chikauji Toku'ami, to a verifiable descendant of the Nitta.[24] The main tactical problem was to find a way physically to transfer the appropriate Nitta from Kōzuke Province to Matsudaira in Mikawa Province. This was done by inventing and inserting the line of Masayoshi, Chikasue, and Arichika and by establishing a tradition of their years of hiding and wandering until Arichika found a home with the Matsudaira family in Mikawa.[25]

The earliest version of the story of the founding of the Matsudaira family is given in the 1622-1639 *Mikawa monogatari* (Tale of Mikawa [Province]) of Ōkubo Hikozaemon Tadataka (1560-1639).[26] According to this somewhat obscure account, one "Tokugawa-dono" followed his relative Nitta Yoshisada (d. 1338) until defeated by Ashikaga Takauji. He was forced out of his native Tokugawa, wandered for some time as a refugee, and became a Jishū or *jishū* monk by the name of Toku'ami.[27] Eventually, he went to Sakai in Mikawa and had a son there, the ancestor of the Sakai family. Later, he was taken as a son-in-law by Tarōzaemon of Matsudaira and became his heir.[28] Surely, the point of the origin of this foundation story was to promote a claim to the common ancestry of the Sakai and Matsudaira.

This story of the process by which the Tokugawa made their way to Mikawa possibly originated at the Jishū temple with strong Matsudaira connections, the temple in Ōhama mentioned above, the Shōmyōji (Hekinan City, Aichi Prefecture).[29] It is probably more correct to say that the Shōmyōji was given the responsibility for validating the story. This temple is the mortuary temple of the ancestor of the Matsudaira, Arichika. According to temple tradition, Tokugawa Arichika Chō'ami, his son Chikauji Toku'ami, and their follower Ishikawa Magosaburō came to the Shōmyōji and stayed there, as the head priest was Saburō's brother.[30] Arichika buried the remains of his father Chikasue at the temple. He himself died in 1452. Chikauji was later adopted into the Matsudaira family.

The Shōmyōji tended to stress its relationship with the Tokugawa as the Matsudaira family of Mikawa rather than with the Tokugawa as Nitta refugees. The temple's traditions seem to do little to attempt to substantiate Tokugawa claims to a Nitta lineage: after all, they say nothing about how and why the Tokugawa came to Matsudaira, only that the connection with the temple was through a brother of the head priest.

The element needed to explain how the Tokugawa came to Mikawa was provided by yet another tradition based on or analogous to the Shōjōkōji battlefield and refugee stories. The narrative tradition can be traced back to the fourteenth-century epic, *Taiheiki*: as mentioned previously, in 1362 the Fujisawa Shōnin (the fourth, Tosen) gave refuge to Hatakeyama Kunikiyo and his brother Yoshihiro, who had fled from their besieged Shuzenji Castle, and, giving them two horses and two *jishū* to guide them, sent them to the Konkōji in the capital. Later, their brother Yoshitō was informed by a *jishū* that they had escaped to Fujisawa, was smuggled out of the enemy camp where he was a hostage, and took refuge at the Shōjōkōji.[31] As seen in chapter 6, the Shōjōkōji narrative tradition of services to the defeated and the dead was expanded by its role in the story of the fall of the Kamakura Ashikaga: there during the revolt of 1416-1417 Uesugi Ujisada committed suicide and Iwamatsu Mitsuzumi was buried, and there in 1439 Uesugi Norizane shaved his head in protest of Ashikaga Mochiuji's actions against him.

The merging of the Shōjōkōji narrative tradition with the foundation story of the Tokugawa found its way into the *Mikawa gofudoki* (Survey of the history of Mikawa [Province]), which explains that Arichika and Chikauji followed the Kamakura *kubō* Mochiuji in his revolt which failed in 1439, distinguished themselves defending his son Yoshihisa, and cut their way back home. Pursued by the shogun Yoshinori, who was intent on destroying the entire Nitta clan, they fled to Shōjōkōji and cut their hair, that is, disguised themselves as monks to save their lives. They stayed for a time with Hayashi Tōsuke Mitsumasa in Shinano and then went to Mikawa.[32]

Another element was added to lend credence to the story of the Tokugawa transfer to Mikawa. This tradition concentrated on the role of the Yugyō Shōnin in protecting the ancestor of the Tokugawa, bringing him to Mikawa, and negotiating his adoption into the Matsudaira family. This was, as future Yugyō Shōnin Donryō so delicately put it, the reason for "the reverence of the shogunal house" for the Jishū.[33]

According to a Tokugawa Jishū source, after the death of Nitta Yoshisada in 1338, his follower, here given the name Serata (another cadet house of the Nitta) no Saburō Mitsuuji, retreated to Tokugawa in Kōzuke. His son Masayoshi, Masayoshi's son Chikasue, and Chikasue's son Arichika lived in various places until 1439. Then, caught in the fight between the Kyoto shogun Ashikaga Yoshinori and the Kamakura *kubō* Mochiuji and pursued by their hereditary enemy the shogun, Chikasue and his son Shōjūmaru fled to the protection of the sixteenth Yugyō Shōnin, Nanyō (YS

1429-1439). Chikasue died the next year and the Yugyō Shōnin (who, according to the official genealogies, became Fujisawa Shōnin in 1439) made the orphaned boy his disciple and renamed him Chō'ami. On *yugyō* with the Shōnin, Chō'ami became ill and the Shōnin sent him to Shōmyōji with the brother of that temple's head priest, Ishikawa Magosaburō. While he was there, Matsudaira Tarōzaemon came to the temple and, on sight, decided that he wanted Chō'ami as his son-in-law. The priest sent him to the Shōnin, who consented to secularize Chō'ami only on the condition that, even if a son were born, Chō'ami would remain heir. And so he became Matsudaira Sakyō no suke Arichika. He died in 1452 and was buried at Shōmyōji. His son Chikauji, who inherited the Matsudaira name Tarōzaemon and the house, died in 1467 and was also buried at Shōmyōji.[34]

To the Shōmyōji tradition has been added a version that makes the savior of the Tokugawa ancestors the sixteenth Yugyō Shōnin. Whereas the Shōmyōji tradition makes no reference to the Yugyō Shōnin, the Shōjōkōji tradition does. This looks like an attempt by the order to take advantage of the tradition of one of its branch temples and, in addition, to create a major role for itself out of it, thereby binding the loyalties of the Tokugawa family to the head of the order rather than to simply only one of the order's temples.

A further "proof" of Minamoto lineage has been inserted into the Tokugawa foundation legend and the Shōjōkōji has enshrined it in the form of an amulet: the Ugajin (or Ukajin), a figurine about 4.8 inches in size, was claimed to be a tutelary god of the Tokugawa. The god is the same as that enshrined at Atsuta Shrine, which connects it with the Minamoto family, from whom the Tokugawa claimed descent.[35] According to the *Toku'ami ganjō* (Written vow of Toku'ami), while in hiding from the Ashikaga shogunate, Toku'ami turned in desperation to this amulet and received a dream revelation, in which an itinerant monk travelling the provinces ("shōkoku hengyōsha") gave him his own grey robe and advised him to disguise himself and to escape danger. The next day, he heard there was an itinerant *hijiri* in the village over the mountain. Arichika went to meet him, found he was indeed wearing the grey robe he had seen in his dream, and was taken into his protection.[36] This vow is an appeal for the revival of the family written and enshrined under the nose of the Kamakura headquarters of the Ashikaga house. A more obscure document could not have been written and, without available commentaries in the *Hannichi kanwa* and *Shimpen Sagami fudoki kō*, literally impossible to decipher. Both commentaries fix the date at 1396 and connect the legend not with the sixteenth but with the twelfth Yugyō Shōnin Sonkan, the imperial prince, and the *Shimpen Sagami* with the Shōrenji in Kiryū (see below).[37] The *Shimpen Sagami,* however, also reports that the image was first brought to the Shōjōkōji only in 1746.[38] Certainly, there is no record of it in catalogues of the Shōjōkōji from c. 1700. Thus, it appears that the setting of the story in the fifteenth century featuring the sixteenth Yugyō Shōnin may be an older level in the development of the story; the integration of the needs of the Tokugawa for a Minamoto genealogy with the Jishū need to strengthen claims of "imperial origins" came later.

It would be a mistake, however, to assume that the order manufactured the tradition out of thin air. First of all, there was an existing tradition of granting protection to defeated warriors and taking them into the service of the order as *kakuryō*. In addition, there were two similar traditions which deserve notice because they represent established motifs in establishing lineage.

The first is that of the Yura family. According to this tradition, the family was descended from a hitherto unknown fourth son of Nitta Yoshisada. On his father's death, he had been rescued by a *jishū* from Fujisawa ("Fujisawa yugyō sō"), taken there to become a monk named Ryō'ami, and later secularized and adopted by one of his father's vassals.[39] This story was recorded perhaps as early as 1591 and certainly by 1641, about the time the Yura submitted their genealogy to the government.[40] The tradition of descent from the Nitta was manufactured in the sixteenth century by Yura Narishige (1506-1578) of Kanayama in Kōzuke Province, a warlord who, like Tokugawa Ieyasu, needed to upgrade his pedigree and for the same reasons: Narishige, like Ieyasu, petitioned to change his name from Yokose to Yura and received permission in 1564 from the shogun Ashikaga Yoshiteru (1536-1565; shogun 1547-).[41] This story was used in 1641 to petition the Tokugawa, as main representative of the Nitta family, to reestablish this cadet house, abolished on the death of its head, because he had had no direct heir.[42] If the Yura claim to Nitta descent, based on the same story as the Tokugawa's, was invalid, then so was the Tokugawa's. Perhaps the Tokugawa used the Yura story or one like it to fill in gaps in its own. The Yura story was later rejected.[43] However, the similarity in the stories, the theme of the rescue of a Nitta by the Yugyō-ha, cannot at this time be dismissed as coincidence especially if one considers that, as discussed below, the Yura, like the Tokugawa, tried to appropriate Nitta temples in order to legitimate their claims.

The second tradition is that of the *Namiaiki*, the account of battles in 1424 and 1435 at a place called Namiai in Shinano Province.[44] The *Namiaiki* is in effect the foundation story of the alliance of the eleven main families of Tsushima in Owari Province, now Tsushima City, Aichi Prefecture. Their alliance, sealed by their common worship of the god of

Tsushima Shrine, is represented in the *Namiaiki* by their defence of the Southern Court descendant Prince Tadayoshi, supposedly the son of Prince Munenaga (1312?-1385?, fourth son of Godaigo) and of his son Yoshiyoki. These eleven families followed Oda Nobunaga. However, when the Oda were defeated in 1590 by Toyotomi Hideyoshi, the families were dispersed, their lands were confiscated, and many became Shinto priests.[45]

The circumstances of the battles are unimportant; of interest to this study are the three motifs which characterize all the versions of the Tokugawa family foundation legend: the defeat in battle of a representative of the Southern Court, the participation of the Tokugawa ancestor, and his rescue by the Yugyō Shōnin. According to the *Namiaiki*, in 1435, at the second battle at Namiai, Serata Ōi no suke Masayoshi was killed. His son Mantokumaru (a name intended to connect him with the Nitta family temple Mantokuji, discussed below) Masachika Kurandō was captured in Matsudaira in Mikawa by a force sent to destroy all traces of the Nitta and taken along with others to the capital the next year. He and two others were sentenced to death. Yoshinori's own commander appealed to him through a disciple of the Yugyō Shōnin, who happened to be in Kyoto at the time. He would not relent, and so the commander executed three criminals, substituted their heads, and slipped Masachika and the two others to the Yugyō Shōnin. They cut their hair, became *jishū*, and toured the country as his disciples until Yoshinori was assassinated in 1441.[46]

Here we have a problem similar to that encountered in the analysis of the Yura tradition: was the *Namiaiki* based on a Yugyō-ha tradition or the tradition based on the *Namiaiki*? The text is presumed to have been written in 1488 but the earliest reference to it is 1709 and it may date from no earlier than the Genroku period.[47] This is borne out by internal evidence. The *Namiaki* reports that the Rendaiji in Tsushima was founded by a Yugyō-ha monk.[48] However, the Rendaiji was a branch temple of the Ikkō-ha Bamba Rengeji.[49] The confusion of the two could only have happened after the Ikkō-ha had been incorporated into the Jishū, sometime in the latter half of the seventeenth century. An earlier variant, the *Shinano no miya den* (written before 1629), contains no reference to the Yugyō Shōnin but the names "Serata Shuri no jin Chikasue" and "Serata Ukyō no suke Arichika" are highlighted.[50] Already, the first attempts were being made to use this particular tradition, the battles at Namiai, to substantiate the Tokugawa claims to an ancestor by the name of Arichika who belonged to the Nitta clan and had fought for a prince of the Southern Court line.

This tradition must have been introduced to both the Tokugawa family and the Yugyō-ha by one of the families celebrated in the *Namiaiki*. This was very likely the Hotta family, whose ancestor was enshrined at the

Tsushima Shrine. Hotta Masayoshi (died 1629, aged forty-nine) first came to serve Tokugawa Ieyasu in 1605. He was an adherent of the Yugyō-ha: his posthumous Buddhist name was Kaku'a and he was buried at the Nichirinji, which maintains memorial monuments of the family.[51] The *Tōtakusan chiji kiroku* records that there were remains of a shrine for the Hotta family at Shōjōkōji and monuments with inscriptions reading Shōseiinden, Jōshōinden, Shōtōinden, and Jōgakuinden.[52] The *Namiaiki*, as well as the entries in Jishū sources such as the *Jishū kekkishū* and the *Shibazaki bunko*, were based on the net result of the Hotta family's contribution to the Tokugawa foundation legend.

The Yugyō-ha made claims on the Tokugawa, both as a private family and as the government, on the bases of personal obligation and precedent established by the previous Ashikaga government. The order, directly or indirectly, used three temples with their connections to the Nitta and the Tokugawa to press their claims: the Mantokuji (dissolved; Serata Village, Nitta District, Gumma Prefecture), the Shōrenji (Ōjima Town, Nitta District, Gumma Prefecture), and the Shōnenji (Maruoka Town, Fukui Prefecture). All three received large government stipends.

Ieyasu, as "Minamoto Ason," issued the Mantokuji its vermilion seal document and endowed it with 100 *koku* in 1591.[53] The claims of the Mantokuji to Tokugawa patronage were based on the tradition that it was a nunnery founded by the Nitta and headed by Nitta and Tokugawa women.[54] According to tradition, Yura (and Yokose, vassals of the Nitta) women were sent to serve at the Mantokuji in the sixteenth century.[55] The *Shibazaki bunko* relates that it was established by Yoshino-ni, the daughter of Chikasue. After Chikasue's second son Arichika had established himself in Matsudaira, he returned to Tokugawa and built a temple and made his sister Yoshino-ni the founder.[56] This tradition goes back at least to 1647.[57] There has been an attempt by the writer of the *Namiaiki* to cross traditions with the Mantokuji, as seen in the use of the name "Mantokumaru" for the Serata protagonist (as above).

Part of the Jishū's propaganda about the Mantokuji was meant to reflect favorably on the Yugyō-ha by demonstrating the esteem in which the Shōjōkōji had traditionally held the Mantokuji. According to the *Shibazaki bunko*, the name of the temple and the right to wear their colored garments had been given by Shōjōkōji, that is, by the Fujisawa Shōnin. Also reported is that the temple had received its name from the Yugyō Shōnin.[58] Some of the information is meant to indicate grateful acknowledgment of the connection with Ieyasu: because Ieyasu endowed the temple, celebrations were held every New Year.[59]

The order considered the nunnery Mantokuji very important in strengthening its own position with the shogunate, and relations go back very early. In 1616, the head of the Mantokuji was received at the shogunal palace to present New Year's compliments.[60] The Jishū, however, did not have jurisdiction over the Mantokuji, despite its claims, and in the eighteenth century the abbesses of the temple drew near the Pure Land or Jōdo sect, the official sect of the Tokugawa family.[61]

The *Shibazaki bunky* entry on Mantokuji ends with a short mention of the Iwamatsu Shōrenji, which had the function of instructing the nuns of the Mantokuji. This temple in Nitta territory was established and patronized by the Nitta and their relatives, the Iwamatsu. Both the thirty-third Yugyō Shōnin Mango and the thirty-fourth Yugyō Shōnin Chōgai served as head priests of the Shōrenji. Emperor Ōgimachi presented the name plaque during Mango's term of office and Ieyasu's representative endowed it with 250 *koku*. It possessed five Tokugawa mortuary tablets.[62]

The temple traditionally associated itself with the Southern Court. According to the *Nitta Iwamatsu Shōrenji engi* (Origins of the Shōrenji of Iwamatsu), from the time Naozumi, a seventh generation descendant of Yoshisada, established himself at the temple (1501-1503), the temple had been a place for praying for the souls of those warriors loyal to the Southern Court.[63] The *Kaisei Mikawa gofudoki* (Revised survey of the history of Mikawa [Province]) reports a tradition that the Yugyō Shōnin (here, Sonkan, the twelfth Yugyō Shōnin, prince of the Southern Court) was staying at this temple when Tokugawa Arichika came with his two sons and became his disciple, thus escaping capture.[64]

The Iwamatsu Shōrenji and its traditions are duplicated by the Kiryū Shōrenji and its traditions. In 1575, Yura Narishige "moved" the Shōrenji to Hisakata Village in what is now Kiryū City, Gumma Prefecture with Mango as its founder (Mango was not elected thirty-third Yugyō Shōnin until 1589).[65] This clearly represents attempts to appropriate the Iwamatsu Shōrenji traditions just as Narishige appropriated a Nitta lineage; the temple is even recorded as being moved to Hisakata Village as early as 1417.[66] It possesses a mortuary tablet for Nitta Yoshisada, supposedly made in the time of the twelfth head: the Southern Court connection is emphasized by calling Yoshisada the "General of the Imperial Forces" (*miyakata taishōgun*) as opposed to the rebels under Ashikaga Takauji.[67] This temple is also named as the temple at which the twelfth Yugyō Shōnin Sonkan was staying when Arichika placed himself under his protection.[68]

Like the Mantokuji and two Shōrenji, yet another temple had the function of validating Tokugawa claims to a Nitta lineage. The Chōrinsan Ōjōin Shōnenji was one of the most important of the Yugyō-ha temples during the middle ages, but it lost land during the sixteenth century due to competition from the precursor of the True Pure Land sect.[69] As mentioned above, in 1458 the Ashikaga shogunate designated the Shōnenji a *kiganjo*, an official temple for prayers for peace and prosperity, as did the imperial court in 1465. In 1536, Gonara conferred the title "Shōnin" on the head of the temple.[70]

The extraordinary success of the temple in the middle ages was in part due to the fact that Nitta Yoshisada, the great hero of the restoration movements of the fourteenth and nineteenth centuries, was buried there until after the Meiji Restoration. According to the *Taiheiki*, his headless body, accompanied by eight *jishū*, had been sent there immediately after his death in battle in 1338.[71] In 1458, the shogun Ashikaga Yoshimasa endowed the temple to provide incense for Yoshisada.[72]

As far as the order was concerned, Nitta Yoshisada was of no consequence; there is rarely mention of him in Jishū sources. What mattered to the order was that the head of one of its branch temples bore the title "Shōnin" and was presented at court. According to the *Shibazaki bunko*, the head of the Shōnenji was first presented at court in the time of the Emperor Gonara and the shogun Manshōin Yoshiharu.[73] Of importance, as is noted, was that copies of documents were presented by the Nichirinji in 1672 in response to a query concerning the precedent for the reception at court of heads of branch temples.

It was only later that the Tokugawa house took an interest in the Shōnenji as the burial place of Nitta Yoshisada. There was some interest on the part of the Fukui Matsudaira house, descended from Ieyasu: in 1732, a Matsudaira vassal erected on the temple grounds a great monument inscribed with a poem to Yoshisada.[74] The eighth shogun Yoshimune (1684-1751; shogun 1716-1745) ordered a great investigation into the Nitta house. One result was the shogunate's sponsorship in 1737 of the ceremonies at Shōnenji for the four hundredth anniversary of Yoshisada's death (repeated in 1785 and 1837) and the acquisition of the Matsudaira, lords of Fukui, as parishioners.[75] Thus, the Tokugawa family and the Yugyō-ha were united in preserving the relics and administering the cult of the champion of the Southern Court, Nitta Yoshisada.

Since the aetiology of the Tokugawa house was constructed within a very short period of perhaps fifty years, it is very difficult to determine the sequence of incorporating the themes or motifs and this is neither the time nor the place to launch a study of the construction, deconstruction, and crossing of themes in traditional narrative that would offer an hypothesis of the development of the legend of the origins of the Tokugawa family. What is important here is the role of Jishū temples of validating Tokugawa claims by means of the aetiologies passing for histories, the monuments, and the ceremonies dedicated to the ancestors of the Tokugawa.

The order certainly profited from its role in the creation of the Tokugawa foundation legends. A Jishū source from 1690 notes that the twenty-first head of the Shichijō Konkōji Ji'a Shōnin met Ieyasu's confidant and religious advisor Tenkai, the superior of Tōeiji. Tenkai is reported as telling Ji'a that Ieyasu's sons, the heads of the three main cadet houses of Owari, Kii, and Mito, had said that their ancestor was under great obligation to the Jishū and that, since there was no document to the effect, they would probably issue one.[76] The order's single greatest patron under the forty-second Yugyō Shōnin was Tokugawa Mitsutomo (1625-1700), head of the Owari house.[77] The Jishū could also rely on other descendants and collateral relatives of Ieyasu.

MONZEKI STATUS

One reward for the Jishū's role in the legitimation of the Tokugawa lineage was the (albeit temporary) recognition of *monzeki* status for the Yugyō Shōnin. The principal basis for claiming *monzeki* status was the claim that the twelfth Yugyō Shōnin Sonkan (b. 1349; YS 1387-1400) had been an imperial prince. There are several traditions concerning Sonkan's ancestry. The two most important are that he was 1) the grandson of Godaigo and 2) Godaigo's cousin, the son of Tokiwai Tsuneakira, second son of the Emperor Kameyama (1249-1305; r. 1260-1274). Since the earliest references to Sonkan's name and imperial lineage date from the Tokugawa period, there is no proof either that the twelfth Yugyō Shōnin was actually called Sonkan or that he was an imperial prince.

The earliest documentation of the name Sonkan or of Jishū interest in Sonkan's imperial lineage dates from 1623.[78] In a letter to the head priest of the Konkōji in Kyoto, the Fujisawa Shōnin Fukō insisted that the twelfth Yugyō Shōnin was not the grandson of the Emperor Godaigo and son of Ōtō no miya (Morinaga Shinnō [Imperial Prince], 1308-1335), but his cousin, the son of Tokiwai Tsuneakira, second son of Kameyama.[79] However, other evidence challenges certain information in the document.[80] Whether or not Sonkan was the son of Tsuneakira has yet to determined. There is also a tradition that Sonkan was the son rather than grandson of Kameyama.[81]

However, the tradition that Sonkan was the grandson of Godaigo seems to have obtained in the seventeenth and eighteenth centuries. The *Jishū kekkishū* records that Sonkan was the son of Ōtō no miya Morinaga Shinnō and that the famous portrait of Godaigo, which is still in the possession of Shōjōkōji, had been given to Sonkan precisely because he was the grandson of Godaigo. It offers a short genealogy as proof.[82] The *Shibazaki bunko* expands on the *Jishū kekkishū* version: when Prince Morinaga was assassinated, his concubine fled with their son to the Southern Court at Yoshino, where he was adopted by the Emperor Gomurakami (1328-1368; r. 1339-) and created crown prince.[83] The strength of this tradition can be seen in the fact that, as the Jishū text *Tōtakusan chiji kiroku* notes, mortuary tablets (*ihai*) to Godaigo, Gomurakami, and Morinaga ("Hyōbu-kyō Shinnō") were at Shōjōkōji, and that they were there because the twelfth Yugyō Shōnin "Sonkan Hōshinnō" was the grandson of Godaigo.[84] Sonnin is also recorded as going to Yoshino for the 350th anniversary of Godaigo's death, apparently because of this connection.[85]

Eventually, it seems, in the end the version that Tokiwai Tsuneakira was Sonkan's father prevailed. This may have been due to the appearance of new court genealogies in the eighteenth century.[86] Two early nineteenth-century Jishū sources, the "Nantei monzeki no koto" (On the *monzeki* of the Southern Court) in the *Hannichi kanwa*, and the *Yugyō Fujisawa ryōshōnin gorekidai keifu*, accept this version.[87]

Whether Sonkan was the son of Tokiwai Tsuneakira or of Ōtō no miya Morinaga was not as important as the claim that he was, indeed, an imperial prince. Throughout the Tokugawa period the following argument was made. An imperial prince of the Southern Court, Sonkan had been the first *monzeki* of the Jishū and had established a precedent and a right to privileges to which later Yugyō Shōnin were entitled. Furthermore, Sonkan, as an imperial prince, had been the first to receive official protection for *yugyō*. The Jishū was, in fact, the surviving "house" of the lost Southern Court.

The principal motive for the argument was the establishment of precedent. The *Jishū kekkishū* maintains that privileges accorded an imperial prince had been enjoyed by Sonkan and therefore by "generations" of Yugyō Shōnin.[88] Whether literally "generations" of Yugyō Shōnin had actually done so is not known. However, the source and the meaning of those privileges are stressed in the *Shibazaki bunko*.[89] A Southern Court Emperor (Gokomatsu) had, in granting the privilege, recognized Sonkan's status as a prince of the Southern Court. "Thus, the rank of Yugyō [Shōnin] is equal to [that of] *monzeki*."[90]

The privileges included that of being seated on two mats, even in the presence of the shogun or the emperor, and that of maintaining *yugyō* at government expense. Both the *Jishū kekkishū* and the *Shibazaki bunko* claim that Sonkan, as an imperial prince, was entitled to sit on two mats, but the *Shibazaki bunko* claims that this privilege had been granted at his interview with Gokomatsu, who had invited him to sit at the same height.[91] A document dated 1627 states explicitly that the privilege of using a palanquin and other paraphernalia began with Sonkan in the time of Shōkō, who reigned 1414-1428, even though Sonkan is supposed to have died in 1400.[92] These privileges included carrying a round court fan and a white cloth umbrella.[93] Dōnen may actually have been the first to carry such a fan at his presentation at court in 1580.[94] Nevertheless, even the precedent of government protection of *yugyō* is credited to Sonkan, the first, it is claimed, to whom documents were issued, even though no such document survives.[95] Donryō repeated his argument in the account of the Jishū submitted to Yanagizawa Yoshiyasu: "on account of this, since then, when the Yugyō Shōnin goes to the imperial palace, his status is equal to that of *monzeki*."[96]

Not only is *monzeki* status claimed for the Yugyō Shōnin, but status of the order as a house descended from the Southern Court. According to the *Yugyō tokumyō no koto* (On the special name of itinerancy, c. 1700), Ashikaga Takauji—and supposedly his descendants—destroyed the supporters of the Southern Court, but the "house of the Yugyō [Shōnin]" (*Yugyō no ie*) survived. Because the Yugyō Shōnin was a "descendant" of the Yoshino court and its crown prince [Sonkan], he was called "Nanmon" (Southern Gate/House) and "Nanmonzeki" (Prince Imperial Abbot of the Southern Court).[97]

In other words, the Yugyō-ha claimed status as a house "descended" from Sonkan, crown prince of the Southern Court, forced into exile and given refuge by the order. The order was, as a Buddhist institution, the last surviving representative of the Southern Court and its only *monzeki* and was honored as such by the court and the military houses.[98] It is not clear exactly when the argument was first put forward. The one first to profit from it was Sonnin, who became the forty-second Yugyō Shōnin in 1668, advanced to nineteenth Fujisawa Shōnin in 1683, and died in 1691 at sixty-seven.[99] Sonnin apparently acquired the highest rank in the official Buddhist hierarchy (Daisōjō or Senior High Priest) and was recognized as Abbot of the Southern Court, with rank equal to that of *monzeki*.[100]

There are only Jishū sources to document when Sonnin was raised to this status. According to the *Jishū kekkishū*, in what might be an entry later than 1848, Sonnin was first received as Sōjō by the shōgun in 1668. When in 1687 Sonnin went to offer the Emperor Higashiyama (1675-1709; r. 1687-) congratulations on his ascension, he was received in the palace wearing crimson, the color of exalted rank. From that time, the *Jishū kekkishū* notes, he was called "Nanmon Sōjō" (Southern Gate/House Abbot).[101] According to a very late source, in 1672 he was permitted to be called "Nanmon" ("Southern Gate/House [Abbot]") and given the title "Daisōjō" by the court; in 1679, this was confirmed and announced by the shogunate—"lest the line of the Southern Court be forgotten."[102]

Sonnin acquired status equal to that of Shinkyō and Donkai as a precedent maker. Even his grave is listed as one of the important "properties" of the Shōjōkōji in the *Tōtakusan chiji kiroku*: "Here is the grave of the forty-second Yugyō [Shōnin] the Nanmonjū Sōjō Sonnin."[103] It was he who so stressed the role of Sonkan in establishing precedent: he changed the succession to the office of Yugyō Shōnin by demanding that the head of the Ichirenji should succeed him because Sonkan had been head of the Ichirenji before becoming Yugyō Shōnin. Sonnin himself took a character from Sonkan's name and started a trend followed by fourteen of the following thirty-eight Yugyō Shōnin. Sonnin became, in effect, as important to the order as Sonkan: Sonnin had won recognition of the order's right to rank and privilege first conferred upon Sonkan. However, no other Yugyō Shōnin is recorded as bearing the rank of Senior High Priest or of the title "Abbot of the Southern Court."

REFORMS UNDER SONNIN

Sonnin is revered because he "tried to revive a stagnant order."[104] Sonnin used his prestige (and, in the time-honored tradition, no doubt the backing of the shogunate) to introduce reforms into the order, most significantly in the areas of organization and succession.[105] By the mid-Muromachi period, from what is known of the Yugyō Shōnin's train, the order had developed a system of organization based on six dormitories for monks and six for nuns. These were called "ryō" and the head of each was called by his position "First Dormitory (Ichi[no]ryō)," "Second dormitory (Ni[no]ryō)," and so forth. The highest ranking was the Sixth Dormitory.[106] By 1500, there were in addition those under the protection of the Shōnin or temples—fugitives, unfilial sons, defeated warriors—organized as Guest Companions or *kakuryō*. They were laymen with shaven heads and religious robes who performed a variety of functions.[107] Some of these became separated from the order when temples were destroyed; in the seventeenth century, however, the order claimed such people as gong ringers (*kaneuchi*) as belonging to the order and the claim was recognized.[108] There were also workshops, staffed either by lay or religious, attached to the temples.

Although most temples in the order were organized in line with this model, there were variations. In the seventeenth century, the organization (and course of promotions) of Fujisawa Shōjōkōji was based on a hierarchy starting with the heads of three dormitories of full religious (Ichinoryō, Ninoryō, and Sannoryō), followed by the First, Second, Third and Sixth Preceptors of Novices (Ichinorushui, Ninorushui, San[no]rushui, and Roku[no]rushui), and rounded off by the heads of six service groups or workshops (guides, chopstick makers, toothpick or toothbrush makers, netters, makers of spindles for scrolls, and coopers.[109]

Sonnin is credited with reorganizing the hierarchy and career of *jishū*.[110] Upon taking up residence in a temple (*zaikan*) for first time (*hatsukannin*), a novice (*hirasō*) was entered and ranked in the roll of monks and nuns called the *Taishūchō*. For three years the novice served as an attendant (*chashitsuji*) on the Fujisawa Shōnin, Yugyō Shōnin, or Konkōji Shōnin. During this period the novice was advanced through "four grades" or "rooms" (Shitsuzen to Keishitsuzen to Tōshitsuzen to Yōshitsuzen). A fee was assessed at promotion to Shitsuzen.

In the fourth year, the novice was advanced and progressed through a further ten grades or "ten rooms" (*jūshitsu*: Keishitsu, Ganshitsu, Junshitsu, Kenshitsu, Denshitsu, Gyōshitsu, Gakushitsu, Ryōshitsu, Monshitsu, and Anshitsu) and received a black surplice (*kesa*). In the fourth year after that, one was advanced over four years through the ranks of "Five Apartments" (*goken*: Jishōken, Garyūken, Bunhōken, Manshōken, and Shūryōken) and was permitted a surplice of burnt orange or brown. A fee was charged for promotion to the "Five Apartments," and the title of Oshō could be granted during this period after at least ten years in orders.

After four years, the monk (or nun) was promoted to the rank of the Two Retreats (*nian*: Jōjūan, Tōkakuan) and permitted a green surplice. Again, a fee was assessed at promotion. At this stage, one was permitted if summoned to be presented at court. In the eighteenth year, one was allowed to write and to preach. If a master, one was promoted through the five ranks named after "chapels" (Shiin, Keikōin, Tōun'in, Kōtokuin, Tōyōin).[111] If acknowledged an authority in practice or learning, one was permitted the position of head priest of a main temple (*kanju*). This was usually the highest rank achieved by a priest of a branch temple. The Yugyō Shōnin was chosen by lot from the three most talented men in the entire order, whether from main temple or branch temple, in a ceremony performed in front of the shrine of the god of Kumano, the Kumano Gongen. This apparently objective system avoided unsightly succession disputes.[112]

Sonnin's immediate successors and disciples furthered the rationalization of the order by organizing a system of higher education. Previously, training had been based on lectures by scholar monks or the Shōnin and by study at Pure Land school seminaries (*danrin*). In 1748 seminaries (*gakuryō*) were established at "both main temples" (*ryō honzan*), the Kyoto Konkōji and the Fujisawa Shōjōkōji. Each was staffed by a principal (*ryōjū*) and his assistants (*jitō*, *shūhai*, and *gakuryō rusui*), all supported by the Shūryōken. The course of study covered works of Ippen and Takuga, basic Pure Land texts, the three Pure Land sutras, and Tendai texts. A seminary was established by the

1770s at the Nichirinji in Edo. Studying at a main temple or *honzan* was called *zaikan* and a student had to finish seven years to become a head priest of a temple. In some cases, as when a student was required to return to a branch temple to become head priest, he could participate in a continuing course of ninety days every year in spring.[113]

Fees were assessed. The cost included an admission fee of 2 *bu* gold or 24 *momme* silver (roughly 2000 *mon*, or about six months' rice rations for one man) and 200 *hiki* (about one year three months' rations) assigned to the endowment. At the Konkōji, the Indai (supervisor for Yugyō Shōnin) and other monks managed the money as a capital fund for acolytes; however, fourteen *momme* (about four months' rice rations) were split between the Konkōji and the Fujisawa seminaries. Residence (*keshaku*) cost each student 6 *momme* silver per year: 3 went to the Yugyō Shōnin when he was in residence at Konkōji or to the Fujisawa Shōnin when at Shōjōkōji; 1 for the head of Konkōji, 1 for the principal, 5 *bu* each to two officials. These expenses were borne by the temple which had sent the student.[114]

This regularization of promotion through a hierarchy—especially in its method of choosing the Yugyō Shōnin—and the establishment of seminaries, although constituting a change, were clearly rational improvements to the order. They can be seen as creating a system which would be attractive as fair and open to *jishū* because of its standardized and objective criteria for advancement through the hierarchy, which itself reflected the benefits of peace and rational organization of the Tokugawa period.

Sonnin also introduced a crucial change in the succession which was directly connected to *monzeki* status. Citing as precedent the case of the twelfth Yugyō Shōnin Sonkan (1387-1400), the first Prince Imperial Abbot, he insisted that, should both the Yugyō Shōnin and Fujisawa Shōnin die, the succession to the office of Shōjōkōji pass directly to the head of the Ichirenji.[115] Again, this temple in Kōfu, Yamanashi Prefecture was the mortuary temple of the Takeda family and had been assigned the responsibility for rebuilding the Shōjōkōji. As a sign of his commitment to the precedent established by Sonkan, in 1685, a year or more after Sonnin had become Fujisawa Shōnin, he appointed as the forty-third Yugyō Shōnin Sonshin (1629-1691; YS 1685-), who had served as head of the Ichirenji. In 1691, first Sonshin and then Sonnin died within three months of each other; in accordance with Sonnin's will, the head of the Ichirenji was appointed directly—without first serving as Yugyō Shōnin—to the position of twentieth Fujisawa Shōnin. The next year he took up the tour (*kaikoku*) as the forty-fourth Yugyō Shōnin. "This was the first time that without [practicing] the career of *yugyō* someone became the [Fujisawa] Shōnin."[116] Sonnin demonstrated his farsightedness in using his prestige to introduce reforms which would strengthen the order and make provisions for emergencies. Although honored for his contributions, he was, nevertheless, the first and last of the Jishū *monzeki*.

8
Epilogue

Sonnin and his successors made further provisions for the succession to the leadership of the order, revised the hierarchy of the order, and established seminaries both to regularize the training of its leadership and to maintain the distinctive characteristics of Ippen school doctrine, which might have been difficult had formal education continued to be conducted in Pure Land school seminaries. Thus, in the seventeenth and eighteenth centuries, the Jishū adapted fully to the principles—the Confucian principles—of rationalization which dominated the society: organization on the basis of the "house" (*ie*), strict hierarchy, the assignment of duties on the basis of one's position in society, and rigorous cultivation of the individual. It also adapted to the historical fact of the absolute power of the Tokugawa shogunate. These developments, as Weber would have argued, were inevitable in the process of the routinization of charisma.[1] They do not necessarily represent a "decline" of the order or even a betrayal of the religious life originally established by Ippen. The confraternity was indeed transformed over a period of more than four hundred years into a monastic institution with fully bureaucratic features virtually indistinguishable from those of others. Nevertheless, this confraternity survived where many others had perished utterly, even to memory, and preserved within an institution fully adapted to the exigencies of historical and social realities Ippen's mission and vision of salvation for all through Rebirth in the Pure Land.

All this notwithstanding, it is important to reexamine the theme of "decline" in the history of the Jishū in order to distinguish its motifs and the evidence adduced to support it. Thus, the following chapter will focus on three principal issues: the charismatic career of the heads of the sect, the economic situation of the temples and *yugyō*, and the effects of the Meiji Restoration.

THE CHARISMATIC CAREER OF THE YUGYŌ SHŌNIN

As noted in chapter 7, Sonnin made a will ordering that, in the case of the deaths of both Yugyō Shōnin and Fujisawa Shōnin, the head of the Kōfu Ichirenji succeed to the position of Fujisawa Shōnin. On the one hand, this can be seen as merely an attempt to underscore the claim to *monzeki* status by incorporating the career of Sonkan, the former crown prince of the Southern Court who had served as head of the Ichirenji, into the career of the head of the order. On the other hand, the decision to elevate the Ichirenji in status may have had something to do with the fact that the Kyoto Konkōji had effectively been demoted in status vis à vis the Shōjōkōji, designated sole collective-main temple of the Jishū, and that the Edo Nichirinji now had considerable influence as the new liaison to the shogunate.

The head of the Ichirenji first succeeded to Shōjōkōji under the stated conditions in 1691. This modification in the career of the Yugyō Shōnin, meant to provide for measures in case of a crisis of succession, resulted in what seems to have been permanent confusion in the traditional charismatic career of the head of the order. Of the twenty-one Fujisawa Shōnin from 1691 to 1867, fourteen came from the Ichirenji; of these, six subsequently undertook *yugyō* and were counted as Yugyō Shōnin after rather than before becoming Fujisawa Shōnin. In 1711, the twenty-fourth Fujisawa Shōnin was brought from the Ichirenji; he did not practice *yugyō*. The twenty-sixth Fujisawa Shōnin, again, was brought in from the Ichirenji in 1725. In 1726, he became the fiftieth Yugyō Shōnin on the very day the twenty-seventh Fujisawa Shōnin, brought in from the Takada Shōnenji (appointed to the Ichirenji but did not actually serve), took office. In 1735, upon the death of the twenty-seventh Fujisawa Shōnin, the twenty-sixth Fujisawa Shōnin and fiftieth Yugyō Shōnin resumed the office of Fujisawa Shōnin. This also happened with the twenty-ninth Fujisawa Shōnin, who came from the Ichirenji in 1756 to assume the position without undertaking itinerancy, took up the function and position of the fifty-second Yugyō Shōnin in 1757, appointed his chief disciple (Indai) to the Ichirenji, and returned to the Fujisawa Shōjōkōji in 1761. The thirtieth Fujisawa Shōnin was promoted from the Ichirenji in 1766 (having passed through the Takada Shōnenji), and the thirty-first in 1769 (four months after the Yugyō Shōnin had taken office).[2] The thirty-third Fujisawa Shōnin came from the Ichirenji in 1779, the thirty-fifth in 1807 (and became the fifty-fifth Yugyō Shōnin in 1812), the thirty-sixth in 1815, and the thirty-seventh in 1821 (fifty-sixth Yugyō Shōnin in 1824). In 1835, the thirty-eighth Fujisawa Shōnin was brought in from the Ichirenji and died suddenly; the thirty-ninth was appointed by the shogunate. The last Fujisawa Shōnin taking office during the Tokugawa period, the forty-first, was appointed in 1855 by the shogunate even though there was a Yugyō Shōnin, who was required to retire to the Konkōji.[3] The relationship between the Yugyō Shōnin and the Fujisawa Shōnin broke down. Often there was one and not the other. There was no Fujisawa Shōnin seven times for a total of roughly thirty-seven years; there was no Yugyō Shōnin twelve time for about seventy-four years.[4] Since it was usually the case that the Fujisawa Shōnin appointed a caretaker for Shōjōkōji and took up *yugyō*, the result was that the Fujisawa Shōnin in effect subsumed the Yugyō Shōnin. Although in the eighteenth century there was an alternating system of succession (Yugyō Shōnin to Fujisawa Shōnin or Ichirenji to Fujisawa Shōnin to Yugyō Shōnin), by 1801, the balance had shifted to the Ichirenji-Shōjōkōji-Yugyō Shōnin pattern of succession.

Since the head of the order was so often drawn directly from the Ichirenji, it is easy to imagine that some Fujisawa Shōnin may have felt that they lacked the religious authority (not to mention the political connections with branch temples) that they might have had had they been chosen by lot in front of the Kumano Shrine at Shōjōkōji and as Yugyō Shōnin carried out Ippen's mission throughout the country. Therefore, they undertook *yugyō*. However, the modification to the succession ordered by Sonnin did not necessarily make inevitable the Fujisawa Shōnin's absorption of the role and identity of the Yugyō Shōnin. There was at least one other factor at work: the Nichirinji.

The Nichirinji, in the Shibazaki district of Edo, was the Jishū temple physically nearest the offices of the Tokugawa shogunate—Edo Castle—and the one with the closest relationship with it. As chief liaison or *furegashira* of the order, it functioned as the temple through which instructions of the shogunate were passed on to all the provincial *furegashira* of the order.[5] Its head priest had been an official participant in the shogun's yearly poetry gathering at the New Year since the Kan'ei period. So highly regarded was he that he was even called the "Shibazaki Shōnin."[6] Therefore, Nichirinji was the order's most important contact with the Tokugawa and became, therefore, its most important temple. The Nichirinji collected the traditions that might prove useful (borrowing texts from the Mito Tokugawa family), kept the documents, and aided other Jishū temples in their petitions to the government.[7] It was the Nichirinji which worked for and finally effected the incorporation of the Pure Land itinerant orders, the Ikkō-ha and Tenryū-ha, into the Jishū.[8]

The strategic importance of the Nichirinji is demonstrated by the fact that between 1660 and 1708 four Yugyō Shōnin were selected from the Nichirinji, three of whom were head priests of the temple: the fortieth, forty-first, forty-second, and forty-eighth.[9] This last, Fukoku (b. 1656; YS 1708-

1711, FS -1711), is better known as Donryō, who wrote two principal sources for the order's propaganda during the seventeenth and early eighteenth centuries, the *Shibazaki bunko* and the *Jishū yōryakufu*, and effected the transfer of the Ikkō-ha and Tenryū-ha to the Jishū.

The Shōjōkōji may have been the collective-main temple of the Jishū with the right to appoint the heads of important branch temples; even so, its political position had been considerably weakened by the shogunate's system of *furegashira*, whereby official relations between shogunate and Jishū were maintained not through the Shōjōkōji but through the Nichirinji. Technically bypassed by the government and thus politically diminished, the Shōjōkōji also found that the political advantage that had once accrued to the Yugyō Shōnin as joint head of the order under the Muromachi shogunate had been lost; indeed, the Yugyō Shōnin's status had been considerably reduced to that of the heads of other important branch temples when the shogunate neglected to recognize the Konkōji as joint headquarters. It is more than probable that, with neither the political clout of official relations with the shogunate nor the religious authority derived from the Yugyō Shōnin's *hijiri* functions, the Ichirenji successors to the Shōjōkōji felt impelled at least to strengthen their relations with the branch temples of the sect by arrogating the functions and therefore the religious authority of the traditional career of the Yugyō Shōnin. It would be a mistake, then, to attribute solely to Sonnin the change in the traditional succession; the Tokugawa shogunate was very clever in its tactics of weakening Buddhist sects, of which breaking down traditional organizational structures, separating out political and religious functions, and redistributing them were but a few used for the Jishū. These changes, however, represent not so much a "decline" as a demonstration of the capacity on the part of the Jishū to adapt.

THE ECONOMIC CONDITION OF THE JISHŪ

There is no clear relationship between change in the tradition of succession and problems at the local level, as Mochizuki Kazan would suggest. The principal problem of local temples seems to have been their poverty. Indeed, evidence of the poverty of Jishū temples can be found in the Yugyō Shōnin's travel diaries, the *Yugyō nikkan*. For example, as Mochizuki notes, off and on appears the term *mushūgan*, a failure to request a new head priest at the death of the last one; this was often due to a lack of or damage to the main hall or priest's quarters. A temple might be vacant for three years: it would be up to parishioners to bring in the harvests, to make the repairs to the temple, and then to send in a request for a priest. Mochizuki assumes that *mushūgan* is just one more indication, along with the 1799 report of monks absconding from both main and branch temples, of the decline in the temples and therefore in the order itself, which is attributed to the absence, physically or spiritually, of priests.[10] Tamamuro Fumio has adduced evidence of the poverty that forced even branch temples to decline the visit of the Yugyō Shōnin on tour or made it a misery to one and all. When informed of the Shōnin's plan to "drop in," branch temples might decline for economic reasons. In 1726, the Takayama Senganji sent a letter to the Yugyō Shōnin Kaison with the excuse that since it was "a small village with a low income, it would be inconvenient" to receive him. At least this temple informed Kaison in good time while he was still at the Nichirinji in Edo. However, while he was at the Kawagoe Tōmyōji, he received a message from the next stop begging to be excused because it was "shabby" and "it would be difficult to make suitable the extremely small temple for the stay." It was extremely rude to wait until the Shōnin's train was practically on the doorstep to decline the visit. Nevertheless, this seems not to have been an isolated case. A worse situation, perhaps, presented itself when an entirely unsuitable temple overestimated its capacities. In 1728, a temple with only fourteen parishioners did its best despite its poverty and poor facilities: the Yugyō Shōnin stayed one night out of courtesy, but a note was made to decline invitations in the future. That was not the only time.[11]

These reports seem to confirm an impression of widespread and systemic problems in the economy that made even life in a temple difficult to endure. The question of whether life in a temple was unendurable or life outside altogether too alluring to resist notwithstanding, one must remember to bear in mind that none of the above indicates any decline or even change in the Jishū. First, despite the preeminence of the ranking and well-connected temples, most of the sect's temples were very small and poor and probably always had been. Second, breaches of discipline were nothing new to the Jishū; indeed, they had plagued even Ippen's confraternity. Third, the whole issue of the traditional historiographic interpretation of the "decline" of Buddhism is now being subjected to the same revision as that of the decline of the national economy.[12]

It is assumed that the development of the Jishū after 1700 was influenced by a serious decline in the agricultural economy in the eighteenth and nineteenth centuries, particularly the north and east, due to volcano eruptions, tsunami, and famine. The order, so the argument goes, was gradually impoverished not only by the general economic shift from agriculture to commerce but also by, among other things, fires which repeatedly demolished Shōjōkōji, Konkōji, and other temples.[13]

It is easy to assume that Buddhist institutions were somehow restricted to limited forms of subsidization. It is true that some Buddhist temples, including Jishū temples, were heavily dependent on stipends received from the government. That does not mean that temples did not have other means of support, including fees for funerals and memorial services, not to mention "money-lending, running lotteries, [and] charging special admission [fees] for [viewing a] sacred image."[14] It is true that the tour of the Yugyō Shōnin was heavily subsidized by the shogunate and domains. That does not mean, however, that the tour was totally dependent on such support. Indeed, as seen below, the harder it was for domains to control (tax) the economy as it shifted to a commercial base, the easier it was for the Jishū, especially for the Yugyō Shōnin, to tap it. After all, Buddhism was just one more service industry; thus, as control of a domain's income shifted from the warrior governments to the peasants, merchants, and workers, those profiting in the new economy used their new wealth to purchase the services of the sect. Nowhere is this so clearly seen as in the case of the tour of the Yugyō Shōnin.

THE DOMAINS AND THE YUGYŌ SHŌNIN

Under the Tokugawa, *yugyō* was a formal affair. On the day of arrival at the border of the domain, low-ranking officials and guards, *yakunin* and *ashigaru*, were sent as escort. When the Shōnin entered the temple assigned to him during his stay, the lord sent a "banquet" of rice and miso. The domainal lord and his family attended services, either out of faith or as a formality.[15]

The train would stay at each temple for ten to fifteen days.[16] During this time, the Shōnin would distribute the *nembutsu* amulets, preside over the dancing *nembutsu*, and perform a variety of services. On the day before last, the Shōnin or a representative called on the castle to express thanks by distributing *nembutsu* amulets to the lord's family, high-ranking vassals, and officials. The next morning, he was escorted to the border where he performed a last "farewell ten nembutsu" (*owakare no jūnen*). There, the escort of the lord of the next domain would be waiting for him.[17]

It is important to consider the economics governing the relations between the Yugyō Shōnin and the domains. It is true that the condition of some domainal administrations was quite desperate. For example, in 1813 the agent of the Akita domain of Miharu sent a message to the Edo Nichirinji asking for exemption from the proposed itinerary:

> We acknowledge your announcement informing us of the Yugyō Shōnin's tour of the [lord's] residence Miharu this year. However, since the previous [year of the] Hare third year of Temmei [1783], [in] Yamashiro no kami's domain there have been bad harvests year after

year; the situation has been serious and [we have suffered an enormous] loss [in income]. Furthermore, not yet a year ago [we] were commanded [by the *bakufu*] to assist in the repair of the Sanmon Shrine [of the Enryakuji] at Sakamoto in the province of Ōmi as well as of various other temples and shrines. There being an enormous need, we ordered contributions from both town and country within the domain; this means that poverty extends to all. Beginning with [Akita] Yamashiro no kami's own entourage the nearest vassals to the most distant are managed strictly with cutbacks and there are cases where even the roof has fallen in.

This being the meaning of the above passage, the point of this is that we are in the process of taxing the domain, striving to the point of such things as forced labor and assigning duties [without pay].

Things being the way they are, we humbly announce Yamashiro no kami's decision regarding the Shōnin's tour this time of the domain.[18]

At issue here are poor harvests and shogunate exactions, the burden of which is being borne by the domain and its warriors. If the nearby Nambu domain of Morioka, economically the area's most backward, offers any analogy, then one can make some assumptions about these complaints: that the domain's troubles were exaggerated to fend off the shogunate's exactions (of which the support of the Yugyō Shōnin was but one); and that the real source of the domainal lord's economic troubles was the successful resistance to attempts to coerce peasants into paying higher taxes and those in the expanding commercial economy to pay any taxes at all.[19] The poverty claimed is that of the lord and his warriors, not that of the people. The answer from the Yugyō Shōnin's representative tactfully announced a change in the itinerary due to heavy snowfall.[20]

The relations between the shogunate and the domains (*bakuhan*) and the Jishū's mission, the tour of the Yugyō Shōnin, was very much dependent on the financial ability of the military houses, dependent on the agricultural economy as a tax base, to subsidize the tour. The tour can be seen as just one more shogunal exaction and it was often a very heavy one. It began with the shogunate's own burden: fifty horses and fifty handlers. Even so, this was not necessarily a yearly commitment. Under the Tokugawa, only one tour or *kaikoku* was permitted each Yugyō Shōnin; when the first tour of the country was finished, the Yugyō Shōnin had to stay at his own temple, the Konkōji in Kyoto. The fifty-first Yugyō Shōnin Fuson (b. 1682?; YS 1742-1754; FS -1756) stayed at the Konkōji for six years between 1748 and 1754 because he had completed his tour; he was not yet able to enter Shōjōkōji because the Fujisawa Shōnin was still alive.[21] In addition, as seen above, only half the Fujisawa Shōnin who had come from Ichirenji went on *yugyō*. For nearly seventy-five years, there was no Yugyō Shōnin at all.

The Tokugawa for the most part observed precedent established by the sixteenth century. Patronage of *yugyō* under the Muromachi shogunate was not economic, but economic support probably was given. In the sixteenth century, independent warlords passed on to their vassals the cost of the support of the trains of the two Shōnin while travelling; nevertheless, vassals made donations over and above demands made by their overlords. As demonstrated in chapter 6, a vassal of a domainal lord might donate as much as forty bales of rice as well as firewood and vegetables to subsidize the tour of a Shōnin. However, these same vassals could expect something from the Shōnin in return: one host, Agei Kakuken, recorded a flat fan (*uchiwa*) and folding fan (*ogi*) to himself from the Fujisawa Shōnin Dōnen; from the messenger a short sword and fan. In return, he feasted them on a meal including fish and saké.[22] In the sixteenth century, at least, *yugyō* was a reciprocal relationship in which the basic costs of supporting the train of the Shōnin were compensated by quite expensive ceremonial gifts. Under the Tokugawa, things were not much different. Most importantly, daimyo, as vassals of the shogun, were expected to bear a heavy burden of the cost of entertaining the Yugyō Shōnin in their domains.

Whatever the size of the Yugyō Shōnin's train, the shogunate's subsidy remained unchanged. Ōhashi observes that even with shogunal protection, there was no increase in the number of horses or personnel.[23] In the sixteenth century, the train had numbered "several hundred" and three or four boats were required to ferry the train of the twenty-fourth Yugyō Shōnin—with its "monks, nuns, lepers, and outcasts." Tamamuro calculates 460 people in Dōnen's train in 1584, religious and teamsters or porters. There were also many hangers-on. A contemporary witness, Agei Kakuken, reported a domainal requisition of eighty riding horses and 300 pack horses for Dōnen: that meant eighty religious as well as 150-310 handlers. Obviously, the Tokugawa shogunate was taking the grand trains of the two Shōnin of the sixteenth century into consideration when considering the size of the train to be subsidized.[24]

Numbers are not always given; nevertheless, the extent of the imposition on a domain boggles the mind. In 1675, as noted above, the train was great enough for one domain to conscript from peasants 1300 bearers and 212 horses. In 1700, there were 75 religious in the train; in 1716, 81 (including cook and 13 menials). In 1731, for Kaison, on *yugyō* in Tango Province, 15 boats and 134 boatmen were conscripted.[25] In 1744, on entering Iwakidaira

Fuson brought a train of 70 horses and 179 people, of whom all but 43 monks and nuns were porters.[26] This number apparently did not include guests and a local escort of perhaps twenty.[27] In effect, the train of the Yugyō Shōnin was a mobile temple, with all religious, guests, craftsmen, and servants thereto appertaining. These included prayer-bead makers, hanging-scroll makers for the large-sized Six Character Name calligraphies produced by the Shōnin, bedding-and-clothes makers, kitchen staff, watchmen and servants—all of whom were religious—and tatami makers, lacquerers, stone cutters and coopers, who may have been lay.[28] The major responsibility for feeding, housing, and policing the train fell to the domain.

The extra demands on the domainal lord's purse might be exacted only once in thirty years.[29] Even so, yugyō was a near monumental undertaking requiring both careful planning and considerable flexibility. As soon as a tour was scheduled, all domains and shogunate officials concerned were notified. According to Mochizuki, messengers were sent at least half a year ahead.[30] However, as little as less than three months notice might be given.[31] Emergencies were handled by the official called Shūryōken serving the Yugyō Shōnin, who was sent ahead to finalize arrangements.[32]

The cost to the domainal lord began with the requirements to assign many men to the train as escort and traffic control: in 1859, one domain supplied 120-130 men every day—from officials down to ashigaru—and lodged the train in twenty-four houses.[33] In addition, the domain was required to repair roads used by the train. The itinerary might follow not only those highways with official post stations but also pass through towns and villages on side roads, such as the route Sonnin used in 1674 from Ōmi Province: to transport the train, the Hikone domain had to conscript porters and horses from surrounding villages.[34]

The Tokugawa government required more: the repair and refurbishment of temples used by the train. For example, the official appointed in late 1743 by the Naitō domain of Iwakidaira received lists of requests for repairs from the three temples assigned to the Yugyō Shōnin's train: 87 items from the Jōsaiji, 23 from the Dairinji, and 22 from the Kōgenji. A month later, domain officials were sent to inspect them: repaired or replaced were 153.5 tatami mats, 14 thin mats, 166 sections of wainscoting, 179 indoor sliding doors, and 669 outdoor sliding doors. At Jōsaiji alone, repairs had been made to the roof of the temple reception room, Shōnin's living room, wood and paper doors (18 rolls of paper were used), the bamboo floor veranda, the plank veranda, the Shōnin's toilet (roof, bowl, and cover), bath, another toilet and bath, the water-supply system, corridor, fences, and gate. In addition, a roofed stage for distributing the nembutsu amulets, a small house of planks for officials and another for the menials of the train had been built—and more.[35] Preparations for the Yugyō Shōnin himself were those for a domainal lord: he was provided wash-cloth stand, bathtub, ladle, toilet paper, small offering stand of plain wood, dresser, candles, rainwear for train, doctor and emergency room.[36]

Repairs were made to any temple, Jishū or not, assigned to the Yugyō Shōnin. For example, in 1731 the Kyōgoku of Toyooka domain (15,000 koku) in Tajima Province ordered the repair and refurbishment (bath, toilet, reception room, etc.) of the Raigoji, which belonged to the Pure Land sect.[37]

The domain even found itself responsible for meals for the train. The Naitō domain was to provide the Yugyō Shōnin the evening meal on the day of arrival, to consist of three main and seven side dishes. Sixty-three religious were to be served according to the custom at Jōsaiji; five escorts, two main and five side dishes; thirty-six novices attached to the Yugyō Shōnin, a main and five side dishes; twelve menials, a main and three side dishes. After the morning meal the next day, the Yugyō Shōnin's kitchen would handle the meals. In addition, the Naitō contributed charcoal, vegetables, and twenty bales of hulled rice (less than .03 percent of its official income).[38] However, the donations did not end with this. From the daimyō came ceremonial gifts of noodles (somen), confectionery, and sugar.[39]

It is nearly impossible to calculate the total outlay of the domain for the Yugyō Shōnin. However, the subsidy made yugyō easier for the Yugyō Shōnin, not possible.

Every attempt was made to lighten the burden of the temples involved in yugyō. In advance of yugyō, letters were also sent by the Shūryōken to branch temples on the proposed itinerary.[40] Instructions called for modest reception ceremonies, simple meals, simple offerings to the Shōnin appropriate to social standing, and the immediate notification of Shōjōkōji of the names of all domainal and village officials to be involved. The Shūryōken also pointed out that the visit would conform to precedent, that the support of the domain would preclude any undue economic hardship on the temple, and that construction, repairs, and replacement of tatami should be undertaken conscientiously because the temple would be under the scrutiny of people from other sects.[41] An important point to consider is that the Yugyō Shōnin also sent (in addition to ceremonial gifts) supplies, about half the value of the domain's donations, to the temple to help cover expenses so that the branch temple was, as promised, not burdened: in the case of the 1744 visit to Iwakidaira, supplies donated included eleven bales of hulled rice and money to the value of 18,000 copper coins (equivalent to rice rations for one man for 1,800 days or nearly five years).[42]

KANJIN

During his stay, the Yugyō Shōnin would engage in a range of activities that would "cement" relations with the domain, the branch temple, important patrons, and the people on the whole—the *kechienshū*. The first and foremost of these activities was the distribution of the small *nembutsu* charms or *fuda*; this was called *fusan*.

From the diaries of *yugyō*, the *Yugyō nikkan*, Tamamuro has gleaned a figure of 70,300 for the number of *nembutsu* amulets distributed by Kaison in 1727 (five entries) but only 2,000 in 1731 (one entry).[43] Just how incomplete these figures are can be demonstrated by the fact that in 1744 at the Jōsaiji in Iwakidaira, 36,300 amulets were distributed in just 10 days (a low of 339 on the last day, a high of 5,996 on the fourth).

The faith in the efficacy and reception of these *fuda* is demonstrated by stories of miracles. The *fuda* cured illness, including eye illness, according to one entry.[44] A three-year old was cured of an eye illness in the Sekiyado domain of Shimōsa Province.[45] Another source reports that the wife of a farmer in Mikawa Province received a *nembutsu fuda* from the Yugyō Shōnin as an amulet for safe childbirth, ate it, and eventually gave birth to a baby holding the amulet in the left hand.[46]

The Yugyō Shōnin distributed not only the *nembutsu* amulets but also a variety of other charms and amulets. From the hands of the Yugyō Shōnin people received the ten *nembutsu*, large Six Character Name, statues, and enrollment in the death register. In twelve days recorded in 1708, 1984 items were distributed, of which 1175 included traditional Six Character Names, *fuda*, enrollment, and "main images" (most likely large copies of the *nembutsu* for altars); the rest were an assortment of charms.[47] The *Yugyō nikkan* reports charms handed out to lords, officials, and commoners. As Ōhashi notes, women wanted charms for love, easy childbirth, and protection against lightning. Men of the samurai class wanted charms for prowess in education and the martial arts. Others wanted charms for wealth and against illness.[48] Whether a price was charged is not clear.

The prices of other benefits and services, however, are clearly stated. Although the complete death register of the Yugyō Shōnin is no longer available (due to various fires, specifically one in the 1850s at the Konkōji), the *Yugyō nikkan* preserves some indication of the fee for having one's name entered into the official death register, or "kakochō iri," also called "kechimyaku," also called "gyakushū," as seen in entries in the *Jishū kakochō* and *Tōtakusan kakochō*.[49] This was not free: it usually cost 100 *hiki* (roughly equivalent to rice rations for 250 days). During a period of forty-one days at the Edo Asakusa Nichirinji, seventy-four names were entered on eleven days in 1726 for a total of 185,000 *mon* (about 50.7 years' worth of rice rations).[50] One Takazawa Tarōbei paid one *ryō* gold (400 days' rations) to have himself and his wife entered by the Yugyō Shōnin while he was at the Hamagawa Raigoji. Members of other sects, especially nobles, had their names entered.[51]

Another way for the order to acknowledge patronage was to grant posthumous religious names (*hōmyō*): *daishi* ("lay sister"), *koji* ("lay brother"), and *in* ("[resident of a] chapel"). These, too, cost, with the price established in the time of the forty-ninth Yugyō Shōnin, Ippō (b. 1660?; YS 1712-1721, FS -1725): for *daishi*, three pieces of silver (1,290 days' rations); for *koji*, three pieces of silver: for *in*, two hundred *hiki* (500 days'). There appears to have been a discount for two or more names. In 1726, one Nagano Jūdayū paid two hundred *hiki* gold for *in*, *koji*, and *daishi* names for his parents. The price dropped to one hundred *hiki* gold for *in*, *koji*, and *daishi* names for a another man and his wife.[52] Or perhaps the order took what was offered rather than establishing a set price. There are also cases of granting garments and Amida names, also in return for sizeable contributions. This is considered an indication of "decline," a sale of office for especially important parishioners.[53] However, the compromise on the price indicates that the relationship represented by the exchange of money for religious names was more important than the amount of money exchanged. It is also important to remember that according to *hijiri* practice—especially in the tradition of the Yūzū *nembutsu* with which the order early identified itself—salvation was a matter of mutual aid and commitments were recorded in registers. All who donated became members of the community who were saved and by their donations assisted others; registration was originally a membership list, not necessarily a guarantee of salvation.

The relationship represented by these exchanges of money for religious dignities as a truly religious one can be seen in the fact that donations were made often not for oneself but for others. In 1727, the daughter of one Onoderamura Heizaemon donated 2,500 *mon* (250 days' rations) for a service for those souls of the dead without family to provide for them, the hungry ghosts ("mizu gaki hōyō"). The parishioners of the Kaneda Anyōji donated 5,000 *mon* for a memorial service ("ekō"). Gotō Goemon donated 2,500 *mon* for a memorial service for his ancestors. And a village donated 5,000 *mon* to the Yugyō Shōnin and 7,500 (for a total of 1250 days' or about 3.4 years' rice rations) to others in his train ("taishū") for a memorial service for hungry ghosts ("segaki kūyō").[54] Peasants even made outright donations: the Shōnin collected 38.5 *ryō* 2 *shū* (gold) (rations for 15,450 days or 42.3 years) at one stop from 131 peasants in what is now Gumma Prefecture.[55] The last two cases deserve comment: they indicate the permeation of cash and commerce into the countryside and the ability of even peasants to accumulate surplus with which, like their betters, they bought luxuries and services. The Yugyō Shōnin also used the tour to reenforce relations with branch temples. As noted above, the Yugyō Shōnin made contributions to the branch temple to cover expenses. Even more helpful was the lending of treasures for display in order to assist the branch temples in raising funds. The treasures brought by the train are not all listed and the number may have been twelve or more. They included the *Ippen Shōnin engi e*, a ritual implement shaped like a lotus bulb on a stalk called the "Kajime no shakushi," a figure of Benten (one of the seven gods of luck and worshipped at Enoshima near Kamakura), the Amida embroidered, it was claimed, by Princess Chūjō at the Taimadera in Yamato Province, and the helmet said to have belonged to the famous and aged warrior of the twelfth century, Saitō no bettō Sanemori.[56]

These treasures were borrowed, for example, by the Shin'ōji in Mito, Hitachi Province to exhibit along with its own famous Kannon specifically to raise funds for its main hall. Other temples borrowing the Yugyō Shōnin's treasure to raise money included the Jōkyūji in Fukui, Echizen Province in 1729 and the Shikajima Shrine in Ichinomiya, Hitachi Province in 1727. While the Yugyō Shōnin was staying at the Shōmyōji in Fuchū in Echizen Province, the Jishinji, which displayed its Kannon once every thirty-three years, displayed it on the occasion of the Yugyō Shōnin's tour. It is not clear whether these religious treasures were used primarily for preaching or for fundraising by the Yugyō Shōnin's train. On the whole, Tamamuro concludes that the main purpose of display or *kaichō* was to gather people to whom to preach and distribute the *nembutsu* amulets. At other times, these were displayed on various occasions to people of all ranks, lords in their castles, officials at temples, and commoners in villages. How or whether admission was charged is not indicated.[57]

The Yugyō Shōnin could be used to build up the number of sub-branch temples. There is at least one example of using the prestige of the Yugyō Shōnin to get a new temple recognized despite the ban on new temples. There was one attempt to revive an abolished temple by building a retreat on farmers' land, attaching a "chapel" or *in* name (as a sub-temple), and getting a sacred image and a calligraphy of the Six Character Name from the Yugyō Shōnin as well as a priest from the Toyama Jōzenji, where the Yugyō Shōnin was staying in 1728.[58] The list of temples in the far north (Tōhoku) to which the Shūryōken sent instructions in 1743 included two which were not on the 1633 list of branch temples submitted to the shogunate.[59]

In addition, the branch temple could also look forward to promotions on the occasion of the Yugyō Shōnin's visit. In 1727, the head of the Kōgakuji was promoted to Nian (2,000 *mon* or rations for 200 days), the head of the Yamagata Kōdaiji was promoted on his retirement (2,500 *mon*), and the head of the Manjūji to Nian (2000 *mon*).[60] Other ceremonies carried out by the Yugyō Shōnin at branch temples increased the prestige of the temple and very likely attracted the public and patronage. The New Year was spent at important temples like the Sendai Shinfukuji (85 days, 1727-1728), the Kanazawa Ōsenji (68 days, 1728-1729), and the Yamaguchi Zenfukuji (53 days, 1731-1732) as well as at temples important in the history of the order: Okudani Hōjōji (area where Ippen was raised), Kōbe Shinkōji (where Ippen is buried) or Kyoto Konkōji (established by Donkai). It offered the temples the opportunity to host one of the order's most important ceremonies, the New Year's ceremony Gomettō (Hitotsubi), which used to be called the *Saimatsu betsuji*.[61]

The *yugyō* subsidized and protected by shogunate and domain presented the Jishū with many opportunities to carry out its principal mission, to build up the community of the saved. Like all communities, especially the *hijiri* communities of the middle ages, the Jishū community was built upon carefully negotiated exchanges of practical assistance. In exchange for the protection and subsidies of the Tokugawa shogunate, the Jishū offered truly practical assistance of a political nature. Like the Ashikaga shoguns and the warlords of the sixteenth century, the Tokugawa shoguns were able to test their authority over its vassals; vassals were given the opportunity to affirm their loyalty. In exchange for patronage expressed in devotion and donations, ordinary people received a variety of material and religious benefits—and, increasingly, opportunities to enhance their status in their own communities through what can be called the purchase of specific religious services from the Yugyō Shōnin, one of the few commodities not prohibited by contemporary sumptuary laws. *Hijiri* practices for community formation clearly had economic implications; the Yugyō Shōnin had at his disposal a variety of strategies for raising funds and they translated easily from the agricultural economy to the slowly but inexorably emerging commercial sector. The Jishū's ability to adapt to the new economy would certainly preclude a "decline" due to economic changes.

Under the Tokugawa, *yugyō* was sometimes criticized for its size and the burden it placed on the people.[62] Mochizuki points out the resentment of domainal lords who were not adherents.[63] (One might ask whether the Yugyō-ha was functioning as a lightning rod for the shogunate from whom, after all, all the orders came.) In 1695, for example, the forty-fourth Yugyō Shōnin Sontsū (b. 1640; YS 1692-1695) was returning to Hyōgo, near modern Kōbe, because of illness. At Sadowara in Hyūga Province, his progress was observed by the Nichiren Fuju-fuse (no give, no take) priest Nikkō, who observed in his diary,

> Today the departure of the Yugyō [Shōnin], the several hundreds of men and horses, the heaviness of the ornaments were just as though they resembled the tour of an imperial prince abbot. I think that in recent years the tour of the Yugyō [Shōnin has become] an extravagant trip [and] violates the custom of creating religious community of the tour of the founder Ippen.[64]

One can only respond that even Ippen had known prosperity and that prosperity was no hindrance to the Jishū's mission. Nevertheless, the times had changed, the economy had changed, and the shogunate and domains were no longer able to afford maintaining the mission. In the Ansei period (1854-1860), too, it was called an unnecessary economic burden.[65] Nevertheless, the expense and trouble to which the domains were put were of use to the Tokugawa shogunate, just as they had been to the lords of domains of the sixteenth century: they were a demonstration and execution of the shogunate's political power over its vassals and can be thought of as just one more obligation—like alternate residence and dredging the shogun's castle moat—that kept them busy and poor. One shogunate political adviser, Ogyū Sorai (1666-1728), understood the value of the Yugyō Shōnin's train when in his *Seidan* he wrote of the Tokugawa subsidy as "a special case which must be honored," although within limits.[66] In the end, however, economic pressures forced the shogunate to rescind part of its subsidy of *yugyō*: in 1835, during the Tempō famine, the shogunate Magistrate for Temples and Shrines, Inoue Kawachi no kami, informed the Shōjōkōji that the Yugyō Shōnin would have to absorb the cost for the porters.[67] That year, the new Fujisawa Shōnin had just been promoted from the Ichirenji, which made *yugyō* unnecessary. In any case, there had not been both a Yugyō Shōnin and a Fujisawa Shōnin since 1800 and there would not again be until 1855.

THE EFFECTS OF THE MEIJI RESTORATION

From around 1800, the problem of the agricultural economy as the tax base for the administrations of shogunate and domains converged with growing anxiety concerning international relations as more and more foreign ships, especially English and Russian, were sighted in Japanese waters. When Commodore Matthew C. Perry first dropped anchor in Uraga Bay in 1853 and a year later persuaded the shogunate to sign a provisional treaty, the shogunate found itself in an untenable position: hampered by its impoverished treasury, unable militarily to keep foreigners out or militarily to suppress recalcitrant domains, and very likely unwilling to risk sacrificing the whole of Japan to a foreign takeover while it waged a long civil war, the shogunate in 1867 surrendered the government of the nation to Emperor Mutsuhito (1852-1912; r. 1867-), subsequently known as the Meiji Emperor.

The Meiji Restoration ended the official position of Buddhism as a state-sponsored religion. Those who depended on the Tokugawa system went under with it.[68] In 1868, the policy of separating Shinto and Buddhism (*shimbutsu bunri*) was adopted. However, for both ideological and economic reasons, the anti-Buddhism movement had already been in full swing among the adherents of the Imperial Restoration, even long-time adherents of the Jishū. For example, the lord of the Satsuma domain Shimazu Hisamitsu (1817-1887) lambasted Buddhism in 1866 in an address to the gods (*saimon*) at Kirishima Shrine:

> As for the coming of the teachings of the so-called Englightened One of filthy countries, the bewitching words of the bewitching monks who study those teachings lead ordinary men astray [to] abandon the hundred and thousand treasures of the [Japanese] past and build thousands of temples [to a foreign religion].

He thus announced his intention to ban Buddhism and to promote Shinto within his own domain. In 1869 a shift was made from Buddhist to Shinto funerals. The Buddhist festivals of Chūgen and Obon were banned and replaced with Shinto worship and ceremonies. All temples were abolished and religious secularized: Buddhist images and texts were burned in front of domain officials; stone images were smashed and used to reinforce river banks.[69]

In the provinces of Satsuma, Ōsumi, and Hyūga, 1066 Buddhist temples were abolished, 15,118 *koku* confiscated, and 2968 religious secularized. Of forty-two temples and fifteen Jishū "chapels" in Hyūga Province listed in the 1788 *Kakuha*, only four remained in post-Restoration Miyazaki Prefecture; in Ōsumi Province not one remained of ten. In Satsuma Province of forty-two (and eighteen other buldings), only the Jōkōmyōji, the mortuary temple of the Shimazu family, remained and not much of it: the greater part of its 554 ken (1002.74 m) by 260 ken (470.6 m) grounds was given over to make a shrine and its graveyard. In 1876, due to True Pure Land (Shinshū) activism permission was finally granted to reestablish temples; the Jōkōmyōji was reestablished and its succession rights recognized.[70]

In the end, after surveying the damage, the Shōjōkōji found that of its own 274 branch temples, of the eighty-five possessing endowments only thirty-one per cent were left; and yet, of those eighty five temples, 65.8% had endowments of less than twenty *koku*, and fifty-five per cent had less than five *koku*. Most of the temples had been very small and poor and they still were. Thus the Jishū found itself reduced from 1008 temples and buildings to 498 temples.[71]

Removal of property was followed by removal of special status: in 1872, monks were officially permitted to eat meat, drink liquor, marry wives, grow hair, and wear lay clothes. In the ninth month of that year, they were instructed to use family names. They were now subject to military service and the draft, not to mention taxation.[72]

The Buddhist institutions united to save Buddhism and Jishū clerics were involved in the efforts: Sonkaku (b. 1817?: YS/FS 1889-1903) head of the sect, tried to mitigate the effects; Kōno Ō'a (1838?-1906) of the Kōbe Shinkōji took part in councils of the Buddhist church, in which he acquitted himself well. Nevertheless, the Jishū itself suffered the permanent loss of government support for *yugyō* and the unique structure of its double leadership when the positions of the Yugyō Shōnin and Fujisawa Shōnin were combined by law in 1885.[73] Over the years, whole schools and individual temples broke away: the Bamba Rengeji broke away and joined the Pure Land or Jōdo sect in 1942 on the occasion of the six hundredth anniversary of its founder Ikkō Shunjō (1239-1287); the Ichirenji, too, broke away in 1952 after a dispute over succession and became independent. The great Kyoto temples were amalgamated: the Konkōji was combined with the Chōrakuji and its lands sold off; one of the most important temples in the religious and cultural life of premodern Japan ceased to be in 1908.[74] There are now only about four hundred temples and many priests have to administer three or four. Even so, the Jishū survives.

The Jishū community in premodern Japan had been based on the network of relationships created and reenforced by generations of Yugyō Shōnin, who always made the mission worthwhile to just about everyone. Local temples made out splendidly: they received donations from the Yugyō Shōnin and because he was there the domain made extensive repairs; they raised funds for projects of their own by receiving donations from those who came to see treasures borrowed from the order. Their head priests received promotions not far away at the main temple but in ceremonies in their own communities, where they could be seen and appreciated. Memorial services for previous Shōnin or New Year's services were that much more special when conducted by the Shōnin.

The local people did well, too. *Nembutsu fuda* and other charms were distributed. Holy images were displayed. Wealthy parishioners could gain status in their own communities by sponsoring services; they could express their devotion with donations and receive expressions of gratitude of handwritten Six Character Names, religious names, and entry in the list of the community of the saved. The ordinary folk got children born safely, eye illnesses cured, hungry ghosts pacified, and tickets to paradise. The exalted took the opportunity to demonstrate their loyalty to the shogun and their virtue to the people, and the shogunate to demonstrate its power. And if the shogunate would not allow the people freely to go on pilgrimage to Buddhist temples, then it would at least bring Buddhist salvation to the people. Everyone belonged one way or the other to this religious community; the Yugyō-ha indeed was one of the very few representatives of a nation-wide community in an otherwise fragmented political system.

So important was the mission of the Yugyō Shōnin to shogunate, domain, and people, that support was only reluctantly withdrawn and only for severe economic or political reasons. Damage to the Jishū was done principally by the supporters of the Meiji government, who tried to destroy its past as well as its future by reducing the sect in terms of its political effectiveness, economic base, and numbers. Even so, the brunt was borne by the temples and not so much by the mission. There might be fewer and smaller trips and fewer attendants, but the mission continued.

The aim of the *hijiri* tradition was to create a religious community and this the Yugyō-ha and Jishū achieved. If it was diminished, it was so in the ideological and economic interests of a new government, whose apologists propagated the tradition of Buddhism in decline as well as that of vilifying in histories the Tokugawa regime with which it had been identified. Nevertheless, the future of Japan could not be so easily rent from its past. Even the Meiji Emperor, like so many before him, passed the night at the Fujisawa Shōjōkōji when travelling the highway between Kyoto and Tokyo.[75]

Appendix

1. "Jikū shojō"[1]

Item: As for the rules for *jishū* accompanying armies, although a letter was sent from the Yugyō Shōnin to several places during the Kan'ō period, there must now be not a single *jishū* who has been able to see it or heard about it from others. Therefore, because there are those who have acted as they pleased, saying it was the wish of their patrons (*danna*) or that it was convenient at the time, they have ended up as objects of scorn of followers of the order and have lost their own [chance of] Rebirth in paradise. Even though they have made themselves useful to their patrons, because they have broken the rules of the order, the path of the jishū is cut off to them, and, moreover, suffering will result even for their patrons. Thus, the following articles must be understood both by laity and religious.

Item: The purpose of *jishū* going on the same road (*dōdō*) is to administer the ten *nembutsu* at the time of death. When in times of war, free passage is denied to the warrior, *jishū* must never be sent to carry a message or a letter for the purposes of battle because, as *jishū*, they will be allowed to pass freely. However, if the reason is to rescue people, women, children, and non-combatants, there is no objection.

Item: In the field, there will be times when you hold your patron's armor. There is no objection concerning articles such as cuirass and helmet. That is because they are things which protect the body. But *jishū* must never touch things like bows and arrows and weapons. That is because they are used to kill.

181

Item: As for the Year End Special Ceremony, there is of course a rule that even if you are in the field, you must perform cold water austerities, prepare the foods, wear *jishū* robes, and chant the *nembutsu*. However, depending on the situation, water may be hard to find. You may not be able to serve the foods you wish. Again, it does no good to be so weak that you cannot attend your patron properly at his death; since you have followed him, eat whenever you can, and perform cold water austerities, and prepare the proper foods as well as you can according to the conditions. In the situation [ ], perform the ceremonies according to the rules.

Item: When a battle is about to begin, you must think. When you joined the *jishū*, you turned over to the Chishiki your very life. Knowing that the reason for which you did this is the Rebirth in paradise at hand, you must not only lead your patron in chanting the *nembutsu* at his death, but achieve your own Rebirth in paradise. These instructions must be proclaimed to *jishū* who may not be aware of them, that they might understand them well.

Respectfully
Namu Amidabutsu
Sixth year of Ōei, eleventh month, twenty-fifth day
Ta'amidabutsu

2. "Nagano gosho"[2]

Letter dispatched concerning Nagano in the province of Ise. Second year of Bunna, ninth month, last day.

In regard to the news that the *jishū* of the Nagano temple must be expelled and replaced; what is the reason for this? For, to call one among the *jishū* friend and one foe is by no means the way of one who has entered religious life. This is the work of devils.[3] However, since there is no estrangement among *jishū* in different places in the many provinces, clearly they all follow the same way. When during times of warfare, *jishū* and their patrons (*ganshū*) hide their traces in mountain and field, accompanying nuns come to their aid. Probably because our monks and nuns follow the same principle, even now warriors requesting our monks and nuns are very many. If they were to abandon this principle, what would happen in the end? That, not knowing the reason, you have tried to make *jishū* your enemy, I feel is most regrettable.

Accompanying *jishū* who, in this way, with prejudiced minds, do not teach this principle and give the patrons the idea that they are on the same side, are not *jishū*. That it results in your becoming an unbeliever is a very sad thing for you. I must submit this religious instruction. As for the shogun, I see only that he surpasses men in bravery. When I last met him in Kayazu, I saw that he knew [the difference between] good and evil. If he should agree with you on such an issue, it would be most regrettable. You must discuss this affair with him at a time convenient to you.
Respectfully

3. On the Fujisawa Shōnin after the loss of Shōjōkōji

   Igyō ("Fujisawa Shōnin" 1514-1518), a member of the Sasaki Kōsaka family of Ōmi Province, first built a temple in Mino and then went to his own family memorial temple of Jōdaiji because of trouble in Mino.[4] Fugai (YS 1520-1526) returned to the Hōdoji in Etchū Province (now Shinminato City in Toyama Prefecture) where he had served more than thirty years and to his converts among the local magnates, including the Vice-military governor (*shugodai*) Jinbō Yoshimune.[5] Forced out by an invasion from Echigo under Nagao Tamekage (d. 1538+, father of the famous Uesugi Kenshin), Fugai sought the protection of Takeda Nobutora (1493-1573, father of the famous Takeda Shingen) and brought the badly-damaged Amida triad of the Fujisawa temple to the Kōfu Ichirenji.[6] Butten (FS 1528-1571 and one of five Shōnin from the Nihonmatsu, a cadet branch of the Hatakeyama, one of the three Kyoto Shogunal Deputy or *kanrei* families), established himself first at the Saihōji in Tsuruga, Echizen Province and then, when it burned down (and with it Shōjōkōji's death register, the *Tōtakusan kakochō*) in 1557, at the Shinzenkōji nearby in Igawa.[7] In fact, he sought the protection of the newly-risen Asakura, vassals of the Shiba, also a Shogunal Deputy family, who had supplanted them and established a base at Ichijōgatani; there he joined other Ashikaga refugees including the last shogun Yoshiaki and his maternal uncle.[8] Yūsan ("FS" 1573-1583) retired to the Saihōji in Echizen, which passed in 1573 from the Asakura to Oda Nobunaga, who gave it to Shibata Katsuie. Dōnen (1584-1587) retired to the Kōshōji in Obi in Tonogōri, Hyūga Province (Saito City), under the protection of the Shimazu (whose own memorial temple, the Jōkōmyōji in Kagoshima, had been converted by Ippen in 1277).[9] And Fukō ("FS" 1589-1626), of a cadet branch of the Satake family, took refuge with his relatives, who in 1591 built the Shin'ōji for him in Mito.[10]

4. "Letter from Yanagiwara Sukesada"[11]

The fact of your many years of ministry has come to the attention of the emperor. Thus, in order that he might make a karmic connection [with you toward his salvation], that there be an interview, that he might deign to cause [you] to come to the capital, he has given the order for this official quickly to notify [you]. Although the distance certainly [will be] a great inconvenience, because it is an imperial order, it is of utmost importance that you thrust aside all obstacles and come quickly to the capital. Because, particularly since summer the emperor has been unwell, it is important that [you] make haste as quickly as possible. Because [your] interview at the palace at this time will [result in] the restoration of your order and perpetuation of your reputation into eternity, this is of course [an opportunity] highly to be appreciated. [The messenger] Matsugi Hyōgo no suke will inform you further. Respectfully sincerely yours 8.4 from [Yanagiwara] Sukesada [to] the honorable priest Fujisawa Shōnin [through his official] Takemuroka.[12]

5. From the *Yugyō sanjūissō Kyō-Ki goshūgyōki*

In the eightieth year of the reign of the late retired Emperor Gonara, how affected he was by [concerns] for the world after his death! Making lord Yanagiwara his envoy [he sent an] imperial message to the twenty-fifth Yugyō Shōnin [then] residing in Echizen. Although under the imperial order to proceed to the palace in order [to grant] the ten *nembutsu* [and make] a karmic connection, considering that [the Shōnin] was bent with age he did not go. Even now this is regretted by all the *jishū* of [our] followers. As for the imperial wish afterwards, what must [the emperor] have thought? Because of his resentment, we are thus [conducting] a memorial service today.[13]

. . . On the thirteenth of the same month he went to the palace; he inquired of the bearer of the imperial order Kajūji-dono as to the present requirements of the palace. The Yugyō [Shōnin] was carrying a "Fushi" fan [*uchiwa*]; even though there were no details of precedent, since Ippen had not received an imperial summons to court, he was now carrying one when he went to court. Two monks of Dormitory (*ryō*) rank and others attended him as far as the steps of the imperial residence and [stayed to await him] in the garden. Then he proceeded to [the residence of] the Crown Prince. At that time he caused many nobles to accept the [*nembutsu*] amulets. Afterwards, when he had visited the throne room and office of the sacred mirror, lower-ranking ladies issued from the palace; he distributed more [*nembutsu*] amulets than had ever been heard of in previous generations."[14]

. . . On the fifth day of the second month, Kajūji Dainagon-dono [came to escort him on] this propitious day to the palace. That is, to the imperial residence itself. The emperor was smiling slightly [and said that] he valued the circumstances highly because he was able [to realize] his desire [to receive] the [*nembutsu*] amulets [and] ten *nembutsu* easily without moving [from the] the imperial residence. He personally inspected the precious treasures of generations of Yugyō [Shōnin], including the ten volume illustrated life [*Ippen Shōnin engi e*], the gong of Ippen, the Tenjin *shinpitsu* Six Character Name, and the star inkstone. From between the screens, remembered as being far to the rear, emerged first one beautiful elderly woman and ten ladies stretched out their hands from the spaces [between] the folding screens, whom [the Shōnin] caused to receive the [*nembutsu*] amulets. From the Nagabashi lady official the Shōnin received paper and fan, aloes and money, and from the nobles court dress. Truly, the scent of the nine-layer blinds wafted faintly as far as the steps, as far as the attendants [and] both Ninoryō and Rokunoryō. Furthermore, the entire party of attendants were waiting in the garden; from there they went to the new Nijō palace [of the Crown Prince]. [His consort] the daughter of Kajūji-dono was there too [and] lady officials came forward to offer *manju* and tea. It was very pleasing that the Crown Prince of the new palace [made] a karmic connection [by receiving] a [*nembutsu*] amulet and the ten *nembutsu*. In time they retired. Ashō [Kajūji Dainagon and] Kōmon [Susuki Chūnagon], the two imperial messengers, [said that] the emperor had heard that because [the Shōnin's] journey to the capital was particularly miraculous they had brought in the New Year at the Shichijō [Konkōji] and had performed cold-water austerities [throughout] the cold days and nights. The rules of the founder Ippen who abandoned the body [in a life] so [difficult] it was hard to bear were proper practices suitable to an age which would not extend as far as the [very] beginning of the [period] of the end of the world (*masse*). From now on he would wear ramie and thinking it a sign of benefits widely [distributed] he bestowed thirty lengths of cloth [which the Shōnin] received. The compassion, doctrines, and prestige of the order were [a source of] envy to other schools. Then [the Shōnin] informed Kajūji Dainagon and Susuki Chūnagon that the *jishū* with whom he was staying certainly would like to see the palace. [They] worshipped the imperial throne, stories about which they had heard while in provinces far and distant. It is difficult to express in words how fine was the architecture of the hundred palaces within the imperial compound. [They were] entranced by the famous garden [with its] pond, standing stones, and deeply [penetrating] scent of plum blossoms—they remembered with deep gratitude. It was the utmost experience of their lives. People expressing their admiration said things such as that Unbō, of the Tōdō [and former head priest] of the Nanzenji, living in the capital for several years, at this time [had remarked] what a destiny [must lie in wait] over and above the itinerancy and circuit [preaching] incompatible with viewing the inner palace. What a miracle was the [granting] of the ten *nembutsu* that inclined the imperial word and head.[15]

6. *Shōnenji okibumi*[16]

(On the back) [*sic*] A book left to posterity on the [document under the] seal of the shogun (*kubō sama*)

Two imperial orders [instructing] designation of this temple (Shōnenji) [and] Kōmyōin as *chokuganjō* 1465/Kanshō 6.11.6. Kajūji [Ujinaga] is the agent; [communications are to be] addressed to Iio Saburōzaemon Hiko[saburō Tameasa][17]

The honorable seventeenth Yugyō Shōnin: when in the capital summoned by the shogun [Ashikaga Yoshimasa], the Shōnin was informed by Ise [Sadachika {1417-1473}]-dono that, in the time of the thirteenth head priest [of Shōnenji], this temple along with Kōmyōin (first built by the head priest Mi'a who had come from the Kōshōji in Hyōgo where he had previously been head priest), the Kōsokuji, and Kōshōji [had] become *gokiganji* 1458/Chōroku 2.12.26.[18]

Conferral of [a document under the shogun's] seal: (At this time the magistrate [administering the document under] the seal was the brother of Ise [Sadachika, Ise] Hyōgo [Sadamune]-dono).

As official gifts, [the choice of] tray and incense container (an article worth four thousand *hiki* of money was [made according] to the plan of Ise [Sadachika]). The Shōnin brought [these as a gift for] the shogun.

1.8 of the third year of the same (Chōroku, 1459), official gifts [from the shogun]: (Portrait of Fukōin'den [Yoshinori], several mortuary tablets, similarly the envoy from the capital was En'a.)[19]

From now hereafter the reign [of the shogunate] shall always endure and like this shall [also] the [document under the] seal. Should by the designs of a single generation there proof be brought that the succession be taken lightly the magistrate will punish. There must be no disrespect in one's attitude. Tribute in the future will often be discussed as before. Every year two hundred wax candles will be presented to the shogun (one hundred to Ise [Sadachika and] thirty candles and one *kan* of [silver] to his secretary this tribute every year for many years will be offered.) The agent will be Ise [Sadachika]-dono. Among [the seals] of the document under the seal are the seal of the submitter Iio Saemon Taifu [Yukishige]-dono (the brother of Shimosa [no kami Tamenori]-dono) and that of Ise-dono the secretary of the shogun. The seal of Iio Shimosa [no kami Tamenori] the enforcer is [included]. This temple [Shōnenji and] the various other [temples] thus are become *gokiganji* [*sic*]. The lord Military Governor is agent (the seal of Yusa-dono; seal of Kai-Buzen-dono). In addition to carrying out shogunal orders, receiving [orders from Iio] Shimosa [no kami Tamenori] the messenger is his son Iio Hikosaburō [Tameasa]-dono (thus this item is here). Besides the [document under the] seal the original documents will be handed down within the year, the first month, twenty-first day (the messenger En'a and the accompanying Rin'a are both from the Kōmyōin community). This is put down as a record of evidence for eternity.

Third year of Chōroku (1459) first month eleventh day.
Ukyō daibu (Hosokawa Katsumoto)
The seal of the Shogunal Deputy will be handed down mid-spring, as above
Attachment forthcoming
(1460) Chōroku 4.11.17 submitted

7. From the *Shōnenji engi utsushi*[20]

Item, [on] this temple [as] gokiganjo: in the second year of Chōroku (1458), an independent monk (arasō) said concerning this province [and] the world, "The origins of this temple [lie with] the receipt of an imperial order. However, the times changed and [the world fell into] decadence. In ancient times of respect the Buddha and monks had dignity. In these times of disbelief, are there not those who hide the virtues of the excellent teachings [of Buddhism]?" Later on, knowing that there was a desire [to designate this temple a] *gokiganjo* in the ancient order of the emperor, when time had passed, on the night of twenty-sixth day of the ninth month of the same year, the present head [of the temple] On'a saw in a dream Ippen and the second founder [Ta'a], who said that this temple must be [designated] a *gokiganjo* and they recommended sending *jishū* called Na'a [and] Shun'a as messengers to the shogun [Yoshimasa]. How very miraculous it was [that] when the seventeenth [Yugyō] Shōnin was in Kyoto, on the twenty-sixth day of the twelfth month of the same year, [a document under the shogun's] seal was handed down. The twenty-sixth day corresponded to the day of the dream revelation . . ."

8. "Letter from the twenty-fourth generation Yugyō [Shōnin] Taikō"[21]

As for [the site of] the ruins [of the Shōjōkōji at] Fujisawa: is it [true what I have heard] that it was on your request that for a monetary donation of one thousand *kanmon* from the lord (Hōjō Ujiyasu; 1515-1570), [we shall be forced to] sell this land [so that it might be used as] fiefs for vassals? That it should come to this [after] so many years of your interceding [for us] is regrettable. Did [Ujiyasu] doubt that this stupid priest would return [as the Fujisawa Shōnin] and rebuild [the temple]? If so, I swear to it with this written pledge. [We are blessed] with the mysterious presence of [Shaka,] the founder of Buddhism; we see clearly the protective deity of this temple [Shōjōkōji], the Great God of Suwa, and the other greater and lesser deities of heaven and earth in the various provinces. [By them all I swear.] There was a promise to hand over the whole of the old site [as] a donation of the domain; when there is a signature [of the lord] attached to an order [to do] as promised [and] without breach, I shall return and rebuild [the temple]. Because I have left the capital [and proceeded only] as far as Tōtomi Province, I am not [travelling with] the speed I had thought. Therefore, as in the letter above. Eiroku 1.8.13, Year of the Elder Brother of the Earth/ Year of the Horse. [From] Ta'amidabutsu. [To] Hōjō Saemon Daibu-dono

Notes

Notes to Chapter 1

1. Max Weber, *Economy and Society: An Outline of Interpretive Sociology*, 2 vols., ed. Guenther Roth and Claus Wittich, tr. Ephraim Fischoff et al. (Berkeley, Los Angeles, London: University of California Press, 1978), 2:1113.

2. Ibid., 2:1123.

3. Ibid., 2:1119.

4. Weber points to self-interest as a principal motivation for transforming "charismatic communities" into perennial institutions. However, Weber points to economic interests as a motivation for transformation rather than part of the process of transformation. Ibid., 1:246.

5. Ibid., 1:241-243, 2:1112-1113.

6. Ibid., 1:242, 2:1121.

7. Alan Bryman, *Charisma and Leadership in Organizations* (London, Newbury Park, CA, and New Delhi: SAGE Publications, 1992), pp. 56-59.

8. See Donal B. Cruise O'Brien and Christian Coulon, eds., *Charisma and Brotherhood in African Islam* (Oxford: Clarendon Press, 1988 and Stanley Jeraraja Tambiah, *The Buddhist Saints of the Forest and the Cult of Amulets: A Study in Charisma, Hagiography, Sectarianism and Millennial Buddhism*, Cambridge Studies in Social Anthropology, no. 49 (Cambridge, UK and New York: Cambridge University Press, 1984).

9. Janet Goodwin, *Alms and Vagabonds: Buddhist Temples and Popular Patronage in Medieval Japan* (Honolulu: University of Hawaii Press, 1994), pp. 142, 145, 146-147, 148, and 149.

10. I am following Bryman's discussion of routinization in terms of succession and organizational structure. *Charisma*, chapter 4.

11. Weber, *Society and Economy*, 1:241-242. See also Bryman, *Charisma*, pp. 22-25, on Weber's analysis of charismatic qualities.

12. Ibid., pp. 50-54.

13. Ibid., p. 51. He notes that "the exchange is an asymmetric one in the end, for it is the charismatic leader who holds the reins of power." However, we shall see that this does not exactly apply in our case.

14. Ibid., pp. 66-67 for a survey of research on the techniques of effecting perception of charisma through media.

15. Ibid., pp. 50-54.

16. Ibid., p. 84 on the "institutionalization" of charisma, citing J. C. Robinson, "Mao after death: charisma and political legitimacy," *Asian Survey* 28: 353-68.

17. Ibid., especially pp. 52-53 for empowerment through participation in the leader's mission.

18. For a survey of Weber's concept of the legitimacy of power and the types of legitimacy, see Bryman, *Leadership*, pp. 23-24. Weber identifies three kinds of legitimate authority: rational, traditional, and charismatic. *Society and Economy*, 1:212-216.

19. Weber, *Society and Economy*, 2:1146-1148, 1173-1176. Weber's discussion does not quite apply to the Yugyō-ha since many of the legitimating functions described were provided the shogunate by the imperial house.

20. Ibid., 2:1164, 1165.

21. Ibid., 1:1148-1150. Weber maintains that in such situations, an organization can "maintain effective superiority . . . only by means of a very strict internal discipline." Ibid., p. 1149. For the similarity of warrior and monk, see ibid., p. 1153.

22. Among the modern scholars are Imai Masaharu, Tamamuro Fumio, Kondō Yoshihiro, Kōno Noriyoshi, Mochizuki Kazan, and many third-generation scholars. For Akamatsu, see Akamatsu Toshihide, "Ippen Shōnin no Jishū ni tsuite," *Shirin* 29, no. 1 (January 1944), cited in Ōhashi Shunnō, *Jishū no seiritsu to tenkai* (Yoshikawa Kōbunkan, 1973), p. 5. For Kanai, see his *Ippen to jishū kyōdan* (Kadokawa Shoten, 1975), *Jishū to chūsei bungaku* (Tōkyō Bijutsu, 1975), *Jishū kyōdan no chihō tenkai* (Tōkyō Bijutsu, 1983), and *Jishū bungei to Ippen hōgo* (Tōkyō Bijutsu, 1987); for many years he edited the journal *Jishū kenkyū,* which he founded. Ōhashi is the editor of *Jishū zensho,* 2 vols. (Kamakura: Geirinsha, 1974) and *Jishū kakochō,* Jishū shiryō 1 (Fujisawa: Jishū Kyōgaku Kenkyūjo, 1964); he wrote *Jishū no seiritsu to tenkai* (Yoshikawa Kōbunkan, 1973), *Ippen to Jishū kyōdan,* Kyōikusha rekishi shinsho (Nihonshi) 172 (1978), and others. Tachibana is the author of *Jishūshi ronkō* (Kyoto: Hōzōkan, 1975), *Yugyōji: chūsei no Jishū sōhonzan,* Fujisawa bunko 1 (Meicho Shuppan, 1978), and editor with Tamamuro Fumio of *Shomin shinkō no genryū: Jishū to yugyō hijiri* (Meicho Shuppan, 1982).

23. See also Yuyama Manabu, "Ta'a Shōnin hōgo ni mieru bushi," parts 1 and 2, *Jishū kenkyū* 63 (February 1975): 23-29; 64 (May 1975): 8-53; idem, "Jishū to Sagami bushi: Ta'a Shōnin hōgo ni mieru bushi, hōron," *Jishū kenkyū* 65 (August 1975): 5-21; idem, "Jishū to Musashi bushi," parts 1 and 2, *Jishū*

kenkyū 68 (May 1976): 1-23; 69 (August 1976): 17-31; Shimoda Tsutomu, "Jishū to Ōgoshi," *Jishū kenkyū* 76 (May 1978):20-27; Kaijima Tomoko, "Kōryū jiki Jishū kyōdan no shiji sō ni tsuite: toku ni bushi kaikyū o chūshin to shite," parts 1 and 2, *Jishū kenkyū* 80 (April 1980): 13-22, and 82 (November 1980): 6-16.

24. For guaranteeing Rebirth, see Imai Masaharu, *Chūsei shakai to Jishū no kenkyū* (Yoshikawa Kōbunkan, 1985), pp. 351-365. For attendance in the field, see ibid., pp. 365-374, Tachibana, *Jishūshi ronkō*, pp. 214-237; and Kanai, *Jishū bungei*, pp. 207-233. For reconciliation of *nembutsu* and other worship, see Kanai, *Ippen*, pp. 85-90; and Ōhashi, *Ippen*, pp. 59-64. For publicity, see Kanai, *Ippen*, pp. 431-432. For cultural life, see ibid., pp. 436-438, 456-459; Ōhashi, *Ippen*, pp. 181-187; and, for a complete survey of *jishū* literary production, Nagai Yoshinori, "Jishū to bungaku geinō," *Kokubungaku kaishaku to kanshō* 25, no. 13 (November 1960): 61-69. For the Tokugawa genealogy, see Yoshikawa Kiyoshi, *Jishū ami kyōdan no kenkyū* (Kamakura: Geirinsha, 1956), pp. 253-257. This last is based on the work of Nakamura Kōya, *Tokugawa ke*, Nihon rekishi shinsho, 2d. ser., 36 (Shibundō, 1961), pp. 4-10; and idem, *Tokugawa Ieyasu monjo no kenkyū* 1 (Nihon Gakujutsu Shinkōkai, 1958), pp. 88-96. See also Imai, *Chūsei shakai*, pp. 109-132; and Tachibana, *Yugyōji*, pp. 88-89.

25. Isogai Tadashi, *Jishū kyōdan no kigen oyobi hattatsu*, Jishūshi kenkyū 1 (Yokohama: [Privately printed?], 1937).

26. For a survey of the characterization of Buddhism as decadent or degenerate throughout the Tokugawa period and the Meiji period, see James E. Ketelaar, *Of Heretics and Martyrs in Meiji Japan: Buddhism and its Persecution* (Princeton, NJ: Princeton University Press, 1990), pp. 11-12, 14, 19, 35, 39, 43, 51, 56, 64, 86, 214

27. Tsuji Zennosuke, *Nihon bukkyōshi* (Iwanami Shoten, 1955), 4:310-351 ("Muromachi Period Monastic Corruption") and 10:404-489 ("The Deterioration of Buddhism and the Corruption of Monks").

28. Isogai, *Jishū*, pp. 66-67. He is citing Tsuji's *Nihon Bukkyōshi no kenkyū*, 2 vols. (Kinkodō Shoseki, 1919-1931), chapters 16 through 20 of the *zokuhen*.

29. Nakamura Nobuyuki, "Jishū no suibiki ni oite," *Bukkyōshi kenkyū* 1 (September 1969): 24-28.

30. Ishida Yoshitō, "Muromachi jidai no jishū ni tsuite," part 2, *Bukkyō shigaku* 11, nos. 3-4 (July 1964): 95-109.

31. As for the accusation of spying, Kanai Kiyomitsu indicates that the basis for this story, the third Patriarch's refusal to "spy" for the Hōjō and the fourth Patriarch's expulsion for agreeing to, is in the *Mazanshū*, but I could not find it. Kanai Kiyomitsu, *Ippen*, p. 297. An unnamed source from the Taima Muryōkōji is cited in *Shimpen Sagami no kuni fudokikō* 5, *Dai Nihon chishi taikei* 22, ed. Ashida Koretō, rev. ed. (Yūzankaku shuppan, 1962), p. 132.

Mazanshū, in *Teihon Jishū shūten*, ed. Teihon Jishū Shūten Hensan Iinkai, (Sankibō Busshorin; Fujisawa: Jishū Shūmusho, 1979), 2:832-854.

32. "Rennyo ga sekkyoku-teki ni minshū to ittai to natte fukyō ni shinshutsu shite kita no de aru." Nakamura, "Suibi," pp. 26-27.

33. Tamamuro Fumio, "Edo jidai no Yugyō Shōnin kaikoku ni tsuite," in *Chihō bunka no dentō to sōzō*, ed. Chihōshi Kyōgikai (Yūzankaku Shuppan, 1976), p. 235.

34. Mochizuki Kazan, *Jishū nempyō* (Kadokawa Shoten, 1970), pp. 202-204.

35. Diana Elizabeth Wright, "The Power of Religion/The Religion of Power: Religious Activities as *Upaya* for Women of the Edo Period—The Case of Mantokuji—" (Ph. D. diss., University of Toronto, 1996).

Notes to Chapter 2

1. For the Kōno, see Kanai, *Ippen*, pp. 10-15; for Takanawa Castle, ibid., p. 10, citing *Azuma kagami*, 1181/Yōwa 1. 2. 12; For Michikiyo, see ibid., citing *Yoshōki*; for Michinobu, see ibid., citing *Azuma kagami*, 1185/Juei 4. 2. 21; for coat of arms, see ibid., citing *Yoshōki*; for rewards, see ibid., pp. 10-11, citing *Azuma kagami*, 1203/ Kennin 3. 4. 6 and 1205/Genkyū 2. 7. 29 as well as an order from Hōjō Yoshitoki dated 1205. 2. 7 in the collection of Ōyamazuma Jinja. Michinobu had also taken a wife from the Shinjō family of Iyo and the daughter of Nikaidō Yukimitsu, a chief official of the shogunate, and so Michinobu's six sons had different mothers. There does not seem to be consensus on the identity of Nyobutsu's mother.

2. Kanai, *Ippen*, p. 14, citing *Kōno keizu* in Nagao Hidenishi, *Yoyō Kōno shikō* (manuscript Tōzenji collection, 1903) and *Kōno shi keizu*, manuscript in the collection of the Hōgonji in Matsuyama.

3. Ibid., p. 15, citing *Ippen hijiri e*, 1. 1-2 (roll and section numbers), *Nihon emakimono zenshū* 10 (Kadokawa Shoten, 1960), p. 64].

4. Ibid., pp. 21-22; for Dōkyō Ken'i, citing *Hōsuibungyūki*.

5. *Ippen Shōnin ekotoba den*, 1. 1, published as *Yugyō Shōnin engi e*, *Nihon emakimono zenshū* 23 (Kadokawa Shoten, 1968), p. 57.

6. This theme is taken up by the *Mazanshū*, a Tokugawa-period text produced by the Taima-ha, and the late Muromachi *Ippen Shōnin nempuryaku*. See Kanai, *Ippen*, pp. 25-27. The *Mazanshū* underscores the problem: Ippen is nearly assassinated when he instead of another is chosen to succeed his brother who has died without a legitimate heir. *Mazanshū*, in *Teihon*, 2:1819.

7. For the life of Ippen see the *Ippen hijiri e*; the *Ippen Shōnin ekotoba den*, the first four volumes; James Foard, *Ippen Shōnin and Popular Buddhism in Kamakura Japan*, Ph. D. dissertation, Stanford University, 1977 (Ann Arbor:

Xerox University Microfilms, 1978); Kanai, *Ippen*; and Ōhashi, *Ippen*, among many others.

8. These included his half-brothers Shōkai and Sen'a. Kanai, *Ippen*, p. 198. The term's meaning at this time is not clear; it could refer to heads of temples as with other Buddhist schools.

9. *Yugyō Shōnin engi e*, 4. 3-5. 1, pp. 68-69; for Awakawa's wife, *Ippen hijiri e*, 12. 2, p. 81; for Ippen's intent to create an order, see Imai Masaharu, *Jishū seiritsushi no kenkyū* (Yoshikawa Kōbunkan, 1981), pp. 226-227, and Ōhashi, *Ippen*, pp. 76-77.

10. Imai, *Jishū seiritsushi*, p. 221.

11. "Yugyō nidai Shinkyō Shōnin shojō," *Shichijō monjo*, no. 1, in *Teihon*, 1:391; Shinkyō gives permission to practice amulet distribution (*fusan*) to Yū'amidabutsu Donkai. See also Kanai, *Ippen*, pp. 256-257 for transcription, p. 264 for discussion.

12. Kanai, *Ippen*, pp. 198-201. Relations, however, were close. Zenkōji had a copy of Shinkyō's poems. Ibid., p. 277, citing his *Jishū bungei kenkyū* [(Kazama Shobō, 1967)], p. 174. Brackets indicate that part of the citation not originally provided but included by myself.

13. Kanai, *Ippen*, pp. 199, 259-263.

14. Ibid., pp. 199-200; for Shinkyō as a poet see ibid., pp. 276-281, and Ōhashi, *Ippen*, pp. 85-88.

15. Letters collected during the *yugyō* of the fifty-third Yugyō Shōnin Sonnyo were published with poems, hymns, and other texts in 1778 (variant text 1794) as the *Nisō Ta'a Shōnin hōgo*. See *Ta'a Shōnin hōgo*, in *Teihon*, 1:122-231.

16. "Hitomi On'amidabutsu e tsukawasaru gohenji," *Ta'a Shōnin hōgo*, 3 (volume number), in *Teihon*, 1:158-160, and "Hitomi no On'amidabutsu e tsukasawaru gohenji," 5, ibid., p. 182-183.

17. The temple is known as the Yasukunisan Hitomiin Ichijōji and is located in Hitomi, Fukadani City, Saitama Prefecture. According to tradition, it was founded by Ippen Shōnin and Hitomi Shirō Yasukuni in 1289 (Shōō 2). *Shimpen Musashi no kuni fudoki kō* 11, Dainihon chishi taikei 11, ed. Ashida Koretō, rev. ed. (Yūzankaku Shuppan, 1960), p. 239.

18. Chapter Six, "Akasaka kassen no koto tsuketari Hitomi Honma nukegake ga koto," *Taiheiki*, 3 vols., ed. Gotō Tanji and Kamada Kisaburō, *Nihon koten bungaku taikei* 34-36 (Iwanami Shoten, 1960), 1:199-208.

19. Kanai, *Ippen*, p. 218.

20. According to the *Mazanshū*, 1303/Kagen 1. *Mazanshū*, in *Teihon*, 2:1822. The date 1304/Kagen 2. 1. 10 is given by the *Jishū kechimyaku sōzoku no shidai*, in Ōhashi, *Jishū*, p. 305.

21. The earliest life of Jō'a is the *Jō'a Shōnin den* (finished in 1463 and bearing the seal of Gohanazono), in *Teihon*, 2:1543-1544. Tachibana Shundō, "*Jō'a Shōnin den* kaisetsu," ibid., 2:1545.

22. Kawahata nyoin Kōgimon'in Fujiwara (Saionji) Yasuko (1292-1357). According to the *Jō'a Shōnin den*, this occurred in the spring of the first year of Ōchō. In *Teihon*, 2:1543. However, other sources give dates for Kōgon's birth between 1311 and 1313. The *Jō'a Shōnin den*'s account should probably be seen as an attempt by the Shijō-ha to assert prerogatives after amalgamation with the Yugyō-ha: thus the disparity in the accounts of Shinkyō's receipt of the title of Shōnin.

23. Kanai, *Ippen*, pp. 255-256, citing Ōhashi Shunnō, "Yugyō rekidai Shōnin den (2)," *Jishū kenkyū* 22 (Feb. 1967), p. []. For Kagehira, see also "Donkai Shōnin," *Yugyō Fujisawa ryōshōnin gorekidai keifu*, ed. Takano Osamu, in *Shomin shinkō*, p. 239 and *Shimpen Sagami*, 5:133.

24. "Rakuyō Konkōji kaiki no koto," *Shibazaki bunko*, in *Teihon*, 2:1802. "Yugyō nidai Shinkyō Shōnin shojō," *Shichijō monjo*, no. 1, in *Teihon*, 1:391.

25. Identified as Fujisawa Shirōtarō. Kanai, *Ippen*, p. 258. Another supporter is identified as Akamatsu Sadanori, son of Norimura Enshin (1277-1350). Ibid., p. 258, citing Kōno Noriyoshi, *Ippen kyōgaku to jishūshi no kenkyū* [(Tōyō Bunka Shuppan, 1981)].

26. He complains in a letter to Donkai of a lack of assistance from those at Muryōkōji even though his eyes were bothering him. "Yudai Chitoku Shōnin shojō," *Shichijō monjo*, no. 5, in *Teihon*, 1:394. See also Tachibana, *Yugyōji*, p. 42.

27. Tachibana, *Yugyōji*, p. 57, citing "Yugyō sandai Chitoku Shōnin shojō," *Shichijō monjo*, [no. 4, in *Teihon*, 1:393]. Muneshige's daughter was the concubine of the last *shikken* Hōjō Takatoki (1301-1333) and mother of his son Sagami Tarō Kunitoki. Entrusted with the care of the boy at the fall of Kamakura, Muneshige revealed the whereabouts of the boy, who was captured and executed. Muneshige died of starvation. Tachibana, *Yugyōji*, pp. 57-58, citing *Taiheiki*.

28. "Yugyō yondai Donkai Shōnin shojō," *Shichijō monjo*, no. 6, in *Teihon*, 1:394-395. For a complete discussion, see Kanai, *Ippen*, pp. 309-316.

29. Tachibana Shundō, *Yugyōji*, p. 47, citing *Donkai Shōnin gohōgo*, [in *Teihon*, 1:267-268], in which it is claimed that a letter from Osaragi had stated that Donkai ("Yugyō") should not come to Taima.

30. Kanai, *Ippen*, p. 259.

31. *Shimpen Sagami*, 5:133, which quotes the entry for Donkai in the *Gorekidai keifu*, [in *Shomin shinkō*, p. 239].

32. Kanai, *Ippen*, p. 383.

33. For "dōdō," see *Shōkei ranrishi*, in *Zoku shiseki shūran* 1, ed. Kondō Heijō (Kondō Shuppanbu, 1930), p. 213. The expression "dōdō" is also used by Jikū. "Yugyō jūichidai Jikū Shōnin shojō," *Shichijō monjo*, no. 9, in *Teihon*, 1:396. It was probably the official term used by the order. For "shōban," see "Seishū Nagano e tsukasawaru no gosho Bunna 2 nen 9 gatsu misoka," *Shichidai Shōnin hōgo*, in *Teihon*, 1:383. In what is better known as his "Nagano gosho,"

he also uses the expression "shōban no nishū" and demonstrates the full participation of women in the battlefield activities.

34. In the "Nagano gosho," Takuga states, "Even now more than ever men requesting monks and nuns are very many." *Shichidai Shōnin hōgo*, in *Teihon*, 1:383. Seconding monks or nuns from individual temples would seem to be less regular and less regularized. According to the *Meitokuki*, the *jishū* who reported the death of Yamana Ujikiyo to his wife was "a *jishū* who had been summoned from the Sakai *dōjō* to follow [the lord of] Ōshū." *Meitokuki*, ed. Tomikura Tokujirō, Iwanami bunko 2899-2900 (1942), p. 115.

35. See the "Jikū shojō," *Shichijō monjo*, no. 9, in *Teihon*, 1:396.

36. The *Ihon Odawara ki* states, "In general, *jishū* monks have from times of old been experts in *waka* and have made their business the treating of weapon wounds. Therefore, they have gone to the front lines, have treated battle wounds; they have disposed of the corpses and have accepted the last ten *nembutsu*. That is why, they say, every general has them accompany him and greatly appreciates them." *Muromachi-dono monogatari*, *Ashikaga jiran ki*, *Ihon Odawara ki*, *Kokushi sōsho* 3, ed. Kurokawa Mamichi (Kokushi Kenkyūkai, 1914), pp. 359-360. This paean to *jishū* follows an entry discussing the Eiroku period (1558-1570). Also, as will be discussed below, there is a tradition that the Saifukuji (Kohama City, Fukui Prefecture) sent out *jishū* as surgeons. Personal communication from Saifukuji.

Examples of informing relatives are found in the *Meitokuki* (see note 34) and the *Taiheiki*, 1:199-208, and 1:387-388. *Jishū* were allowed even to carry letters to save the lives of the aged, women, and children, according to the "Jikū shojō." See *Shichijō monjo*, no. 9, in *Teihon*, 1:396.

37. I have concluded that serious lobbying by the Yugyō-ha must have begun with Jikū. It was Jikū who gained the support of the shogun in permanently resolving the problem of chaplains being seconded for paramilitary duties by their warrior patrons, and Jikū did carry on with the duties of Yugyō Shōnin for years after becoming Fujisawa Shōnin, presumably, among other reasons, to keep in close touch with his contacts in Kyoto. "YS" is the abbreviation for "Yugyō Shōnin" and "FS" is the abbreviation for "Fujisawa Shōnin." I have not indicated these titles for Donkai above even though he is traditionally recognize as Yugyō Shōnin and first Fujisawa Shōnin.

38. *Jishū kakochō*, pp. 54-55. To be discussed more fully in chapter 6.

39. In 1430, the shogun Ashikaga Yoshinori (Muromachi-dono) went to the Konrenji for *renga*. *Mansai jugō nikki* 2, *Zoku gunsho ruijū*, suppl. vol. 2, comp. Hanawa Hokinoichi (Zoku Gunsho Ruijū Kanseikai, 1928), p. 153, under Eikyō 2. 6. 11. He heard sermons at the Konkōji later the same year. Ibid., p. 170, under Eikyō 2. 8. 28. In 1435, Yoshinori watched *odori nembutsu* at the Konkōji. Ibid., p. 656, under Eikyō 7. 3. 18.

40. The document, dated Ōei 7. 4. 7, is transcribed and discussed, as summarized above, in Tachibana, *Jishūshi ronkō*, p. 256.

41. "Ashikaga Yoshimochi migyōsho," *Shōjōkōji monjo*, no. 16 in *Fujisawa shishi 1: Shiryōhen*, ed. Fujisawa Shishi Hensan Iinkai (Fujisawa: Fujisawa Shiyakusho, 1970), p. 652. It is dated Ōei 23. 4. 3.

42. "Ashikaga Yoshinori migyōsho," *Shōjōkōji monjo*, no. 21 in *Fujisawa shishi*, 1:657. It is dated Eikyō 8. 12. 5.

43. For text of Ōuchi document, dated Eishō 10. 1. 15, see "Yugyō nijūyonsō Shōnin [no] toki Eirin'in Yoshitane shōgun yori shokoku shugonin no migyōsho," in *Jishū kekkishū*, in *Teihon*, 2:1262; for text of Uesugi document, dated Tenshō 17. 9. 7, see "Fukō Shōnin," *Gorekidai keifu*, in *Shomin shinkō*, p. 247; for the text of first Tokugawa license, issued in 1613 or Keichū 18. 3. 11, see "Chōgai Shōnin," ibid., p. 248.

44. Tachibana, *Jishūshi ronkō*, pp. 324-325. See *Yugyō sanjūissō Kyō-Ki goshugyō ki*, in *Teihon*, 2:1495.

45. For the story, see *Yūki senjō monogatari*, in *Gunsho ruijū* 20, comp. Hanawa Hokinoichi (1898-1902; reprint, Zoku Gunsho Ruijū Kanseikai, 1940), pp. 720-734 (*maki* 383, *kassenbu*).

Technically, the Kamakura Ashikaga were the Kantō *kanrei*. However, they appropriated the title *kubō* and passed on the position of *kanrei* to the Uesugi. Depending on what was going on politically and who had power (or pretensions), the Uesugi variously held the position of *kanrei* or *shitsuji* (First Minister) to the *kanrei*.

46. *Denchū ika nenchū gyōji*, in *Gunsho ruijū* 22, comp. Hanawa Hokinoichi (Zoku Gunsho Ruijū Kanseikai, 1928), p. 342 (*maki* 408, *bukebu*).

47. *Yugyō nijūyonsō goshugyō ki*, in *Teihon*, 2:1476.

48. Konrenji was occupied by Miyoshi Motonaga in 1527 and by Matsunaga Nagahide in 1558. Konkōji was occupied by Miyoshi Motonaga in 1558 and 1569. Shōnenji was occupied by the leader of a farmers' revolt in 1574. Mochizuki, *Jishū nempyō*, pp. 71, 77, 79, 80.

49. For the date, see ibid., p. 64, citing the *Myōhōjiki*.

50. The temple was caught between the forces of Hōjō Sōun (Nagauji, 1432-1519) and Miura Dōsun (Yoshiatsu, d. 1516). "Chiren Shōnin," *Gorekidai keifu*, in *Shomin shinkō*, p. 244.

51. For death register, see *Tōtakusan kakochō: monmatsu kechienshū*, ed. Tachibana Shundō (Fujisawa: Jishū Shūmusho Kyōgakubu, 1981), p. 5. For main image, see *Yugyō nijūyonsō*, in *Teihon*, 2:1480.

52. For more on the "Fujisawa Shōnin," see Appendix, no. 3. Fukō took up residence in 1607. "Fukō Shōnin," *Gorekidai keifu*, in *Shomin shinkō*, p. 246, and Ōhashi, *Ippen*, pp. 193-198. Fugai called himself the "twenty-fourth Ta'a, head priest of [Tō]takusan [Shōjōkōji]" (*[Tō]takusan tō jūji nijūyon se Ta'a*). Ōhashi, *Ippen*, p. 194, citing *Yugyō nijūyonsō*, [in *Teihon*, 2:1480]. Yūsan, thirtieth Yugyō Shōnin, was called "Sunshū Fujisawa Shōnin" because he resided as Fujisawa Shōnin at the Chōzenji in Sumpu, Suruga Province. Ōhashi, *Ippen*, p. 198, citing "Ta'a Shōnin shojō," *Horiuchi monjo*, [no. 9, in *Fujisawa shishi*,

1:645]. "Yū'amidabutsu shojō," *Horiuchi monjo*, no. 10 in ibid., p. 646, also refers to "Sunshū Fujisawa." Both are dated 9. 23; Ōhashi suggests the year 1577. *Ippen*, p. 201.

53. ". . . taishū sōni . . . hinin raisha . . ." (lay followers, monks and nuns . . . pariahs [possibly unattached ascetics and religious practitioners] and lepers). *Yugyō nijūyonsō*, in *Teihon*, 2:1470.

54. In 1579, Dōnen was received at court. *Oyu-dono no ue no nikki* 7, *Gunsho ruijū* suppl. vol. 3 bk. 7, comp. Hanawa Hokinoichi (Zoku Gunsho Ruijū Kanseikai, 1934), p. 278, under Tenshō 7. 9. 13. See also *Yugyō sanjūissō*, in *Teihon*, 2:1499. He was received again in 1580/Tenshō 8. 2. 5. Ibid., 2:1500 and *Oyu-dono* 7, pp. 296-297. See chapter 6.

55. Mochizuki, *Jishū nempyō*, pp. 80, 82, citing the *Igawa Shinzenkōji monjo*.

56. Tachibana, *Yugyōji*, pp. 131-133, citing letter dated Eiroku 1. 8. 13 in Takase collection. Tsunanari was an adopted son and son-in-law of Ujitsuna. His father had been Fukushima Masanari, lord of Hijikata Castle in Tōtōmi and vassal of the Imagawa. A mere child when his father was killed in the campaign against the Takeda in 1521, he had been taken by a vassal to Suruga. Tachibana, *Yugyōji*, pp. 126-127, citing the *Odawara Hōjō keizu betsuhon*, in *Zoku gunsho ruijū* [vol. 6 bk. 1, comp. Hanawa Hokinoichi (Zoku Gunsho Ruijū Kanseikai, 1925), p. 96] (*maki* 140). The vassal in question was Horiuchi Tango no kami Shigechika, whose own father Izu no kami Chikamoto had also been killed in the same 1521 campaign. The Horiuchi served the Hōjō and after their fall stayed in Fujisawa and, as a prominent family, continued to support the Shōjōkōji.

57. Tachibana, *Yugyōji*, pp. 134-135, citing the *Odawara shūsho ryōyaku-chō*, with colophon dated 1559/Eiroku 2. 2. 12, in *Nihon shiryō sensho*.

58. Tachibana, *Jishūshi ronkō*, p. 279, citing *Tōtakusan kakochō*, [pp. 8, 11] ("Kaku'amidabutsu moto Fujisawa kanbō [1560] Eiroku 3. 4. 19" under Taikō and "Go'amidabutsu moto Rokuryō Fujisawa kanshu 87 sai [1593] Bunroku 2 nen 12 gatsu 8 nichi ōjō" under Fukō).

59. Ibid., pp. 279-280. In 1588/Tenshō 16. 3. 6 a fire destroyed a chapel enshrining an image of Donkai; 7. 13 both were replaced probably by the same *kanshu* Go'amidabutsu. Ibid., citing inscription on wood inside image in *Fujisawa shishi* 1.

60. He was the seventeenth head and seventeenth Hō'amidabutsu. Tachibana, *Jishūshi ronkō*, p. 283. His death is recorded in *Tōtakusan kakochō*, p. 11, and *Shiryō: Ichirenji kakochō*, *Fujisawashi kenkyū* 16, special volume (February 1983), p. 72.

61. For the endowment, see Tachibana, *Jishūshi ronkō*, p. 283; and "Mango Shōnin," *Gorekidai keifu*, in *Shomin shinkō*, p. 247. For Fushimi, Tachibana, *Yugyōji*, citing *Tokugawa jikki*, 5.

Wealth was officially assessed and taxed in terms of *koku* (about five bushels) of rice. Rice at this time was considerably more valuable than in the eighteenth century, when one *koku* rice was equivalent (given sometimes wide fluctations in the rate of exchange) to about one gold *ryō*.

62. "Yugyō sanjūnidai Fukō shojō," *Shichijō monjo*, no. 23, in *Teihon*, 1:402. Tachibana posits powerful figures behind the recalcitrant priest: Toyotomi Hideyori and Yodo gimi. *Yugyōji*, p. 166.

63. From 540,000 to 205,000. Originally 800,000 according to E. Papinot, *Historical and Geographical Dictionary of Japan* (1910; reprint, with an introduction by Terence Barrow, Rutland, Vermont and Tokyo: Charles E. Tuttle Company, Inc., 1972), s. v. "Satake Yoshinobu." 540,000 *koku*, according to Tachibana, *Jishūshi ronkō*, p. 284.

64. "Chōgai Shōnin," *Gorekidai keifu*, in *Shomin shinkō*, p. 248, in entry for Chōgai.

65. In the laws for shrines and temples passed between 1601 and 1615, the Jishū, along with the Ikkō or True Pure Land sect and the Nichiren sect, were left out of the ranking system that was being developed. However, the relationship between main and branch temple was strengthened, and practices of the temples and the careers of the religious were regulated. The lists which survive name roughly 12,000 temples. Tamamuro, "Edo jidai," pp. 165-166.

66. Tamamuro Fumio, "Edo jidai no Yugyō Shōnin," in *Ippen Shōnin to Jishū*, ed. Tachibana Shundō and Imai Masaharu, Nihon Bukkyō shūshi ronkō 10 (Yoshikawa Kōbunkan, 1984), p. 224. However, in the Jishū itself, the Konkōji was always recognized as one of two main temples. Documents refer to "ryōhonzan," or "both head temples." Hasegawa Masatoshi, "Jishū no gakuryō to shūgaku seikatsu," in *Yugyō nikkan 3*, ed. Tamamuro Fumio (Kadokawa Shoten, 1979), p. 627, citing two documents from 1721 and 1774.

67. Tamamuro, "Edo Shōnin," p. 224, citing the *Jikakuchō*. For *furegashira*, see Ōhashi, *Ippen*, p. 233.

68. According to Ōhashi, by 1697. *Ippen*, p. 235.

69. Temmei 8. 10. Ōhashi, *Ippen*, p. 235. See also "Kōchōji shiryō (3): Jishū jūni ha honmatsu sōjiin renmyōbo tadashi Hōreki nenchū shahon," *Jishū kenkyū* (February 1965): 1-15.

70. See Donryō, *Jishū yōrakufu*, in *Teihon*, 2:1219.

71. For Yoshino, see Mochizuki, *Jishū nempyō*, p. 102, citing *Kubota monjo*; for reception at court, ibid, p. 103, citing *Nanmon Shōnin kōjō shō*.

72. For Shijō-ha, Kanai, *Ippen*, pp. 438, and for Ikkō- and Tenryū-ha, both founded by Ikkō Shunjō, see ibid, pp. 392, 412 (both returned to Pure Land school in 1942).

73. For Mt. Kōya, see Mochizuki, *Jishū nempyō*, pp. 87, 88, citing the *Kōya shunshū shūroku*; for Zenkōji, see Sakai Kōhei, *Zenkōjishi*, 2 vols. (Tōkyō Bijutsu, 1969), 2:1157. See also *Shibazaki bunko* for mention of the *jishū* community at Zenkōji. "Ōko jishū no fugō no koto," in *Teihon*, 2:1798.

74. "Bateren no sonin gin shi nihyakumai, iruman no sonin onajiku hyakumai, kirishitan no sonin onajiku gojūmai mata wa sanjūmai sonin ni yoru beshi." Cited in Tamamuro, "Edo jidai," p. 167.

75. For example, in 1635 (Kanei 12. 10. 15), the Shūkōin of Ōbamura in Takakura District (Fujisawa City) in Sagami Province sent an order requiring proof of rejection of Christianity to the headman (*myōshū*) of Hatori Village ("Kondo kirishitan shū onaratame ni tsuki, danna bōzu shōmon shijō . . .") And the next day, the branch temple of the Shōjōkōji, the Jōkōji, sent an official list of seven parishioners to the *daikan* ("Hatori mura: Hitotsu, hidari no monodomo waga ishhū no badai no danna ni te goza sōrō koto jisshō nari. Moshi Kirishitan shūshi ni sōrō to waki yori sonin goza sōrō wa, gusō makari de mōshibun sōrō beshi. Kanei 15 Tora nen 10 gatsu 16 nichi Fujisawa Jōkōji. Saemon Shin'emon Giemon Chōbei Monzaemon Sukekurō. Naruse Goemon"). Cited in Tamamuro, "Edo jidai," p. 167.

76. Ibid., pp. 167-168.

77. Ibid., pp. 169-170.

78. For a complete description of the Yugyō Shōnin's *yugyō* during the Tokugawa period, see Tamamuro Fumio, "Edo jidai," pp. 163-178 and "Edo Shōnin," pp. 214-236.

79. For Masakado, see Sasaki Kyōdō, "Ōkurashō nai Masakado zuka to Nichirinji," in *Kanda, Musashino shōsho* 1 (Musashinokai, 1935), pp. 30-39. As for the Nichirinji, the head priest was called "Shibazaki Shōnin," (quoting the *Tenshō nikki*, Tenshō 18. 10. 6) and he took part in the New Year *renga* at the shogun's palace. *Tōkyō-tō meisho zue: Asakusa-ku no bu*, ed. Miyao Shigeo (Bokushobō, 1968), p. 66. The forty-eighth Yugyō Shōnin Fukoku (b. 1656; YS 1708-1711, FS -1711), who came from the Nichirinji, was a member of the Satomura family, *renga* masters to the shogunal house. For genealogy and poetry activities, see Takano Osamu, "Jishū bungei to Yugyō sō (5: Bakufu rengashi Satomura-ke to Fukoku Shōnin)," in *Shomin shinkō*, pp. 137-146.

Notes to Chapter 3

1. Following A. K. Warder, *Indian Buddhism*, 2d. rev. ed. (Delhi, Varanasi, Patna, India: Motilal Banarsidass, 1980), pp. 28-31, 37-39; Govind Chandra Pande, *Studies in the Origins of Buddhism*, 2d. rev. ed. (Delhi, Varanasi, Patna, India: Motilal Banarsidass, 1974), pp. 310-317; Uma Chakravarti, *The Social Dimensions of Early Buddhism* (Bombay, Calcutta, Madras, India: Oxford University Press, 1987), for a full study of the process, especially pp. 12-16 for warriors and decline in the face of monarchism, p. 87 for the custom of assembly and joint ownership of property transferred to the monastery, and pp. 167-173, 177-176 for the separation of king and *sangha*.

2. The three main texts are the Longer Pure Land Sutra ("scripture;" Skt. *Sukhāvatīvyūha* ["description of place of happiness"], Ch. *Wu-liang-shou ching*, Jp. *Muryōjukyō*), Shorter Pure Land Sutra (Skt. *Amitābha-Sūtra* ["Amida scripture"], Ch. *O-mi-t'o ching*, Jp. *Amidakyō*), and the Sutra on the Contemplation of Amitāyus ("Limitless Life;" Skt. *Amitāyurdhyana-Sūtra*, Ch. *Kuan wu-lian-shou-fo ching*, Jp. *Kanmuryōjukyō*). *Oxford Dictionary of World Religions*, ed. John Bowker (Oxford and New York: Oxford University Press, 1977), s. v. "Amitābha-Sūtra," "Pure Land," and "Sukhāvatīvyūha." See also ibid., s. v. "Avalokiteśvara," and "Amida."

3. *Oxford Dictionary*, s. v. "Hui-yuan," "T'an-luan," "Pure Land schools," "San-lun," and "Sanron-shū."

4. Ibid., s. v. "Pure Land schools," "Tendai-shū," and "Shingon-shū."

5. The very invocation of *mappō*, the Latter Age of Buddhist Doctrine, indicates that the major catalyst of Pure Land Buddhism was the social environment of China: the Pure Land movement began in the period of the breakup of the Han empire and culminated in the period of the unification and active expansion of the T'ang empire.

6. *A Tale of Flowering Fortunes: Annals of Japanese Aristocratic Life in the Heian Period*, 2 vols., translated with an introduction and notes by William H. and Helen Craig McCullough (Stanford: Stanford University Press, 1980), 2:71-72, for the death of Emperor Horikawa in 1107. See also Fujiwara no Nagako, *Emperor Horikawa Diary (Sanchi no Suke nikki)*, translated with an introduction by Jennifer Brewster (Honolulu: University Press of Hawaii, 1977), pp. 762-763, for the death of Fujiwara Michinaga, at which his adopted son the Mii Novice Narinobu functioned as *chishiki* by "exhort[ing] him to invoke the holy name."

7. Attacked in 1207 and suppressed again in 1227. Imai, *Jishū seiritsushi*, pp. 181-182.

8. Keiko Hartwieg-Hiratsuka, *Saigyō-Rezeption: Das von Saigyō verkörperte Eremiten-Ideal in der japanischen Literaturgeschichte*, European University Studies, Asian and African Studies, vol. 27 no. 10 (Bern, Frankfurt, Nancy, and New York: Peter Lang, 1984), pp. 67-68.

9. Hartwieg, *Saigyō*, p. 69.

10. What really distinguished them from *tonsei no mono* was their preservation of social organization and functions: they organized in groups, were often laymen, and engaged in fundraising and in preaching. Hartwieg, *Saigyō*, p. 171, citing Gorai Shigeru, *Kōya hijiri* (Kadokawa Shoten, 1965). For a complete study of *kanjin hijiri*, upon which the following discussion is based, see Goodwin, *Alms*.

11. Goodwin, *Alms*, p. 80.

12. Kanai, *Ippen*, p. 46.

13. See Kanai, *Chūsei bungaku*, p. 43, and Sakai Kōhei, *Zenkōji-shi*, 2 vols. (Tōkyō Bijutsu, 1969), 2:809-810, for a list of Shinzenkōji, including those,

founded by families such as the Takeda, Shishidō, Ōi, and Asakura, which were converted by *jishū.*

14. They were, indeed, the harbingers of peasant alliances and guilds that become so prominent in the social history of the fifteenth and sixteenth centuries. Goodwin, *Alms,* pp. 150-151. It should be no surprise that the breakdown of those same hierarchical, land-based relationships supporting the Buddhist institutions based in Nara should result in the same kind of voluntary associations of free-lance technical experts and entrepreneurs in the religious economy that also characterized the secular economy.

15. For Saigyō, see Hartwieg, *Saigyō,* pp. 166-171. For Saigyō as the product of identification and the choice of Saigyō by the *hijiri* movement to represent it, see ibid., pp. 173-176. For the reconfiguration of the biography of Saigyō in the model of that of the Buddha's, see William LaFleur, "The Death and 'Lives' of the Poet-Monk Saigyō," in *The Biographical Process: Studies in the History and Psychology of Religions,* ed. Frank E. Reynolds and Donald Capps (The Hague: Mouton, 1976), pp. 342-361.

16. For Saigyō as literary hermit, see Hartwieg, *Saigyō,* p. 69; for texts, ibid., pp. 73-86; for Saigyō as outsider, ibid., pp. 172-173. The *Senzaishū* was compiled by Fujiwara Toshinari Shunzei (1114-1204), the *Shin kokinshū* by Fujiwara Sadaie Teika (1162-1241), former Emperor Gotoba (1180-1259, r. 1183-1198), et alii, and the *Shin chokusenshū* by Teika. Dates for collections vary according to source, including *Japan: An Illustrated Encyclopedia,* 2 vols. (Kodansha, 1995), s. v. "Imperial anthologies," etc.

17. For Saigyō and fundraising, Hartwieg, *Saigyō,* p. 47, citing Gorai, *Kōya-hijiri* and *Kokonchomonjū, Nihon koten bungaku taikei* 84, pp. 93 ff. For Saigyō as fundraiser from a letter ("En'i Shōnin shojō") in his own hand dated 1178/Chishō 1. 3. 15, see ibid., p. 66, citing *Kōya-san hōkanshū* (Collection of valuable letters from Kōya) vol. 23, cited in Gorai, *Kōya-hijiri,* p. 167, and Mezaki Tokue, *Saigyō no shisōshi-teki kenkyū* ([], 1978), pp. 328-229. See also Hartwieg, *Saigyō,* p. 172. For Saigyō at Ōmine, see ibid., p. 48, citing *Sankashū* (Collection of Poems from the Mountain Hut [1191-1206]), *Nihon koten bungaku taikei* 29.

18. Hartwieg, *Saigyō,* pp. 166-169

19. Hartwieg, *Saigyō,* p. 105. It shares material with about half the legends about him in the *Hosshinshū, Myōe Shōnin denki, Imamonogatari, Jikkinshō, Kokonchomonjū, Gempeiseisuiki* (or *jōsuiki), Shasekishū,* and *Seiashō,* compiled between 1250-1280. Ibid., pp. 87, 88, 110.

20. There Saigyō finds an old cherry, under which the Emperor Kazan (968-1008; r. 984-986) had performed religious exercises and composed a poem, and sees Buddha there. Hartwieg, *Saigyō,* p. 112. *Saigyō monogatari emaki,* in *Saigyō monogatari engi, Taima mandara engi, Nihon emakimono zenshū* 11 (Kadokawa Shoten, 1958). For date of 1219, Hartwieg, *Saigyō,* p. 97. The *Bunmei bon,* 1480, the definitive and most widely circulated text of the *Saigyō*

monogatari, is in *Saigyō zenshū*, ed. Sasaki Nobutsuna, Kawada Jun, Itō Yoshio and Kyūsojin Hitaku (1941), 2:235-410.

21. For discussion, see Hartwieg, *Saigyō*, pp. 117-166. It was compiled ten to twenty years after *Saigyō monogatari* or *Saigyō monogatari emaki*. Ibid., p. 122.

22. Hartwieg, *Saigyō*, p. 171

23. *Ippen hijiri e*, 3. 1, p. 66.

24. James H. Foard, "Prefiguration and Narrative in Medieval Hagiography: The *Ippen Hijiri-e*," in *Flowing Traces: Buddhism in the Literary and Visual Arts of Japan*, ed. James H. Sanford, William R. LaFleur, and Masatoshi Nagatomi (Princeton: Princeton University Press, 1992), pp. 77-92.

25. *Ippen hijiri e*, 1. 3, 2. 1, 2. 3, and 2. 4, pp. 65-67; Foard, "Prefiguration," p. 82. Foard surveys the ten standard narrative forms of which the *Ippen hijiri e* is comprised: chronologies, legends (*setsuwa*), histories of religious insitutions and objects (*engi*), poetry (*waka*), creeds, doctrines, poetic travel descriptions (*michiyuki*), documents, Shōkai's narrative, and sermons and commentaries (*hōgo*). "Prefiguration," pp. 81-84.

26. Laura S. Kaufman, *Ippen hijirie: Artistic and Literary Sources in a Buddhist Handscroll Painting of Thirteenth-Century Japan*, New York University Ph. D. dissertation (Ann Arbor: University Microfilms International, 1980), pp. 272, 280. Also see idem, "Nature, Courtly Imagery, and Sacred Meaning in the *Ippen Hijiri-e*," in *Flowing Traces*, pp. 47-75.

27. Hartwieg, *Saigyō*, pp. 106, 109.

28. Kaufman, "Nature," p. 60.

29. Hartwieg, *Saigyō*, p. 46.

30. Nōin's poem is number 515 in the *Goshūishū*, vol. 9: "Miyako wo ba / kasumi to tomo ni / tachi shikado / Akikaze zo fuku / Shirakawa no seki." Kaufman, "Nature," p. 58, with translation and citing Watanabe Tamotsu, *Saigyō Sanka-shū zenchūkai* (Kazama Shobō, 1971), p. 633. Saigyō's poem is found in the private anthology of Fujiwara Tametsune, the *Goyō wakashū*, of 1155. Hartweig, *Saigyō* p. 46, 75n and 76n.

31. Hartwieg, *Saigyō*, p. 114, and *Saigyō monogatari emaki*, color plate 3. For Sanetaka's exile, see William LaFleur, *Mirror for the Moon: A Selection of Poems by Saigyō (1118-1190)* (New York: New Directions Publishing Corporation, 1978), p. xxi.

32. *Ippen hijiri e*, 5. 3, p. 4 for illustration, and p. 69 for text.

33. Kaufman, "Nature," pp. 58-60.

34. Shinkyō is credited with saving Ippen's poems. Kanai, *Ippen*, p. 276. Certainly, he attracted patronage through his own reputation as a poet. It is not unreasonable that he would seek to identify himself with a poetic tradition, especially that of itinerant recluse/poet.

35. *Yugyō engi e*, 2. 2, p. 60. The entry is cited as the basis of the play, but neither analysis and nor explanation is given. Koresawa Kyōzō, "Yugyō Shōnin: *Yugyō yanagi* ni yosete," *Kanze* (September 1967), p. 12.

36. *Yugyō no bijutsu*, ed. Kanagawa Kenritsu Hakubutsukan (Yokohama: Kanagawaken Bunkazai Kyōkai, 1985), p. 136 for information, and p. 18 for illustration. There is no representation of anyone writing on the pillar in the *Ippen hijiri e* (although someone is looking at a pillar) or the *Ippen Shōnin ekotoba den*. A comparison of the illustrations of the scene in the *Ekotoba den* shows the writing figure to be Ippen except for the Kōmyōji version and the *Fujisawa dōjō koengi*. *Yugyō engi e*, pp. 7-8.

37. Koresawa seems to think that the association comes from the illustration of the previous section, on the first *odori nembutsu* at Tomono in Shinano, because it shows a river or stream and next to it two willow trees; a party rests there with their horses. "Yugyō Shōnin," p. 12.

38. I might mention, almost parenthetically, the role in this identification between Saigyō and the heads of the Yugyō-ha that might have been played by the Kyoto temple Sōrinji in Higashiyama. A branch temple of the Tendai school Enryakuji, it had been built for Saichō on his return from China. During the Heian period, it became famous as a retreat. It was here that, according to the *Saigyō monogatari*, Saigyō decided to die in middle of the night of the fifteenth day of the second month (the date of the Buddha's death). He did die with all the signs of Amida's appearance to welcome him into the Pure Land (*raigo*). Hartwieg, *Saigyō*, pp. 115-116. It was to the Shōrinji that Taira Yasuyori retreated on his return from exile on Kikaigashima (Devil's Island) and wrote the *Hōbutsushū*, a collection of tales (*setsuwa*). It was here, too, that the famous poet Ton'a (1301-1384) died. Ton'a, born Nikaidō Sadamune, was of a family very close to the Yugyō-ha. Ten *nembutsu* were chanted at Shōjōkōji every evening for "Nikaidō Shikibu Taifu nyūdo Shū'amidabutsu" because of the order's obligation to him. *Shinshū yōhōki*, 3, in *Teihon*, 2:990. A disciple of Jō'a of the Fourth Avenue Konrenji, Ton'a also spent time at Mt. Kōya. *Kōya nikki*, in *Teihon*, 2:1692-1694. Kōno Noriyoshi, "Ton'a chōsakushū kaidai," in *Teihon*, 2:1700-1701 and *Kōya nikki*, in *Teihon*, 2:1692-1694. If identification with Saigyō and Ippen was initiated by court circles, then it was strengthened and extended to the Yugyō-ha through the Konrenji.

39. *Ippen hijiri e*, 1. 1, p. 64. Again, the sister of Ōi Tarō sees a dream in which a tall figure is practicing surrounded by small buddhas ("seeing he was called Ippen Shōnin" [*Ippen Shōnin to mō(su) to mite*]). Ibid., 5. 1, p. 69. Just before his death, Ninomiya nyūdo saw a vision of Ippen ("jindō chishiki no sō ni Ippen Shōnin no irasetamaitari wa mitatematsuruka, ushiromukite owashimasu zo to mōshikereba"), and in the same place, a letter and poem are addressed to "Ippen Shōnin." Ibid., 6. 3, p. 71. The text reports an oracle referring to "Ippen Shōnin." Ibid., 10. 3, p. 78.

40. Foard refers to this as the "citation of the Ryōnin legend as precedent for Ippen's Kumano experience." "Prefiguration," p. 85.

41. For Kōya as guide, see *Ippen hijiri e*, 7. 3, p. 73. For Kōya and *odori nembutsu*, see ibid., 4. 5, p. 68. The *emakimono* of Ryōnin states actually that the sanction came some years after he started his mission, in contradistinction to Ippen, who received his oracle as a correction certainly within a few months of beginning his mission. The relationship between the two traditions is problematic due to the fact that the oldest existing recording of Ryōnin's story was made after the *Ippen hijiri e*.

42. *Ippen hijiri e*, 9. 3, p. 76, and 11. 3, p. 80.

43. Goodwin, *Alms*, p. 115. For the campaign and Chōgen's role, see ibid, pp. 67-106.

44. Goodwin, *Alms*, p. 83.

45. Goodwin, *Alms*, pp. 81, 100-103. Sources for his life include the autobiography *Namuamidabutsu sazenshū*, *Bukkyō geijutsu* 30 (1934): 42-51 and *Tōdaiji zoku yōroku*, in *Zokuzoku gunsho ruijū* 11, comp. Hanawa Hokinoichi (Kokusho Kankōkai, 1907), pp. 208-209. Quotation, ibid., p. 82.

46. Kanai, *Ippen*, pp. 31-33 (for Zenkōji) and pp. 46, 63 (for Mt. Kōya); and Imai, *Jishū seiritsushi*, pp. 82-83.

47. *Ippen hijiri e*, 2. 3, p. 66.

48. For Kōya *hijiri*, see Kanai, *Ippen*, p. 46. Kanai also notes two legends in the *Ōei engi* (1427, *Zoku gunsho ruijū*) which would indicate that Zenkōji also distributed amulets, called *goinbun*, as far back as the Heian period. Such amulets were distributed by the temple in the Edo period and presently they carry the imprint "Honji nyōrai: ōjō ketsujō." Ibid., pp. 31-33. I find this inconclusive as evidence for the practice before Ippen's time.

49. This, noted Shinkyō, refers to the whole of humanity saved. "Hitomi no On'amidabutsu e tsukawasaru gohenji," *Ta'a Shōnin hōgo*, 5, in *Teihon*, 1:182. While at the Shingū Shrine of Kumano, after receiving his oracle at the Hongū, Ippen composed a poem expressing his view of the single chanting of the *nembutsu*, the *ichinen*. *Ippen hijiri e*, 3. 1, p. 66. The first character of each of the four lines read together "rokujūmannin," or "six hundred thousand people." Kanai, *Ippen*, pp. 89-90. This is only a general Pure Land translation. The next chapter gives the Seizan school interpretation.

50. The letter is dated 6. 13. *Ippen hijiri e*, 3. 2, p. 66. Kanai argues that, since Ippen had sent the *katagi* and thus the right to *fusan* to Shōkai in Iyo, *fusan* is coterminous with *yugyo* and that, even though Shinkan was *dokuju*, he too practiced *fusan* and thus that *fusan* always means *fusan* and *yugyo*. Kanai, *Ippen*, p. 299. I disagree: *fusan* and *yugyo* must be treated separately.

51. ". . . myōgo kakite tamai, jūnen sazuke nado shitamau." *Ippen hijiri e*, 2. 2, p. 65.

52. *Ippen hijiri e*, 3. 1, p. 66 ("kanjin"); ibid., 4. 2, p. 67 ("nembutsu o kanjin shitamaikeru"); ibid., 5. 5, p. 70 ("kanjin hijiri"); ibid., 3. 1, p. 66 ("Yūzū

nembutsu susumuru hijiri"); and ibid., 12. 2, p. 81 ("rokujūmannin yūzū nembutsu").

53. See Tamamuro Fumio, "Edo jidai," pp. 164-178, especially 175-177. His analysis makes no mention of money accepted for the regular *fuda*, but for others. Neither did I observe any exchange of money when participants accepted the *fuda* from the Yugyō Shōnin at the Year End Ceremony (Hitotsubi) at Shōjōkōji in December, 1995.

54. Kanai, *Ippen*, pp. 48-49, quoting Hirata Michiyoshi (Teizen), *Jishū kyōgaku no kenkyū*, p. 46. Sources include the "Greater Amida Sutra" (Larger Pure Land Sutra) and the Lotus Sutra. *Yugyō tokumyō no koto*, in *Teihon*, 2:1811. "Yūge" means the free movement of a Bodhisattva from buddhaland to buddhaland and "gyōbō" means the effort of walking or austerities. Nakamura, *Bukkyō daijiten*, s. v. "Yuge" (2:1379) and "Gyōbō" (1:245).

55. *Ippen hijiri e*, 4. 5, p. 68.

56. Ōhashi Shunnō, *Odori nembutsu*, Daizō sensho 12 (1974), p. 85.

57. "Kūya shōnin waga sendatsu nari" (Kūya Shōnin is my guide). *Ippen hijiri e*, 7. 3, p. 73. "Odori nembutsu wa Ichiya arui wa Shijō no tsuji ni te shugyō shitamaikeri." Ibid., 4. 5, p. 68.

58. Ōhashi, *Odori nembutsu*, pp. 65-68. Even so, as long as one looks at dancing *nembutsu* as a fusion of *nembutsu* belief and the native tradition of dance as magic to pacify the angry spirits of the dead, one can trace a history going back to the early preaching *hijiri* as well as to practices in Korea and China as a form of meditation, an expression of joy with scriptural authority. Ibid., pp. 13-18; and *Ippen hijiri e*, 4. 5, p. 68, which quotes the *Muryōjukyō*. See also Ōhashi, *Odori nembutsu*, p. 65. It is in this connection that dancing *nembutsu* must be discussed along with itinerancy (see next chapter).

59. For Ippen at Iwayaji, see *Ippen hijiri e*, 2. 1, p. 65; for Ippen and the three female companions ("dōgyō"), see ibid., 2. 2, p. 65. Names are written over the figures in the illustrations for 2. 2. Ibid., p. 85 (plate four) for description.

60. Foard, *Ippen*, p. 196.

61. "Ta'amidabutsu hajimete dōgyō sōshin no chigiri o musubitatematsurinu." *Ippen hijiri e*, 4. 3, p. 67.

62. *Ippen hijiri e*, 11. 4, p. 82.

63. Imai defines *dōgyō* as Same Practice ("onajiku gyōzuru"). Imai, *Chūsei shakai*, p. 225.

64. The term appears in the works of Shan-tao, Eshin, and even Shinran. See Kanai, *Ippen*, pp. 107-108 and Ōhashi, *Tenkai*, p. 40. Although the *rokuji nembutsu* was a practice common to all Pure Land groups, the term *jishū* eventually was not. Rennyo was clear in stating that the term *jishū* was reserved for followers of Ippen and Ikkō Shunjō: "Kano Ikkōshū to iu wa jishū kata no na nari. Ippen Ikkō kore nari." *Chōmyō ofumi* 4, cited in Ōhashi, ibid., p. 41.

65. See Imai, *Jishū seiritsushi*, p. 283.

66. Goodwin, *Alms*, pp. 102-103, citing Mōri Hisashi, "Shunjōbō Chōgen to busshi Kaikei," *Bukkyō geijutsu* 105 (1976), pp. 68-70, *Sazenshū*, p. 50, and Mizukami Ichikyū, *Chūsei no shōen to shakai* (Yoshikawa Kōbunkan, 1969), pp. 340-343, 357-358.

67. Kōan 2. *Jishū kakochō*, p. 14.

68. *Jishū kakochō*, p. 22 ("Dōnen [Bumpō 2] shōgatsu 14 nichi kechienshū E'amidabutsu dōnen 10 gatsu 8 ka kechienshū Bun'amidabutsu"). "Kechienshū" appears throughout here as well as in the *Tōtakusan kakochō*. In the *Ippen hijiri e*, for example, both verbal and nominal forms appear: 3. 2, p. 66 ("kechien arubeki"); 4. 4, p. 68 ("kechien subeshi"); 6. 3, p. 71 ("kechien no tame"); 7. 2, p. 74 ("kechien no tame"), and 12. 3, p. 81 ("kechienshū").

69. Kanai, *Ippen*, pp. 112, 119-120, for forty-eight vows and names, respectively.

70. Kōan 2, in the collection of Shōjōkōji. Kanai, *Ippen*, pp 114-118.

71. According to Kanai, when Ippen named Shōkai, he ordered him to "'accept the precepts of the Greater Vehicle and bring salvation to mankind,'" thus making him a Bodhisattva and never Amida Buddha. Kanai, *Ippen*, p. 453, quoting the *Kaisan Mi'a Shōnin gyōjō* [in *Teihon*, 2:1571-1573].

72. For Mt. Kōya, see Gorai Shigeru, *Kōya hijiri* (Kadokawa Shoten, 1965), pp. 134, 137, 153, 201-247; for Zenkōji, see Sakai, *Zenkōjishi*, 1:240-243, 2:843-845.

73. ". . . mochitamaeru kyō shosho Shoshazan no jisō no haberishi ni watashitamau. Tsune ni waga kadō wa ichigo bakari zo to notamaishi ga . . . Amidakyō o yomite tezukara yakitamaishikaba, denbō ni hito nakushite shi to tomo ni horoboshinuru ka to . . . Namuamidabutsu ni narihatenu to notamaishi wa . . ." *Ippen hijiri e*, 11. 4, p. 80. For discussion, see Imai, *Jishū seiritsushi*, p. 226-227, and Ōhashi, *Ippen*, pp. 76-77.

74. Kanai, *Ippen*, pp. 198, 201.

75. Kanai calls Shinkyō the real founder of the Jishū. See Kanai, *Ippen*, p. 200. He also states that Shinkyō established an order separate from that of Ippen's successor Shōkai. Ibid., p. 201.

76. See Kanai, *Ippen*, pp. 197-198.

77. *Yugyō engi e*, I. 3, p. 59; 2. 4, p. 61; 3. 2, p. 63; 4. 3, p. 66 (four times); 4. 5, p. 67 (by Ta'a); 4. 5, p. 68 (twice).

78. *Yugyō engi e*, for Mishima Shrine, 4. 3, p. 66; for shedding tears, 4. 5, p. 67; for "tears of attachment," 5. 1, p. 67; for "late hijiri," 5. 1, p. 68, and 6. 3, p. 72; for "late Shōnin," 10. 1, p. 82; and *Hōnō engi ki, San dai sōshi hōgo*, in *Teihon*, 1:237-238. As for the title of the *Ekotoba den*, various copies have various names: *Ippen Shōnin e den, Ippen Shōnin engi-e, Ippen Shōnin onden*, and *Yugyō engi*. Miya Tsugio, "Sōshunhon Yugyō Shōnin engie shohon ryakkai," in *Yugyō engi e*, pp. 52-55, 92.

79. *Yugyō engi e,* for "sutehijiri," 6. 1, p. 71, and 7. 4, p. 75; for "tashū no hijiri," 9. 1, p. 80; and for "Shōnin," 4. 5, p. 68 (twice), 5. 3, p. 69, 5. 5, p. 70, 9. 1, p. 80, 9. 2, p. 81, 10. 2, p. 83 (three times), and 5. 5, p. 70.

80. Miya, "Sōshunhon," in *Yugyō engi e,* p. 52.

81. *Yugyō engi e,* 9. 1, p. 80 ("gojitsu ni jingū yori Shōnin e susumeserarekeru to namu").

82. Imai, *Chūsei shakai,* pp. 349-351. For the definition, see *Bukkyōgo daijiten,* ed. Nakamura Hajime, 2 vols. (Tōkyō Shobō, 1975), 2:948 and 850 (for "Zenchishiki").

83. It has also been used for the members of communities serviced by *kanjin hijiri.* For *chishiki* as lay believers, see Goodwin, *Alms,* pp. 26-27, 74, 159.

84. *Ippen hijiri e,* 6. 2, p. 71 (letter to Hōin Kōchō).

85. *Ippen hijiri e,* 4. 3, p. 68 ("chishiki o shite shukke o toge"); 6. 3, p. 71 ("Namuamidabutsu rokujūmannin chishiki Ippen . . . chishiki no yakusoku mōshite; saigo no kisami tada hitori mae ni kitamaitarikeru o, nyūdō chishiki no sō ni Ippen Shōnin no irasetamaitaru wa mitatematsuru ga, ushiro mukite owashimasu zo to mōshikereba, chishiki no sō tadaima rinjū ni te mashimaseba"); 10. 1, pp. 77-78 ("Chishiki no oshie no gotoku rinjū seinen ni shite ōjō o togenikeri"); 12. 2, p. 81 ("Saigū no Daimyōjin no saigo no kechien semu . . . Saigū no kanjū mairite mōsu yō . . . chishiki to tanomimairasete sōrō ga"); and *jishū* drown themselves in 12. 3, p. 81 ("chishiki o shitau kokorozashi"). *Yugyō engi e,* 1. 3, p. 59, at the Kehi Shrine ("hijiri o chishiki ni shite shukke o togenu"); 2. 4, p. 61 ("Namuamidabutsu rokujūmannin chishiki Ippen"); *jishū* commit suicide in 4. 5, p. 68 ("chishiki o shitau kokorozashi"); *jishū* make their farewells in 5. 1, p. 68 ("chishiki ni okuretatematsurinuru ue wa, sumiyaka ni nembutsu shite rinjū subeshi to te").

86. Imai, *Chūsei,* pp. 349-351. See also Nakamura, *Bukkyōgo daijiten,* 2:948, and 850 (for "Zenchishiki").

87. For Ajisaka Nyūdo, *Yugyō engi e,* 2. 5, p. 61; for Ippen and *saigo no jūnen,* see 3. 1, p. 63.

88. ". . . hijiri yori jūnen susumeraretatematsuru yoshi . . ." *Yugyō engi e,* 7. 3, p. 74.

89. *Yugyō engi e,* 9. 1, p. 80. The practice of receiving the ten *nembutsu* from the head of the order would become an important ritual in the Yugyō-ha. Chiren, *Shinshū yōhōki,* 17, in *Teihon,* 2:992.

90. *Yugyō engi e,* 1. 1, p. 57.

91. *Yugyō engi e,* 6. 3, p. 71. The passage describes the death of the lay priest Ninomiya.

92. *Yugyō engi e,* 5. 1, p. 69.

93. *Yugyō engi e,* 7. 3, p. 74 ("makoto no chishiki ni aitatematsurinuru koto"); 7. 4, p. 75 ("chishiki to tanomitatematsuru beshi"); 8. 1, p. 77 ("chishiki

ni au koto"); and 8. 3, p. 78 ("makoto no chishiki ni aitatematsurite, ōjō togehaberan koto").

94. "Ima chishiki o motte, butsu no onshi to nashi, hatsugan seikai no kotoba o uketori, shikakushite gonkaikon utau." *Hōnō engi ki*, in *Teihon*, 1:238. Also, "chishiki no kinshi o kataku kuwabaru . . . chishiki no ikku ni yotte shimmei o chishiki ni yuzuru no kotoba wa kimyō no niji kore nari." Ibid.

95. ". . . chishiki no kurai ni narite wa . . . Ryōamidabutsu o sutete Ta'-amidabutsu to gō seraru beshi." "Onaji Shōnin e tsukawasaru ofumi," *Ta'a Shōnin hōgo*, 1, in *Teihon*, 1:125.

96. *Dōjo seimon*, *Ta'a Shōnin hōgo*, 1, in *Teihon*, 1:122 ("kaneguchi no chigiri, shimmei o chishiki ni yuzuru no namu no tōtai kore nari"); "Sansō Shōnin e tsukawasaru ofumi," ibid., p. 124 ("Shimmei o butsu ni kimyō shite, chishiki no mei ni yotte"); and "Onaji Shōnin e tsukawasaru ofumi," ibid., p. 125 ("chishiki no muro ni hairi, shimmei o Mida ni ki su to iedomo").

What I call here "variants of a formulaic expression" is actually close to what is called a "formulaic system" in oral composition. Fry defines "formulaic system" as "the identical relative placement of two elements, one a variable word or element of a compound . . . and the other constant word or element of a compound." Donald K. Fry, Jr., "Old English Formulas and System," *English Studies* 48 (1967): 203, cited in John Miles Foley, *Traditional Oral Epic: The "Odyssey," "Beowulf," and the Serbo-Croation Return Song* (Berkeley, Los Angeles, and Oxford, U. K. : University of California Press, 1990), p. 206. The difference is that in the Japanese example both elements of the compound are variable in diction if absolutely the same in meaning.

97. For Ippen, see *Yugyō engi e*, 1. 2, p. 58 ("kuniguni o shugyō shi") and 1. 3, p. 58 ("Kyūgoku o shugyō shitamaikeru toki"). For Shinkyō, see 6. 3, p. 72 ("Kōzuke no kuni o shugyō arikeru ni") and 9. 2, pp. 80-81 ("shokoku shugyō no nembutsu kanjin hijiri Ta'amidabutsu").

98. *Ippen hijiri e*, 9. 3, p. 77; and *Ippen Shōnin goroku*, 2. 89, in *Teihon*, 2:36 ("shokoku yugyō no omoide"); *Yugyō engi e*, 9. 1, p. 80 ("yugyō tashū no hijiri").

99. "Onaji Shōnin e tsukawasaru ofumi," *Ta'a Shōnin hōgo*, 1, in *Teihon*, 1:125 (letter to Chitoku promoting him to Chishiki). See note 96.

100. "Shisō Shichijō Konkōji sumu no toki tsukawaseru gosho," *Yugyō hōgo*, in *Teihon*, 1:330.

101. *Yugyō Shōnin engi e*, 1. 1, p. 57 ("nembutsu kanjin"); 1. 2, p. 57 ("fuda o uketamae"); 1. 2, p. 58 ("nembutsu o ukeba . . . nembutsu to mōshite fuda o uketamau beshi. . . . Yūzū nembutsu susumeraruru hijiri . . . nembutsu . . . susumeraruru zo. . . . fuda o kuba(ri)te . . . nembutsu no fuda o ukete . . . nembutsu kanjin no chikai . . . nembutsu o susume tamau. . . . nembutsu no fuda o kubaru tamau").

102. *Yugyō engi e*, 5. 1, p. 68 ("hajimete nembutsu no fuda o tama(i)nu"); 5. 3, p. 69 ("Uriu . . . o shugyō shite . . . nembutsu susume tamau"); and 8. 1, p. 77 ("nembutsu kanjin").

103. "Shichidai Shōnin e Rokudai Shōnin yori," *Yugyō daidai hōgo*, in *Teihon*, 1:353. In one line Itchin writes "fuda o kubar[u]" with characters for *san* and *fu* and in another what could be "fusan tama[i]ki" or "fuda o kuba[ri]tama[i]ki." This is the earliest recording I could find of "fusan." It appears very rarely and in *kanbun* texts, which means that "fuda o kubaru" could still be the correct reading. Even so, it is definitely found in the chronicle of Tosen (b. 1305; YS 1354-1356, FS -1381), which is mixed *kana* and *kanji*. *Yugyō hachidai Tosen Shōnin kaikoku ki*, in *Teihon*, 2:1447 ("gomyō sōzoku shi fusan o kubari tamau").

104. There is no indication that Shōkai or his successors actually practiced amulet distribution until the seventeenth century even though it is assumed that he did indeed do so. Kanai, *Ippen*, pp. 460, 198, 302.

105. According to the *Mazanshū*, 1313/Kagen 1. Rōhō, *Mazanshū*, in *Teihon*, 2:836. The date 1304/Kagen 2. 1. 10 is given by the *Jishū kechimyaku sōzoku no shidai*, in Ōhashi, *Jishū no seiritsu*, p. 305.

106. "Onaji Shōnin e tsukawasaru ofumi," *Ta'a Shōnin hōgo*, in *Teihon*, 1:125. A manuscript of *Shinkyō hōgo shū* has a note "ninth month last day [from] Ta'amidabutsu received Kagen 2/1304 tenth month twelfth day." Kanai, *Ippen*, p. 254, citing Kōno, *Ippen kyōgaku*, p. 260.

107. *Shichijō monjo*, no. 1, *Teihon*, 1:391. The date is 2. 13. The address, "Yū'amidabutsu [e] Daiichi Ta'amidabutsu [yori]," is in the same hand. Kanai, *Ippen*, p. 257.

108. *Shichijō monjo*, no. 1, *Teihon*, 1:391.

109. The earliest life of Jō'a is the *Jō'a Shōnin den* (finished in 1463 and bearing the seal of Gohanazono) in *Teihon*, 2:1543-1544. Tachibana Shundō, "*Jō'a Shōnin den* kaisetsu," ibid., 2:1545. I am not certain what sort of problem is presented by the fact that the year of Kōgon's birth is more generally given as 1313.

110. *Shichijō monjo*, no. 1, in *Teihon*, 1:391.

111. Kanai, *Ippen*, p. 422, for the limit of activities to Kyoto. He also cites a Muromachi copy of a what is called the *inka jō* (letter conferring certification) of the Konrenji which states that the founder of the temple, Jō'a, was assigned to preaching activities ("kadō") within the capital ("Rakuchū") as the representative of the Great Shōnin ("Daishōnin").

112. Kanai, *Ippen*, p. 296. Ibid., p. 421.

113. Chitoku, *Chishin shuyōki*, in *San daisōshi hōgo*, in *Teihon*, 1:240.

114. Ibid., in *Teihon*, 1:240; idem, *Nembutsu ōjō kōyō*, in *San dai*, in *Teihon*, 1:243; and idem, *Sanshinryōkengi*, in *San dai*, in *Teihon*, 1:244.

115. "Chūshō gosho," in *Yugyō hōgo*, in *Teihon*, 1:331.

116. "Shichisō Shōnin e tsukawasaru ofumi," *Ta'a Shōnin hōgo*, 1, in *Teihon*, 1:127; "Chūshō gosho," *Yugyō hōgo*, in *Teihon*, 1:331; "Yugyō sandai Chitoku Shōnin shojō," *Shichijō monjo*, no. 3, in *Teihon*, 1:392-393. See also no. 4 for "yugyō."

117. For "sandai" and "Chishiki," *Shichijō monjo*, no. 4, in *Teihon*, 1:393; for "Ta'amidabutsu," ibid., no. 3, p. 392.

118. *Shichijō monjo*, no. 3, in *Teihon*, 1:392 (dated 10. 4) and 5, 1:394 (dated 8. 26). Based on the dating of sending and receipt, Kanai concludes that Donkai was already on tour distributing amulets. *Ippen*, p. 296.

119. *Shichijō monjo*, no. 6, in *Teihon*, 1:394-395, and *Donkai hōgo*, in *Teihon*, 1:268.

120. *Donkai hōgo*, in *Teihon*, 1:265. See also Kanai, *Ippen*, p. 313.

121. *Donkai hōgo*, in *Teihon*, 1:265.

122. "[Shijō] Jō'amidabutsu (onaji [Ryakuō] onaji [2] ka)." *Jishū kakochō*, p. 27.

123. "Shikaraba yondai no sōzoku ichiri no kaeki narubeshi, yue ni Daishō iwaku sutehijiri no monka ni yuiseki sōzoku no gi arubekarazu to ieri. . . . kaeki wa funi ni shite gojūnenyo toshi nari." *Donkai hōgo*, in *Teihon*, 1:267.

124. *Yugyō keizu*, in *Teihon*, 2:1574; Kanai, *Ippen*, pp. 317-318, 348.

125. Kanai, *Ippen*, p. 326-7, citing *Shichijō kakochō*. Kanai thinks it more than likely that Chitoku sent both Ankoku and Takuga to help Donkai, and thus Donkai made Ankoku head of Konkōji when he went to Fujisawa. Ibid., p. 327.

126. Ibid., p. 334.

127. Ibid., p. 348, citing Takuga's "Saishū waden yō" [*San dai*, in *Teihon* 1:253-260]. ("Zaikyō no hajime Bumpō no koro ni ya").

128. "Hakuboku Shōnin," *Gorekidai keifu*, in *Shomin shinkō*, p. 240.

129. Kanai, *Ippen*, pp. 334-335.

130. Letter beginning "Yugyō . . ." and dated the twenty-fifth, in *Yugyō hōgo*, in *Teihon*, 1:336; Kanai, *Ippen*, p. 346-347.

131. *Yugyō hachidai Tosen Shōnin kaikoku ki*, in *Teihon*, 2:1447-1448, and also in Kanai, *Ippen*, pp. 367-370.

132. *Yugyō hachidai*, in *Teihon*, 2:1447. See commentary by Makino Sozan for explanation. Ibid., 2:1449, 5n.

133. According to another source, he came directly from the Hakuseki Jōrinji. "Hakuboku Shōnin," *Gorekidai keifu*, in *Shomin shinkō*, p. 240.

134. Tosen is apparently at the Ōshōji in Echigo. I am not sure where Hakuboku is. The text reads "Shichijō no Kai'amidabutsu" and the *Gorekidai keifu* says that Hakuboku distributed amulets for the first time here on this date. The use of the term "gomyōgo" differs from that used above, "myōji."

135. Takuga died as Yugyō Shōnin and Tosen's succession ceremony took place at Fujisawa. Hakuboku (ninth) died as Yugyō Shōnin and his successor Gengu (tenth; b. 1324; YS 1367-1381, YS -1387) succeeded at Ōshōji or Shōnenji in Echizen Province. Sonmyō (thirteenth; b. 1349; YS 1401-1412, YS

-1417) and Nanyō (sixteenth; b. 1387; YS 1429-1439, FS -1470) succeeded at Fujisawa, but Nyoshō (eighteenth; b. 1419; YS 1467-1471, FS -1494) had his ceremony at the Tarui Konrenji. "Gengu Shōnin," "Sonmyō Shōnin," "Nanyō Shōnin," and Nyōshō Shōnin," *Gorekidai keifu*, in *Shomin Shinkō*, pp. 240-243.

136. Also known as the *Ōko kakochō*. Although all the entries up to and including Shinkyō's name Ta'amidabutsu are in Shinkyō's hand, the number of names recorded between 1279 and 1304 (Kōan 2. 6 and Kagen 1. 2), 135, does not match that recorded in the *Ekotoba den*, 269. The number of names recorded by 1306 does not match the 275 recorded in Shinkyō's *Dōjō seimon*, dated by him Kagen 4. 9. 15. The numbers cited in the *Ekotoba den* and *Dōjō seimon* were not based on the present *Jishū kakochō*, which, because the first twenty-eight names appear to have been written in all at once, Kanai thinks, is not the original but a copy. Kanai, *Ippen*, pp. 225-227, citing p. 226 on the twenty-eight names. Ōhashi Shunnō (Toshio), *"Jishū kakochō* ni tsuite," in *Jishū kakochō*, pp. 1-2.

137. The *Betsuji banchō, Gokuraku rokuji san, Ajiki mondō*, in Shinkyō's hand, and the *Ippen Shōnin ekotoba den*, later sent to the Saku Kondaiji, all ended up at the Konkōji. Kanai, *Ippen*, p. 292-295.

138. A piece of paper has been added on with six names in a different hand. Kanai, *Ippen*, p. 330. Ōhashi says twelve, but I counted six. *"Jishū kakochō* ni tsuite," p. 6. There seem to be other problems in the numbers cited.

139. Kanai, *Ippen*, pp. 336-337. Kanai thought that the title "Yondai Shōnin" had also been entered by Itchin, but a paleographic investigation published in 1969 determined that all such entries had been made by a single hand, that of the thirty-seventh Yugyō Shōnin Takushi. Tachibana, *Jishūshi ronkō*, pp. 128-129.

140. Kanai thinks the number too small and that therefore the names are those of the most important. Kanai, *Ippen*, p. 337. For entry of Ankoku's name and date of death, see ibid., p. 345.

141. For Takuga, see Kanai, *Ippen*, p. 346; for Tosen, see ibid., p. 366.

142. *Jishū kakochō*, pp. 14, 19, 21, 23, etc. ("fu"); p. 22 ("kechienshū"); pp. 44, 48, etc. ("gyakushū"); pp. 37, 170 ("genzon"); p. 87 ("Mi'amidabutsu [Benkei]"), p. 91 ("Antoku Tennō Go'amidabutsu"), p. 95 ("Go'amidabutsu [Taira Sōgoku]"), and p. 110 ("Go'amidabutsu [Shonagon Shinzei]"); p. 105 ("Sen'amidabutsu [Echizen sarugaku]"), p. 110 ("Jiki'amidabutsu [Manzai]"), p. 114 ("Rai'amidabutsu [Kanze Saburō] Sei'amidabutsu [onaji Shirō]"), and p. 119 ("Sō'amidabutsu [Manzai Yamato nyūdo]"). For artisans, stonecutters, sculptors, religious performers, and pirates, see Ōhashi, *"Jishū kakochō* ni tsuite," pp. 7-8. The Ashikaga family will be discussed in chapter 6.

143. The thirteenth Yugyō Shōnin Sonmyō spent a long time in Kyoto. When he tried to go on *yugyō*, he got only as far as Moriyasu in Etchū when he was called back by the shogun. *Yugyō engi*, in *Teihon*, 2:1451.

144. Ōhashi, "*Jishū kakochō* ni tsuite," p. 5, citing Akamatsu Toshihide, "Fujisawashi Shōjōkōji no *Jishū kakochō*," *Shirin* 35 [], p. 481.

145. According to Ōhashi's calculations. "*Jishū kakochō* ni tsuite," pp. 6-7.

146. Ōhashi, "*Jishū kakochō* ni tsuite," pp. 5-6. Ōhashi notes a difference in calligraphy between the entry "Yugyō 22 dai Eishō 10 nen mizu no to tori 5 gatsu mikka kore o haji[meru]" and twenty-four entries (including one "gyakushū). *Jishū kakochō*, p. 144. I am inclined to propose that if the entry, like so many, was entered by a later hand, then it is possible that the above-mentioned twenty-four were indeed entered by Igyō. I have before me a printed edition. Until I have the chance to see a photographic facsimile or the original, I have to depend on the estimations of other scholars.

147. Tachibana, *Jishūshi ronkō*, pp. 124-125.

148. "Saikoku," according to the inscription in the *Jishū kakochō* by thirty-seventh Yugyō Shōnin Takushi (p. 152). "Bizen," according to an inscription by the thirty-second Yugyō Shōnin Fukō on the back of a portrait of Ippen (portrait of Ippen, private collection), which notes that it as well as one of Shinkyō had been taken. An inscription by Fukō on a copy of the *Ta'a Shōnin wasan shū* in Shinkyō's hand indicates that it too had been taken. Tachibana, *Jishūshi ronkō*, pp. 121-124. Dōnen's travel diary, *Yugyō sanjūissō Kyō-Ki goshugyō ki*, last reports the date 1580/Tenshō 8. 3 and his visit to Taimadera in Yamato. In *Teihon*, 2:1502.

149. Inscriptions on the reverse side of the *Yugyō Fujisawa gorekidai reibo* indicate registration in a "kakochō" (thirty-fifth) and "Yugyō no kakochō." Tachibana, *Jishūshi ronkō*, p. 125. These inscriptions are not included in the text, edited by Tachibana, published in the *Teihon*, 2:1583-1600.

150. Tachibana, *Jishūshi ronkō*, p. 122. Takushi's inscription, *Jishū kakochō*, p. 152.

151. For dimensions, see Ōhashi, "*Jishū kakochō* ni tsuite," p. 1. Discussion on explanatory comments given by Tachibana, who cites an inscription by Takushi in the *Jishū kakochō* which I could not find in the printed version. *Jishūshi ronkō*, p. 127. He is using a photographic facsimile *Jishū kakochō* ([]: Jishū Kyōgakubu, 1969) with an introduction by the head of the research team. He lists Takushi's additions, the results of the Jishū Kyōgakubu's research results, on pp. 128-129. He also summarizes the additions of other Tokugawa Yugyō Shōnin/Fujisawa Shōnin to the text on p. 130.

152. Shōhō 1. 3. 16. Tachibana, *Jishūshi ronkō*, 128-130, citing Mochizuki, *Jishū nempyō*, p. 94, which cites ["Nyotan Shōnin,"] *Gorekidai keifu* [in *Shomin shinkō*, p. 249] and *Shichijō dōjō kiroku*.

153. Tachibana, *Jishūshi ronkō*, p. 126. He notes that a copy of the *Ippen Shōnin engi e* donated by Emperor Higashiyama (1675-1709; r. 1687-1709) was also burned. His source is Mochizuki, *Jishū nempyō*, p. 137, citing *Shichijō dōjō kiroku*.

154. Kanai, *Ippen*, pp. 293-295.

NOTES TO CHAPTER 3 213

155. Butten's inscription in *Tōtakusan kakochō: monmatsu sōryo kechienshū*, ed. Tachibana Shundō (Fujisawa: Jishū Shūmusho Kyōgakubu, 1981), p. 5.
This would have been between 1513. 5. 8, when Chiren died (b. 1459; YS 1497-
1512, FS -1513), and 1514. 9. 3, when Shōgu succeeded (b. 1470; YS 1518-
1520, FS -1526). For the dates, see Mochizuki, *Jishū nempyō*, p. 68, citing *Jishū
kakochō* [p. 149] and ["Chiren Shōnin," "Igyō Shōnin," and "Shōgu Shōnin,"]
Gorekidai keifu [in *Shomin shinkō*, p. 244].
    156. Kōji 3. 3. 24. Butten's inscription, *Jishū kakochō*, p. 5.
    157. For last entries, *Tōtakusan kakochō*, pp. 46, 105. For "gyakushū," ibid.,
p. 51 ("Bun'ichibō"), p. 52 ("Rei'butsubō" and "Hō'amidabutsu"), etc.
    158. *Tōtakusan kakochō*, p. 51; for Satake, pp. 58, 60, 61, etc.
    159. "In the Jishū of this country are three *shōnin*. One is the Shichijō
Shōnin, who ministers to the three *ri* of the capital. The second is the Fujisawa
Shōnin, who ministers to the six provinces of the north. And the third is the
Yugyō Shōnin, who ministers to the whole country of Japan." Kanai, *Ippen*, p.
436, citing "Shūkokuan Bun'ami shōzōsan," *Kanrin koroshū* 11. For Jō'a, see
Shichijō monjo, no. 1, in *Teihon*, 1:391.

Notes to Chapter 4

1. See for example Alicia Matsunaga and Daigan Matsunaga, *Foundation
of Japanese Buddhism*, vol. 2, *The Mass Movement (Kamakura and Muromachi
Periods)* (Los Angeles and Tokyo: Buddhist Books International, 1976), p. 7
("the path of salvation for even common man, who had been totally neglected
by the older sects . . . embracing the majority of the populace").
    2. For meditation, see *The Encyclopedia of Religion*, ed. Mircea Eliade
(New York: Macmillan Publishing Company; London: Collier Macmillan
Publishers, 1987), s. v. "Nien-fo" and "Ching-t'u;" for main text, Matsunaga and
Matsunaga, *Foundation*, 2:32-34.
    3. Allan A. Andrews, *The Teachings Essential for Rebirth: A Study of
Genshin's Ōjōyōshū* (Sophia University, 1970), pp. 78-79 for description of
practices, and p. 86 for discussion of benefits of *nembutsu*.
    4. For recording visions, Matsunaga and Matsunaga, *Foundation*, 2:61,
citing *Hōnen Shōnin zenshū*, pp. 865-867; for quote, *Encyclopedia of Religion*,
s. v. "Hōnen."
    5. Matsunaga and Matsunaga, *Foundation*, 2:85-86 and 91, citing Eshin-ni's
letter of 1263, in Ishida, *Shinran to sono tsuma no tegami*, pp. 224-225.
    6. The following discussion is based on the definition of mystic in *The
Encyclopedia of Religion*, s. v. "Mystical Union."
    7. For Tendai meditation practices, see Imai, *Jishū seiritsushi*, pp. 50-53.
Jōgyō zanmai is based on the *Hanju sanmai kyō* (Pratyutpanna-buddha-
sammukhāvastita-samādhi sūtra); it was "devised by Chih-I and brought to Japan

by Saichō and Ennin." Matsunaga and Matsunaga, *Foundation*, 2:34. For Shōkū, Imai, *Jishū seiritsushi*, pp. 182-183.

8. Imai, *Jishū seiritsushi*, p. 210.

9. ". . . if mysticism is an interior pilgrimage, pilgrimage is an externalized mysticism." Victor and Edith Turner, *Image and Pilgrimage in Christian Culture: Anthropological Perspectives*,Lectures on the History of Religions, new ser. no. 11 (New York: Columbia University Press, 1978), p. 6. If Buddhist pilgrimage reflects the idea of Buddha as the external world, then Buddhist mysticism reflects the idea of Buddha in the mind; for Ippen, there would be no difference. The following discussion is based on the Turners' book.

10. Following Genshin (Andrews, *Essentials*, p. 86), Shan-tao, Hōnen, and the Pure Land Meditation Sutra (Matsunaga and Matsunaga, *Foundation*, pp. 61-62).

11. See Kanai's discussion of *ōjō* and *fuōjō* in *Ippen*, pp. 228-229.

12. Imai, *Jishū seiritsushi*, p. 53, and *Ippen hijiri e*, 4. 2, p. 67 ("dōgyō shichi hachi nin").

13. *Ippen hijiri e*, 4. 5, p. 68. There are seven illustrations of *odori nembutsu* in the *Hijiri e*. The first shows a pretty wild dance. The illustration of the *odori nembutsu* at Katase in Kamakura three years later shows a stage and a formal, organized dance. Kanai, *Ippen*, p. 125.

14. Imai, *Jishū seiritsushi*, p. 54. See for example, Ohashi, *Odori nembutsu*.

15. Matsunaga and Matsunaga, *Foundation*, 2:246.

16. Ibid., 2:53, 57 for Amida as Buddha Nature.

17. *Ippen hijiri e*, 1. 2-3, p. 64. The following discussion on the doctrines expressed in the poems is based on Imai, *Jishū seiritsushi*, pp. 183-195 for Shōkū, and pp. 195-217 for Ippen. Transliteration is based on Kanai, *Ippen hōgo*, pp. 345-346, translation on ibid., pp. 336-346 and idem, *Ippen*, pp. 35-36.

18. Kanai, *Ippen*, pp. 35-36. See also idem, *Ippen hōgo*, pp. 345-346.

19. For Ippen, especially, Rebirth in Amida's land is achieved in and for the moment of a single *nembutsu*. There is no question of one and many invocations: the very problem suggests effort on the part of the individual, which is not reliance on another, Amida, and therefore not Rebirth as understood in the Pure Land school.

20. Kanai, *Ippen hōgo*, p. 352.

21. *Ippen hijiri e*, 3. 1-2, pp. 66-67. Transliteration and translation based on Kanai's translation and commentary in *Ippen hōgo*, pp. 346-352.

22. Imai, *Jishū seiritsushi*, p. 189.

23. Ibid., pp. 186-187.

24. Kanai, *Ippen hōgo*, pp. 345-346.

25. Imai, *Jishū seiritsushi*, pp. 203, 207, 208 and 210.

26. For Amida's reward, Imai, *Jishū seiritsushi*, p. 215; for Amida and the Name, ibid., pp. 203, 207, 208.

27. For a study of the transfer of charisma to amulets, see Tambiah, *Buddhist Saints*.

28. Kanai, *Ippen hōgo*, p. 346.

29. Ibid., p. 350.

30. For an English language translation, see Dennis Hirota, trans., *No Abode: The Record of Ippen* (Kyoto: Ryukoku University, 1986), pp. 63-65.

31. *Ippen hijiri e*, 9. 4, p. 77. For commentary, see Kanai, *Ippen hōgo*, pp. 507-533.

32. For description and text, see Kanai, *Ippen*, pp. 112-115. The date is Kōan 1.

33. *Ippen hijiri e*, 10. 1, p. 75 ("sōshū yonjūhachinin nishū yonjūhachinin").

34. It is dated Kyōhō 6. 8. 23. Recorded in the *Jimyōchō chūshaku* of the future twenty-sixth Yugyō Shōnin Kaison. *Teihon*, 1:951-953. He claims Shinkyō as a source. See also Kanai, *Ippen*, pp. 115-116. A manuscript of the Chōanji in Ōtsu titled the *Jishū banchō* has a list for male religious (six groups of eight), for male [?] lay (six groups, two of fifteen, one of sixteen, one of eighteen, and two of nineteen) for female religious (six of eight), and for female [?] lay (one of twenty-three, three of twenty-four, one of twenty five, and one of twenty-six). There is a very great deal of correspondence in the sets of names and thus are obviously related. Kanai, *Ippen*, pp. 116-118.

35. *San daisōshi hōgo*, in *Teihon*, 1:237.

36. Kanai, *Ippen*, pp. 114-115. It is dated Kagen 4. 1. 25.

37. In *Teihon*, 1:947-954. See Kanai, *Ippen*, pp. 115-119.

38. "Ima Ippen o motte moto to nasu. Ima no Fujisawa Ippen yori yondaime ni ataru nari." Kanai, *Jishū bungei kenkyū*, pp. 204-205, citing the Muromachi manuscript (compiled after Bunnan 1. 6) of Tokyo University National Language Research Seminar. This would date the text to the mid-1320s (Donkai is traditionally given as in residence at Fujisawa 1325-1327). For an overview of the studies, see ibid., pp. 199-206.

39. Dated Kōan 10. 3. 1. *Ippen hijiri e*, 10. 1, p. 78.

40. In *Teihon*, 1:6-7. See also a translation in Hirota, *No Abode*. The list, titled the "Dōgu hishaku" (The Deep Significance of the Tools of the Way), is found ibid., pp. 79-83.

41. For transliterations, see Kanai, *Ippen*, p. 120.

42. In the *Ippen hijiri e*, the boxes look like those carried by Kōya *hijiri*. Kanai, *Ippen*, p. 121. *Hōnō engi ki, Sandai sōshi hōgo*, in *Teihon*, 1:237.

43. *Yugyō Shōnin engi e*, 3. 1, p. 62, and *Hōnō engi ki*, in *Teihon*, 1:237.

44. *Yugyō Shōnin engi e*, 10. 3, p. 83, and Kanai, *Ippen*, p. 121.

45. *Teihon*, 2:1224, and Kanai, *Ippen*, pp. 121-122.

46. Called The Larger Sutra of Immeasurable Life in Hirota, *No Abode*, p. 198.

47. Hirota, *No Abode*, p. 80.

48. *Ippen hijiri e*, 8. 5, p. 75; *Yugyō Shōnin engi e*, 3. 1, p. 62; *Teihon*, 1:6. Translated by Hirota as "Verse of Aspiration." *No Abode*, pp. 74-75.

49. Hirota indicates that this line can be read "My disciples" or "Disciples and I," but that in Pure Land tradition, *nembutsu* practitioners are disciples of Shakyamuni or Amida, as with Ippen. *No Abode*, pp. 196-197.

50. Imai, *Jishū seiritsushi*, p. 239. The discussion is taken from Imai.

51. *Hijiri e*, 7. 1, p. 72, and Imai, *Jishū seiritsushi*, p. 238. What is not clear in the meaning of *kechien* in the Ippen schools compared with other *hijiri* groups is whether the connection toward salvation is made only with the leader of the group or with other members of the group. I will take this up later in a separate article.

52. *Ippen hijiri e*, 1. 2, p. 64.

53. Imai, *Jishū seiritushi*, p. 31. In the *Ippen Shōnin nempuryaku* the date given is for 1273 and the wives those of a close relative. The Dōshin-Karukaya story from Zenkōji is a related story.

54. Kōan 7. *Ippen hijiri e*, 7. 4, in p. 73. See also Imai, *Jishū seiritsushi*, pp. 240-241.

55. For Ippen and authority, see Imai, *Jishū seiritsushi*, p. 239; for absolute authority and the Name, ibid., p. 244. Assuming that Ippen actually confronted problems in his confraternity, Imai asserts that Ippen was unable to deal effectively with the problems of *fushin* and sex. Ibid., p. 246

56. *Ippen hijiri e*, 11. 4, p. 80.

57. The *Ippen Shōnin ekotoba den* has been renamed the *Yugyō Shōnin engi e* (The illustrated biographies of the Yugyō Shōnin).

58. An attempt has been made to identify him as the son of Ōgo (or Awakawa) Tokitoshi. Shimoda, "Ōgo-shi," pp. 25-26. However, Imai notes that the name Sōshun/Munetoshi does not appear in Hōjō genealogies and, although a "Taira Munetoshi" is listed as sponsor ("hatsugan shū") of 1323 on the colophon of the *Ippen Shōnin yugyō engi emaki* (ten volumes) of the Kobe Shinkōji (where Ippen is buried), there is no proof that the two are the same. Imai Masaharu, "Tokifusa-ryū no Hōjō-shi to jishū," in *Kamakura jidai bunka denpa no kenkyū* (Yoshikawa Kōbunkan, 1993), pp. 182-183.

59. Shōan 1, according to the colophon at the end of the text. *Ippen hijiri e*, 1. 1, p. 82. *Yugyō Shōnin engi e*, 1. 1, p. 57. Miya, "About the Engi-e," pp. 1, 4.

60. See Miya, "About the Engi-e," pp. 1-4. Japanese and more complete version, ibid., pp. 52-56. For the rivalry, see Imai, *Jishū seiritsushi*, pp. 255, 266, 271.

61. Imai, *Jishū seiritsushi*, p. 271. In the *Hōnō engi ki*, Shinkyō asks rhetorically whether honoring Ippen's admonitions and continuing the mission had not been due to the *gongen*'s protection. In *Teihon*, 1:238.

62. Stressed by various scholars, for example, Imai, *Jishū seiritsushi*, pp. 255, 271.

63. *Ippen hijiri e*, 4. 3, p. 67, 11. 4, p. 80, and 12. 2, p. 81.

64. *Ippen hijiri e*, 11. 4, p. 80; *Yugyō engi e*, 4. 5, p. 67.

65. *Yugyō Shōnin engi e*, 4. 5, pp. 67-68.

66. Ibid., 5. 1, pp. 68-69, and Imai, *Jishū seiritsushi*, p. 252.

67. *Yugyō Shōnin engi e*, 4. 5, p. 67.

68. See Imai, *Jishū seiritsushi*, pp. 253-254 for a comparison of discussions.

69. *Yugyō Shōnin engi e*, 5. 1, p. 69, and Imai, *Jishū seiritsushi*, p. 252.

70. *Yugyō Shōnin engi e*, 4. 5, p. 68.

71. For a comparison of the *Ekotoba den* and *Hijiri e* on who had the special relationship with Ippen, see Imai, *Jishū seiritsushi*, pp. 254-55.

72. *Ippen hijiri e*, 11. 4, p. 80.

73. *Yugyō Shōnin engi e*, 5. 1, pp. 68-69.

74. "Sono toki hijiri ware ni shimeshite iwaku . . ." *Hōnō engi ki*, in *Teihon*, 1:238.

75. Imai, *Jishū seiritsushi*, p. 273.

76. See Hirota, *No Abode*, 18n, pp. 196-197, citing Shan-tao's *Commentary on the Meditation Sutra* (*Kangyōsho*), T37, 271b.

77. See Kanai, *Ippen*, pp. 201-212.

78. *Yugyō Shōnin engi e*, 9. 2, pp. 80-81.

79. Ibid., 10. 2, p. 83.

80. See Kanai, *Ippen*, pp. 204-208.

81. *Hōnō engi ki*, in *Teihon*, 1:238.

82. For Bishamon, *Yugyō Shōnin engi e*, 3. 1, pp. 61-62; for Bishamon and Fudō, ibid., 5. 5, p. 70; and for Echizen Sōsha, ibid., 5. 3, p. 69.

83. For Ajisaka Nyūdo, *Yugyō Shōnin engi e*, 2. 5, p. 61; for priest of Gokurakuji, ibid., 7. 4, p. 75; for Shinkyō at Shinzenkōji, ibid., 6. 4, p. 73; and for Chūjō, 8. 3, pp. 78-79. For the significance of folded hands, see "Shinano no kuni Uehara Saemon nyūdo Ren'amidabutsu jōjō no fushin o kakite tazunetatematsurikereba shimeshitamau gohenji jūni shō," *Ta'a hōgo*, 4, in *Teihon*, 1:174.

84. *Ippen hijiri e*, 12. 3, p. 81.

85. *Yugyō Shōnin engi e*, 5. 1, p. 69 ("makoto ni gongen no hito nara de wa").

86. Ibid., 3. 4, p. 64.

87. Ibid., 10. 3, p. 84.

88. "Ta'amidabutsu o hajimete dōgyō sōshin no chigiri o musubitatematsurinu." *Ippen hijiri e*, 4. 3, p. 67. There is no indication that Ippen made a vow with the women *dōgyō* who accompanied him to Kumano.

89. *Yugyō Shōnin engi e*, 1. 3, p. 58.

90. *Hōnō engi ki*, in *Teihon*, 1:237.

91. Imai notes the dependence on the patterns of existing Buddhist organizations in the transition from what must be called Ippen's confraternity and Shinkyō's order. Imai, *Jishūshi seiritsushi*, p. 283.

92. "Ima chishiki o motte, butsu no onshi to nashi, hatsugan seikai no kotoba o uketori, shikakushite gonkaikon utsu." *Hōnō engi ki*, in *Teihon*, 1:238.

93. "Chishiki wa tōtai ni sono imashime aru yue ni ōjō no shinan shutsuri no yōro wa Chishiki no ikku ni sugitaru koto nashi kore ni yotte shimmei o Chishiki ni yuzuru no kotoba wa kimyō no niji kore nari iu iu." *Hōnō engi ki*, in *Teihon*, 1:238.

94. See also *Yugyō Shōnin engi e*, 6. 3, p. 72 for the whole ritual.

95. "... ima yori miraisai o tsukushite shimmei o chishiki no yuzuri" and "ikinagara shinite, shimmei o chishiki ni yuzuri." *Yugyō Shōnin engi e*, 6. 3, p. 72.

96. *Hōnō engi ki*, in *Teihon*, 1:238.

97. "... nihōshi shimmei o chishiki ni yuzurite chikai o nashi, kane o uchite, waga kokoro ni ninsezushite ... chishiki no myō ni shitagaite, kane no dōri yaburazareba, ketsujō ōjō o togu beki." "Omimi Sa'amidabutsu e tsukawasaru gohenji," *Ta'a hōgo*, 2, in *Teihon*, 1:145.

98. "Chishiki wa tōtai ni sono imashime aru yue ni ōjō no shinan shutsuri no yōro wa Chishiki no ikku ni sugitaru koto nashi kore ni yotte shimmei o Chishiki ni yuzuru no kotoba wa kimyō no niji kore nari iu iu." *Hōnō engi ki*, in *Teihon*, 1:238.

99. "Namu to iu wa sunawachi kore kimyō nari. Mata kore hatsugan ekō no gi nari. Amidabutsu to iu wa sunawachi kore sono gyō nari. Sono gi o motte no yue ni kanarazu ōjō suru koto o uru." *Shinshū yōhōki*, 16, in *Teihon*, 2:992. Shinkyō explains that "namu" is the body or essence (*tōtai*) of swearing the oath and giving up one's life to the Chishiki. *Dōjō seimon*, in *Teihon*, 1:239. Shinkyō explains that this oath and giving up one's life to the Chishiki are "kimyō" in the *Hōnō engi ki*, in *Teihon*, 1:238.

100. Nakamura, *Bukkyōgo daijiten*, s. v. "Ki," "Kie," "Kimyō," "Kimyō Muryōju kaku," (1:214-216) "Namu," and "Namuamidabutsu" (2:1029-1030).

101. This oath of obedience is now called *kimyōkai* or *chishiki kimyō*. The first to use the phrase *chishiki kimyō* seems to have been Takuga in his *Jōjō gyōgi hōsoku*, in *San dai*, in *Teihon*, 1:253 ("Chishiki kimyō no kane no naka").

102. *Hōnō engi ki*, in *Teihon* 1:237-238; both quotes p. 238.

103.". . . shimmei o motte Amidabutsu o kuyō shi tatematsuru ... kono mi wa shibaraku edo ni ari to iedomo kokoro wa sude ni Jodo no bosatsu naru beshi." *Hōnō engi ki*, in *Teihon*, 1:238.

104. "Fuse no So'amidabutsu shūchū no koto ni tsukite mōsu mune arikeru ni tsukawasaru gohenji," *Ta'a hōgo*, 1, in *Teihon*, 1:132 ("Manji o butsu/hotoke ni ninsete . . . manji o butsu/hotoke ni ninsetatematsurite" [in the first example, the character for Buddha is given "Ta," the same as that for Ta'amidabutsu]); "Utsunomiya Yo'amidabutsu e tsukawasaru gohenji," *Ta'a hōgo*, 1, in *Teihon*, 1:128 ("manji butsu/hotoke ni makasete"); "Ōmimi Sa'amidabutsu," *Ta'a hōgo*, 2, in *Teihon*, 1:146 ("manji o butsu/hotoke ni makasete"). In the last two examples, the character is for "butsu" is again that for "Ta." "Umeda no

Shi'amidabutsu tsukawasaru gohenji," *Ta'a hōgo*, 2, in *Teihon*, 1:143 ("manji o Chishiki ni ninzuru nari").

The same is seen for the formula "shimmei o Chishiki/hotoke ni kimyō s[u]." For "Chishiki," see "Oda Kai'amidabutsu e tsukawasaru gohenji," *Ta'a hōgo*, 2, in *Teihon*, 1:142. For "butsu/hotoke," see "Sansō Shōnin e tsukawasaru onfumi," *Ta'a hōgo*, 1, in *Teihon*, 1:124; "Shinano no kuni Uehara Saemon," *Ta'a hōgo*, 4, in *Teihon*, 1:173; and "Homma Gen'amidabutsu e tsukawasaru gohenji," *Ta'a hōgo*, 6, in *Teihon*, 1:192. There is one variation of this formula in "Amagasaki Ji'amidabutsu mōsu mune arikereba kakite shimeshitamau gokyōkai," *Ta'a hōgo*, 2, in *Teihon*, 1:138 ("Amidabutsu ni kimyō shitatematsuru wa").

105. "Ware yuiteira matsudai ni itarite kono mune o mamorite . . ." *Hōnō engi ki*, in *Teihon*, 1:238.

106. For English translation, see Hirota, *No Abode*, pp. 76-78.

107. *Yugyō Shōnin engi e*, 7. 1, p. 74. The date is Einin 6. The title is later. Takuga wrote a commentary called *Ta'amidabutsu dōgyō yōshin taikō chū*, in *San daisōshi hōgo*, in *Teihon*, 1:245-250.

108. See, for example, Turner on St. Francis. Victor Turner, *The Ritual Process: Structure and Anti-Structure* (Chicago: Aldine's Publishing Company, 1969), p. 143.

109. Imai, *Jishū seiritsushi*, p. 271.

110. *Hōnō engi ki*, in *Teihon*, 1:237; *Ippen hijiri e*, 10. 1, p. 78; *Yugyō Shōnin engi e*, 3. 1, p. 62.

111. *Hōnō engi ki*, in *Teihon*, 1:237 ("toshi tsuide o kasaneru hoto ni sōni tashū ni oyobu").

112. "Jishū mo banchō ni wa sōshū yonjū hachinin, nishū yonjūhachi nin sono hoka no yonbu no shū wa kazu o shirazu." *Hijiri e*, 10. 1, p. 78.

113. Imai is right when he says that the exact words are not in the *Hijiri e*, but the idea in contracted form is. *Jishū seiritsushi*, p. 271. The question is whether "jishū" also means members of the wider community or people taking part in the ceremony, rather than just members of the confraternity.

114. "Koshō no toki yori kono shita no sōni no betsu shite ni kawarite, hosshin mo chie mo suguretaru kono wa nashi." "Shimojō Ren'amidabutsu e tsukawasaru gohenji," *Ta'a hōgo*, 6, in *Teihon*, 1:195.

115. "Ni hōshi no aida, midari ga hashiki yō ni . . ." "Echigo no kuni Kokkyō Hongō e no gohenji," *Ta'a hōgo*, 6, in *Teihon*, 1:194.

116. Kanai, *Ippen*, p. 272.

117. "Dōjin [Utsunomiya Yo'amidabutsu] e no gohenji," *Ta'a hōgo*, 1, in *Teihon*, 1:128 ("mudōshin no yagara o ba, seimon ni ninsete, shūchū o taishutsu sarubeshi"). See also Kanai, *Ippen*, p. 269.

118. For example, "Umeda no Shi'amidabutsu," *Ta'a hōgo*, 2, in *Teihon*, 1:143. See also "Shōnin yori yori dōzoku ni taishite shimeshitamau onkotoba," ibid., 2, p. 147 ("shukke hosshin shite chishiki ni kimyō su to iinagara . . . [if

you fall in love with a nun], chishiki ni wa kimyō sezu shite, kore wa ni ni kimyō shite, wareware o aiketsu no fujin ni ate ga hitaru nari"). See also Kanai, *Ippen*, p. 271.

119. "Amagasaki Ji'amidabutsu," *Ta'a hōgo*, 2, in *Teihon*, 1:137.

120. "Shōnin yori yori dōzoku," *Ta'a hōgo*, 2, in *Teihon*, 1:149.

121. "Umeda," *Ta'a hōgo*, 2, in *Teihon*, 1:143. See also "Echigo no kuni," ibid., 6, p. 194 ("issho ni te sankyō o kibishiku okite, kōgan wa nasu to mo te utsushi ni mono o mo torikawasazushite shikaru beshi to oboyu").

122. *San daisōshi hōgo*, in *Teihon*, 1:239-240. Dated Kagen 4. 9. 15. "Seimon" means oath; I translate it as "regulation" for the title. See, for example, the letter "Umeda," *Ta'a hōgo*, 2, in *Teihon*, 1:143, where he mentions writing and sending it to the *dōjō*. See also Imai, *Jishū seiritsushi*, p. 282.

123. See "Shōnin yori yori dōzoku," *Ta'a hōgo*, in *Teihon*, 1:149. See also *Hōnō engi ki*, in *Teihon*, 1:238, where he states that once having broken the precepts and accepted the Chishiki's stern admonitions, "if one repents and undertakes practice one's good roots will be the same as before" (*eshin shugyō seba zenne mae ni onajiku nari*).

124. Between Kōan 4 and Meitoku 5. In one case, the "fu" was cancelled because of repentence and the name entered while still alive in 1281 (Ōei 3. 9. 8, Tōbutsubō). *Jishū kakochō*, p. 175.

125. A letter from Itchin to Takuga confirms the date. See Kanai, *Ippen*, p. 346. Death is confirmed in *Jishū kakochō*. Takuga mentions that he had been in Kyoto since the Bunpō era (1317-1319) in the *Saishū waden yō*, cited in Kanai, *Ippen*, p. 348. Apparently, Shinkyō's successor Chitoku had sent him along with Ankoku to assist Donkai in the management of the Konkōji in the year or so after Shinkyō had granted Donkai the right to distribute amulets.

126. In *Teihon*, 1:990-1004. For example, section 6 (p. 5),

127. "Takuga Shōnin," *Gorekidai keifu*, in *Shomin shinkō*, p. 239. Soseki was raised by a priest by the name of Kū'a of the temple Hirashio-yama in Kai Province. Papinot, *Historical Dictionary*, s. v. "Soseki."

128. In the *Taiheiki*, Chapter Twenty, "Yoshisada jisatsu no koto," eight *jishū* accompany Nitta Yoshisada's body to the Yugyō-ha Nagasaki dōjō Ōjōin Shōnenji for burial. Many of his men enter the same temple. *Taiheiki*, 3:321. In Chapter Twenty-seven, "Uesugi Hatakeyama ruzai shikei no koto," the wife of Uesugi Shigeyoshi, who had been exiled and assassinated by Kō no Moronao in 1349, is rescued from a suicide attempt and is brought by her long-time chaplain ("chishiki . . . hijiri") to the Ōjōin to become a nun. *Taiheiki*, 3:77-80.

129. *Teihon*, 2:1719-1729.

130. "Dōgyō tsune ni aishitashi mite tōzakaru koto nakare." *Tōzai sayō shō* (number 30), in *Teihon*, 2:1720.

131. *Ta'amidabutsu dōgyō yōshin taikō chū*, in *San daisōshi hōgo*, in *Teihon*, 1:245-249; *Jōjō gyōgi hōsoku*, ibid., pp. 250-253.

132. "Yoku chishiki ni kimyō su to iedomo shoki wa buttai nari. Kono yue ni kakechigau tokoro no kane wa butsu no yonjūhachi gan chishiki to butsu to ittai naru koto o shirubeshite jihi o motte shujō o sessu kore sunawachi busshin nari. Chishiki to butsu to jihi o motte kokoro to naru mono nari." *Jōjō*, introduction, *San dai*, in *Teihon*, 1:251.

133. "... iwayuru Ta to wa jūman shūjō nari Amida to iu wa shōwa myōgo nari butsu to wa gan jōju no gakutai nari." *Ta'a dōgyō*, introduction, *San dai*, in *Teihon*, 1:245.

134. This term "shōbutsu ittai" is not found in Nakamura. Nakamura, *Bukkyōgo daijiten*, s. v. "Shōbutsu ichinyo," "Shōbutsu funi" (1:710), and "Ittai" (1:64).

135. Imai, *Jishū seiritsushi*, p. 215.

136. For a complete survey of *kihō ittai*, see Hirata Teizen, "Kihō ittai ron no kenkyū," in *Jishū kyōgaku no kenkyū*, rev. ed. (Sankibo Busshorin, 1977), pp. 145-166. Takuga used variants. *Ta'a dōgyō*, introduction, *San dai*, in *Teihon*, 1:245 ("nōsho ittai"), and commentary to addendum, p. 248 ("Nembutsu no chishiki ni oite yugaku mugaku o ronsezu noke shoke o iwarezu butsu no hongan ni josuru"). For attribution to Ippen, see *Ippen goroku*, 1 (*sosoku hogo*) ("kihō"), and 2 (*monjin densetsu*) ("kihō ittai"). It derives from Shan-tao's "kihō nishu shinjin" (two kinds of faith [in] Sentient Beings and Amida; also invoked by Shinkyō and Takuga). *Ta'a dōgyō*, commentary on eighth couplet, *San dai*, in *Teihon*, 1:248 ("Iwayuru kihō nishu no shinjin ketsujō suru ga yue ni") and *Jōjō*, 7, *San dai*, in *Teihon*, 1:251 ("kihō nishu no shinjin o hosshite").

137. Nakamura, *Bukkyōgo daijiten*, s. v., "Ki," "Kihō," "Nōki," and "Nōki ittai."

138. *Jōjō*, 9, *San dai*, in *Teihon*, 1:252.

139. "... iwayuru chishiki wa kore shōjin no buttai jishū wa kore tokujin no bosatsu nari." *Ta'a dōgyō*, commentary to addendum, *San dai*, in *Teihon*, 1:249.

140. "... monka no jishū wa kimyō no toku o gyōshite . . . bosatsu nar[i]." *Jōjō*, 9, *San dai*, in *Teihon*, 1:252.

141. "... jishū no sōni o motte futai no bosatsu to nasu nari." Ibid.

142. Ibid. ("yue ni jishū no sōni o motte futai no bosatsu to nasuru. Dokujū mata keshin taru ga yue ni"), or again, ibid., p. 253 ("chishiki kimyō no kane no naka ni bosatsu no i ni itari . . . bosatsu to wa dōshin no na nari").

143. Imai Masaharu has traced the movement to provide chaplains back to the rise in Pure Land Buddhism of the practice of having a *chishiki*, a friend or monk, at one's deathbed to make sure one chanted the *nembutsu* and thus attain Rebirth in the Pure Land. *Chūsei shakai*, pp. 349-351.

144. *Muromachi-dono monogatari*, *Kokushi sōsho* 3, pp. 359-360. This paean to *jishū* follows an entry discussing the Eiroku period (1558-1570).

145. Ai'a of Fukudadera, in what is now Odawara City, Kanagawa Prefecture. Negita Shūzen, *Jishū no teradera* (Mishima: Negita Shūzen, 1980), p. 10.

146. For "dōdo," *Shōkei ranrishi*, in *Zoku shiseki* 1, p. 213. The expression "dōdo" is also used by Jikū. *Shichijō monjo*, no. 9, in *Teihon*, 1:396 ("jishū dōdō no koto wa"). This seems to be the official use of the term in the Yugyō-ha. For "shōban," see "Takuga's "Seishū Nagano e tsukasawaru no gosho Bunna 2 nen 9 gatsu misoka (Nagano gosho)," *Shichidai Shōnin hōgo*, in *Teihon*, 1: 383. He also uses the expression "shōban no nishū," which demonstrates the participation of women in the battlefield activities.

147. According to the "Jikū shojō," "a letter was sent from the Yugyō [Shōnin] to several places during the Kan'ō period." *Shichijō monjo*, no. 9, in *Teihon*, 1:396. See Appendix, no. 1.

148. *Shichidai Shōnin hōgo*, in *Teihon*, 1:383. See Appendix, no. 2.

149. See note 115.

150. For Moronao and Morofuyu, "[Kano] 2 gatsu 26 nichi Shu'amidabutsu Musashi no kami [Moronao] onajiku musuko [Mikawa no kami Morofuyu]." A Kai *jishū* brought the news to Moronao 1351/Shōhei 6. 2. 25 that his brother, on the run, had been killed In Kai Province the twelfth month of the previous year. Tachibana, *Jishūshi ronkō*, pp. 225-226, citing *Taiheiki*, Chapter Twenty-nine. The same chapter also describes the deaths of Moronao and Moroyasu. For Moroyasu and Moroyo, "dōgetsu dōjitsu Sen'amidabutsu (Echigo no kami onajiku musuko nado)." *Jishū kakochō*, p. 29. Tachibana thinks Takuga was informed by their *jishū* chaplain. Tachibana, *Jishūshi ronkō*, p. 225.

151. For Tadayoshi ("Daitaiji Kan'ō 3 nen 2 gatsu 26 nichi"), Motouji ("Zuisenjiden Jōji 6 nen 4 gatsu 28 nichi"), and Takauji ("Chōjūjiden Enbun 2 nen 4 gatsu misoka [last day]"), *Jishū kakochō*, pp. 54-55.

The Kō appear to have been long-time adherents. A "Butsu'amidabutsu (Kō Uemon nyūdō)" is entered in the fifth Yugyō Shōnin's section sometime in the 1320s [1324?]. *Jishū kakochō*, p. 23 and Takuga wrote a letter to one Kō Suruga-dono Ji'amidabutsu (father of Moronao and Moroyasu). *Takuga Shōnin hōgo*, in *Teihon*, 1:358. Another entry made was "Kanō 2 nen Shōgatsu 17 nichi Shō'amidabutsu (Kō Banshū [Harima]). *Jishū kakochō*, p. 54.

152. *Shinshū yōhō ki*, 18, in *Teihon*, 2:993-994 ("jishū wa tada Chishiki no isshin nari. . . . Shikaredomo Butsu Chishiki no funi no dōri o motte no yue ni Chishiki ni kisuru tokoro wa hikkyō shite Mida ni kisuru nari").

Notes to Chapter 5

1. Bryman, *Charisma*, pp. 50-54.

2. *Ekotoba den*, 4. 5, p. 67 ("Shikaru ni tokorodokoro no chōrōtachi ide-kitarite").

3. "As for [making] karmic connections to salvation, since the laity are indeed important, from today one must become [as a daimyo's] personal retainer and follow the essential point" (*Kechien wa zaike no hito koso taisechi nareba, kyō yori yō ni shitagaite kinjū subeshi*). *Ippen hijiri e*, 11. 3, p. 80.

4. ". . . dōzoku wa shū no shōmyō no hoka ni kimyō no tai arazu shite, monka no jishū wa kimyō no toku o gyōshite . . . bosatsu nari." *Jōjō*, 9, *San dai*, in *Teihon*, 1:252.

5. Imai, *Jishū seiritsushi*, p. 231.

6. Ibid., pp. 124-127.

7. Kōan 5. 3. 2. *Ippen hijiri e*, 5. 5, p. 70.

8. "Mi'amidabutsu e tsukawasaru gohenji," *Ta'a hōgo*, 1, in *Teihon*, 1:134. For a reference to several requests, see also "Ōmimi Sa'amidabutsu," ibid., 2, p. 146.

9. "Ōmimi Sa'amidabutsu," *Ta'a hōgo*, 2, in *Teihon*, 1:145.

10. Ibid.

11. "Aru hito no moto yori . . . mōshiageru toki no gohenji," *Ta'a hōgo*, 3, in *Teihon*, 1:157.

12. "Yugyō nidai Shinkyō Shōnin shojō," *Shichijō monjo*, no. 2, in *Teihon*, 1:392. See also Kanai, *Ippen*, p. 265.

13. "Takanomiya no Setsu'amidabutsu . . . gohenji," *Ta'a hōgo*, 3, in *Teihon*, 1:156.

14. "Aru toki jishū tasho no dōjo o taikutsu shi idekitarite . . . shimeshite iu," *Ta'a hōgo*, 3, in *Teihon*, 1:165.

15. "Ōmimi Sa'amidabutsu," *Ta'a hōgo*, 2, in *Teihon*, 1:145.

16. From the Lotus Sutra, according to Takuga in the *Kibokuron*, 14, in *Teihon*, 1:301. The text goes on: "As for the Chishiki, he is none other than the mercy of the Buddha. . . . As for the Name, it is the Cause for Release. As for the Chishiki, he is the connection to Release. As you know, faith in the *kihō noshū* is the principle (*gi*) of belief in the Chishiki, belief in the Name. . . . That one does not believe in the Chishiki diminishes the Three Hearts [of faith]. The Chishiki is the connection to Release. Therefore, reliance on the connection of the Chishiki creates the cause of Rebirth. . . . Therefore they call this the Great Cause. . . . Again, the Chishiki of Rebirth does not discuss learning or lack of learning."

17. "Shōnin yori yori dōzoku," *Ta'a hōgo*, 3, in *Teihon*, 1:149-150.

18. "Mi'amidabutsu," *Ta'a hōgo*, 2, in *Teihon*, 1:134.

19. "Ōmimi Sa'amidabutsu," *Ta'a hōgo*, 2, in *Teihon*, 1:145.

20. "Etchū no kuni Yoshie dōjō . . . tsukawasaru gohenji," *Ta'a hōgo*, 1, *Teihon*, 1:131.

21. "Ōmimi Sa'amidabutsu," *Ta'a hōgo*, 2, in *Teihon*, 1:145.

22. Kanai, *Ippen*, p. 268, citing a letter first introduced by Kōno Noriyoshi, "Shōki jishū shujusō," *Shimane daigaku kaigaku jūshūnen kinen ronbunshū* (Feb. 1960).

23. "Ōmimi Sa'amidabutsu," *Ta'a hōgo*, 2, in *Teihon*, 1:145.

24. "Mi'amidabutsu," *Ta'a hōgo*, 1, in *Teihon*, 1:134.

25. *Taiheiki*, 3:77-80 ("Uesugi Hatakeyama ruzai shikei no koto").

26. In the "In Praise of the Nonduality of the ten and one," Ippen expressed his affirmation of the Seizan school doctrine.

27. See also "Shimojō Ren'amidabutsu," *Ta'a hōgo*, 6, *Teihon*, 1:196 ("Kannon and Seishi [are] the messengers/representatives of Amidabutsu").

28. "Tōshū nikushin buttai o tatete, Chishiki o motte saison to nasu." *Shinshū yōhō ki*, 38, in *Teihon*, 2:998.

29. ". . . iwayuru chishiki wa kore shōjin no buttai jishū wa kore tokunin no bosatsu nari." *Dōgyō yōshin, San dai*, in *Teihon*, 1:249; ". . . eshin ōjō seshimu yue ni jishū no sō ni o motte futai bosatsu to suru nari." *Jōjō*, 9, *San dai*, in *Teihon*, 1:252. According to Chiren, citing this latter passage, "this school makes the Chishiki the buddha in human form; the *jishū* it makes a non-retrograding Bodhisattva" (*kono shū wa chishiki o motte shōjin buttai to nasu. Jishū o motte futai bosatsu to nasu no iware nari*). *Shinshū yōhō ki*, 18, in *Teihon*, 2:993.

30. *Jōjō*, 9, *San dai*, in *Teihon*, 1:252.

31. Nakamura, *Bukkyōgo daijiten*, s. v. "Ōjin," (1:132) "Keshin," (1:292) and "Funjin" (2:1199).

32. Ibid. See also Hirota, *No Abode*, pp. 190, 195, 196.

33. *Shinshū yōhō ki*, 41, in *Teihon*, 2:1000.

34. When one considers the way Takuga taps into the concept of Amida's Enlightenment as eternal, rather than merely ten *kalpa*s since, so that even the Buddha Shaka and Amida (Muryōjubutsu) are one, then the order of *jishū* is the corporate body of buddhahood itself. *Jōjō*, 4, in *Teihon*, 1:251 ("honmon no Shaka wa Muryōjubutsu").

35. "Yoku chishiki ni kimyō su to iedomo shōki wa buttai nari. Kore no yue ni kakechikau tokoro no kane wa butsu no yonjūhachi gan *chishiki to butsu to ittai naru koto* [my emphasis] o shiru beshite jihi o motte shūjō o sessu kore sunawachi busshin nari. Chishiki to butsu to jihi o motte kokoro to naru mono nari." *Jōjō*, introduction, *San dai*, in *Teihon*, 1:251. "Yue ni aru tokoro no *jishū wa yui chishiki no isshin nari* [my emphasis]." *Shinshū yōhō ki*, 19, in *Teihon*, 2:993.

36. "Shūji wa sunawachi ittai funjin no gi o motte, Chishiki no go o ukuru yue nari." *Shinshū yōhō ki*, 19, in *Teihon*, 2:994. See also ibid., 41 ("temple heads are all parts of the Chishiki as buddha" (*shūji wa mina Chishiki no [fun]shin nari*). *Teihon*, 2:1000. One variant of the text does have "funjin" rather than "shin."

37. "Ōmimi Sa'amidabutsu," *Ta'a hōgo*, 2, in *Teihon*, 1:145.

38. "Chishiki no isshin ni oite wa sunawachi Mida no katoku o ukete yoku shūjō o watasu." *Shinshū yōhō ki*, 19, in *Teihon*, 2:993.

39. *Shinshū yōhō ki*, 16, in *Teihon*, 2:993 ("Shakka hokken").

40. Ibid., 41, p. 1000 ("hokken Shaka").

41. "Omou ni seikai no kotoba o hakari, shimmei o Chishiki ni yuzuru to iu. Yue ni aru tokoro no jishū wa yui Chishiki no isshin nari. . . . Chishiki no isshin ni oite wa sunawachi Mida no katoku o ukete uoku shujō o watasu." *Shinshū yōhō ki*, 19, *Teihon*, 2:993.

42. Kanai, *Ippen*, p. 266, citing "Kondō no Shin'amidabutsu e tsukasawaru gohenji," *Ta'a hōgo*, [1, in *Teihon*, 1:127].

43. *Shinshū yōhō ki*, 19 and 20, in *Teihon*, 2:994, and 18, p. 993.

44. "Andō Saemon nyūdō Shōken e tsukawasaru gohenji," *Ta'a hōgo*, 4, in *Teihon*, 1:162-163. See also *Shinshū yōhō ki*, 18, *Teihon*, 2:993.

45. For absolute dependency, *Hōnō engi ki*, in *Teihon*, 1:238 ("shimmei Chishiki ni yuzuru").

46. *Ippen hijiri e*, 6. 2, p. 71. See Imai, *Jishū seiritsushi*, p. 268.

47. "Ueda no Jū'amidabutsu e tsukawasaru gohenji," *Ta'a hōgo*, 1, in *Teihon*, 1:133.

48. *Shinshū yōhō ki*, 38, *Teihon*, 2:998.

49. Ibid., 17, p. 993.

50. Ōei 31. 8. 10 and 11, *Kanmon gyoki* 1, *Zoku gunsho ruijū* suppl. vol. 3, comp. Hanawa Hokinoichi (Zoku Gunsho Ruijū Kanseikai, 1930), p. 277, and Ōei. 31. 8. 10, *Mansai* 1, p. 450.

51. *Jōjō*, in *Teihon*, 1:252.

52. "Shinano no kuni Uehara," *Ta'a hōgo*, 4, in *Teihon*, 1:174.

53. "Anjiki mondō," *Ta'a hōgo*, 7, in *Teihon*, 1:206.

54. In Ōhashi, *Ippen*, pp. 145-146, citing the letter in the Kondaiji collection.

55. "Jiku shojō," *Shichijō monjo*, no. 9, in *Teihon*, 1:396.

56. The date is Genkō 3. 1. 30. *Taiheiki*, 1:201.

57. "Akasaka kassen no koto tsuketari Hitomi Honma nukegake ga koto," *Taiheiki*, 1:199-208; direct quotation, p. 201. There is reason to believe that this particular story is modelled on the famous story in the *Heike monogatari* of Kumagae Naozane who slipped out ahead of others to attack the enemy, for the text relates, "Kumagae Hirayama ga Ichinotani no sakigake o tsutae kikite, urayamashiku omoeru monodomo nari. Ato o miru ni tsuzuku musha mo nashi." Naozane was famous as wanting to be first in the charge and then first in religion as a disciple of Hōnen.

58. "Hitomi On'amidabutsu e tsukawasaru gohenji," *Ta'a hōgo*, 2, in *Teihon*, 1:158-160, and 5, pp. 182-183; "Homma Gen'amidabutsu e tsukawasaru gohenji," *Ta'a hōgo*, 6, in *Teihon*, 1:192-193.

59. For Okamoto, who died Jōji 2. 6. 17, see "Haga Hyōe nyūdō ikusa no koto," *Taiheiki*, 3:438. For the *jishū*, see Kadokawa Gen'yoshi, "Katarimono to kanrisha," *Kokugo to kokubun* 13, no. 12 (December 1943), pp. 11-12. For the temple, see Negita Shūzen, *Jishū no teradera* (Mishima: privately published by Negita Shūzen, 1980), p. 143.

60. "Yaki Kurō no koto," *Meitokuki*, pp. 87-92; direct quotation, p. 89; for his wife and mother, p. 89; for the lock of hair, p. 91.

61. "Yamana Ujikiyo midai no koto," *Meitokuki*, pp. 114-119; direct quotation, p. 115.

62. For the Sanmyōji, see Kanai, *Chūsei bungaku*, pp. 114-129 ("*Meitokuki* to Hōki Sanmyōji"). The Yamana are entered in the *Jishū kakochō* at some time between 1418 and 1423 ("Yamana Miyata [Tokikiyo] . . . Gorō [Tokimasa] . . . Iyo [Tokiyoshi] . . . Sanshū [Yoshiyuki] . . . Saihō [Ujifuyu] . . . Ōyamana [Yoshimasa] . . . Banshū [Mitsuyuki] . . . Jurō [Ujiyori] . . . Kōjirō [Tokinaga] . . . Ōshū [Ujikiyo] . . . Kazusa [Yoshinori]"). *Jishū kakochō*, p. 101. There are other Yamana entries.

63. It was abolished in 1875 and combined with the Pure Land Seizan school Shōhōji. Negita, *Jishū no teradera*, p. 431.

64. "Kongōsan no yosetera chōserareru koto tsuketari Sakai Sadatoshi ga koto," *Taiheiki*, 1:386-388; direct quotation, p. 387.

65. "Sasuke Aki no kami Sadatoshi-dono e tsukuwasaru gohenji," *Ta'a hōgo*, 4, in *Teihon*, 1:167, and 8, p. 219. At the end of the year 1313/Shōwa 2, Sadatoshi had visited Shinkyō and they had composed poetry.

66. "Yoshisada jisatsu no koto," *Taiheiki*, 3:321-322.

67. "Yamana Mitsuyuki chūseraru koto," *Meitokuki*, pp. 131-134 (Ōei 1. 3. 10). "Toribeno no dōjō" is mentioned on pp. 133 and 134. For the temple, see Kanai, *Ippen*, p. 430, and Kadokawa Gen'yoshi, "*Meitokuki* no seiritsu," *Dentō bungaku kenkyū* 2 (May 1962), p. 8. He cites the *Sanshū meiseki shi* on Toribeno ("Nakagoro Ta'a Shōnin tera o tatete Hōfukuji to gosu"). It was also a branch temple of the Konrenji. See also Negita, *Jishū no teradera*, p. 346. Only the foundations are left.

68. "Uesugi Hatakeyama ruzai shikei no koto," *Taiheiki*, 3:77-80; direct quotation, p. 80. The Uesugi would become intimately connected with the Shōjōkōji. See chapter 6.

69. "Morofuyu jigai no koto tsuketari Suwa Gorō no koto," *Taiheiki*, 3:138-139; direct quotation, p. 138.

70. "Hatakeyama kyōdai Shuzenji no jō ni tatekomuru koto tsuketari Yusa nyūdō no koto," *Taiheiki*, 3:408-411.

71. Kanai, *Jishū bungei*, p. 228, citing the *Entairyaku*, Kanō 2. 2. 27

72. Sonmyō acknowledged that it was difficult to refuse a patron when discussing the problem of unsanctioned pilgrimage and substitute pilgrimage. "Yugyō sanjūsandai Sonmyō Shōnin shujō," *Shichijō monjo*, 13, in *Teihon*, 1:398. See also nos. 12, 14, 15, ibid., pp. 398-399.

73. The first two temples are in Yamanashi Prefecture, the third in Iwate Prefecture, moved when the Nambu were transferred to the north. See Negita, *Jishū no teradera*, pp. 482, 487-488, and 228-229. Another main Nambu temple, the Kyōjōji, is in Morioka City, Iwate Prefecture. Ibid., pp. 226-227.

74. Kanai, *Ippen*, p. 218.

75. Negita, *Jishū no teradera*, p. 484.

76. Ishida Yoshitō, "Muromachi jidai no jishū ni tsuite," part 1, *Bukkyō shigaku* 10, no. 4 (March 1963), p. 200.

77. Ōhashi, *Ippen*, pp. 187-188, citing *Zenfukuji kyūzō monjo*. Apparently, the temple is no longer extant; it is not listed among the order's temples.

78. Ōhashi, *Ippen*, p. 215.

79. For Fukō as Satake, see "Fukō Shōnin," *Gorekidai keifu*, in *Shomin shinkō*, p. 246; for Ryūzenji, see Negita, *Jishū no teradera*, p. 232.

80. See Takano's introduction, *Ichirenji kakochō*, pp. 1-5.

81. For dates of first part for monks, *Ichirenji kakochō*, pp. 7, 77; for dates of first part for nuns, pp. 78, 133; for Hō'a, Takano's introduction, p. 2 (Takano observes that the number "seven" in the inscription at the beginning of the monks' section seems to have been altered to "eight" and that the calligraphy of both inscriptions seem to be the same. This is from a colophon by the fifty-eighth head in 1881, p. 78; for third part, p. 147.

82. For a complete analysis of people and workers involved in the rebuilding of the temple of Shōjōkōji, see Tachibana, *Jishūshi ronkō*, pp. 263-288 (Chapter Fifteen, "Tōtakusan no shōbō to sono saikō: Eishō kara Keichō made").

83. *Ichirenji kakochō*, pp. 133-135, 147.

84. Ibid., pp. 26, 141.

85. Ishida, "Muromachi jidai," 1, p. 205.

86. *Ichirenji kakochō*, p. 37, for those killed "Ogasawara gassen," battle with or at Ogasawara, and "Baba gassen" in 1487/Chōkyō 1; for Suwa Yorishige, *Ichirenji*, p. 64 (see also entry for Suwa Aki no kami three years before, ibid.); for Kurogoma or Hemi, two in the Eikyō period (1429-1441), p. 25; for villages, p. 86 ("Dai'ichibō"). Ishida counts nineteen persons or place names "Hemi." "Muromachi jidai," 1, p. 204. For head priests, *Ichirenji kakochō*, p. 56, (Eishō 6-7/1509-1510).

87. For nuns' section, *Ichirenji kakochō*, pp. 101-105; for monks' section, pp. 43-49.

88. *Ichirenji kakochō*, p. 46 ("Gon'amidabutsu Kudō gyakushū").

Notes to Chapter 6

1. "Senior High Priest," "High Priest," "Senior Assistant High Priest," "Provisional Senior Assistant High Priest," "Junior Assistant High Priest," "Provisional Junior Assistant High Priest," "Senior Master of Buddhist Asceticism," "Middle Master of Buddhist Asceticism," and "Provisional Master of Buddhist Asceticism." Jean Reischauer and Robert Karl Reischauer, *Early Japanese History (c. 40 B. C. -A. D. 1167): Part B* (Princeton: Princeton University Press, 1937) and Papinot, *Historical* (s. v. each title in Japanese),

with some emendation by myself. Other titles, *sōi*, in use included Hōkyō, Hōin, Hōgen, Ajari, Zasu, and Shuza. The titles conferred posthumously were Hōshi, Kokushi, and Daishi. Papinot, *Historical*, p. 601, s. v. "Sō-kwan."

2. "Great Master," "National Master," "Master of the Buddhist Law," "Meditation Master," and "Superior Person." Reischauer and Reischauer, *Early Japanese History: Part B* and Papinot, *Historical* (s. v. each title in Japanese), with some emendation by myself.

3. "Shūmon matsuji Shōnin go chokkyo rinji no utsushi," *Shibazaki bunko*, in *Teihon*, 2:1802.

4. The use of the title is especially characteristic of the True Pure Land and Nichiren schools: however, in the Nichiren school, the founders are distinguished by the use of another character for "shō" ("pure" rather than "above"). *Komonjo yōgo jiten*, ed. Arai Eiji et al. (Hakubshobō, 1983), s. v. "Shōnin" (p. 239).

5. For title for monks, evangelists, and ordained monks, see *Koji ruien* 27: *Shukkyō-bu* 2 (1911; photographic reproduction, Yoshikawa Kōbunkan, 1981), p. 830, citing *Irohaji ruisho* (early Kamakura); Nakamura, *Bukkyōgo*, 1:693, s. v. "Shōnin;" and *Komonjo*, p. 239, s. v. "Shōnin." For title and emperors, see *Koji ruien* 27, p. 831, citing *Shinchō gōki*, 1495/Meiō 4. 9. 21. For official inquiry, see ibid., pp. 830-831, citing *Sakkaiki*, 1494/Ōei. 33. 10. 17, *Kōfūki*, 1149/Hōtoku 1. 10. 13, and *Shinchō gōki*, 1495/Meiō 4. 9. 21 (especially for reference to "birdcatchers"). For title and Ieyasu, ibid., pp. 831-832, citing *Kinrikō gohōshiki*, "Kinchū hōgo gojōmoku 17 kajō," 1597/Keichō 2. 7. For Chion'in, see ibid., p. 832, citing *Kenkyō ruiten* 4/13b *Jisha*, 1627/Kan'ei 4. 7. 27.

6. "Gofushimiin inzen," *Kyōtō Shijō dōjō Konrenji monjo—chūsei hen*, 2, no. 1, ed. Abe Yukihiro, in *Shōmin shinko*, p. 224, and *Jō'a Shōnin den*, in *Teihon*, 2:1544. The version in the *Jō'a Shōnin den* has the date, the *Konrenji monjo* version does not. The latter's editor gives the name Takashina. The characters for "Masa" differ.

7. *Teihon*, 2:1544 and "Gokōgon rinji," *Konrenji monjo*, 2, no. 5, p. 225 ("Gokitō itaserubeki wa tenki kono gotoshi, yotte shittatsu kudan no gotoshi. Sangatsu 24 nichi [Yanagiwara] Sachūben Tadamitsu Jō'a Shōnin gobō").

8. *Jō'a Shōnin den*, in *Teihon*, 2:1544.

9. Ishida, "Muromachi jidai," part 2, pp. 103-104.

10. "Gonara tennō rinji," *Shōnenji monjo*, no. 8, in *Fukui kenshi shiryōhen* 4: *Chū kinsei* 2, ed. Fukuiken (Fukui: Fukuiken, 1984), p. 702. Dated Temmon 5. 12. 20. See also "Echizen Shōnenji On'a Shōnin rinji no utsushi," *Shibazaki bunko*, in *Teihon*, 2:1801.

11. "Yoshisada jisatsu no koto," *Taiheiki*, 3:321 (Chapter Twenty). There is also a legend that Yoshisada's horse, which had brought him so often to the Shōnenji, had run to the temple bearing his body. Umedani Shigeki and Takaō Sairyō, *Nitta Yoshisada-kō to jishū: Shōnenji* (Maruoka: Nitta-kō 650 Nenki Bozensai Hōsankai, 1987), p. 10.

12. By Yoshimasa and by Gotsuchimikado. *Shōnenji okibumi, Shōnenji monjo*, no. 5, in *Fukui kenshi*, 4:701. The date given is Chōroku 2. 12. 26. For Gotsuchimikado, "Gotsuchimikado tennō rinji," ibid., no. 6, p. 702. It is dated Kanshō 6. 11. 6.

13. Mochizuki, *Jishū nempyō*, p. 57, citing the *Echizen meishoshi* and *Dainihon shiryō*.

14. First in the time of the emperor Gonara and the shogun Manshōin Yoshiharu (1511-1550; shogun 1522-1547).

15. "Nijūgo dai Butten Shōnin chokujō ni yoru sandai no koto," *Jishū kekkishū*, in *Teihon*, 2:1264. Gomizunoo retired Meishō 6. 11. 8. "Onaji densō tensho no utsushi," *Shibazaki bunko*, in *Teihon*, 2:1801.

16. Meireki 2. 2. 19. The edict conferring the title is transcribed in the *Shibazaki bunko*, in *Teihon*, 2:1801. The deaths of several heads of the Kyōkōji while in office are recorded. The four entered between the 1580s and 1640, that is before the conferral of the title, are listed without the title Shōnin. However, of the three entered subsequently, two are listed as Shōnin (twenty-third, died 1700, and twenty-eighth, died 1765 and one not (twenty-fourth, died 1705). *Tōtakusan kakochō*, pp. 12, 16, 17, 24, 27, and 35.

17. Negita, *Jishū no teradera*, pp. 460-461.

18. *Shinshū yōhōki*, 32, in *Teihon*, 2:996.

19. "Yugyō sanjūnidai Fukō Shōnin shōjō," *Shichijō monjo*, no. 20, in *Teihon*, 1:401.

20. "Shūmon matsuji," *Shibazaki bunko*, in *Teihon*, 2:1801.

21. *Tōtakusan kakochō*, pp. 22-26. From the ranks held (Kōtokuin, Tōkaku'an, and Manshōken), it appears the title "Oshō" was given to those at least ten years in orders, as in the Zen school.

22. Ibid., p. 22 (Ōganji in Sado), p. 23 (Echizen Iwaki Seiganji, Kyoto Hōkokuji, Jōshū Amidabutsudera), p. 24 (Kōshū Kurogoma Shōganji [Oshō], Kazusa Manpukuji, Satsuma Jōkōmyōji), p. 25 (Musashi Shōmyōji [Oshō], Kyoto Bummyōji [Oshō]).

23. Ibid., p. 10 ([before 1584] "Kaku'a [Tōshū Kyōkōji jūji]"), p. 12 ("Kaku'amidabutsu [1604] Keichō 9 . . . 2 gatsu 27 nichi Hamamatsu Kyōkōji jūgo dai"), p. 16 ("[1640] Kan'ei 17 nen 10 ka 15 nichi Kaku'amidabutsu Kyōkōji Hamamatsu"), p. 17 ("Kan'ei 17 nen gokugetsu 9 ka Kaku'amidabutsu Hamamatsu"), p. 24 ("Tōshū Hamamatsu Kyōkōji nijūsandai Kaku'a Tanseki Oshō [1700] Genroku 13 . . . 7 gatsu 22 nichi"), p. 27 ("Tōshū Hamamatsu Kyōkōji nijūyondai zen Keikōin Go'a Shōnin Keikan Oshō [1705] Hōei 2 . . . nen 9 gatsu 6 ka").

24. Ibid., pp. 27 (d. 1706), 29 (d. 1714), 41 (d. 1779), 24 (d. 1689), 27 (d. 1704), 34 (d. 1762), and 42 (d. 1782).

25. Ibid., p. 28. There is a problem with the dating: the twenty-third is noted as dying in An'ei 6, which I believe is a mistake for Hōei 6, although the astrological sign is for the year before (1708). The one who died in 1529 or

1544 (depending on whether one reads vertically or horizontally) is not listed as a Shōnin. Ibid., p. 6. Since only Yugyō Shōnin are listed as Shōnin, it would not be unusual.

26. Ibid., p. 41. A complete study of this phenomenon needs to be made. Certainly, it is clear that the abbesses of Mantokuji in Tokugawa Village, a Jishū temple which claimed administrative independence from the sect, used the title Shōnin (as well as the privileges of a *monzeki*). See Wright, *The Power of Religion*, pp. 273, 433.

27. *Koji ruien* 28: *Shukkyō-bu* 3 (1912; photographic reproduction, Yoshikawa Kōbunkan, 1981), p. 182, citing *Shomonzekifu*, "jō." The list does not seem either comprehensive or even correct, with at least one replication: Ninnaji, Shōren'in, Zuishin'in, Rengekōin, Jōdoji, Byōdōin, Hongakuji, Hōjūji, Anjōji, Myōkōin, Zenrinji, Jōjūji, Nyoonji, Bishamondō, Shōgoin, Kajiiden (Kajii no miya, the Enyūin), Sanbōin, Kajūji, Emmain (the Byōdōin), Ichijōin, Daijōin, Rinnōji Jigain, Myōhōin, Jissōin, Manjin, Daikakuji, Tōnan'in, Jōjōin, and Chion'in. A source dated 1852 (Kaiei 7) lists as *miya monzeki* Rinnōji, Ninnaji, Daikakuji, Myōhōin, Shōgoin, Shōren'in, Chion'in, Kanshūji, Kajii no miya, Manjin, and Emmain; as *sekke monzeki*, the Yugateiin of the Daikakuji, Daijōin, Ichijōin, Jissōin, Sanbōin, Zuishin'in, and Rengekōin, making a total of eighteen. Ibid., pp. 182-184, citing *Kaiei shichinen Unjō myōran*.

28. For *sekke*, see Papinot, *Historical*, s. v. "Go-sekke." For *seika*, see *Koji ruien* 28, p. 182, citing *Kenkyōruiten*, 3. 4, "Shosatsu: Hōsho no shidai" and Papinot, *Historical*, pp. 550-551, s. v. "Seikwa." These families were the Sanjō, Saionji, Tokudaiji, Kazan'in, Ōimikado, Kuga, Imadegawa, Hirohata, and Daigo.

29. *Koji ruien* 28, p. 187, citing *Wakinkan, zenhen*, 33 *mō*.

30. "Sonnin Shōnin," *Gorekidai keifu*, in *Shomin shinkō*, p. 251.

31. *Komonjo*, s. v. "Kigan," "Goganji," and "Chokugan." Distinct from *goganjo/goganji*, temples built for private purposes.

32. For Tōdaiji, see *Koji ruien* 28, p. 177, citing *Tōdaiji yōroku*; for private reasons, see ibid., p. 176, citing *Shingishiki: Gorinji*.

33. See G. Cameron Hurst III, *Insei: Abdicated Sovereigns in the Politics of Late Heian Japan 1086-1185* (New York and London: Columbia University Press, 1976), pp. 263-270 for the land holdings of *goganji*.

34. Papinot, *Historical*, s. v. "Engakuji" and "Onjōji." For Onjōji, see also *Koji ruien* 28, p. 176, citing *Shingishiki: Gorinji*.

35. For mortuary tablet, see *Koji ruien* 28, p. 177, citing *Kennyō Shōnin zakki*; for Nara temples, ibid., p. 176; for documents, ibid., p. 178, citing the *Tōfuku kinenroku*, according to which Tōkōji received the distinction of *chokuganji* in 1329/Karyaku 4. 5. 14 and *Reigenji monjo*, according to which the Reigenji received the imperial decree to become a *chokuganji* in 1677/Empō 6. 5. 29. The *Koji ruien* seems to consider the *goganji* as *chokuganjo*, but according to strict definition, it is not.

36. For document creating Shōnenji a *kiganjo*, see "Ashikaga Yoshimasa shūhan migyōsho," *Shōnenji monjo*, no. 2

37. This is how Nakayama Nobuyuki characterizes the Shōnenji. "Jishū no seisuiki," p. 25. (dated Chōroku 2. 12. 26), in *Fukui kenshi*, 4:693. For On'a and his dream, see *Shōnenji engi utsushi*, ibid., p. 700. For shogunal authority in Echizen, see "Kaidai," ibid., p. 706. For Gotsuchimikado, see "Gotsuchimikado tennō rinji," *Shōnenji monjo*, no. 6, ibid., p. 702 ("Echizen no kuni Nagasaki Shōnenji gokitō itasu beki wa tenki kono gotoku, kore [o] tsubusa ni, jō o motte, Kanshō 6 nen 11 gatsu 6 ka [seal of Kajūji Ujinaga]"). For Gonara, see "Gonara tennō rinji," *Shōnenji monjo*, no. 8, ibid., p. 702 ("Kokka anzen hōso chōkyū [no tame ni] inori [o] notamai tatematsuru wa, tenki kono gotoku, kore [o] tsubusa ni, jō [o] motte, Temmon 5 nen 12 gatsu hatsuka [seal of Madenokōji Korefusa]").

38. "Gokōgon rinji," *Shōjōkōji monjo*, no. 18 in *Fujisawa shishi*, 1:654.

39. At the Hōshōin in Yuki-no-shita. Papinot, *Historical*, s. v. "Ashikaga Mochiuji" and "Uesugi (Inukake) Ujinori" and *Fujisawa shishi*, 1:654.

40. Tachibana, *Yugyōji*, p. 101. See also Mochizuki, *Jishū nempyō*, p. 49, citing *Kamakura ōzoshi*.

41. *Shimpen Sagami*, 5:141. These names are not on the present monument. Yoshikawa Kiyoshi assumed that the list of names in the *Shimpen Sagami* had for some reason been erased. *Jishū ami*, p. 256. It is clear from the *Tōtakusan chiji kiroku* (Record of the administration of the Fujisawa temple) that the original, set up by the fourteenth Yugyō Shōnin Taikū in 1425, had been replaced by the "thirty-seventh Shōnin," Takushi (YS 1645-1647, FS 1647-1658). The *Tōtakusan chiji kiroku* notes that the inscription was written by the thirty-seventh Shōnin for those killed in some past disturbance and that there had been one whose inscription had been written by the fourteenth Shōnin. Dates are noted as unknown. In *Teihon*, 2:1807.

42. This is the part of the text on the present monument. *Fujisawa shishi* 3: *Shiryōhen* (Fujisawa: Fujisawashi yakusho, 1973), p. 288. Tachibana notes that Uesugi Norimoto (1383-1418), Mochiuji's *shitsuji* after Ujinori was dismissed, endowed the Engakuji in Kamakura for prayers for the "mikata narabi ni onteki nado" who had died in the revolt which had ended the year before. Tachibana, *Yugyōji*, p. 102, citing document from the temple collection.

43. "Ankoku Shōnin," *Gorekidai keifu*, in *Shomin shinkō*, p. 239.

44. S. A. Thornton, "The Propaganda Traditions of the Yugyō-ha: The Campaign to Establish the Jishū as an Independent School of Japanese Buddhism (1300-1700)," (Ph. D. Thesis, University of Cambridge, 1989), pp. 127-137.

45. *Yugyō nijūyonsō*, in *Teihon*, 2:1476.

46. "Gokomatsuin inzen," *Shōjōkōji monjo*, no. 20 in *Fujisawa shishi*, 1:656.

47. Nakayama, "Jishū no seisuiki," p. 25. See also "Itchin Shōnin," *Gorekidai keifu*, in *Shomin shinkō*, p. 23ᵒ.

48. *Kizuregawa hangan*, in *Zoku gunsho ruijū* 5:1 (Keizai Zasshi Sha, 1905), p. 339. There is no mention of tonsure.

49. *Konrenji monjo*, 2, in *Shomin shinkō*, pp. 224-230 (twenty-eight documents).

50. Papinot, *Historical*, s. v., "*Kokinshū*."

51. For political interference, see Robert N. Huey, *Kyōgoku Tamekane: Poetry and Politics in Late Kamakura Japan* (Stanford: Stanford University Press, 1989), p. 21.

52. "The one who relies on Mida, seeing the moon in the evening sky even though not cleared of clouds, still heads West (Mida tanomu hito wa ama yoru no tsuki nare ya kumo harenedomo nishi ni koso yuke)." *Gyokuyō wakashū*, 19, no. 2620 [2607], in *Shimpen kokka taikan* 1: *Chokusenshūhen*, ed. Shimpen Kokka Taikan Henshū Iinkai (Kadokawa Shoten, 1983), p. 476. The anthology was commissioned in 1311 by the former Emperor Fushimi, edited by Kyōgoku Tamekane, and finished in 1312.

53. Tachibana, *Yugyōji*, p. 37. The preface records, "Kore wa, aru hito onaji yashiro [Ishikiyomizu] nembutsu no sūhen wa ōku kuru koso suguretare to mōsu hito haberikeru o, mata shizuka ni hitotsu zutsu koso mōsubekere hito haberikereba, izure ka makoto ni yokinaran to obotsukanaku omoite netaru yume ni kaku miekeru to nan." *Gyokuyō wakashū*, p. 476.

54. Tachibana, *Yugyōji*, p. 38. *Gyokuyō wakashū*, 19, no. 2702 [2689], p. 478 ("Nani toshite mo naki mi no uki kumo ni kokoro no tsuki o hedate somekemu").

55. For Shinkyō as a poet, see Kanai, *Ippen*, pp. 276-281 and Ōhashi, *Ippen*, pp. 85-88.

56. "Yomi hito shirazu." 18, no. 2529/2516, in *Shimpen kokka taikan*, 1:474. See also Kanai, *Ippen*, p. 279 and *Waka daijiten*, ed. Inukai Kiyoshi et al. (Meiji Shoten, 1986), pp. 235-236 (as no. 2516).

57. Tachibana, *Yugyōji*, p. 37.

58. Enkei 3. *Ta'a hōgo*, 8, in *Teihon*, 1:215.

59. Kanai, *Ippen*, pp. 279-80. *Ta'a hōgo*, 8, in *Teihon*, 1:217, 224 (Enkei 3. 9, or 1310, and sometime between 1308 and 1310 ["Enkei no koro"]).

60. For Tamesuke, Showa 5. 6. *Ta'a hōgo*, 8, in *Teihon*, 1:221. For Tamemori, Shōwa 2. 8. 1. Ibid., p. 218.

61. Kanai, *Ippen*, p. 279. One might note that "the work's criticism is couched in anti-Zen, anti-Jōdo, pro-Tendai religious terms. In other words its religious stance is as orthodox as its poetic one." Huey, *Tamekane*, p. 34.

62. For Shinkyō's poem, see *Ta'a hōgo*, 8, in *Teihon*, 1:223 (dated 1318/Bumpō 2). For play, see *Yugyō yanagi*, in *Yōkyokushū* 2, ed. Yokomichi Mario and Omote Akira, *Nihon koten bungaku taikei* 41 (Iwanami Shoten, 1963), p. 128, line 11, which also uses the theme of old age.

63. Kanai, *Ippen*, p. 423. 9, no. 889, in *Shimpen kokka taikan*, 1:618 ("Oroka naru mi wa shimonagara murasaki no kumo no mukae o mataru hi wa nashi").

64. For Shinkan's death, see Mochizuki, *Jishū nempyō*, p. 34, citing *Jishū kakochō*, and for death of second Jō'a, see ibid., p. 37, citing *Jishū kakochō*.

65. Kanai, *Ippen*, p. 425. For poem, 8, no. 774, in *Shimpen kokka taikan*, 1:616.

66. Commissioned in 1375 by Emperor Goenyū (1359-1393; r. 1371-1382); compiled by Nijō Tametō and Tameshige, finished in 1383 and revised in 1384. Kanai, *Ippen*, p. 426. For poem, 8, no. 800, in *Shimpen kokka taikan*, 1:706.

67. For temple tradition, see Kanai, *Ippen*, p. 426, citing *Enfukuji rakuengi* of the Enfukuji in Nagoya.

68. Ōan 3. 9. 27. His death is recorded in the *Jishū kakochō* and the *Jōrakki* (on the twenty-sixth). Kanai, *Ippen*, p. 426. For his poetry activities, see also Negita, *Jishū no teradera*, p. 446. On the request of the head of the Atsuta Shrine head Owari Nakamune, he copied the *Nihon shoki* and on the back of the pages he recorded 483 poems, the *Shihai waka*. It was presented 1377/Eiwa 3. 11. 4, according to the colophon. See also Kanai, *Ippen*, p. 427.

69. *Shimpen kokka taikan*, 1:702 (no. 600), 704 (no. 692), 716 (no. 1299).

70. *Shimpen kokka taikan*, 1:658, (no. 374), 666 (no. 777), 669 (no. 911), 670 (no. 986), 674 (no. 1143), 674 (no. 1177), 687 (no. 1810), 688 (no. 1835). The *Shinshūi wakashū* was commissioned in 1363 by Emperor Gokōgon, begun by Fujiwara Tameaki, and completed 1364. Robert H. Brower and Earl Miner, *Japanese Court Poetry* (Stanford: Stanford University Press, 1961), p. 486.

71. *Shinshū yōhōki*, 3, in *Teihon*, 2:990.

72. "Ton'amidabutsu e tsukawasaru gohenji," *Ta'a hōgo*, 4, in *Teihon*, 1:177-178.

73. Kanai, *Ippen*, p. 423-424, citing the *Sōanshū* (for poetry meetings) and *Gyokuseki zasshi* (for living at Konrenji). Shinkan died Kōkoku 2. 6. 2.

74. "Sonkan hōshinnō," *Gorekidai keifu*, in *Shomin shinkō*, p. 241.

75. *Jō'a Shōnin ekotoba den*, in *Teihon* 2:1541. The emperor died Engen 1. 4. 6.

76. For the nineteenth as the last to court, see *Yugyō sanjūissō*, in *Teihon* 2:1496. For invitation to court, see "Yanagiwara Sukesada shojō," *Shōjōkōji monjo*, no. 33 in *Fujisawa shishi*, 1:669. For the text of the letter of invitation, see Appendix, no. 4.

77. *Yugyō sanjūissō*, in *Teihon*, 2:1496. For full text, see Appendix, no. 5. The number for the year of Gonara's reign should be "sanjū" or thirty, according to editor Tachibana Shundō.

78. "Butten Shōnin," *Gorekidai keifu*, in *Shomin shinkō*, p. 254.

79. Tachibana, following the *Gorekidai reibo* ["Butten Shōnin," in *Teihon*, 2:1588] and Mochizuki, *Jishū nempyō*, [p. 77], accepts the date 1557/Kōji 3 and thus thinks the failure to wait on the emperor was a result of the fire. *Jishūshi*

ronkō, p. 313. The precise date for the fire, Kōji 3. 3. 24, comes from Butten's inscription in the *Tōtakusan kakochō*, p. 5.

80. "Nijō-dono and Kujō-dono," Fujiwara Terumitsu (the future Nanoin Kampaku [regent]) and Fujiwara Kanenori (the future Getsurin Kampaku), the Kampaku-Sesshō Konoe Harutsugi, and the wife of the famous Hosokawa Fujitaka (Yūsai). *Yugyō sanjūissō*, in *Teihon*, 2:1496. See also p. 1504, 89n.

81. *Yugyō sanjūissō*, in *Teihon*, 2:1500. For full text, see Appendix, no. 5. The crown prince was Masahito, 1552-1586, posthumously Dajō tennō and Yōkōin. Ibid., p. 1504, 105n and Papinot, *Historical*, s. v. "Masahito-shinnō."

82. "Yugyō Shōnin gorei mairu. Kajūji Chūnagon mōshitsugi. Hikiawase jūjō ni aogi makimono ittan shinjō. Onajiku miya no onkata e mo gorei mōsaruru." *Oyu-dono no ue no nikki*, 7:278; also cited in Tachibana, *Jishūshi ronkō*, p. 328. Note that the ranks for Kajūji are different in the texts. *Hikiawase* paper was used for official documents. *Komonjo*, s. v. "Hikiawasegami."

83. *Yugyō sanjūissō*, in *Teihon*, 2:1500. For full text, see Appendix, no. 5. The crown prince's consort was Fujiwara Haruko, Shinjōtōmon'in; Kōmon Susuki Chūnagon was the son of Yamashina Akitsugi. Ibid., p. 1504, 132n, 134n.

84. *Oyu no ue no nikki*, 7:296-297. The imperial princess had the religious name Seishū and was called Bikuni gosho, Taijikōin, Dongein. The new palace had been built by Oda Nobunaga for the Crown Prince and his son. Tachibana, *Jishūshi ronkō*, p. 330. *Sugiwara* paper was a fine paper made in Sugiwara Village, Harima Province. *Shinmeikai kogo jiten*, ed. Kindaichi Haruhiko (Sanseidō, 1972), s. v. "Sugiharagami."

85. "Nyotan Shōnin," *Gorekidai keifu*, in *Shomin shinkō*, p. 249. For Sonnin, see Mochizuki, *Jishū nempyō*, p. 100, citing *Yugyō Shōnin yūi sho* and *Jishū kōyō*.

86. 1339/Enbun 4[Ryakuō 2]. 10. 18. Mochizuki, *Jishū nempyō*, p. 33, citing document of the Konkōji. For Takauji's motivations and text, Tachibana, *Jishūshi ronkō*, p. 252 ("Shichijō dōjō Konkōji ryōsho rakuchū hendo sanzai [no] senki no gotoku mattaku jinō [suru] mono nari. Ryakuō 2 nen 10 gatsu 18 nichi. Kaō [Ashikaga Takauji]").

87. A Tokugawa period entry. Kanai, *Ippen*, p. 347, citing the *Ontemoto kakochō*. I have found no such entry in the *Jishū kakochō*. However, it is in "Itchin Shōnin," *Gorekidai keifu*, in *Shomin shinkō*, p. 239. For the interpretation of Takauji's motives, see Kanai, *Ippen*, p. 348.

88. "Nagano gosho," *Shichidai Shōnin hōgo*, in *Teihon*, 1:383.

89. ". . . hayaku Shōjōkōin gonyūin arubeki . . ." *Yugyō hachidai*, in *Teihon*, 2:1448.

90. *Yugyō engi*, in *Teihon*, 2:1451.

91. For donation, see "Taikū Shōnin," *Gorekidai keifu*, in *Shomin shinkō*, p. 242; for ten *nembutsu*, see *Shinshū yōhōki*, in *Teihon*, 2:990; for entry, see *Jishū kakochō*, p. 129. For entry, see also *Ichirenji kakochō*, p. 26 ("Eikyō 11

nen 2 gatsu 13 nichi Go'amidabutsu Chōshun'inden Dōnō jūsan'i Mochiuji kō").

92. *Yugyō engi*, in *Teihon*, 2:1451; *Yūki senjō monogatari*, in *Gunsho ruijū* 20: *Kassenbu* (Zoku Gunsho Ruijū Kanseikai, 1929) (vol. 383). See Thornton, "Propaganda," pp. 104-109.

93. For Konrenji, see *Mansai jugō nikki*, 2:153 (Eikyō 2. 6. 11); for Konrenji and Konkōji, see *Inryōken nichiroku* 1, *Zōho zoku shiryō taisei* 21, ed. Takeuchi Rizō (Kyoto: Rinsen Shoten 1954), p. 78 (Eikyō 10. 10. 8).

94. Kaijima, "Kōryū jiki," part 1, p. 14, 12n, citing Konkōji document dated Eikyō 4. 10. 8.

95. *Nochikagami* 2, *Shintei zōho kokushi taikei* 35, ed. Kuroita Katsumi (Kokushi Taikei Kankōkai, Yoshikawa Kōbunkan, Nichiyo Shobō, 1932), p. 1081 (Eikyō 12. 3. 29), citing the *Gonaishoan*.

96. Kaijima, "Kōryū jiki," part 2, p. 15, 18n, citing *Yugyō yuisho*.

97. *Jishū kakochō*, p. 138. The entry states that Yoshinori (who was assassinated in 1441) died Kakitsu 1. 6. 24, but it was placed among dates for 1466 or 1467. However, the entry is claimed to be a Tokugawa period entry. Tachibana, *Jishūshi ronkō*, pp. 128-129.

98. The document transcribed by Tachibana is the one sent to the Konkōji; I have added the name of the second temple. Tachibana, *Jishūshi ronkō*, p. 256. The discussion below follows Tachibana.

99. "Ashikaga Yoshimochi migyōshō," *Shōjōkōji monjo*, no. 16 in *Fujisawa shishi*, 1:652. The meaning of the passage as "without charging a fee" follows Tachibana, *Yugyōji*, pp. 82-83.

100. "Miidera shūto Benchō-ra rensho shojō," *Shōjōkōji monjo*, no. 17 in *Fujisawa shishi*, 1:653. The Togashi were *shugo* of Kaga before the Shiba. This Togashi might be Mitsunari. Ibid. The "tradition" of the temple is that this letter was sent to the Miidera. However, Tachibana identifies the temple as Enryakuji because of the seals identified as those of officials of Enryakuji. Tachibana, *Yugyōji*, p. 187.

101. "Ashikaga Yoshimochi kyōsho [*sic*]," *Shōjōkōji monjo*, no. 19 in *Fujisawa shishi*, 1:655.

102. "Ashikaga Yoshinori migyōsho," *Shōjōkōji monjo*, no. 21 in *Fujisawa shishi*, 1:657.

103. "Chiren Shōnin," *Gorekidai keifu*, in *Shomin shinkō*, p. 244.

104. It appears that this assigning of the Yugyō-ha jurisdiction over the Shijō-ha was the result of years of lobbying on the part of the former. Relations between the two appear to have been good until the beginning of the Ōei period (1394-1427). The first five Jō'a are entered in the *Jishū kakochō*, the last of them entered in 1396 ("Ōei 3 nen 9 gatsu 15 nichi Shijō Jō'amidabutsu." *Jishū kakochō*, p. 53. Because the sixth Jō'a, who died in 1415 (Ōei 22. 6, according to the *Shijō dōjō Konrenji rekidai yofuki*, in Kanai, *Ippen*, p. 440.) and his successors were not entered, Kanai thinks that relations were definitely strained by this time, strained by the pressure the Yugyō-ha was exerting on the

shogunate to make the Shijō-ha subordinate to the Yugyō-ha. Kanai, *Ippen*, p. 431.

105. For the burning of Konrenji, see *Kanmon*, 1:277 (Ōei 31. 8. 10 and 11) and *Mansai*, 1:450 (Ōei. 31. 8. 10). For *renga* at Konrenji, see *Mansai*, 2:153 (Eikyō 2. 6. 11).

106. At the end of the year (*shimotsuki*) and at New Year's, first the head of Konrenji was received and then the head of Konkōji, one or more days later. See *Denchū moshitsugiki*, in *Gunsho ruijū* 21 (Zoku Gunsho Ruijū Kanseikai, 1928), p. 260 and *Nenchū jōreiki*, ibid., p. 290.

107. *Denchū ika nenchū gyōshi*, pp. 318 (receiving Fujisawa Shōnin), 340 (receiving ten *nembutsu* and leaving the palace).

108. *Koga kubō nidai Ashikaga Masauji monjoshū*, ed. Satō Hironobu, Kenkyū shiryō gaihen 1 (Chigazaki: Gohōjōshi Kenkyūkai, 1973), no. 125, pp. 30-31 and no. 126, pp. 32-34.

109. *Nochikagami*, 2:565 (Ōei 18. 4. 10), 699 (Ōei 30. 6. 9), 714 (Ōei 31. 4. 7). All citing the *Gonaishoan*.

110. *Inryōken nichiroku*, 1:417. The entry is Kanshō 4. 8. 12, which describes the incident of the day before.

111. Chōkyō 3. 4. 9. *Inryōken nichiroku* 3, *Zōho soku shiryō taisei* 23, ed. Takeuchi Rizō (Kyoto: Rinsen Shoten, 1954), p. 378.

112. Entoku 2. 1. 14. *Inryōken nichiroku* 4, *Zōho zoku shiryō taisei* 24, ed. Takeuchi Rizō (Kyoto: Rinsen Shoten, 1954), p. 12 and *Nochikagami* 3, *Shintei shōho kokushi taikei* 36, ed. Kuroita Katsumi (Kokushi Taikei Kankōkai, Yoshikawa Kōbunkan, Nichiyo Shobō, 1933), p. 924 (Entoku 2. 1. 23, quoting *Ryōanshōbo*).

113. Kanai, *Ippen*, p. 384, citing *Mansai jugō nikki* (Eikyō 3. 2, for Hachiman Shrine) and *Daijōin jisha zatsuji ki* (Bummei 10. 2. 16, for the nineteenth, for Konkōji).

114. For Yoshimitsu (Ōei 2. 5. 6), see Tachibana, *Jishūshi ronkō*, p. 255, citing Konkōji document ("Kifu Konkōji: Shichijō yori minami, Shiokoji yori kita. Higashitōin yori higashi, Takakura yori nishi [no] chi. Migi [no] tōji [ni] kifu [suru] tokoro no jō kudan no gotoshi"). For Yoshimochi, ibid., p. 257, citing another Konkōji document and Kaijima, "Kōryū jiki," part 2, p. 14, 6n, citing Konkōji document dated Ōei 16. 11. 6.

It is not possible to determine whether Yoshimochi's son Yoshikazu was also a devotee and patron of the Yugyō Shōnin. Kaijima considers the directives regarding the Yugyō-ha which came out in Yoshikazu's short term of office as actually coming from his retired father. Kaijima, "Kōryū jiki," part 1, p. 15. The *Kanmon gyoki* (Ōei 31. 8. 10) and the *Mansai jugō nikki* (Ōei 31. 8. 11) both state that the order to Konrenji came from the "Kubō" ("Prince," the title of the shogun). However, the *Kanmon gyoki* also stresses that the converts to the Yugyō Shōnin included "Muromachi-dono" (lord of the palace at Muromachi), or Yoshimochi. *Kanmon gyoki*, 1:277; *Mansai jugō nikki*, 1:450.

115. *Shōnenji okibumi, Shōnenji monjo*, no. 5, in *Fukui kenshi*, 4:701.
116. "Ashikaga Yoshimasa shūhan migyōsho," *Shōnenji monjo*, no. 2, in *Fukui kenshi*, 4:693.
117. *Shōnenji engi utsushi*, no. 4, in *Fukui kenshi*, 4:694 (for Genshō), 700 (for dream). See Appendix, no. 7 for text.
118. *Fukui kenshi*, 4:706.
119. Papinot, *Historical*, s. v. "Shiba Yoshitake," "Shiba Yoshikado," and "Shiba Yoshitoshi."
120. *Shōnenji okibumi, Shōnenji monjo*, no. 5, *Fukui kenshi*, 4:701-702. See the Appendix, no. 6 for full text.
121. *Shōnenji engi utsushi, Shōnenji monjo*, no. 4, *Fukui kenshi*, 4:700 ("Tōji gokiganjo no koto").
122. As noted in note 14, the head of the Shōnenji was first presented at court in the time of Emperor Gonara and the thirteenth shogun, Manshōin Yoshiharu. "Onaji densō," *Shibazaki bunko*, in *Teihon*, 2:1801. Yoshiharu was actually the twelfth. If this is the case, he must have been presented between 1546, the year Yoshiharu abdicated in favor of this son, and 1550, the year Yoshiharu died. In 1672, the order had received an enquiry from the court on the precedent of heads of branch temples being presented at court.
123. Ishida, "Muromachi jidai," part 2, p. 103.
124. Tachibana, *Jishūshi ronkō*, p. 249.
125. For Chōshun'in, see Negita, *Jishū teradera*, p. 29; for Mochiuji as Chōshun'inden, see *Kizuregawa hangan*, p. 339.
126. "Ashikaga Mochiuji shojō," *Shōjōkōji monjo*, no. 26 in *Fujisawa shishi*, 1:662. No year is given, but Tachibana argues for Taikū. *Jishūshi ronkō*, p. 250.
127. For Ujimitsu, see "Kamakura gosho (Ujimitsu) kishinjō," no. 1280 (Eitoku 2. 10. 9) in *Sōshū komonjo* 4, ed. Nuki Tatsuto (Kadokawa shoten, 1969), p. 75. He also made another significant contribution in 1391. "Kamakura gosho (Ujimitsu) kishinjō," no. 1281 (Meitoku 2. 9. 8), ibid. For Mitsukane, see "Kamakura gosho (Mitsukane) kishinjō," no. 1283 (Ōei 7. 12. 30), ibid. Mitsukane also made a second contribution in 1406. "Kamakura gosho (Mitsukane) kishinjō," no. 1284 (Ōei 13. 5. 12), ibid., p. 76. For Mochiuji, see "Ashikaga Mochiuji shojō," no. 1286 (Ōei 27. 11. 19), ibid. The temple collection also includes a 1415 confirmation of holdings and a letter in thanks for a branch of flowering cherry presented to him. "Kamakura gosho (Mochiuji) migyōsho," no. 1285 (Ōei 21. 12. 20) and "Ashikaga Mochiuji shojō," no. 1287 ([]. 3. 4), ibid.
128. Negita, *Jishū teradera*, p. 25 and *Shimpen Sagami*, 4:300 (vol. 87, Kamakura kōri 19, "Betsuganji").
129. Nuki Tatsuto, *Kamakura haiji jiten* (Yokohama: Yūrindō, 1980), p. 233; *Shimpen Kamakura shi, Dai Nihon chishi taikei* 19, ed. Ashida Koreto (Bokushobō, 1915), pp. 28-29; Tachibana, *Jishūshi ronkō*, p. 249.

130. "The next day a letter arrived this time from Kamakura-dono. The content was the same as that of the letter [from the shogun]." *Yugyō hachidai*, in *Teihon*, 2:1448.

131. "Words are not enough to express [my] sorrow [at my father's death] last year. I cannot express my gratitude [for your letter of condolence] concerning this. Sixth month, twenty-fourth day. [From] Mitsukane. [To the] Yugyō Shōnin." Dated 6. 24, the letter arrived 1399/Ōei 6. 9. 15. Tachibana, *Jishūshi ronkō*, p. 247.

132. "How wonderful the news that in recent years you have built a temple in Mino Province. Sincerely yours. Seal. [To] Ta'a Shōnin." Tachibana, *Yugyōji*, p. 121, citing *Gonaishoan*, in *Zoku gunsho ruijū* (vol. 664).

133. "The three gō of candles have arrived. I am delighted [with them]. Yours sincerely. Fifth month fourteenth day. Signature Ashikaga Yoshizumi." "Ashikaga Yoshizumi gonaisho," *Shōjōkōji monjo*, no. 29 in *Fujisawa shishi*, 1:665. "The twenty lengths of silk and five hundred candles have arrived. I am delighted [with them]. I am sending gold brocade and a tray. Sincerely yours. Fourth month seventeenth day. Signature Ashikaga Yoshizumi." "Ashikaga Yoshizumi gonaisho," no. 27 in ibid., p. 663.

134. He died at sixty-four. See Tachibana, *Jishūshi ronkō*, pp. 314-316. Butten entered Gishun in the *Tōtakusan kakochō* ("Shōnen'in zenjugō Gishun Go'amidabutsu [died] at Tsuruga in Eiroku Junior brother of the fire/Hare tenth year first month twelfth day the twenty-fifth Yugyō [Shōnin] conducted the funeral service. He accompanied the shogun Samanotō Yoshiaki when he arrived in Echizen. He was the uncle of the shogun"). *Tōtakusan kakochō*, p. 47. Tachibana points out that Gishun had left Kyoto in 1562 and had been in Tsuruga for some years before Yoshiaki, who arrived in 1566. Tachibana, *Jishūshi ronkō*, p. 315.

135. *Fujisawa shishi*, 1:666-668 and Tachibana, *Jishūshi ronkō*, pp. 315-317.

136. "Ashikaga Yoshiaki gonaisho," *Shōjōkōji monjo*, no. 32 in *Fujisawa shishi*, 1:668. For Dōnen's possible visit, see Tachibana, *Jishūshi ronkō*, p. 317. This Terumitsu is identified as Makijima Terumitsu of Uji, south of Kyoto. In the seventh month of 1573/Tenshō 1, Yoshiaki raised his standard against Nobunaga for the second time at Makijima Castle. Terumitsu was with him until Yoshiaki died in Osaka in 1597/Keichō 2. 8. 28. Tachibana, *Jishūshi ronkō*, p. 317, citing Okuno Takahiro, *Ashikaga Yoshiaki*. Something might be said of the fact that both use the same character in their personal names (mitsu/aki).

137. "How very wonderful the news that the Shichijō [temple] Konkōji in Yamashiro Province is to be rebuilt. You must [provide] the details to [my messengers] Terumitsu [and] Sadanaga. Sincerely yours. Fifth month seventeenth day. Signature Ashikaga Yoshiaki." "Ashikaga Yoshiaki gonaisho," *Shōjōkōji monjo*, no. 30 in *Fujisawa shishi*, 1:666. In 1569 (1. 5) Miyoshi forces used the

Shichijō temple a as military camp. Mochizuki, *Jishū nempyō*, p. 79, citing *Nochikagami*.

138. "Two hundred candles have arrived. I am delighted [with them]. Therefore I am sending an incense container (red lacquer) [and] tray (crimson engraving). Sincerely yours. Sixth month second day. Signature (*kaō*) (Ashikaga Yoshiaki) [To] Ta'a Shōnin." "Ashikaga Yoshiaki gonaisho," *Shōjōkōji monjo*, no. 31 in *Fujisawa shishi*, 1:667.

139. For permission, Tamamuro Fumio, "Edo Shōnin," pp. 218, citing *Agei Kakuken nikki* (Tenshō 10. 12. 12); for mounts, ibid., p. 216 (Tenshō 11. 5. 21); for provisions, ibid., p. 217 (Tenshō 12. 8. 22); for vegetables and firewood, ibid. (Tenshō 12. 8. 15).

140. For approval and subsidy, see Tamamuro, "Edo Shōnin," p. 228, citing *Agei Kakuken nikki* (Tenshō 12. 8. 12). For Fujisawa, see ibid., p. 229 (Tenshō 12. 8. 20: "kano ryōji o Fujisawa ni nasaruru yoshi nari").

141. Tamamuro, "Edo Shōnin," p. 216, citing *Agei Kakuken nikki*.

142. Negita, *Jishū teradera*, p. 397.

143. "(Kudō) Mi'amidabutsu (Kudō nai) Rin'amidabutsu." *Jishū kakochō*, p. 119. The Soga brothers are also entered: "(Soga Jūrō) Kaku'amidabutsu (onaji Gorō) Jū'amidabutsu." Ibid., p. 40.

144. Papinot, *Historical*, s. v. "Itō Yoshisuke," "Shimazu Yoshihisa," and "Ōtomo Yoshishige."

145. "Ōuchi Yoshitaka shojō," *Shōjōkōji monjo*, no. 34 in *Fujisawa shishi*, 1:670.

146. *Tōtakusan kakochō*, p. 52.

147. *Yugyō nijūyonsō*, in *Teihon*, 2:1480.

148. For details on the battle, see Tachibana, *Yugyōji*, pp. 125-127, citing especially *Kōyō gunkan* for Masanari's betrayal of the Imagawa in attacking the Takeda and *Hōjō keizu beppon* [*sic*], in *Zoku gunsho ruijū* (vol. 140) under "Tsunanari" for Masanari's son, who was adopted by Hōjō Ujitsuna, married to his daughter, and made master of Tamanawa Castle—it is with him that much correspondence concerning the reconstruction of Shōjōkōji is conducted. *Odawara Hōjō keizu beppon*, in *Zoku gunsho ruijū* vol. 6 bk. 1, comp. Hanawa Hokinochi (Zoku Gunsho Ruijū Kanseikai, 1926), p. 96.

149. "Nobunaga gose ichidaiji de aru kara Ichirenji e oide itadakitai." *Yugyō nijūyonsō*, in *Teihon*, 2:1486-1487.

150. "Takeda Nobutora shojō," *Shōjōkōji monjo*, no. 35 in *Fujisawa shishi*, 1:671.

151. For letter to Ujikatsu, see "Ta'amidabutsu shojō," *Horiuchi monjo*, no. 9 in *Fujisawa shishi*, 1:645. See also Tachibana, *Jishūshi ronkō*, pp. 272 and 275, for identification of addressee. Letter to Horiuchi, see "Ta'amidabutsu shojō," no. 8, ibid., p. 644. See also ibid., p. 271 for text and p. 274, which identifies sender as Dōnen in 1577. For letter to temples, see "Yū'amidabutsu shojō," no. 10, p. 646. See also ibid., p. 273 for text and p. 275, which identifies

sender as Fukō. For letter from Ujishige, see "Iinuma jōshū Hōjō Ujishige inban [no] jō," (*Mori ke monjo*), ibid., p. 277.

152. Tachibana, *Jishūshi ronkō*, pp. 267-268, citing "Yugyō nijūkyūdai Taikō shojō" (Takase collection). See Appendix, no. 8 for text.

153. Tachibana, *Yugyōji*, pp. 126-127, citing *Odawara Hōjō keizu beppon*, in *Zoku gunsho ruijū* (vol. 140), under "Tsunanari."

154. Masanari's chief vassal (*karō*) Horiuchi Izu no kami Chikamoto had died in the same campaign; his son Horiuchi Tango no kami Shigechika had escorted Tsunanari to the Hōjō. Descendants of the Horiuchi would be involved with the Shōjōkōji for generations. Tachibana, *Yugyōji*, pp. 135-136. Many of the documents relating to the temple and its reconstruction are still held by the family. These two families did much toward saving the site and reconstructing the Shōjōkōji.

155. "Hōjō Ujinao hanmotsu," *Shōjōkōji monjo*, no. 23 in *Fujisawa shishi*, 1:659 ("Dōjō zōei ni tsuite, tarebito no ryōchū ni oite mo, yōmoku miatari shidai, kore o toru beku sōrō. Yotte jō kudan no gotoshi. Tenshō jūgonen kugatsu mikka [kaō] [Hōjō Ujinao]").

156. For confiscation, see Tachibana, *Jishūshi ronkō*, p. 270, citing Takuan's *Kamakura henrei ki* (in *Tōhō bukkyō sōshō*), which describes his journey of 1633 and the considerable diminishment of the temples of Kamakura: Kenchōji and Engakuji had been left with land worth only 100 *kan*. For division of temple land between Yugyō Shōnin and sawyers, see ibid., pp. 269-270 and idem, *Yugyōji*, pp. 134-135, citing the *Odawara shūsho ryōyaku chō* (dated Eiroku 2. 2. 12, according to the colophon), in *Nihon shiryō senshō*. For the twenty-five houses, see idem, *Jishūshi ronkō*, pp. 340-341, citing "Tamanawajō shū Hōjō Tsunanari hanmotsu," in *Mori ke monjo* (dated 1556/Kōji 2. 5. 28). For the total number of houses, see Ōhashi, *Ippen*, p. 204, calculated from the amount of tax levied.

157. *Shinshū yōhōki*, 13, in *Teihon*, 2:992 and Tachibana, *Jishūshi ronkō*, p. 338.

158. Tachibana, *Jishūshi ronkō*, pp. 342-343, citing the "Hōjō Ujiyasu inban [no] jō," in *Mori ke monjo* (see note 155) which specifies the daily stipend for various workers summoned for thirty days' service in one of Ujiyasu's campaigns.

159. Mochizuki, *Jishū nempyō*, pp. 80 (for Nobunaga), 82 (for Nomura), citing *Igawa Shinzenkōji monjo*. The town is Tsuruga City, Fukui Prefecture.

160. *Yugyō sanjūissō*, in *Teihon*, 2:1495.

161. As with the twenty-fourth Yugyō Shōnin, who had eighty or so monks and nuns as well as porters, horses, outcasts, and lepers ("taishū sōni . . . hinin raisha . . ." [lay followers, monks and nuns . . . pariahs (possibly unattached ascetics and religious practitioners) and lepers]). *Yugyō nijūyonsō*, in *Teihon*, 2:1470.

162. *Yugyō sanjūissō*, in *Teihon*, 2:1495-1496 (for Nobunaga's relatives and vassals) and 1498-1499 (for Nichirenites and invitation from Nobunaga). The location of Matsugashima Castle is Matsuzaka City, Mie Prefecture, of Anotsu Castle, Tsu City, Mie Prefecture, and Kayatsu, Ama District, Aichi Prefecture. For discussion, see Tachibana, *Jishūshi ronkō*, pp. 324-326.

163. Negita, *Jishū no teradera*, p. 443 and Papinot, *Historical*, s. v. "Toyotomi Hideyoshi."

164. "Fukō Shōnin," *Gorekidai keifu*, in *Shomin shinkō*, p. 247. Although this document is usually cited as being in the Shōjōkōji collection (as with Mochizuki, *Jishū nempyō*, p. 83), I have not seen it printed separately. Kanetsugu served Uesugi Kagekatsu. Papinot, *Historical*, s. v. "Naoe Kanetsugu."

165. "Taikō Hideyoshi kō yori . . ." "Fukō Shōnin," *Gorekidai keifu*, in *Shomin shinkō*, p. 247.

166. For Konkōji, see Mochizuki, *Jishū nempyō*, p. 84, citing *Shichijō monjo* (Tenshō 19. 9. 13); for Hōkokuji, ibid., p. 85, citing the *Shichijō dōjō kiroku* and *Kyō Hōkokuji kiroku*.

167. Sited at Higashiyama-Gojō in Kyoto. Kanai, *Ippen*, p. 460.

168. *Kyōtō shi no chimei, Nihon rekishi chimei taikei* 27 (Heibonsha, 1979), s. v. "Hōkōji."

Notes to Chapter 7

1. "Kishin: Sagami [no] kuni Higashigun Fujisawa no uchi hyaku koku no koto, migi senki no gotoku kifu seshime owaru. Koto ni jichū funyū taru beshi. Iyoiyo kono mune o mamori, buppō sōzoku taiman aru bekarazaru mono nari. Yotte kudan no gotoshi. Tenshō 19 nen kanoto u (Junior Brother of Metal/Hare) 11 gatsu [] hi." Tachibana, *Yugyōji*, pp. 160-161, citing *Shōjōkōji monjo*. See also "Mango Shōnin," *Gorekidai keifu*, in *Shomin shinkō*, p. 247.

2. Tachibana, *Yugyōji*, p. 161, calculating from 1660 figures of 29 *chō*, 1 *tan*, 3 *se*, and 13 *bu* given in *Manji sannen suichō*, collection of Aoki Shirō of Fujisawa.

3. "On this day [Fukō, head priest of] the Shōjōkōji of Fujisawa and [Mango] the Yugyō [Shōnin] came to Fushimi for an audience [with the shogun]. In the middle of the night there was an earthquake and afterwards the quaking of heaven and earth was tremendous." Tachibana, *Yugyōji*, p. 163, citing *Tokugawa jikki*, 5 (Keichō 8).

4. "Yugyō sanjūnidai Fukō Shōnin shōjō," *Shichijō monjo*, no. 23, in *Teihon*, 1:402. As for the current head of the Konkōji, Tachibana says it was the twentieth. *Yugyōji*, p. 164. However, the *Yugyō Fujisawa ryōshōnin gorekidai keifu* states that Yūsan, thirtieth Yugyō Shōnin, was the twentieth head of the Konkōji. "Hōni Shōnin," in *Shomin shinkō*, p. 248.

Just what the nature of this "insurrection" by the head of the Konkōji was is not known. It has been suggested that if indeed there were political motives or powerful people behind the recalcitrant head priest of the Yugyō Shōnin's temple, the likely suspects were Toyotomi Hideyori and his mother Yodogimi. Tachibana, *Yugyōji*, p. 166. As the focus of resistance to a Tokugawa shogunate, they would understand the political advantage of capturing the joint headquarters of one of the most highly-regarded Buddhist orders in Japan.

5. *Tōtakusan kakochō*, p. 11. An inscription notes that the real reviver of the Shōjōkōji was the seventeenth head or Hō'a of the Ichirenji and that, while he was engaged in rebuilding the temple, Fukō was at the Shin'ōji in Mito and only took up residence after Hō'a died.

6. Tachibana, *Yugyōji*, p. 164.

7. "Chōgai Shōnin," *Gorekidai keifu*, in *Shomin shinkō*, p. 248.

8. Tamamuro, "Edo jidai," p. 220. For privileges equivalent to those of a daimyo, see ibid., citing Kodama Kōta, *Yugyō* [], p. 6.

9. "Nantei no miya Sonkan hōshinnō no kei ni tsuite," *Shibazaki bunko*, in *Teihon*, 2:1799.

10. "Shūmon yori: gotōke gosonkei no koto," *Jishū yōrakufu*, in *Teihon*, 2:1220.

11. *Jishū kekishū*, in *Teihon*, 2:1261-1262. The second is the "Document from the sixth generation Shogun Fukōin Yoshinori in the time of the sixteenth Yugyō [Shōnin]" of 1436. This is an exact copy of the 1416 document.

12. Ibid., 2:1261-1262.

13. Ieyasu is entered as "Nikkōsan Tōshō Daigongen Dajō daijin ju ichi i Ieyasu seiitaishogun" and Cha'a as "Chōkakuinden." *Jishū kakochō*, pp. 227 and 150 respectively. Hidetada and his wife, the daughter of Asai Nagamasa, are entered after Ieyasu.

14. *Ōhama Shōmyōji*, introduction, unnumbered pages.

15. Ōhashi, *Ippen*, pp. 189-190, citing *Tōkoku kikō* (for Sōboku and Go'a),

16. *Hannichi kanwa* (for Go'a and Hirotada), and inscription on writing desk at Shōmyōji (used at *renga* party at which the name Takechiyo was chosen). *Ōhama Shōmyōji*, unnumbered page (5). Needless to say, the authenticity of the equipment has never been investigated.

17. For claim to lineage, see Shingyō Norikazu, "Ieyasu keizu to 14 Matsudaira," [], p. 125.

18. Eiroku 9. 12. 29. Yamashina Tokitsugu, *Rekimei dodai*, in *Gunsho ruijū* 29, ed. by Hanawa Hokinoichi (Zoku Gunsho Ruijū Kanseikai, 1939), p. 143. Nakamura insists that the name was not changed but that it was reassumed on the basis that the Matsudaira were a cadet branch of the Tokugawa. Nakamura, *Tokugawa ke*, p. 8. For a complete discussion of the change of name and the background, see idem, *Tokugawa Ieyasu monjo*, pp. 88-97.

19. The text of the document reads "five" but is emended to "nine." The original manuscript gives "Fujiwara Ieyasu" but is emended to "Minamoto."

Nakamura, *Tokugawa ke*, p. 9. For continued use of the Fujiwara name, see Wright, *Power of Religion*, citing Hagiwara Susumu, *Gunma kenjin* (Shinjinbutsu, 1975), pp. 144-146. A document from Tenshō 14. 9. 7 is signed "San'i chūjō Fujiwara Ieyasu."

20. Nakamura, *Tokugawa Ieyasu monjo*, p. 91. Taiō, or Keishin, was a familiar of the Konoe family. For the Seiganji, see Negita, *Jishū no teradera*, p. 455.

21. Kitajima Masamoto, "Tokugawa shi no shutsuji," [ ], pp. 44-45.

22. Kitajima, "Tokugawa shi," p. 45, citing *Tokitsugukyō ki*, Bunroku 4. 5. 29.

23. For *Sompi bummyaku*, see Nakamura, *Tokugawa ke*, p. 8. Keichō 16. 3. 22, Ieyasu applied for and won for the ancestor of the Nitta, Nitta Yoshishige, the rank of Chinjūfu Shōgun. Ibid., p. 5. The temple was the Taikōin in Ōda City, Gumma Prefecture.

24. The line from Chikauji is verified in the *Daijuji kakochō* and the *Mikawa monogatari*, while the Tokugawa line can be verified through Mitsuyoshi by the *Azuma kagami* and *Chōrakuji Nitta keizu*. Yoshikawa, *Jishū ami*, p. 254.

25. As for the line of Masayoshi, in one genealogy the father is Ietoki. *Chōrakuji Kai Genji keizu*, in *Gumma kenshi: Shiryōhen* 5, ed. Gumma Kenshi Hensan Iinkai (Maebashi, Gumma ken, 1978), p. 893. Most often, and in the standard references, his father is given as Mitsuyoshi. *Tokugawa jikki* 1, *Shintei zōho kokushi taikei* 38, ed. Kuroita Katsumi (Kokushi Taikei Kankōkai, Yoshikawa Kōbunkan, Nichiyo Shobō, 1929), p. 16. The text is actually taken directly from the *Kaisei Mikawa gofudoki* 1, ed. Kuwada Tadachika (Akita Shoten, 1976), pp. 96-99. See also *Mikawa kaitōki* in *Mikawa bunken shūsei chūseihen*, ed. Kyūsojin Hitaku (Toyohashi: Kokusho Kankōkai, 1980), pp. 191-193.

As for Arishige, the line is given as Yoshishige-Yoshisue-Yoriuji (Serata no Yajirō)-Noriuji (Serata Jirō)-Ietoki (Matajirō)-Mitsuyoshi (Yajirō)-Masayoshi (Ukyōnosuke)-Chikasue (Surinosuke)-Arichika (Sakyōnosuke)-Chikauji (Matsudaira Tarōzaemonnojō). *Kanei shoka keizuden* 1, ed. Saiki Kazuma et al. (Zoku Gunsho Ruijū Kanseikai, 1980), pp. 97-100.

26. *Genbon Mikawa monogatari* 2: *Kenkyū shakubunhen*, ed. Nakada Norio (Benzeisha, 1970), pp. 11-12. It was begun in 1622 (Genna 8) and finished sometime before 1639, the year of Hikozaemon's death. Ibid., p. 34.

27. Their Amidabutsu names could be said to indicate their status as *jishū* or some other low-ranking religious specialists. In this, the temple does appear to preserve the original tradition of the founding of the Tokugawa family. However, these *ami* names do conveniently resonate the tradition of *kakuryō*, refugees of all kinds protected by the order.

28. *Mikawa monogatari*, 2:11.

244 NOTES TO CHAPTER 7

29. Negita, *Jishū no teradera*, pp. 449-451. The Shōmyōji's claims were recorded over and over again in the diary (*Daigan seishūki*) of the twenty-eighth head priest who in the 1820s and 1830s spent several years in Edo appealing to the shogunate for assistance to the temple. *Ōhama Shōmyōji*, introduction, unnumbered page (6).

30. The twenty-seventh Yugyō Shōnin (d. 1548 at forty nine) is reported as being of the Ishikawa family of Echigo. It might be a clue to the construction of the story. "Shinjaku Shōnin," in *Gorekidai keifu*, in *Shomin shinkō*, p. 245.

31. *Taiheiki*, 3:408-411, Chapter Thirty-eight "Hatakeyama kyōdai Shuzenji no jō ni tatekomuru koto tsuketari Yusa nyūdō no koto." Hatakeyama Kunikiyo, ancestor of the Wada, is also said to have endowed the Ōhama Shōmyōji in 1356. Negita, *Jishū no teradera*, p. 449.

32. The *Mikawa gofudoki* is attributed to Hiraiwa Chikayoshi (1542-1611), one of Ieyasu's most trusted generals. However, this attribution was challenged by the text's principal editor, Narushima Motonao. See 1746-1750 manuscript in University of Cambridge library and *Kaisei Mikawa gofudoki*, ed. Narushima Motonao (Konreidō, 1886), 1:99-101 (4). *Kōya shunshū hennen shūroku* reports that the head of the *jishū* on Mt. Kōya met Tokugawa Chikauji at Shōjōkōji in 1439. Mochizuki, *Jishū nempyō*, p. 53. The issue is further confused by the claim that Arichika's hair is said to be buried at the Muryōkōji. Negita, *Jishū no teradera*, p. 18.

33. *Jishū yōrakufu*, in *Teihon*, 2:1220.

34. "Matsudaira no keifu no koto," *Shibazaki bunko*, in *Teihon*, 2:1800-1801. A version is also carried by the "Shokoku ichiryū shami yūrai no koto." Yoshikawa gives a collation of two documents, from the collection of an "ami" house in Saitama and from the collection of the Mummyōji in Gumma Prefecture. Yoshikawa, *Jishū ami*, pp. 246-249. They relate that Chikasue Toku'ami and his son Arichika Chō'ami became disciples of the sixteenth Yugyō Shōnin before Arichika was adopted into the Matsudaira house. Ibid., p. 248. Yoshikawa thinks the documents are both from the Edo period despite the 1585 and 1637 dates in the colophons. Both have the name of the *furegashira* Nichirinji, which position was created in 1633. The words "jisha gobugyō" also appear in the text, which indicates a later provenance.

The Serata and Tokugawa were cadet branches of the Nitta, as were the Iwamatsu. In the variations, the names are used almost interchangeably. "Mitsuuji" seems to be an alternative name for "Mitsuyoshi." Ibid., p. 253. Chikauji died in the year given as 1362/Kōan 2. 4. 20. The astrological year is wrong: it could only be for 1347, 1407, 1467, 1527, 1587, 1647, and 1707; 1467 is Ōnin gannen, which could be mistaken for Kōan 2 nen. His posthumous name is Hōjūinden Jun'a Shunsan Tokuō kyōshi. Amano Sadakage noted the discrepancies and impossibilities of the death dates given in different traditions in *Shiojiri* 1, *Nihon zuihitsu taisei*, 3rd. series, vol. 9, ed. Nihon Zuihitsu Taisei

Henshūbu (Nihon Zuihitsu Kankōkai, 1930), p. 246 (vol. 15). He noted that in Ōkubō's book, Chikauji died Ōei 1 (1394) and Yasuchika in Eikyō 2 (1430). Chikasue died 1440 or Eikyō 12. 1. 15; his posthumous name is Iwamatsuin den Toku'a Dōun koji. Arichika died Kyōtoku 1. 7. 14; his posthumous name is given as Shōjūinden Chō'a Taiun koji.

35. Also Uka no kami. Nakamura, *Bukkyō daijiten*, 1:79. This god is reported as having the face of an old man and the body of a snake and is enshrined, for example, at Atsuta Shrine. *Shiojiri* 2, *Nihon zuihitsu taisei*, 3rd. series, vol. 10, ed. Nihon Zuihitsu Taisei Henshūbu (Nihon Zuihitsu Kankōkai, 1930), pp. 834-835. Atsuta Shrine is connected with the Minamoto, since Yoritomo's mother was daughter of the chief priest. It enshrines the great sword which was found in the tail of the monster *Yamato no orochi*, whence the form of the snake, and became one of the three imperial insignia. Papinot, *Historical*, s. v. "Atsuta" and "Ame-no-murakumo-no-tsurugi." Since this god is associated with the Atsuta Shrine, closely connected with the Minamoto, claiming it as a tutelary deity can be seen as another way of appropriating a Minamoto lineage.

36. "Toku'ami gansho," *Sōshū komonjo*, no. 1897, 4:100.

37. *Hannichi kanwa*, *Nihon zuihitsu taisei*, 1st. series, vol. 4, ed. Nihon Zuihitsu Taisei Henshūbu (Nihon Zuihitsu Kankōkai, 1932), pp. 323-328 (vol. 5); for dating as Ōei 3/1396, p. 327; and *Shimpan Sagami*, 5:140-141, s. v. "Shōjōkōji."

38. *Shimpen Sagami*, 5:141, citing *Goganbun denki* (text? oral?).

39. *Yura keizu*, in *Gunsho ruijū* 5, comp. Hanawa Hokinoichi (Keizai Zasshi Sha, 1904), p. 433, under "Sadauji" (vol. 116).

40. "*Yura keizu*," in *Gunsho kaidai* 14, ed. Zoku Gunsho Ruijū Kanseikai (Zoku Gunsho Ruijū Kanseikai, 1961), p. 60.

41. *Yura keizu*, p. 434 and *Shintei Kansei chōshū shokafu* 2, ed. Hotta Masaatsu, rev. Zoku Gunsho Ruijū Kanseikai (Zoku Gunsho Ruijū Kanseikai, 1964), p. 113 (vol. 77). The rescuing monk is identified as "Rokunoryō." Ibid., p. 112.

42. *Yura shojō*, in *Kaitei shiseki shūran* 16: *Bekkirui*, ed. Kondō Heijō (Kondō Shuppanbu, 1902), p. 478 (*bekki* 254).

43. *Shintei Kansei*, 2:112.

44. *Namiaiki*, in *Kaitei zoku shiseki shūran* 3, ed. Kondō Heijō (Kondō Shuppanbu, 1900), pp. 1-16 (*tsūki* 13).

45. *Tsushima chōshi*, ed. Tsushima chō (1938; reprint Meicho Shuppan, 1972), p. 722.

46. *Namiaiki*, pp. 11-12.

47. The colophon gives the date Chōkyō 2. 9. 18. *Namiaiki*, p. 16. Amano Sadakage, author of *Shiojiri*, copied the text in the collection of the Takasu Matsudaira family in this year. *Shiseki kaidai jiten* 1: *Kōdai chūsei hen*, ed. Takeuchi Rizō and Takizawa Takeo (Tōkyōdō Shuppan, 1986), p. 205. See also

Yoshida Tōgo, *Dai Nihon chimei jisho*, rev. ed. (Fusanbō, 1911), 3:2345, s. v. "Namiai."

48. *Namiaiki*, p. 10.

49. Okada Kei, *Owari meisho zue* 2, *Dai Nihon meisho zue* o. s., vol. 9, ed. Nihon Meishō Zue Kankōkai (Nihon Meisho Zue Kankōkai, 1919), p. 301.

50. *Shinano no miya den*, in *Katei zoku shiseki shūran* 3, ed. Kondō Heijō (Kondō Shuppanbu, 1900), pp. 1-10 (*tsūki* 14). For names, ibid., pp. 3, 5.

51. *Shintei Kansei chōshū shokafu* 10, ed. Hotta Masaatsu, rev. Zoku Gunsho Ruijū Kanseikai (Zoku Gunsho Kanseikai, 1965), p. 408, s. v. "Hotta," (vol. 643) for ancestor and p. 410 (vol. 644) for Masayoshi.

52. In *Teihon*, 2:1808.

53. Wright, *The Power of Religion*, citing Document 8, "Copy of Mantokuji Domain's Vermillion-Seal Document," 1591. 11, in *Tokugawa Mantokuji*, p. 197. See also "Tokugawa Mantokuji kiritsu no koto," *Shibazaki bunko*, in *Teihon*, 2:1801.

54. *Tokugawa kinreikō* 5, ed. Kikuchi Shunsuke (Yoshikawa Kobunkō, 1932), pp. 118-119, citing the *Kochōshi*.

55. Wright, *The Power of Religion*, p. 111, citing Document 25, "Registration [of holdings] from Iwabi Prefecture Officials [prompted by] the Investigation of [Mantokuji's] Vermillion-Seal Lands," 1868; Document 5, "Mantokuji's Entire History," undated, in Ojimamachi Shisenshū Iinkai, eds., *Tokugawa Mantokujishi: Ojimamachi shi shiryōshū* 3 (Ojimamachi, Gunma: Ojimamachi Shisenshū Iinkai, 1984), p. 220, 178-81 respectively. The Yura were vassals of and claimed descent from the Yokose and through them from the Nitta.

56. In *Teihon*, 2:1801.

57. *Daigan seishūki*, 3, in *Ōhama Shōmyōji*, p. 89, Tempō 7. 10. 13. The text notes that the document submitted and transcribed was copied from a document submitted in Shōhō 4.

58. *Shiojiri*, 1:463 (vol. 27).

59. In *Teihon*, 2:1801. What the early documents do not report is that the Mantokuji was a "divorce temple," a *kakekomidera*. According to an 1808 document submitted to the government, the second shogun Hidetada's daughter Senhime ordered a lady in waiting (Gyōbu Tsubone who took the name Shunchō Shōnin) to become head of the temple and to revive it. Because Senhime had herself supposedly entered the temple as Tenjūin after the fall of Osaka Castle and had then left to marry into the Honda family, this was taken as confirmation of a precedent and the temple became an official "divorce" temple: a woman who stayed for three years as a nun was considered divorced and could remarry. The temple was rebuilt by Iemitsu in 1636 for Tenjūin's afterlife. *Tokugawa kinreikō*, 5:118-119, citing the *Kochōshi*. Just why none of this is mentioned in the *Shibazaki bunko* is not clear: either the order did not consider it of any importance or it was indeed not a divorce temple until long after the *Shibazaki bunko* entry, and the tradition had not yet been "developed." The *Shiojiri*, a

contemporary source, discusses the Mantokuji foundation legends, but makes no mention of it as a divorce temple. *Shiojiri*, 1:463 (vol. 27). Both Senhime's father Hidetada and mother, the daughter of Asai Nagamasa, are entered in the *Jishū kakochō*: "Daitokuin den ippin taisōkoku kō Songi narabi ni onajiku Hidetada mae ni onajiku Sūgen'in den ippin Daifujin shōyo daizentei hōni songi." *Jishū kakochō*, p. 227.

60. Genna 2. 1. 6. Mochizuki, *Jishū nempyō*, p. 89, citing the *Tokugawa jikki*.

61. *Jishū kekkishū*, "Matsudaira ke yori Yugyō sonkei yūrai no koto," in *Teihon*, 2:1262. For rejection of claims and independence of Mantokuji, see Wright, *The Power of Religion*, pp. 128-129. For move to Jōdo, see ibid., pp. 130-131 and Negita, *Jishū no teradera*, p. 138.

62. Negita, *Jishū no teradera*, p. 139-140.

63. *Kiryū shishi* 1, ed. Kiryū Shishi Hensan Iinkai (Kiryū: Kiryūshi, 1958), p. 365.

64. *Kaisei Mikawa gofudoki*, 1:102.

65. Negita, *Jishū no teradera*, p. 141.

66. Mochizuki, *Jishū nempyō*, p. 49, citing the *Fujisawa dōjōki* and *Nitta gunshi*.

67. Negita, *Jishū no teradera*, p. 141.

68. *Shimpen Sagami*, 5:140.

69. Ishida, "Muromachi jidai," part 2, pp. 103-104.

70. For shogunal *kiganjo*, see "Ashikaga Yoshimasa shūhan migyōsho," *Shōnenji monjo*, no. 2, in *Fukui kenshi*, 4:692-693 (dated Chōroku 2. 12. 26); for imperial *kiganjo*, see "Gotsuchimikado tennō rinji," ibid., no. 6, p. 702 (dated Kanshō 6. 11. 6); for Shōnin title, see "Gonara tennō rinji," no. 8, ibid. (dated Temmon 5. 12. 20) and also "Onaji densō," *Shibazaki bunko*, in *Teihon*, 2:1801

71. *Taiheiki*, 3:321 (Chapter Twenty, "Yoshisada jisatsu no koto").

72. Mochizuki, *Jishū nempyō*, p. 57, citing the *Echizen meishoshi* and *Dai Nihon shiryō*.

73. In *Teihon*, 2:1801.

74. Mochizuki, *Jishū nempyō*, p. 112. For text, see Yoshida, *Dai Nihon chimei jisho*, 3:1897, s. v. "Shōnenji."

75. Umedani and Takaō, *Nitta Yoshisada-kō*, p. 14. Photographs of the three *bakufu* documents listing contributions are on the fourth (unnumbered) page of photographs.

76. "Matsudaira ke yori Yugyō [Shōnin] sonkei yurai no koto," *Jishū kekkishū*, in *Teihon*, 2:1262-1263.

77. For relations between the forty-second Yugyō Shōnin and the Owari Dainagon Mitsutomo, see Ōta, *Hannichi kanwa*, 5, pp. 333-334 and "Sonnin Shōnin," *Gorekidai keifu*, in *Shomin shinkō*, p. 252.

78. Tachinaba, *Yugyōji*, p. 76. See also Imai, *Chūsei shakai*, pp. 120-121.

79. He refers to the portrait of Godaigo and three accompanying documents (still in the possession of Shōjōkōji) presented, according to tradition, to the twelfth Yugyō Shōnin. One of these, the "Details of the Inheritance of the Portrait" (*Miei shōshō shidai no koto*), a copy by Fukō of another copy and containing a genealogy, was the proof. "Yugyō sanjūnidai Fukō Shōnin shojō," *Shichijō monjo*, no. 24, in *Teihon*, 1:403 (letter to the twentieth head of the Konkōji). This gives a list of three heads of Daigoji, Kōshin, Shinshō, and Kōson who have owned the portrait and notes that it was presented to the twelfth Yugyō Shōnin. It bears the seal of Kōson. Following we find the genealogy, which shows that Shinshō, Kōson, and Sonkan were brothers, the sons of Tokiwai Tsuneakira, second son of Emperor Kameyama. Imai, *Chūsei shakai*, pp. 124-125. Kōson is entered in the *Jishū kakochō* as the brother of the twelfth Yugyō Shōnin, though by a later hand: "12 dai Shōnin no goshatei Daigoji zashu 2 hin Hōshinnō Kōson." P. 57.

80. According to Tachibana, Kōson was actually Sonshin, a son of Godaigo, neither Shinshō nor Kōson are listed among the heads of Daigoji, and one cannot be certain that Kōson's seal was on the original document. Tachibana, *Yugyōji*, pp. 80-81, cited in Imai, *Chūsei shakai*, p. 125.

81. *Jishū kechimyaku*, in Ōhashi, *Tenkai*, p. 307.

82. In *Teihon*, 2:1261. Same in "Shami yūrai no koto" (1585/1627). Yoshikawa, *Jishū ami*, p. 247.

83. In *Teihon*, 2:1799-1800. The official title, as indicated in the text, is "tōgū" or "Haru no miya."

84. In *Teihon*, 2:1809. *Hannichi kanwa*, 5 records the tradition that Godaigo had revered Takuga (their dates do overlap) and that Gomurakami had made the son of Tokiwai Tsuneakira his crown prince and later given him to the eighth Yugyō Shōnin as his disciple to pacify the realm. P. 328.

85. In *Teihon*, 2:1264.

86. *Nanchō jōunroku* (Tsukui Naoshige, 1785), *Nanchō jōunzu* (Amano Tōkage, 1708), etc. They identify Sonkan as Shinshō Hōshinnō and adopted son of Gomurakami. The *Kōshinkei* says he was Shinshō's brother. Imai, *Chūsei shakai*, p. 116.

87. *Hannichi kanwa*, 5, p. 328; *Gorekidai keifu*, in *Shomin shinkō*, p. 241. A source obviously based on the *Gorekidai keifu*, makes him the third son rather than the fourth. *Shimpen Sagami* 5, p. 134

88. In *Teihon*, 2:1261.

89. Ibid., 2:1799.

90. According to the *Shimpen Sagami no kuni fudoki kō*, it was Jiku who in 1396 was received by Gokomatsu, complained about the lack of places to stay and of porters and horses on *yugyō*; the order was passed down from the emperor to the shogun and to the deputy, who issued the document. *Shimpen Sagami*, 5:134.

91. "Jūnidai Sonkan Shōnin yūrai no koto," *Jishū kekkishū*, in *Teihon*, 2:1261 and "Nantei no miya Sonkan Hōshinnō no keifu," *Shibazaki bunko*, ibid., p. 1799.

92. "Shami yūrai no koto," in Yoshikawa, *Jishū ami*, pp. 246-249. The entry is on p. 247. The date of the document is Kan'ei 4. 3. 19. Ibid., p. 249.

93. A Chinese-style court fan (illustrated) is noted as having been presented to the thirty-sixth Yugyō Shōnin by Kajūji Gondainagon Kiyohiro on the order of the emperor in 1644; a document accompanies it. *Shimpen Sagami*, 5:138; see also "Gokōmyōin yori sanjūrokudai Shōnin uchiwa hairyō no koto," *Jishū kekkishū*, in *Teihon*, 2:1254; for white umbrella, see "Nantei no miya," *Shibazaki bunko*, in *Teihon*, 2:1799.

94. "The Yugyō [Shōnin] was carrying a "Fushi" fan [*uchiwa*]; even though there were no details of precedent, since Ippen had not received an imperial summons to court, he was now carrying one when he went to court." *Yugyō sanjūissō*, in *Teihon*, 2:1500.

95. "Nantei no miya," *Shibazaki bunko*, in *Teihon*, 2:1799.

96. "Shūmon yori," *Jishū yōrakufu*, in *Teihon*, 2:1220.

97. What is interesting, of course, is that the basis for this claim is the status in Pure Land Buddhism of *nanmon* as *yugyō*, derived from one of four practices named after the cardinal directions. *Yugyō tokumyō no koto*, in *Teihon*, 2:811.

98. The *Hannichi kanwa*, pp. 328-329 rehearses this argument of precedent.

99. "Sonnin Shōnin," *Gorekidai keifu*, in *Shomin shinkō*, p. 251.

100. Apparently, these conferral of these honors was based on objects connected to Sonkan Hōshinnō at Shōjōkōji. Ōhashi, *Ippen*, p. 233, citing *Yugyō yuishō*.

101. In *Teihon*, 2:1264-1265. It also records that when Ietsuna died in 1680, Sonnin participated in the services at Tōeisan and from that time Yugyō Shōnin have had the seat of Sōjō.

102. Kōno Ō'a, *Jishū kōyō*, in *Teihon*, 2:1310. It is documented by an entry in the *Tōtakusan kakochō*, p. 22. Sonnin appears to have been very conscious of the importance of *monzeki* status to the order. He entered, in his own hand, "Namuamidabutsu, the sixty-seventh [the number refers to his position in the Pure Land line] Yugyō [Shōnin] the Abbot of the Southern Court and Grand Abbot (Nanbō monjū Daisōjō) Sonnin recorded this." *Tōtakusan kakochō*, p. 22 and Imai, *Chūsei shakai*, p. 129). Another inscription calls him the "Southern Court Prince Imperial Abbot." *Tōtakusan kakochō*, p. 91. On his portrait is inscribed, "Great guide in the spreading of the Buddhist Law throughout the land of Japan, the forty-second Yugyō Shōnin, Abbot of the Southern Court and Grand Abbot, Sonnin (Nihon kokuchū buppō kōdō no daidōshi Yugyō yonjūnidai Nanbō monjū Sōjō Sonnin." "Sonnin Shōnin," *Gorekidai keifu*, in *Shōmin shinkō*, p. 252.

103. In *Teihon*, 2:1808.

104. Ōhashi, *Ippen*, p. 233.

105. *Shiojiri*, 1:154-155.

106. Ōhashi, *Ippen*, p. 231, chart.

107. *Shinshū yōhōki*, 13, in *Teihon*, 2:992.

108. Ōhashi, *Ippen*, p. 215, citing *Sōshū komonjo*. Mochizuki, *Jishū nempyō*, p. 91 (1627), citing *Tōtakusan kinjisha kiroku*. The basis must be the oft-mentioned "Shokoku ichiryū shami yūrai no koto," which explains that those people called *shami* bearing religious names Amidabutsu or *hijiri* or *kaneuchi* had originally been defeated warriors who had followed Ippen. They kept wives and did not keep precepts although they cut their hair and had Amidabutsu names. After Ippen's death, they dispersed or went to Fujisawa. They rang gongs, sang hymns, and chanted the *nembutsu*. Although they travelled from place to place they kept some sort of connection with the Yugyō Shōnin. Yoshikawa, *Jishū ami*, pp. 246-247.

109. *Shiojiri*, 2:154-155.

110. Ibid. Also cited in Ōhashi, *Ippen*, p. 232.

111. Ōhashi, *Ippen*, pp. 232-233. See also Tamamuro, "Edo Shōnin," pp. 225-227, citing *Soshū kaikyū*, and Hasegawa Masatoshi, "*Taishūchō* kara mita Jishū no gakuryō to shūgaku seikatsu," in *Shomin shinkō*, pp. 44-81.

112. Tamamuro, "Edo Shōnin," p. 225, citing *Sōshū kaikyū*. For promotion fees, see Hasegawa Masatoshi, "Jishū no gakuryō to shūgaku seikatsu," in *Yugyō nikkan* 3 (Kadokawa Shoten, 1979), p. 645, chart. A fee corresponding to each promotion was charged.

113. Ōhashi, *Ippen*, pp. 236-238. For "ryō honzan," see Hasegawa, "Gakuryō," in *Yugyō nikkan*, 3:627-628; for Nichirinji, ibid., p. 630.

114. Ōhashi, *Ippen*, p. 238 and Hasegawa, "Gakuryō," in *Yugyō nikkan*, 3:643-647, citing *Tōtakusan nikkan* and *Gakuryō jōmoku*. The chart notes the sums paid to the officials of the school when, it seems, the Yugyō Shōnin or Fujisawa Shōnin was not in residence. Also, fee waivers are also noted. Ibid., p. 644.

115. "Sonnin Shōnin," *Gorekidai keifu*, pp. 252-253. See also Tamamuro, "Edo Shōnin," p. 226, citing *Soshū kaikyū*.

116. "Yugyō no kiyaria (career) o motanai hito ga dokujū Shōnin to natta no wa kore ga saisho de aru." Mochizuki, *Jishū nempyō*, p. 202.

Notes to Chapter 8

1. On routinization due to the economy, see *SE*, 1:254 and 2:1121; on bureaucratization and office, ibid., 1:250-251 and 2:1139-1141; on education, ibid., 2:1143-1145; and on rationalization in monasticism, ibid., 2:1116-1117, 1169-1170; see also on bureaucracy, ibid., 2:956-1003.

2. That same year (4. 12), the official name for *yugyō* (*shokumei*) was changed. The meaning of this is not given, nor any indication of what the new title was. Mochizuki continues to use the word "yugyō." Mochizuki, *Jishū nempyō*, p. 119, citing *Yugyō nikkan*. Apparently, "goindai" and "indai" meant representative for absent Fujisawa Shōnin (p. 120, 1773. 3,2 and p. 121, 1776. 5. 13). If there both the Fujisawa Shōnin and Yugyō Shōnin died, the "Indai" as the head of Ichirenji was the successor. If he died and the Fujisawa and Yugyō Shōnin died, the next head of Ichirenji was automatically successor.

3. Mochizuki, *Jishū nempyō*, pp. 108, 110, 111, 112, 117, 118, 119, 121, 127, 128, 131, 132, 136, and 137, citing *Tōtakusan kakochō*, *Yugyō nikkan*, *Yugyō Fujisawa gorekidai keifu*, *Tōtakusan kinjisha kiroku*, and *Tōtakusan nikkan*.

4. There was no Fujisawa Shōnin 1708-1711, 1757-1761, 1773-1776, 1812-1815, 1824-1835, 1848-1855, 1862-1870; no Yugyō Shōnin 1700-1702, 1707-1708 (six months), 1721-1726, 1735-1742, 1754-1757, 1761-1769, 1776-1791, 1800-1812, 1815-1824, 1835-1848, 1858, and 1862.

5. Ōhashi, *Ippen*, p. 233.

6. *Tōkyōtō meisho zue*, p. 66, citing the *Tenshō nikki* (Tenshō 18. 10. 6).

7. The *Shibazaki bunko* twice makes a reference to texts borrowed from Mito: "Mito sōkō Kamakuraki ni iwaku . . ." and "Mata sōkō no Kamakurashi . . ." In *Teihon*, 1:1797, 1802. For the case of the Shōmyōji, see *Daigan seishūki*, 3, in *Ōhama Shōmyōji*, p. 95, 1824 (Tempō 7. 11. 15), mentioning a chronicle from Nichirenji submitted to the government in 1743 (Kampō 3. 3) and subsequently copied and submitted by the Shōmyōji.

8. Fukuda Akira, "Oguri Terute dan no hassei," *Kokugakuin zasshi* 66, no. 11 (November 1965), pp. 54-55, citing Ōhashi Shunnō, *Bamba jishū no ayumi*.

9. Kōno Noriyoshi, "*Shibazaki bunko* kaisetsu," in *Teihon*, 2:1803.

10. For *mushūgan*, see Mochizuki, *Jishū nempyō*, p. 202. For reports of absconding, see ibid., pp. 125, 203, citing *Tōtakusan nikkan*.

11. For Takayama Senganji, see Tamamuro Fumio, "Yugyō gojūdai Kaison Shōnin no kaikoku ni tsuite," in *Shomin shinkō*, p. 89, citing *Yugyō nikkan*, Kyōhō 11. 5. 24. For letter received in Kawagoe, see ibid., p. 90, citing *Yugyō nikkan*, Kyōhō 11. 6. 20. For the temple with only fourteen parishioners, see ibid., p. 90, citing *Yugyō nikkan*, Kyōhō 13. 8. 13. Another temple also proved to be impossible and a note was made of it: "When we entered Inamitsu, [we found it] inconvenient in a thousand ways; it caused difficulties [to everyone] from the [Shōnin] to the ordinary monks [and nuns]. For future visits [this place] will be of no use. On account of this I am recording this." Ibid., p. 91, citing *Yugyō nikkan*, 1731/Kyōhō 7. 10.

12. For a more recent survey of pejorative characterizations of Buddhism by premodern and modern Japanese scholars, see Wright, "The Power of Religion," pp. 31-32.

13. The order was even responsible for issuing loans for the government after a terrible typhoon which had also damaged the main temple (1856). The typhoon was 1856/Ansei 3. 8. 25; the distribution of government loans is dated 1856. 10. 16. Mochizuki, *Jishū nempyō*, p. 137, citing *Tōtakusan nikkan* and, I think, *Tōtakusan kinjisha kiroku*.

14. Wright, "The Power of Religion," p. 42.

15. Mochizuki, *Jishū nempyō*, p. 195.

16. Tamamuro, "Edo jidai," p. 172.

17. Mochizuki, *Jishū nempyō*, p. 195.

18. Bunka 10. The agent's name was Hasegawa Masaaki. Mochizuki, *Jishū nempyō*, pp. 204-205. From 1645 to 1868, Miharu was the domain of Akita family with 50,000 *koku*. Papinot, *Historical*, s. v. "Miharu."

19. See Susan B. Hanley and Kozo Yamamura, *Economic and Demographic Change ini Preindustrial Japan 1600-1868* (Princeton: Princeton University Press, 1977), pp. 126-160.

20. The agent, the Shūryōken, was in Toriyama. Mochizuki, *Jishū nempyō*, p. 204.

21. Tamamuro, "Kaison," pp. 84-85.

22. Tamamuro, "Edo Shōnin," p. 217, citing *Agei Kakuken nikki*, Tenshō 12. 8. 22 (for lord of Miyazaki), Tenshō 12. 8. 15 (for daily supplies), and (perhaps) Tenshō 11. 5. 21 (for receipt of gifts). Tamamuro also characterizes the gifts as of appropriate value. Ibid.

23. For following precedent in terms of train size, see Ōhashi, *Ippen*, p. 219. For omitting to increase size, see ibid., p. 218.

24. Tamamuro, "Edo Shōnin," pp. 216-218.

25. Ōhashi, *Ippen*, pp. 217-218, citing *Kanmon zakki* for 1675, *Nishimura monjo* for 1731, and (perhaps) *Yugyō nikkan* for 1716.

26. Tamamuro, "Edo Shōnin," p. 230. According to Tamamuro's chart, 50 horses (*tenma goshuin*), 50 horse handlers, 20 horses, 20 horse handlers, 43 monks and nuns, 32 porters carrying 4-pole boxes, 3 porters for treasures, 2 porters for hanging scrolls, 4 porters for 1-pole boxes, 3 porters for mountain palanquin, 4 porters for low table and equipment, 8 porters for Kumano Gongen shrine, 1 porter for ceremonial umbrella, 2 porters for carrying pole box, 1 porter for *dairyū*, 3 porters for *kenryū*, 8 porters for palanquin, 1 porter for *yōkasamibako*, 6 porters as alternates, 2 porters for tea and lunch, 2 porters for carrying pole box, 4 porters for raincoats, etc., 2 porters for stilts. Ibid., pp. 230-231 and Tamamuro, "Edo jidai," p. 174.

27. The instructions to Naitō han give the number of religious as sixty-three. Tamamuro, "Edo Shōnin," p. 231.

28. *Nenju-ya, jiku-ya, kamigoromo-ya* and *monotachi-shū, shokusho, katōsho, fuse-ya, tatami-ya, nushi-ya, ishi-daiku*, and *kagami-ya*. Ōhashi, *Ippen*, pp. 220-222.

29. In 1743 (Kanpō 3. 10. 13), upon being informed that their domain was on the Yugyō Shōnin's itinerary, the Naitō of Iwakidaira sent a letter to their Jishū temple Jōsaiji asking for information on the previous visit of 1712. Tamamuro, "Edo jidai," p. 172.

30. Mochizuki, *Jishū nempyō*, p. 195.

31. It is likely that some previous notification was given. It is not clear who was notified first. According to Tamamuro, notification was sent first to the temple and from there to the *han* official. Tamamuro, "Edo jidai," p. 172.

32. He was in Shirakawa in the tenth month of 1743. Tamamuro, "Edo Shōnin," p. 231. According to the *Tōtakusan nikkan*, the Shūryōken died before *yugyō* on 1744/Enkyō 1. 6. 19. Mochizuki, *Jishū nempyō*, p. 114. This is confusing, since Kaison was at the first temple on the Tōhoku itinerary in the first month of the new year. Ibid., p. 228, itinerary chart.

33. Kansei 6. Mochizuki, *Jishū nempyō*, p. 203, citing Kamiichi Rondō, *Ishimi Manpukuji-shi*.

34. Enpō 4. Ōhashi, *Ippen*, pp. 229-230.

35. Tamamuro, "Edo Shōnin," pp. 229-232 and idem, "Edo jidai," pp. 172-173.

36. Ōhashi, *Ippen*, pp. 228-229, citing Kobayashi house *Shiju nikki*.

37. Kyōhō 16. 10. Tamamuro, "Kaison," p. 87.

38. 70,000 *koku*. Papinot, *Historical*, s. v. "Naitō Masanaga." The Shirakawa domain donated ten bales of hulled rice, one barrel white miso, one barrel miso, one barrel Nara pickles, vegetables, and fifteen *ryō* gold. Tamamuro, "Edo Shōnin," pp. 231-232, citing *han* documents. For a comparison with the donations of other domains,

Kanazawa	Maeda	1,020,000 *koku*	60. 0 *koku*
Sendai	Date	620,000 *koku*	30. 0 *koku*
Yamaguchi	Mōri	400,000 *koku*	24. 0 *koku*
Akita	Satake	340,000 *koku*	20. 0 *koku*
Fukui	Matsudaira	320,000 *koku*	17. 6 *koku*
Hiroshima	Asano	420,000 *koku*	15. 0 *koku*

Idem, "Kaison," p. 84. Kanazawa had 1,027,000 *koku* according to Papinot, *Historical*, s. v. "Maeda Toshitsune." On the basis of this, the Naitō domain calculated their own donation, which included twenty bales of hulled rice. Compared with the donation of the Shirakawa domain, it was a heavy burden. Idem, "Edo Shōnin," p. 232. Tamamuro lists 20 bales of hulled rice, 60 bundles of charcoal, 100 carrots, 60 large burdocks, 30 bundles of sweet potatoes, and 30 bundles of *wakame* (seaweed).

39. Laymen in the train were not bound by religious dietary restrictions and demanded saké and side dishes. Ōhashi, *Ippen*, p. 219. He is using Tamamuro's work but cites the Nakamura house *Shishuku nikki* for the demand for saké and side dishes.

40. The letter came from Shōjōkōji, but the official was more than likely a member of the Yugyō Shōnin's entourage. This Shūryōken apparently died (Enkyō 1. 6. 19) just before the tour was undertaken. Mochizuki, *Jishū nempyō*, p. 114, citing the *Tōtakusan nikkan*.

41. Kanpō 3. 10. 13. Tamamuro, "Edo Shōnin," pp. 228-229, citing the *Yugyō gojūissei gokaikoku soshoku-kō* (a Naitō *han* document in the collection of Meiji University Library [idem, "Edo jidai," p. 171]). Tamamuro thinks that the mention of gifts is not a warning but a solicitation. Since the Naitō were informed on the day that the Shūryōken sent Kaison's itinerary to the Tōhoku temples, questions come to mind: Were the domains informed before the temples? Or had notification been sent earlier to the temples?

42. 11 bales of hulled rice, 18 *kanmon* money, 1 box of noodles, 2 sacks of confectionery, and 1 *kyoku* of sugar. Tamamuro, "Edo Shōnin," p. 232. All calculations have been based on the very crude equivalence of 1 *ryō* gold=4000 *mon* copper or 60 *momme* silver, but 1 *momme* silver=100 *mon* (even though actually 95 in the eighteenth century) and 25 *mon* per *hiki* (Tamamuro uses this calculation, although it means that 1 *ryō* is worth 10,000 *mon*). Correspondence between rice and money is based on an equivalence of 20 *mon* per *shō* rice. If 5 *gō* (1.6 pints) of rice constituted the daily ration of rice for one man, then one year's rations were 1.8 *koku* or 3650 *mon*. The rough calculation of 1 *koku* rice per gold *ryō* is too rough for me. Hanley and Yamamura, *Economic and Demographic*, pp. 155 (citing Morai Jinsuke, "Kanyō kōbenki," in Iwate-ken, *Iwate kenshi*, vol. 5 [Morioka: Iwate Prefecture, 1962], pp. 787-789), 193, 193 (citing E. S. Crawcour and Kozo Yamamura, "The Tokugawa Monetary System, 1787-1868," *Cultural Change*, vol. 18, no. 4, part 1 [July 1970]), 348 (23n), and 367 (32n).

43. Kyōhō 12. 7. 5 (50,000), Kyōhō 12. 8. 26 (2-300), Kyōhō 12. 9. 6 (2,000), Kyōhō 12. 10. 2 (8,000), Kyōhō 12. 10. 7 (1,500), Kyōhō 16. 9. 19 (2,000). Tamamuro, "Kaison," pp. 96-97.

44. Tamamuro, "Edo Shōnin," p. 234, citing *Yugyō nikkan*, Kyōhō 12. 1. 19.

45. Tamamuro, "Edo jidai," p. 176.

46. Ōhashi, *Ippen*, p. 224, citing *Sennen ōjōshū*. The story sounds precariously close to that of Jō'a and the birth of Gokōgon.

47. Six Character Name (749), Ten *nembutsu* (296), Daikoku (wealth, 158), Benten (152), *yayo* (arrow, 130), *raiyo* (lightning, 110), *onfuda* (104), *yokomono* (59), *yobyō* (illness, 58), *jushi* (charm, 56), *omamori* (29), Tenjin (calligraphy, 21), *aizen* (love, 19), *kechimyaku* (enrollment, 14), *hōso* (smallpox, 10), *rinjū shōnin myōgo* (Name in Shōnin's hand at death, 9), *anzan* (easy birth, 7), *honzon* (main image, 3) for a total of 1984. Tamamuro, "Edo jidai," p. 175, citing *Yugyō nikkan*.

48. For charms, 1709/Kyōhō 6. 2. 24 and 1727. 8. 27, to lords, officials, commoners. Ōhashi, *Ippen*, pp. 226-227, citing *Yugyō nikkan*.

49. For *kakochō iri*, see Tamamuro, "Kaison," p. 96, citing *Yugyō nikkan*, Kyōhō 11. 7. 5; for *kechimyaku*, see idem, "Edo jidai," p. 175.

50. Kyōhō 11. 5. 6 (2), 5. 7 (1), 5. 8 (6), 5. 9 (3), 5. 10 (2), 5. 30 (11), 6. 1 (7), 6. 2 (11), 6. 3 (9), 6. 4 (15), 6. 8 (7). Tamamuro, "Kaison," p. 97. Tamamuro calculates at 25 *mon* per *hiki*.

51. Tamamuro, "Kaison," pp. 97-98, citing *Yugyō nikkan*, 1726/Kyōhō 11. 9. 28 (for Tarōbei). Tamamuro thinks it clear one had to be a rich or powerful patron. Ibid., p. 98.

52. For prices of posthumous names, see Tamamuro, "Kaison," p. 98 (citation not clear but most likely *Yugyō nikkan*). For Jūdayū, see ibid., p. 99 (at the Hamagawa Raigoji). For further drop in price, see ibid., p. 99, citing *Yugyō nikkan*, 1726/Kyōhō 11. 12. 7.

53. Tamamuro, "Edo jidai," p. 176, for example when at Hitachi in 1708, citing the *Yugyō nikkan*, Hōei 5. 6. 1.

54. Tamamuro, "Edo Shōnin," p. 234, citing *Yugyō nikkan*, Kyōhō 12. 1. 16, 2. 6, 3. 9, 1. 19.

55. Wright, "The Power of Religion," p. 103, citing Gunma-ken Shihensan Iinkai, eds., *Gunmakenshi, tsushihen 6: Kinsei 3* (Maebashi, Gunma-ken: Gunma-ken, 1992), p. 689.

56. The *Yugyō nikkan* 1728/Kyōhō 13. 8. 11 notes that twelve objects were shown at the Echigo Kamo Saihōji to the Magistrate for Temples and Shrines Matsui Kuemon and the District Magistrate Katō Tomoemon. Cited in Tamamuro, "Kaison," p. 92. For the illustrated scroll, see ibid., citing *Yugyō nikkan*, 1726/Kyōhō 11. 5. 27 ("goengi") and p. 93 citing *Yugyō nikkan*, 1731/Kyōhō 16. 4. 2. For the ritual implement ("goshakushi"), see ibid., citing *Yugyō nikkan*, 1728/Kyōhō 13. 8. 11. Several are listed among the gifts at Shōjōkōji presented by Tokugawa Mitsutomo, head of the Owari branch. *Hannichi kanwa*, p. 333. For Benten, see ibid., citing *Yugyō nikkan*, 1726/Kyōhō 11. 12. 1. Also known as Benzaiten. An Indian goddess, she is often "represented mounted on a dragon or serpent." Papinot, *Historical*, s. v. "Benten." She was originally a water deity. Nakamura, *Bukkyō daijiten*, 2:1217, s. v. "Benzaiten." For Taimadera mandala and Sanemori's helmet, see ibid., p. 93, citing *Yugyō nikkan*, 1731/Kyōhō 16. 4. 2.

57. For Shin'ōji: "[Shinōji] e gohōbutsu myōnichi yori okashi asobasare sōrō, hondō konryū ni tsuki Raijin honji Shōkannon kaichō ni tsuki josei to shite gotōryūchū gojūhō o kashi sōrō." Tamamuro, "Kaison," p. 94, citing *Yugyō nikkan*, 1727/Kyōhō 12. 5. 11. For Jōkyūji, see ibid., citing *Yugyō nikkan*, 1729/Kyōhō 14. 2. 15; for Shikajima Shrine, see ibid, citing *Yugyō nikkan*, 1727/Kyōhō 12. 3. 23. For the Jishinji Kannon, see ibid., p. 95, citing *Yugyō nikkan*, 1729/Kyōhō 14. 4. 16. For purpose of display, see ibid., citing *Yugyō nikkan*, 1727/Kyōhō 12. 6. 10, 1731/Kyōhō 16. 5. 26, and 1731/Kyōhō 16. 10. 14. Lords included Aoyama Yukihide, lord of Miyazu (40,000 *koku*) in Tango Province. Ibid., p. 93. For officials, see ibid., p. 92, citing *Yugyō nikkan*,

1728/Kyōhō 13. 8. 11. For commoners, see ibid., p. 92, citing *Yugyō nikkan*, 1726/Kyōhō 11. 12. 1, showing the Benten to Kumakura Seisaemon in Shinsatomura in Shimotsuke Province while on the way from the Onodera Jōrinji to the Shinya Hōōji. For the question of admission or other charges, see ibid., pp. 92-93.

58. Tamamuro, "Kaison," pp. 88-89, citing *Yugyō nikkan*, Kyōhō 13. 10. 39.

59. Tamamuro, "Edo jidai," p. 228.

60. Ibid., p. 233, citing *Yugyō nikkan*, Kyōhō 1. 12, 1. 15, and 1. 18.

61. Tamamuro, "Kaison," p. 84. This ceremony acts out the fundamentals of Pure Land Buddhism. A light representing the historical Buddha Shaka is put out; the darkness in which the temple is plunged represents the darkness of the world without a Buddha. Then another light is lit to represent Amida. Similarly, at Zenkōji, for example, one enters a subterranean passage to experience the world of darkness without Shaka and emerges after a time into full daylight in order to experience the light of Amida.

62. Mochizuki points out the questioning of *yugyō* under Confucian and Shintō influence and notes the anti-Buddhist wing. Mochizuki, *Jishū nempyō*, p. 203. Even the need for a night watch has been interpreted as a precaution taken because of fear of criticism or opposition. Ōhashi, *Ippen*, p. 229. Policing was part of the duties of the vassals when Fukō was in Satsuma, however, and there is no suggestion of opposition to his tour. Considering the number of goods and money carried by train, it would be reasonable to take precautions to prevent theft.

63. Mochizuki, *Jishū nempyō*, p. 203.

64. Genroku 8. Mochizuki, *Jishū nempyō*, p. 210, 16n, citing Tsuji Zennosuke, *Nihon Bukkkyōshi*. Sadowara was the seat of a branch of the Shimazu with a stipend of 27,000 *koku*. Papinot, *Dictionary*, s. v. "Sadowara."

65. Mochizuki, *Jishū nempyō*, p. 210, citing Tsuji Zennosuke, *Nihon Bukkyōshi*.

66. Wright, "The Power of Religion," p. 103, citing *Seidan*, in *Ogyū Sorai*, *Nihon shisō taikei* 36 (Iwanami Shoten, 1973), p. 435.

67. Tempō 6. Mochizuki, *Jishū nempyō*, pp. 205, 132, citing *Tōtakusan kiroku*.

68. Mochizuki, *Jishū nempyō*, p. 204.

69. Ōhashi, *Ippen*, p. 242. The temple is located on the mountain where Ninigi no mikoto first set foot upon his descent from heaven. Papinot, *Historical*, s. v. "Higashi-Kirishima-yama." Mochizuki also points to Shimazu anti-Buddhism. Mochizuki, *Jishū nempyō*, p. 204. For further discussion on the history of the persecution of Buddhism, see Ketelaar, *Heretics* and Martin Collcutt, "Buddhism: The Threat of Eradication," in *Japan in Transition: From Tokugawa to Meiji*, ed. Marius B. Jansen and Gilbert Rozman (Princeton: Princeton University Press, 1986).

70. Ōhashi, *Ippen*, p. 243. Mochizuki points to Shinshū apologists' emphasis on *kakure nembutsu* in Shimazu territory and concomitant ignoring of Jishū activities in the area for the past several hundred years. Mochizuki, *Jishū nempyō*, p. 204. Ketelaar asserts all Pure Land sects had been banned in Satsuma during the Tokugawa period. *Heretics*, p. 244, 35n. However, only the True Pure Land sect had been banned.

71. Ōhashi, *Ippen*, pp. 243-244, citing for Sado, *Goisshin hōchū kiroku*.

72. Ōhashi, *Ippen*, p. 244.

73. For defense of Buddhism, see Ōhashi, *Ippen*, pp. 244-245. For combination of leadership, Meiji 18. 10. 16, see Mochizuki, *Jishū nempyō*, p. 142.

74. For Rengeji, see Kanai, *Ippen*, p. 413; for Ichirenji, see ibid., p. 220; for Konkōji and Chōrakuji, see ibid., p. 224.

75. In 1868/Meiji 1. 10. 10 and 12. 9. Mochizuki, *Jishū nempyō*, p. 139, citing *Shōjōkōji kiroku*.

Notes to Appendix

1. *Shichijō monjo*, no. 9, in *Teihon*, 1:396.

2. *Shichidai Shōnin hōgo*, in *Teihon*, 1:383.

3. Those who try to destroy Buddhism.

4. Also, Tachibana, *Yugyōji*, pp. 120-121 and *Jishūshi ronkō*, p. 265 citing the Ashikaga shogunate *Gonaishoan* (*Zoku Gunsho Ruijū* 664), document dated 1513/Eishō 10. 6. 2. "Igyō Shōnin," *Gorekidai keifu*, in *Shomin shinkō*, p. 244, for 1518 as the year for taking up residence at Jōdaiji.

5. Tachibana, *Yugyōji*, pp. 122-123 and *Jishūshi ronkō*, p. 266. For Echizen no kami Yoshimune, see especially *Yugyō nijūsō*, in *Teihon*, 2:1482, 1483.

6. Tachibana, *Yugyōji*, p. 123 and *Jishūshi ronkō*, p. 266-267. Both based on *Yugyō nijūsō*, in *Teihon*, 2:1480. Fugai later proceeded to the Saikyōji in Ōita in Bungo Province, territory of the Ōtomo, long-time supporters of the Jishū, where he died in 1526. Tachibana, *Yugyōji*, pp. 130-131. See also "Fugai Shōnin," *Gorekidai keifu*, in *Shomin shinkō*, p. 244.

7. For the genealogy, see Tachibana, *Jishūshi ronkō*, pp. 298-299. See "Butten Shōnin," *Gorekidai keifu*, in *Shomin shinkō*, p. 245 and *Tōtakusan kakochō*, p. 5. Further, see Tachibana, *Jishūshi ronkō*, pp. 306-307. He cites the entry in the *Tōtakusan kakochō* by Butten. He also points to the fact that the twenty-sixth and twenty-ninth (another Nihonmatsu, a nephew perhaps) Yugyō Shōnin succeeded to office at Saihōji and not at Shinzenkōji. The *Gorekidai keifu*, p. 245, then is wrong. For Nihonmatsu entries, see also *Tōtakusan kakochō*, p. 51.

8. Tachibana, *Jishūshi ronkō*, pp. 308-309. For Asakura entries, see *Tōtakusan kakochō*, pp. 9, 51, 53.

9. The Kōshōji was built in 1202 by Itō Sukekuni. Negi, *Jishū teradera*, p. 397. For the Jōkōmyōji, see Negi, *Jishū teradera*, p. 393.

10. Ibid., p. 95.

11. "Yanagiwara Sukesada shojō," *Shōjōkōji monjo* no. 33, in *Fujisawa shishi*, 1:669. Also, Ōhashi, *Ippen*, p. 197. However, he emends "nagerare" to "nageutare." Also, Ōhashi, *Ippen*, p. 197. Tachibana, *Jishūshi ronkō*, p. 312 preserves the *kanbun* and accepts the date 1557/Kōji 3 from *Yugyō keifu*, actually *Yugyō Fujisawa gorekidai reibo*, in *Teihon*, 2:1588. However, the astrological sign given, Kinoto/U (Junior brother of the wood/Hare) corresponds to 1555/Kōji 1.

12. Tachibana, *Jishūshi ronkō*, pp. 313-314 discusses the identity of Matsugi in terms of his position in the Arsenal and the relationship of iron forgers and the illness of an emperor. Date of 1557/Kōji 3 is given in *Yugyō Fujisawa gorekidai reibo*, in *Teihon*, 2:1602 and in *Tōtakusan kakochō*, p. 5. However, only the date in the *Tōtakusan kakochō* gives the correct astrological years for 1557. Yanagiwara Sukesada was Gondainagon in 1539 and died 1578. *Fujisawa shishi*, p. 669.

13. *Yugyō sanjūissō Kyō-Ki goshugyō ki*, in *Teihon*, 2:1496. The number for the year of Gonara's reign should be "sanjū" or thirty, according to editor Tachibana Shundō.

14. *Yugyō sanjūissō*, in *Teihon*, 2:1500.

15. Ibid.

16. *Shōnenji okibumi, Shōnenji monjo*, no. 5, *Fukui kenshi*, 4:701-702.

17. The editor notes that this may be in a different hand. The appearance of the Iio is very interesting because of the connection with a temple possibly connected with the *Yugyō yanagi* legend. See Watanabe Ryūzui, "Yugyō yanagi no kenkyū," part 2, *Nō* (December 1949), pp. 16-17. See also Thornton, "Propaganda Traditions," p. 165.

18. Kōsokuji is a temple in Kamakura, originally Shingon, converted 1282 by Ippen. According to tradition, the temple plaque was conferred by Godaigo. Negita, *Jishū no teradera*, p. 29. The Kōshōji is not yet identified, unless the temple in Hyūga Province is meant.

19. Ishida thinks this person is one of the *dobōshū*. Ishida, "Muromachi," part 2, p. 231/103. However, the text itself goes on to say that En'a was from the Kōmyōin.

20. *Shōnenji monjo*, no. 4, in *Fukui kenshi*, 4:700. The date is unclear; the date on the colophon at the end is 1752/Hōreki 2 under the seal of Kaison, fifty-first Shōnin. *Ibid.*, p. 701.

21. "Yugyō nijūkyūdai Taikō shojō," cited in Tachibana, *Jishūshi ronkō*, pp. 267-268. Transcription adapted from Tachibana, *Yugyōji*, pp. 131-132.

Glossary

amigō	阿弥吾	Religious name formed by adding -ami or -amidabutsu to one syllable; also *amidabutsugō* and *agō*.
bodaiji	菩提時	Temple built to ensure the rebirth of a soul as a buddha; family mortuary temple.
butsubō	仏房	Suffix added to a single syllable to form a religious name for a nun.
chishiki	知識	Religious guide to salvation.
Chishiki	知識	Title of the head of the orders deriving from Ippen's confraternity, including Shinkyō's and the Yugyō-ha.
chokuganjo	勅願所	A temple built for the private purposes of members of the imperial family.
chōshō	調声	Leader of the chant in *nembutsu* rituals.
danna	檀那	Patron of the order or individual *jishū*.
dōdō no jishū	同道の時衆	*Jishū* accompanying warrior into the field.
dōgyō	同行	Same Practice or Fellow Practitioner of the *nembutsu*.

259

dokujū	独住	Retirement and permanent residence of the head of the order at Shōjōkōji; temple residence.
dōjō	道場	Temple.
fuda	札	Charm, amulet; slip of paper printed with sacred words or image.
fuda o kubaru	札をくばる	"Distributing the amulet(s)." In the *Ippen hijiri e*.
	算を賦る	In the *Ippen Shōnin ekotoba den*.
fudan nembutsu	不断念仏	Continuous Nembutsu; walking meditation practice of the Tendai school.
funjin	分身	A sub-classification of the Historical Body of the Buddha; a manifestation.
fusan	賦算	Distribution of *nembutsu* charms; distribution of salvation.
Fujisawa Shōnin	藤沢上人	Former Yugyō Shōnin in residence at the head temple in Fujisawa.
funi	不二	Nonduality.
gyakushū	逆修	Entry while still alive in a death register.
ha	派	Group or school.
hijiri	聖	Holy man; ordained or not, a religious practitioner.
hosshin	報身	Enjoyment Body of the Buddha.
ichibō	一房	Suffix appended to single syllable to form a religious name for a nun in Ippen school orders.

indai, goindai	院代, 御院代	Priest in charge of the temple for an absent Fujisawa Shōnin or Yugyō Shōnin.
isshin	一身	Having identical form.
ittai	一体	A single entity. Single Beings and Amida Buddha as a single entity; Nonduality of Sentient Beings and Amida Buddha.
jishū	時衆	*Nembutsu* practitioner; religious of orders founded by Ippen and Ikkō Shunjō.
Jishū	時宗	Name of the sect in the Tokugawa period; probably in use in the late Muromachi period.
jōgyō zanmai	常行三昧	Perpetual Meditation; walking meditation practice of the Tendai school.
kakochō	過去帳	Temple death register; roll of the saved.
kakuryō	客僚	Guest companion; refugees and outcasts of all sorts under the protection of the Yugyō-ha.
kanjin	勧進	Originally, fundraising; for Ippen and his followers, *nembutsu* propation.
katagi	形木	Printing block for *nembutsu fuda*.
kanrei	管領	Or *kanryō*. Deputy of the shogun; office held by the Hatakeyama, Hosokawa, and Shiba. Also the office of the head of the Kamakura military government.
kihō ittai	機法一体	In the Seizan school, the single entity of Sentient Beings and Amida.

kechien	結縁	Making a connection with Buddhism or salvation.
kechienshū	結縁衆	The people together with whom one has made a connection with salvation.
keshin	化身	Historical Body of the Buddha; that form taken to lead Sentient Beings to salvation.
kiganji	祈願寺	See below.
kiganjo, *gokiganjo*	祈願所, 御祈願所	Temple at which prayers are made on behalf of the emperor for the peace of the realm and perpetuation of imperial rule.
kimyō	帰命	Oath of obedience to the Chishiki upon entry into the religious community of Ippen school orders derived from Shinkyō's order.
monzeki	門跡	Literally, "traces of a lineage"; title conferred on certain privileged temples and extended to their heads, usually members of the imperial family of high-ranking aristocracy. In the Jishū, it means most likely "Prince Imperial Abbot" because the first was supposed to have been an imperial prince of the Southern Court.
myōgō	名号	The Name, specifically the Six Character (or syllable) Name "Namuamida-butsu."
nanmon	南門	Southern Gate, which refers first to itinerncy and second to the *monzeki* established by the Southern Court. As a title, borne only by Sonnin.

nembutsu zanmai	念仏三昧	Nembutsu Meditation; practice of the Tendai school.
niga byakudō	二河白道	Parable of the Two Rivers and White Path of Shan-tao.
nikushinbutsu	肉身仏	Buddha having the same body as Sentient Beings; Buddha in human form.
nishū	尼衆	Nuns.
nōki shoki ittai	能帰所帰一体	Another expression used by Ippen to mean the Nonduality of Sentient Beings and Amida Buddha; the one who relies and the one who is relied upon.
odori nembutsu	踊り念仏	Practice of chanting the *nembutsu* while dancing in a circle; a form of walking meditation.
ōjin	応身	Historical Body of the Buddha; form taken to preach to Sentient Beings according to their abilities.
ōjō	往生	Rebirth in Amida's pure Land in the west; the Seizan and Ippen schools recognize two kinds, while alive and at death.
oshō	和尚	Title given qualified priests after more than ten years in orders; a Tokugawa-period custom.
ryō	寮	Dormitory. There were six under the Yugyō Shōnin and Fujisawa Shōnin as well as other, larger temples; the head of the sixth was the highest ranking.
saigo no jūnen	最後/最期 の十念	Last ten *nembutsu* chanted in anticipation of death.

saimatsu betsuji 歳末別時   *Nembutsu* ceremony conducted at the end of the year.

shōban no jishū 相伴の時衆   *Jishū* accompanying a warrior into the field.

shōbutsu ittai 生仏一体   Single entity of Sentient Beings and Buddha.

shōjin 生身   Body given by parents; human form of a Buddha or Bodhisattva.

Shōkū 性空   910-1007; founder of Enkyōji on Mt. Shosha.

Shōkū 証空   1177-1247; disciple of Hōnen and founder of the Seizan school of Pure Land Buddhism.

Shōnin 上人   Saint; title conferred by the emperor.

sutehijiri 捨て聖   Holy man who abandons everything.

Tōtaku 藤沢   *On* reading of "Fujisawa."

yuge gyōbō 遊戯行法   Expression of which *yugyō* is an abbreviation; it refers to the easy movement to and from worlds by Bodhisattva and walking, and, therefore, itinerancy.

yugyō 遊行   Travel especially for the purpose of preaching; itinerant preaching.

Yugyō Shōnin 遊行上人   Leader of the travelling mission of the Yugyō-ha; joint head of the order.

Bibliography

Unless otherwise indicated, the place of publication is Tokyo, Japan.

PRIMARY SOURCES

Amano Sadakage. *Shiojiri*. 2 vols. *Nihon zuihitsu taisei*, 3rd. series, 9, 10. Ed. Nihon Zuihitsu Taisei Henshūbu. Nihon Zuihitsu Kankōkai, 1930.

Chiren. *Shinshū yōhōki*. In *Teihon Jishū shūten* 2. Ed. Teihon Jishū Shūten Hensan Iinkai. Sankibō Busshorin; Fujisawa: Jishū Shūmusho, 1979.

Chitoku. *Chishin shuyōki*. In *Sandai sōshi hōgo*. In *Teihon Jishū shūten* 1. Ed. Teihon Jishū Shūten Hensan Iinkai. Sankibō Busshorin; Fujisawa: Jishū Shūmusho, 1979.

———. *Nembutsu ōjō kōyō*. In In *Sandai sōshi hōgo*. In *Teihon Jishū shūten* 1. Ed. Teihon Jishū Shūten Hensan Iinkai. Sankibō Busshorin; Fujisawa: Jishū Shūmusho, 1979.

———. *Sanshin ryōkengi*. In *Sandai sōshi hōgo*. In *Teihon Jishū shūten* 1. Ed. Teihon Jishū Shūten Hensan Iinkai. Sankibō Busshorin; Fujisawa: Jishū Shūmusho, 1979.

Chōrakuji Kai Genji keizu, in *Gumma kenshi: Shiryōhen* 5, ed. Gumma Kenshi Hensan Iinkai (Maebashi, Gumma ken, 1978)

Dai Nihon chishi taikei. 39 vols. Ed. Ashida Koreto. Yūzankaku Shuppan, 1923-1933.

Dai Nihon chishi taikei. 29 vols. Ed. Ashida Koreto. Rev. ed. Yūzankaku Shuppan, 1957-1960.

Denchū moshitsugiki. In *Gunsho ruijū* 21. Comp. Hanawa Hokinoichi. Zokugunsho Ruijū Kanseikai, 1928.

Denchū ika nenchū gyōshi. In *Gunsho ruijū* 22. Comp. Hanawa Hokinoichi. Zoku Gunsho Ruijū Kanseikai, 1928.

Donkai. *Donkai Shōnin gohōgo*. In *Teihon Jishū shūten* 1. Ed. Jishū Shūten Hensan Iinkai. Sankibō Busshorin; Fujisawa: Jishū Shūmusho, 1979.

Donryō. *Shibazaki bunko.* In *Teihon Jishū shūten* 2. Ed. Teihon Jishū Shūten Hensan Iinkai. Sankibō Busshorin; Fujisawa: Jishū Shūmusho, 1979.

————. *Jishū yōryakufu.* In *Teihon Jishū shūten* 2. Ed. Teihon Jishū Shūten Hensan Iinkai. Sankibō Busshorin; Fujisawa: Jishū Shūmusho, 1979.

Fujisawa shishi 1: Shiryō hen. Ed. Fujisawa Shishi Hensan Iinkai. Fujisawa: Fujisawa Shiyakusho, 1970.

Fujisawa shishi 3: Shiryōhen. Fujisawa: Fujisawa Shiyakusho, 1973.

Fujiwara no Nagako. *Emperor Horikawa Diary (Sanchi no Suke nikki).* Translated with an introduction by Jennifer Brewster. Honolulu: University Press of Hawaii, 1977.

Fukui kenshi shiryôhen 4: Chū kinsei 2. Ed. Fukuiken. Fukui: Fukuiken, 1984.

Genbon Mikawa monogatari. 2 vols. Ed. Nakada Norio. Benzeisha, 1970.

Ihon Odawara ki. In *Muromachi-dono monogatari, Ashikaga jiran ki, Ihon Odawara ki, Kokushi sōsho* 3. Ed. Kurokawa Mamichi. Kokushi Kenkyūkai, 1914.

Inryōken nichiroku. Edited by Takeuchi Rizō. 5 vols. *Zōho zoku shiryō taisei* 21-25. Kyoto: Rinsen Shoten, 1954.

Ippen hijiri e. Nihon emakimono zenshū 10. Kadokawa Shoten, 1960.

Ippen Shōnin goroku. In *Teihon Jishū shūten* 1. Ed. Teihon Jishū Shūten Hensan Iinkai. Sankibō Busshorin; Fujisawa: Jishū Shūmusho, 1979.

Jishū kakochō. Ed. Ōhashi Shunnō. *Jishū shiryō* 1. Fujisawa: Jishū Kyōgaku Kenkyūjo, 1964.

Jishū kechimyaku sōzoku no shidai. In Ōhashi Shunnō. *Jishū no seiritsu to tenkai.* Yoshikawa Kōbunkan, 1973.

Jishū kekkishū. In *Teihon Jishū shūten* 2. Ed. Teihon Jishū Shūten Hensan Iinkai. Sankibō Busshorin; Fujisawa: Jishū Shūmusho, 1979.

Jishū yōgi monben. In *Teihon Jishū shūten* 2. Ed. Teihon Jishū Shūten Hensan Iinkai. Sankibō Busshorin; Fujisawa: Jishū Shūmusho, 1979.

Jishū zensho. 2 vols. Ed. Ōhashi Shunnō. Kamakura: Geirinsha, 1974.

Jō'a Shōnin den. In *Teihon Jishū shūten* 2. Ed. Teihon Jishū Shūten Hensan Iinkai. Sankibō Busshorin; Fujisawa: Jishū Shūmusho, 1979.

Jō'a Shōnin ekotoba den. In *Teihon Jishū shūten* 2. Ed. Teihon Jishū Shūten Hensan Iinkai. Sankibō Busshorin; Fujisawa: Jishū Shūmusho, 1979.

Kaisei Mikawa gofudoki. 2 vols. Ed. Kuwada Tadachika. Akita Shoten, 1976.

Kaitei shiseki shūran. 33 vols. Ed. Kondō Heijō. Kondō Shuppanbu, 1903.

Kaison. *Jimyō chō chūshaku.* In *Teihon Jishū shūten* 1. Ed. Teihon Jishū Shūten Hensan Iinkai. Sankibō Busshorin; Fujisawa: Jishū Shūmusho, 1979.

Kan'ei shoka keizuden 1. Ed. Saiki Kazuma et al. Zoku Gunsho Ruijū Kanseikai, 1980.

Kanmon gyoki 1. *Zoku gunsho ruijū* supplementary vol. 3. Comp. Hanawa Hokinoichi. Zoku Gunsho Ruijū Kanseikai, 1930.

Kizuregawa hangan. In *Zoku gunsho ruijū* 5:1. Keizai Zasshi Sha, 1905.

"Kōchōji shiryō (3): Jishū jūni ha honmatsu sōjiin renmyōbo tadashi Hōreki nenchū shahon." *Jishū kenkyū* (February 1965): 1-15.

Koga kubō nidai Ashikaga Masauji monjoshū. Ed. Satō Hironobu. *Kenkyū shiryō gaihen* 1. Chigazaki: Gohōjōshi Kenkyūkai, 1973.

Kokushi sōsho. 35 vols. Ed. Kurokawa Mamichi. Kokushi Kenkyūkai, 1914-1917.

Kōnō Ō'a. *Jishū kōyō.* In *Teihon Jishū shūten* 2. Ed. Teihon Jishū Shūten Hensan Iinkai. Sankibō Busshorin; Fujisawa: Jishū Shūmusho, 1979.

Kyōtō Shijō dōjō Konrenji monjo—chūsei hen. Ed. Abe Yukihiro. In *Shomin shinkō no genryū: Jishū to yugyō hijiri*, ed. Tachibana Shundō and Tamamuro Fumio. Meicho Shuppan, 1982.

Mansai jugō nikki 1. *Zoku gunsho ruijū* supplementary vol. 1. Comp. Hanawa Hokinoichi. Zoku Gunsho Ruijūkai, 1928.

Mansai jugō nikki 2. *Zoku gunsho ruijū* supplementary vol. 2. Comp. Hanawa Hokinoichi. Zoku Gunsho Ruijū Kanseikai, 1928.

Meitokuki. Ed. Tomikura Tokujirō. Iwanami Bunko 2899-2900. Iwanami Shoten, 1942.

Mikawa bunken shūsei. 3 vols. Ed. Kyūsojin Hitaku. Toyohashi: Kokusho Kankōkai, 1980.

Namiaiki. In *Kaitei zoku shiseki shūran* 3. Ed. Kondō Heijō. Kondō Shuppanbu, 1900.

Nenchū jōreiki. In *Gunsho ruijū* 21. Comp. Hanawa Hokinoichi. Zoku Gunsho Ruijū Kanseikai, 1928.

Nochikagami 2. *Shintei zōho kokushi taikei* 35. Ed. Kuroita Katsumi. Kokushi Taikei Kankōkai, Yoshikawa Kōbunkan, Nichiyo Shobō, 1932.

Nochikagami 3. *Shintei shōho kokushi taikei* 36. Ed. Kuroita Katsumi. Kokushi Taikei Kankōkai, Yoshikawa Kōbunkan, Nichiyo Shobō, 1933.

Ōhama Shōmyōji rekishi: Shiryō 1. Ed. Nakamura Takeshi and Yamoto Kinji. Hekinan: Tōshōsan Shōmyōji, 1982.

Okada Kei. *Owari meisho zue* 2. *Dai Nihon meisho zue*, o.s., vol. 9. Ed. Nihon Meishō Zue Kankōkai. Nihon Meisho Zue Kankōkai, 1919.

Ōta Nanpō. *Hannichi kanwa. Nihon zuihitsu taisei*, o.s., vol. 4. Nihon Zuihitsu Kankōkai, 1932.

Oyu-dono no ue no nikki 7. *Gunsho ruijū* supplementary vol. 7. Comp. Hanawa Hokinoichi. Zokugunsho Ruijū Kanseikai, 1934)

Rohō. *Mazanshū.* Ed. Zemyō Shōnin. In *Teihon Jishū shūten* 2. Ed. Teihon Jishū Shūten Hensan Iinkai. Sankibō Busshorin; Fujisawa: Jishū Shūmusho, 1979.

Saigyō monogatari emaki. Nihon emakimono zenshū 11. Kadokawa Shoten, 1958.

Sandai sōshi hōgo. In *Teihon Jishū shūten* 1. Ed. Teihon Jishū Shūten Hensan Iinkai. Sankibō Busshorin; Fujisawa: Jishū shūmusho, 1979.

Shichijō monjo. In *Teihon Jishū shūten* 1. Ed. Teihon Jishū Shūten Hensan Iinkai. Sankibō Busshorin; Fujisawa: Jishū Shūmusho, 1979.

Shimpen Kamakura shi. *Dai Nihon chishi taikei* 19. Ed. Ashida Koreto. Boku shobō, 1915.

Shimpen kokka taikan. 2 vols. Ed. Shimpen Kokka Taikan Henshū Iinkai. Kadokawa Shoten, 1983.

Shimpen Musashi no kuni fudoki kō 11. *Dai nihon chishi taikei* 1. Ed. Ashida Koreto. Rev. ed. Yūzankaku Shuppan, 1960.

Shimpen Sagami no kuni fudoki kō 4. *Dai Nihon chishi taikei* 39. Ed. Ashida Koreto. Yūzankaku Shuppan, 1933.

Shimpen Sagami no kuni fudoki kō 5. *Dai Nihon chishi taikei* 22. Ed. Ashida Koretō. Rev. ed. Yūzankaku Shuppan, 1962.

Shinano no miya den. In *Katei zoku shiseki shūran* 3. Ed. Kondō Heijō. Kondō Shuppanbu, 1900.

Shinkyō. *Dōjō seimon*. In *Sandai sōshi hōgo*. In *Teihon Jishū shūten* 1. Ed. Teihon Jishū Shūten Hensan Iinkai. Sankibō Busshorin; Fujisawa: Jishū shūmusho, 1979.

———. *Hōnō engi ki*. In *Sandai sōshi hōgo*. In *Teihon Jishū shūten* 1. Ed. Teihon Jishū Shūten Hensan Iinkai. Sankibō Busshorin; Fujisawa: Jishū Shūmusho, 1979.

———. *Ta'a Shōnin hōgo*. In In *Teihon Jishū shūten* 1. Ed. Teihon Jishū Shūten Hensan Iinkai. Sankibō Busshorin; Fujisawa: Jishū Shūmusho, 1979.

Shinsen Tōkyōtō meisho zue: Asakusa-ku no bu. Ed. Miya Shigeo. Bokushobō, 1968. Originally printed as special issues of *Fūzoku gahō*, 1896-1911.

Shintei Kansei chōshū shokafu. 26 vols. Ed. Hotta Masaatsu. Rev. Zoku Gunsho Rujijū Kanseikai. Zoku Gunsho Ruijū Kanseikai, 1964-1967.

Shiryō: Ichirenji kakochō. Ed. Takano Osamu. *Fujisawashi kenkyū* 16, special volume (February 1983).

Shōkei ranrishi. In *Zoku shiseki shūran* 1. Ed. Kondō Heijō. Kondō Shuppanbu, 1930.

Sōshū komonjo 4. Ed. Nuki Tatsuto. Kadokawa Shoten, 1969.

Taiheiki. 3 vols. Ed. Gotō Tanji and Kamada Kisaburō. *Nihon koten bungaku taikei* 34-36. Iwanami Shoten, 1960.

Takuga. *Jōjō hōsoku gyōgi*. In *Sandai sōshi hōgo*. In *Teihon Jishū shūten* 1. Ed. Teihon Jishū Shūten Hensan Iinkai. Sankibō Busshorin; Fujisawa: Jishū Shūmusho, 1979.

———. *Kibokuron*. In *Teihon Jishū shūten* 1. Ed. Teihon Jishū Shūten Hensan Iinkai. Sankibō Busshorin; Fujisawa: Jishū Shūmusho, 1979.

———. *Shichidai Shōnin hōgo*. In *Teihon Jishū shūten* 1. Ed. Teihon Jishū Shūten Hensan Iinkai. Sankibō Busshorin; Fujisawa: Jishū Shūmusho, 1979.

———. *Ta'amidabutsu dōgyō yōshin taikō chū*. In *Sandai sōshi hōgo*. In *Teihon Jishū shūten* 1. Ed. Teihon Jishū Shūten Hensan Iinkai. Sankibō Busshorin; Fujisawa: Jishū Shūmusho, 1979.

———. *Tōzai sayō shō*. In *Teihon Jishū shūten* 2. Ed. Teihon Jishū Shūten Hensan Iinkai. Sankibō Busshorin; Fujisawa: Jishū Shūmusho, 1979.

Teihon Jishū shūten. 2 vols. Edited by Teihon Jishū Shūten Hensan Iinkai. Sankibō Busshorin; Fujisawa: Jishū Shūmusho, 1979.

Tokugawa jikki 1. *Shintei zōho kokushi taikei* 38. Ed. Kuroita Katsumi. Kokushi Taikei Kankōkai, Yoshikawa Kōbunkan, Nichiyo Shobō, 1929.

Tokugawa kinreikō. 6 vols. Ed. Kikuchi Shunsuke. Yoshikawa Kōbunko, 1931-1932.

Tokugawa shoka keifu 1. Ed. Saiki Kazuma and Isawa Yoshihiko. Zoku Gunsho Ruijū Kanseikai, 1970.

Ton'a. *Kōya nikki.* In *Teihon Jishū shūten* 2. Ed. Teihon Jishū Shūten Hensan Iinkai. Sankibō Busshorin; Fujisawa: Jishū Shūmusho, 1979.

Tōtakusan chiji kiroku. In *Teihon Jishū shūten* 2. Ed. Teihon Jishū Shūten Hensan Iinkai. Sankibō Busshorin; Fujisawa: Jishū Shūmusho, 1979.

Tōtakusan kakochō: monmatsu kechienshū. Ed. Tachibana Shundō. Fujisawa: Jishū Shūmusho Kyōgakubu, 1981.

Yugyō daidai hōgo. In *Teihon Jishū shūten* 1. Ed. Teihon Jishū Shūten Hensan Iinkai. Sankibō Busshorin; Fujisawa: Jishū Shūmusho, 1979.

Yugyō engi. In *Teihon Jishū shūten* 2. Ed. Teihon Jishū Shūten Hensan Iinkai. Sankibō Busshorin; Fujisawa: Jishū Shūmusho, 1979.

Yugyō Fujisawa ryōshōnin gorekidai keifu. Ed. Takano Osamu. In *Shomin shinkō no genryū: Jishū to yugyō hijiri,* ed. Tachibana Shundō and Tamamuro Fumio. Meichō Shuppan, 1982.

Yugyō Fujisawa ryōshōnin gorekidai reibo. In *Teihon Jishū shūten* 2. Ed. Teihon Jishū Shūten Hensan Iinkai. Sankibō Busshorin; Fujisawa: Jishū Shūmusho, 1979.

Yugyō hachidai Tosen Shōnin kaikoku ki. In *Teihon Jishū shūten* 2. Ed. Teihon Jishū Shūten Hensan Iinkai. Sankibō Busshorin; Fujisawa: Jishū Shūmusho, 1979.

Yugyō hōgoshū. In *Teihon Jishū shūten* 1. Ed. Teihon Jishū Shūten Hensan Iinkai. Sankibō Busshorin; Fujisawa: Jishū Shūmusho, 1979.

Yugyō keizu. In *Teihon Jishū shūten* 2. Ed. Teihon Jishū Shūten Hensan Iinkai. Sankibō Busshorin; Fujisawa: Jishū Shūmusho, 1979.

Yugyō nijūyonsō goshugyō ki. In *Teihon Jishū shūten* 2. Ed. Teihon Jishū Shūten Hensan Iinkai. Sankibō Busshorin; Fujisawa: Jishū Shūmusho, 1979.

Yugyō nikkan. 3 vols. Ed. Tamamuro Fumio. Kadokawa Shoten, 1977-1979.

Yugyō sanjūissō Kyō-Ki goshugyō ki. In *Teihon Jishū shūten* 2. Ed. Teihon Jishū Shūten Hensan Iinkai. Sankibō Busshorin; Fujisawa: Jishū Shūmusho, 1979.

Yugyō Shōnin engi e. *Nihon emakimono zenshū* 23. Kadokawa Shoten, 1968.

Yugyō tokumei no koto. In *Teihon Jishū shūten* 2. Ed. Teihon Jishū Shūten Hensan Iinkai. Sankibō Busshorin; Fujisawa: Jishū Shūmusho, 1979.

Yūki senjō monogatari. In *Gunsho ruijū* 20. Comp. Hanawa Hokinoichi Zoku Gunsho Ruijū Kanseikai, 1940.

"*Yura keizu.*" In *Gunsho kaidai* 1. Ed. Zoku Gunsho Ruijū Kanseikai. Zoku Gunsho Ruijū Kanseikai, 1961.

Yura keizu. In *Gunsho ruijū* 5. Comp. Hanawa Hokinoichi. Keizai Zasshi Sha, 1904.

Yura shojō. In *Kaitei shiseki shūran* 16. Ed. Kondō Heijō. Kondō Shuppanbu, 1902.

SECONDARY SOURCES

Brower, Robert H., and Earl Miner. *Japanese Court Poetry.* Stanford: Stanford University Press, 1961.

Bryman, Alan. *Charisma and Leadership in Organizations.* London, Newbury Park, CA, and New Delhi: SAGE Publications, 1992.

Bukkyōgo daijiten. 2 vols. Ed. Nakamura Hajime. Tōkyō Shobō, 1975.

Butler, Kenneth Dean. "The Textual Evolution of the *Heike monogatari.*" *Harvard Journal of Asiatic Studies* 26 (1966): 5-31.

Chakravarti, Uma. *The Social Dimensions of Early Buddhism.* Bombay, Calcutta, Madras, India: Oxford University Press, 1987.

Cruise O'Brien, Donal B. and Christian Coulon, ed. *Charisma and Brotherhood in African Islam.* Oxford: Clarendon Press, 1988.

Chihō bunka no dentō to sōzō. Ed. Chihōshi Kenkyū Kyōgikai. Yūzankaku Shuppan, 1976.

Collcutt, Martin. "Buddhism: The Threat of Eradication." In *Japan in Transition: From Tokugawa to Meiji,* ed. Marius B. Jansen and Gilbert Rozman. Princeton: Princeton University Press, 1986.

The Encylcopedia of Religion. Ed. Mircea Eliade. New York: Macmillan Publishing Company; London: Collier Macmillan Publishers, 1987.

Foard, James H. *Ippen and Popular Buddhism in Kamakura Japan.* Stanford University Ph.D. dissertation, 1977. Ann Arbor, Michigan: Xerox University Microfilms, 1978.

————. "Prefiguration and Narrative in Medieval Hagiography: The *Ippen Hirjie.*" In *Flowing Traces: Buddhism in the Literary and Visual Arts of Japan,* ed. James H. Sanford, William R. LaFleur, and Masatoshi Nagatomi. Princeton: Princeton Uniersity Press, 1992.

Fujisawa shishi. 7 vols. Ed. Fujisawa Shishi Hensan Iinkai. Fujisawa: Fujisawashi Yakusho, 1970-1980.

Donald K. Fry, Jr., "Old English Formulas and System," *English Studies* 48 (1967): 193-204. Cited in John Miles Foley, *Traditional Oral Epic: The "Odyssey," "Beowulf," and the Serbo-Croation Return Song.* Berkeley, Los Angeles, and Oxford, U.K.: University of California Press, 1990.

Fukuda Akira. "Oguri Terute dan no hassei." *Kokugakuin zasshi* 66, no. 11 (November 1965): 29-62.

Gorai Shigeru. *Kōya hijiri.* Kadokawa Shoten, 1965.

Goodwin, Janet. *Alms and Vagabonds: Buddhist Temples and Popular Patronage in Medieval Japan.* Honolulu: University of Hawaii Press, 1994.

Gunsho kaidai. 30 vols. Ed. Zoku Gunsho Ruijū Kanseikai. Zoku Gunsho Ruijū Kanseikai, 1960-1967.

Hanley, Susan B., and Kozo Yamamura. *Economic and Demographic Change in Preindustrial Japan 1600-1868.* Princeton: Princeton University Press, 1977.

Hartwieg-Hiratsuka, Keiko. *Saigyō-Rezeption: Das von Saigyō verkörperte Eremiten-Ideal in der japanischen Literaturgeschichte.European University Studies, Asian and African Studies,* vol. 27, no. 10. Bern, Frankfurt, Nancy, New York: Peter Lang, 1984.

Hasegawa Masatoshi. "Jishū no gakuryō to shūgaku seikatsu."In *Yugyō nikkan* 3, ed. Tamamuro Fumio. Kadokawa Shoten, 1979.

————. *"Taishūchō* kara mita Jishū no gakuryō to shūgaku seikatsu." In *Shomin shinkō no genryū: Jishū to yugyō hijiri,* ed. Tachibana Shundō and Tamamuro Fumio. Meicho Shuppan, 1982.

Hirata Teizen. *Jishū kyōgaku no kenkyū.* Rev. ed. Sankibō Busshorin, 1977.

Hirota, Dennis, trans. *No Abode: The Record of Ippen.* Kyoto: Ryukoku University, 1986.

Huey, Robert N. *Kyōgoku Tamekane: Poetry and Politics in Late Kamakura Japan.* Stanford: Stanford University Press, 1989.

Hurst, G. Cameron III. *Insei: Abdicated Sovereigns in the Politics of Late Heian Japan 1086-1185.* New York and London: Columbia University Press, 1976.

Imai Masahru. "Tokifusa-ryū no Hōjō-shi to jishū."In *Kamakura jidai bunka denpa no kenkyū.* Yoshikawa Kōbunkan, 1993.

————. *Chūsei shakai to Jishū no kenkyū.* Yoshikawa Kōbunkan, 1985.

————. *Jishū seiritsushi no kenkyū.* Yoshikawa Kōbunkan, 1981.

———— and Tachibana Shundō, ed. *Ippen Shōnin to Jishū.* Nihon Bukkyō shūshi ronkō 10. Yoshikawa Kōbunkan, 1984.

Ishida Yoshitō. "Muromachi jidai no jishū ni tsuite." Parts 1 and 2. *Bukkyō shigaku* 10, no. 4 (March 1963): 195-208; 11, no. 3-4 (July 1964): 83-113.

Kadokawa chimei daijiten 14: *Kanagawa ken.* Ed. Kadokawa Chimei Daijiten Hensan Iinka. Kadokawa Shoten, 1984.

Kadokawa Genyoshi. "Katarimono to kanrisha." *Kokugo kokubun* 13, no. 12 (December 1943): 1-19.

————. *"Meitokuki* no seiritsu." *Denshō bungaku kenkyū* 2 (March 1962): 1-13.

Kaijima Tomoko. "Kōryū jiki Jishū kyōdan no shiji sō ni tsuite: toku ni bushi kaikyū o chūshin to shite." Parts 1 and 2. *Jishū kenkyū* 80 (April 1980): 13-22; 82 (November 1980): 6-16.

Kanai Kiyomitsu. *Jishū bungei kenkyū.* Kazama Shobō, 1967.

————. *Ippen to jishū kyōdan.* Kadokawa Shoten, 1975.

————. *Jishū to chūsei bungaku.* Tōkyō Bijutsu, 1975.

————. *Jishū kyōdan no chihō tenkai.* Tōkyō Bijutsu, 1983.

————. *Jishū bungei to Ippen hōgo.* Tōkyō Bijutsu, 1987.

Kanze Nobumitsu. *Yugyō yanagi*. In *Yōkyokushū* 2, ed. Yokomichi Mario and Omote Akira. *Nihon koten bungaku taikei* 41. Iwanami Shoten, 1963.

Kaufman, Laura S. *Ippen Hijirie: Artistic and Literary Sources in a Buddhist Handscroll Painting of Thirteenth-Century Japan*. New York University Ph.D. dissertation. Ann Arbor: University Microfilms International, 1980.

————. "Nature, Courtly Imagery, and Sacred Meaning in the *Ippen Hijiri-e*." In *Flowing Traces: Buddhism in the Literary and Visual Arts of Japan*, ed. James H. Sanford, William R. LaFleur, and Masatoshi Nagatomi. Princeton: Princeton University Press, 1992.

Ketelaar, James E. *Of Heretics and Martyrs in Meiji Japan: Buddhism and its Persecution*. Princeton, NJ: Princeton University Press, 1990.

Kiryū shishi 1. Ed. Kiryū Shishi Hensan Iinkai. Kiryū: Kiryūshi, 1958.

Kitajima, Masamoto. "Tokugawa shi no shutsuji." [ ].

Koji ruien 27: *Shukkyō-bu* 2. 1911. Photographic reproduction, Yoshikawa Kōbunkan, 1981.

Koji ruien 28: *Shukkyō-bu* 3. 1912. Photographic reproduction, Yoshikawa Kōbunkan, 1981.

Komonjo yōgo jiten. Ed. Arai Eiji et al. Hakushobō, 1983.

Kōno Noriyoshi. "*Shibazaki bunko* kaisetsu." In *Teihon Jishū shūten* 2. Ed. Teihon Jishū Shūten Hensan Iinkai. Sankibō Busshorin; Fujisawa: Jishū Shūmusho, 1979.

————. "Ton'a chōsakushū kaidai." In *Teihon Jishū shūten* 1. Ed. Teihon Jishū Shūten Hensan Iinkai. Sankibō Busshorin; Fujisawa: Jishū Shūmusho, 1979.

————. *Ippen kyōgaku to jishūshi no kenkyū*. Tōyō Bunka Shuppan, 1981.

Koresawa Kyōzō. "Yugyō Shōnin: *Yugyō yanagi* ni yosete. "*Kanze* (September 1967): 11-15.

Kyōtō shi no chimei. Nihon rekishi chimei taikei 27. Heibonsha, 1979.

LaFleur, William. "The Death and 'Lives' of the Poet-Monk Saigyō," in *The Biographical Process: Studies in the History and Psychology of Religions*, ed. E. Reynolds and Donald Capps. The Hague: Mouton, 1976.

————. *Mirror for the Moon: A Selection of Poems by Saigyō (1118- 1190)*. New York: New Directions Publishing Corporation, 1978.

Miya Tsugio. "Sōshunhon Yugyō Shōnin engie shohon ryakkai." In *Yugyō Shōnin engi e. Nihon emakimono zenshū* 23. Kadokawa Shoten, 1968.

Mochizuki Kazan. *Jishū nempyō*. Kadokawa Shoten, 1970.

Nagai Yoshinori. "Jishū to bungaku geinō." *Kokubungaku kaishaku to kanshō* 25. no. 13 (November 1960): 61-69.

Nakamura Kōya. *Tokugawa Ieyasu monjo no kenkyū*. 4 vols. Nihon Gakujutsu Shinkōkai, 1958-1961.

————. *Tokugawa ke.* Nihon rekishi shinsho 2d. series, vol. 36. Shibundō, 1961.

Nakamura Nobuyuki. "Jishū no suibiki ni oite." *Bukkyōshi kenkyū* 1 (September 1969): 24-28

Negita Shūzen. *Jishū no teradera*. Mishima: privately published by Negita Shūzen, 1980.

Nuki Tatsuto. *Kamakura haiji jiten*. Yokohama: Yūrindō, 1980.

Ōhashi Shunnō. *"Jishū kakochō* ni tsuite." In *Jishū kakochō*. Ed. Ōhashi Shunnō.

Jishū shiryō 1. Fujisawa: Jishū Kyōgaku Kenkyūjo, 1964.

————. *Jishū no seiritsu to tenkai*. Yoshikawa Kōbunkan, 1973.

————. *Odori nembutsu*. Daizō sensho 12. Daizō Shuppan, 1974.

————. *Ippen to Jishū kyōdan*. Kyōikusha Rekishi Shinsho (Nihonshi) 172. 1978.

Pande, Govind Chandra. *Studies in the Origins of Buddhism*. 2d. rev. ed. Delhi, Varanasi, Patna, India: Motilal Banarsidass, 1974.

Papinot, E. *Historical and Geographical Dictionary of Japan*. 1910. Reprint, with an introduction by Terence Barrow, Rutland, Vermont and Tokyo: Charles E. Tuttle Company, Inc., 1972.

Reischauer, Jean, and Robert Karl Reischauer. *Early Japanese History (c. 40 B.C.-A.D. 1167)*. 2 vols. Princeton: Princeton University Press, 1937.

Sakai Kōhei. *Zenkōjishi*. 2 vols. Tōkyō Bijutsu, 1969.

Sasaki Kyōdō. "Ōkurashō nai Masakado zuka to Nichirinji." In *Kanda. Musashino sōsho* 1. Musashino Kai, 1935.

Shimoda Tsutomu. "Jishū to Ōgoshi." *Jishū kenkyū* 76 (May 1978): 20-27.

Shingyō Norikazu. "Ieyasu keizu to 14 Matsudaira."[ ].

Shinmeikai kogo jiten. Ed. Kindaichi Haruhiko. Sanseidō, 1972.

Shirahata Yoshi. *"Saigyō monogatari emaki* to *Taima mandara engi* ni tsuite." In *Saigyō monogatari emaki, Taima mandara engi*. *Nihon emaki zenshū* 11. Kadokawa Shoten, 1958.

Shiseki kaidai jiten. 2 vols. Ed. Takeuchi Rizō and Takizawa Takeo. Tōkyōdō Shuppan, 1985-1986.

Tachibana Shundō. *Jishūshi ronkō*. Kyoto: Hōzōkan, 1975.

————. *Yugyōji: chūsei no Jishū sōhonzan*. Fujisawa bunko 1. Meicho Shuppan, 1978.

————. *"Jō'a Shōnin den* kaisetsu." In *Teihon Jishū shūten* 2. Ed. Teihon Jishū Shūten Hensan Iinkai. Sankibō Busshorin; Fujisawa: Jishū Shūmusho, 1979.

———— and Tamamuro Fumio, ed. *Shomin shinkō no genryū: Jishū to yugyō hijiri*. Meicho Shuppan, 1982.

Takano Osamu. "Jishū bungei to Yugyō sō (5: Bakufu rengashi Satomura-ke to Fukoku Shōnin)." In *Shomin shinkō no genryū: Jishū to yugyō hijiri*, ed. Tachibana Shundō and Tamamuro Fumio. Meicho Shuppan, 1982.

A Tale of Flowering Fortunes: Annals of Japanese Aristocratic Life in the Heian Period. 2 vols. Translated, with an Introduction and Notes by William H. and Helen Craig McCullough. Stanford: Stanford University Press, 1980.

Tamamuro Fumio. "Edo jidai no Yugyō Shōnin." In *Ippen Shōnin to Jishū*, ed. Tachibana Shundō and Imai Masaharu. Nihon Bukkyō shūshi ronkō, vol.

10. Yoshikawa Kōbunkan, 1984. Originally published in *Miura kōbunkan* 18 (November 1975).

―――. "Edo jidai no Yugyō Shōnin kaikoku ni tsuite." In *Chihō bunka no dentō to sōzō*, ed. Chihōshi Kenkyū Kyōgikai. Yūzankaku Shuppan, 1976.

―――. "Yugyō gojūdai Kaison Shōnin no kaikoku ni tsuite." In *Shomin Shinkō no genryū: Jishū to yugyō hijiri*, ed. Tachibana Shundō and Tamamuro Fumio. Meichō shuppan, 1982.

Tambiah, Stanley Jeraraja. *The Buddhist Saints of the Forest and the Cult of Amulets: A Study in Charisma, Hagiography, Sectarianism and Millenial Buddhism*. Cambridge Studies in Social Anthropology, no. 49. Cambridge, UK and New York: Cambridge University Press, 1984.

Thornton, S.A. "The Propaganda Traditions of the Yugyō-ha: The Campaign to Establish the Jishū as an Independent School of Japanese Buddhism (1300-1700)." Ph.D. Thesis, University of Cambridge, 1990.

Tsuji Zennosuke. *Nihon bukkyōshi*. 10 vols. Iwanami Shoten, 1944-1955.

Tsushima chōshi. Ed. Tsushima chō. 1938. Reprint, Meicho Shuppan, 1973.

Umedani Shigeki, and Takaō Sairyō. *Nitta Yoshisada-kō to jishū: Shōnenji*. Maruoka: Nitta-kō 650 Nenki Bozensai Hōsankai, 1987.

Turner, Victor. *The Ritual Process: Structure and Anti-Structure*. Chicago: Aldine's Publishing Company, 1969.

―――― and Edith Turner. *Image and Pilgrimage in Christian Culture: Anthropological Perspectives*.Lectures on the History of Religions, new ser. no. 11. New York: Columbia University Press, 1978.

Waka daijiten. Ed. Inukai Kiyoshi et al. Meiji Shoten, 1986.

Warder, A.K. *Indian Buddhism*. 2d. rev. ed. Delhi, Varanasi, Patna, India: Motilal Banarsidass, 1980.

Watanabe Ryūzui. "Yugyō yanagi no kenkyū." Part 2. *Nō* (December 1949): 15-18.

Weber, Max. *Economy and Society: An Outline of Interpretive Sociology*. 2 vols. Ed. Guenther Roth and Claus Wittich. Tr. Ephraim Fischoff et al. Berkeley, Los Angeles, London: University of California Press, 1978.

Wright, Diana Elizabeth. "The Power of Religion/The Religion of Power: Religious Activities as *Upaya* for Women of the Edo Period—The Case of Mantokuji—. Ph.D. dissertation, University of Toronto, 1996.

Yoshida Tōgo. *Dai Nihon chimei jisho*. 7 vols. Rev. ed. Fusanbō, 1907.

Yoshikawa Kiyoshi. *Jishū ami kyōdan no kenkyū.* Kamakura: Geirinsha, 1956.

Yugyō no bijutsu. Ed. Kanagawa Kenritsu Hakubutsukan. Yokohama: Kanagawa-ken Bunkazai Kyōkai, 1985.

Yuyama Manabu. "*Ta'a Shōnin hōgo* ni mieru bushi." Parts 1 and 2. *Jishū kenkyū* 63 (February 1975): 23-39; 64 (May 1975): 8-53.

―――. "Jishū to Sagami bushi: *Ta'a Shōnin hōgo* ni mieru bushi, hōron." *Jishū kenkyū* 65 (August 1975): 5-21.

————. "Jishū to Musashi bushi." Parts 1 and 2. *Jishū kenkyū* 68 (May 1976): 1-23; 69 (August 1976): 17-31.

Index

CORNELL EAST ASIA SERIES

FORTHCOMING

To order, please contact the Cornell East Asia Series, East Asia Program, Cornell University, 140 Uris Hall, Ithaca, NY 14853-7601, USA; phone (607) 255-6222, fax (607) 255-1388, internet: ceas@cornell.edu, http://www.einaudi.cornell.edu/eastasia/EastAsiaSeries.html.

3-99/.5 M pb/.2M hc